The Task Planner

The Task Planner

An Intervention Resource for Human Service Professionals

William J. Reid

Columbia University Press
New York

Columbia University Press
Publishers Since 1893
New York   Chichester, West Sussex
Copyright © 2000 Columbia University Press
All rights reserved

Library of Congress Cataloging-in-Publication Data

Reid, William James, 1928 –
    The task planner : an intervention resource for human service professionals /
    William J. Reid.
        p.   cm.
    Includes bibliographical references and index.
    ISBN 0-231-10646-7 (cloth).—ISBN 0-231-10647-5 (paper)
    1. Task-centered social work.   2. Social case work—Planning.   I. Title.
    HV43.R3826   2000
    361.3′2′0684—dc21   99–38236

Printed in the United States of America

c   10   9   8   7   6   5   4   3   2   1
p   10   9   8   7   6   5   4   3   2   1

To Ricky

Contents

Acknowledgments

Although my name appears as its sole author, this book is the work of many authors. Following each task planner are the names of those who contributed to its creation at different stages in its development. This book owes its existence to their special knowledge and creative efforts.

I am especially indebted to one of these individuals—Pamela Zettergren, my research assistant throughout much of the period during which this volume was written. A perusal of the book will reveal her substantial contribution to the drafting and revising of the task planners.

I am also in debt to a number of other contributors whose enhancement of the book is only partially reflected in their credits for particular task planners. Included are Mary Corrigan, James Golden, Jennifer Hescheles, Miranda Koss, Matthias Naleppa, Darren O'Leary, and Blanca Ramos. For their able assistance in word processing, my thanks are also due to Mary Ann Burke and Paula Marion.

I owe much to the student practitioners who both applied the task planners in their field instruction settings and critiqued them in my classes on task-centered practice. As a result of their valuable feedback, existing task planners were improved and new ones added.

Finally, my grateful acknowledgement to two very supportive administrators—Lynn Videka-Sherman and Anne E. Fortune, the Dean and Associate Dean of the School of Social Welfare during the time the book was created.

William J. Reid
School of Social Welfare

List of Task Planners

The Task Planner

Simplified Guidelines

1. Locate the problem of interest to you in the **List of Task Planners.** If you can't locate the problem by this means, check the index. Task planners are alphabetized, but the problem may not be referred to in the terms you might have in mind. For example, marital problems are found under COUPLE PROBLEMS. The accompanying disk can also be used to search task planners using key terms.

2. The **Task Menus** provide a variety of tasks that may be used with your clients and that will stimulate your thinking about other possibilities. However, the menus are by no means exhaustive.

3. Indication is given when tasks may be logically used in the order in which they are listed.

4. Terms or letters in *italics* are explained in the **Common Procedures** section at the end of the volume.

5. When a task calls for the client to engage in an activity that may require instruction or facilitation, such as *progressive relaxation, exposure,* or *cognitive restructuring,* it is assumed that the practitioner will provide whatever instruction or facilitation may be necessary. Such standard activities will not be mentioned under **Practitioner's Role.** Technical details regarding the practitioner's helping efforts as part of any *italicized* method are found in the **Common Procedures** section.

6. Detailed guidelines for use of the task planners may be found in **Task Planners: Overview and Applications.**

Task Planners:
Overview and Applications

This work provides a resource for answering questions of perennial concern to practitioners and students in the human services, such as "What kind of problem is my client facing?" "What can he or she do to resolve it?" "What can I do to facilitate the resolution?" The volume covers a large array of common problems that human service practitioners attempt to help their clients resolve. Although we emphasize problems dealt with by social workers, most are also encountered by other practitioners in the human services, including psychologists, psychiatrists, guidance counselors, teachers, and nurses.

For each type of problem, we provide a **Task Menu** that contains possible actions that the client can take to resolve the problem as well as suggestions for what the practitioner can do to facilitate these actions or initiate others. These problem–task menu combinations are referred to as "task planners." Basic principles and methods for using tasks are set forth later in this overview. In addition, frequently used procedures for task implementation that can be used by clients, in collaboration with practitioners or on their own, are contained in the **Common Procedures** section at the end of the volume.

The Nature and Purpose of Task Planners

Actions or tasks clients can undertake to resolve their difficulties are becoming increasingly important in the human services, due in part to greater emphasis on action-oriented methods of helping, such as cognitive-behavioral, problem-solving, solution-focused, task-centered, strategic, and family structural approaches (Reid 1997). In addition, there has been growing recognition that tasks carried out by clients can augment virtually any helping approach (Burns & Nolen-Hoeksma 1992; Gelso & Johnson 1983; Lambert & Bergin 1994; Neimeyer & Feixas 1990).

In the framework of this book, clients are seen as actively engaged in reaching solutions to their own problems; in other words, clients respond to problems with various "coping tasks" (Zeidner & Saklofske 1995). For a given problem we map out a range of such tasks a person might need to accomplish to achieve a successful resolution. In their development of this notion Zeidner and Saklofske (1995:509) use the example of the tasks that might need to be undertaken by children coming to grips with their parents' divorce. As these authors put it, such tasks include "acknowledging the marriage breakup, disengagement from the parental conflict, coming to terms with multiple losses associated with divorce, and resolving feelings of self-blame and anger." From these general coping tasks more specific tasks can be derived, for example, getting information from parents about the reason for the divorce or attending a therapeutic group for children of divorce. Practitioners are viewed as the clients' collaborators and facilitators in their coping efforts. Thus if the client's problem is awkwardness in social situations, one of his or her tasks might be to learn appropriate social skills. The practitioner's role would be to help the client identify and learn the skills.

As the preceding example suggests, tasks can be viewed at different levels of abstraction. Tasks stated at a more general level, such as "resolving feelings of self-blame and anger," may often be seen as goals since they do not state particular actions to be taken but describe a general direction for action. Task planners provide the client with suggestions for problem solving at both general and specific levels, with the latter predominating. Specifics of more general tasks are usually indicated under the **Elaboration** and **Practitioner's Role** subheadings.

Tasks are construed as direct problem-solving efforts that can be worked on outside the counseling session. An activity that requires interaction with a practitioner (e.g., "Discuss the problem with your therapist") would not be considered a task in this framework. However, some tasks can be undertaken both outside and within the session. For example, a coping task for depressed clients may be to challenge negative beliefs about their self-worth. The task could be done by a client on his or her own as well as with the practitioner. Because such efforts may be guided by the practitioner, they have not usually been thought of as the client's task work. However, studies of the therapeutic process have suggested that such in-session activity may be advantageously seen as the client's attempt to accomplish tasks (Berlin, Mann, & Grossman 1991; Greenberg 1984; Rice & Saperia 1984). In fact, these studies use methods of "task analysis" to examine these activities.

Many of the tasks presented here are drawn from developments in the behavioral, cognitive-behavioral, task-centered, and other action-oriented systems of intervention. In our framework they can still be seen as sophisticated expressions of client coping. Throughout history people have tried to master social skills, learn more effective techniques for managing their children, overcome fears through exposing themselves to feared situations, and so on. What advances in action-oriented treatments have added are often especially efficient, effective, and well-tested means of achieving these goals.

The clients' tasks in this framework are much more than simply "homework assignments." They can become a central organizing force in problem remediation. They can provide the focus for treatment sessions with the client and serve as the basis for problem-solving actions clients may carry out in their life situations between sessions.

This framework emphasizes the reality that in most cases it is ultimately the client who must bring about change, even though the practitioner has a key part to play in providing stimulation, expertise, a caring relationship, and other support. Indeed, the practitioner may assume strong guiding and teaching roles, as needed. But no matter what techniques or approaches the practitioner uses, they will generally accomplish little unless the client becomes involved in an active effort to alter his or her behavior or situation. Then the critical paths to problem resolution can be seen as client tasks.

To be sure, some problems require actions that the client is not able to carry out. For example, a frail elderly client confined to a hospital bed may need a discharge plan, which might call for the exploration of nursing homes in the area. The client may not be able to do the exploration, even though he or she, if mentally competent, should be able to decide what home to go to on the basis of information provided. Thus task planners may include tasks in which the "leg work" is undertaken by practitioners serving the client or by other professionals, caregivers, etc.

In sum, the emphasis on client tasks, as I have defined them, is meant to accomplish two purposes: to center the responsibility and means of change in the client, and to stress the role of the practitioner as a facilitator of the client's coping actions both within and outside the session. Any action to be considered must be one clients can take in their life situations on their own, even though they may prepare for and even work on tasks with the practitioner. In these respects, this book may be distinguished from practice planners oriented toward practitioner goals and related interventions. (See, for example, Jongsma et al. 1996; Jongsma & Peterson 1995; Perkinson & Jongsma 1998).

Task planners are meant to supplement basic knowledge users might have or be acquiring about human behavior and intervention methods, the kind of knowledge taught in introductory courses in human services curricula. Users who have such a background should be able to obtain from the task planners key ideas about what actions clients might take to solve given problems.

Task planners are not designed to provide full assessment or intervention information about a problem or to be used as service prescriptions. They simply provide ways of identifying, defining, and describing selected client problems; summarize a range of potentially useful client and practitioner activities for such problems; and provide bridges to additional source material. They should help the practitioner in the same way a reference tool helps a writer—as an aid to creative efforts. Practitioners who have expertise about certain problems may not learn a great deal from the task planners about solutions to those problems. But in most caseloads practitioners encounter client problems with which they are not very familiar. For example, regardless of settings or clients' primary complaints, the practitioner may have to deal with problems of alcohol abuse, caregiving, child management, and so on. Task planners are a useful resource in such situations, providing new information or refreshers about problems, client tasks, and practitioner interventions. By the same token, supervisors and educators, who perhaps have an even greater need for general knowledge about client problems and related interventions, can find task planners helpful, as can students, given their relative lack of knowledge about most problems and possible ways of resolving them. In fact, the majority of students who have used task planners have reported in anonymous questionnaires that they "provided a useful overview of possible actions that could be taken for a particular problem" and that they "stimulated thinking about other possible actions."

In addition to presenting possible interventions for particular problems, task planners "map" and specify common problems in particular areas of practice, problems that may not have occurred to the practitioner (note the breakdowns under ALCOHOLISM/ADDICTION and SCHOOL PROBLEMS). Finally, task planners provide access to the literature relating to a wide range of problems and associated tasks.

Developing the Task Planners

The task planners were created according to a detailed protocol developed by the author and then went through several drafts, written by the author, masters and doctoral students (in independent studies and course work), practitioners, educators, and staff assistants. The writers reviewed relevant literature, made use of their own practice experience and expertise, and consulted with experts in the relevant practice areas. The initial drafts of the planners were revised by the author and his assistants and students; whenever feasible, additional expert consultation was obtained. At the end of each planner are the names of those (aside from the author) who contributed to its development.

The developers of some task planners did more than the protocol required, in the amount of detail they included in the problem descriptions and tasks and in the number of references in the **Literature** section. Thus some task planners are more extensively developed than others regardless of the salience of the problem. It was assumed that the resulting unevenness in length and embellishment was more than offset by the added information.

In selecting tasks, priority was given to those whose effectiveness has been supported by research and those that have been used with apparent success in clinical practice. Theoretical or other kinds of consistency among tasks was not a criterion since our interest was in presenting a broad range of possibilities. It will be up to the user to select, adapt, and combine tasks in ways that make theoretical and clinical sense.

Problem Selection

The selection and formulation of problems for the task planners was guided by three considerations. First, we aimed for a broad representation of problems frequently encountered by human service practitioners. Problems dealt with by social workers were of particular interest since the task planner project was developed in a school of social work and was designed to serve the needs of social workers. At the same time, care was taken to ensure that most of the problems selected would also be of concern to related helping professionals.

A second consideration concerned the informative value of the tasks that might be related to possible problems and their definitions. Problems too broad in scope might result in an excessive variety of tasks or in tasks too generally stated to be useful; in other problems tasks might be too obvious to be informative.

A final consideration had to do with the expertise and interests of some of the authors of the task planners. Problems selected might not be as common as some that were not included, but the authors knew a good deal about them and could generate tasks that were particularly useful.

The application of these criteria has resulted, it is hoped, in a presentation of most of the common problems dealt with by social workers and other helping professionals, along with some problems that might not meet the criterion of "most common" but are still important and reflect special knowledge in their descriptions and related tasks. Suffice it to say, however, that the volume by no means covers all client problems of importance to human service workers.

The Task Planner in Detail

In this section we take up specific components of the task planner. Readers may wish to refer to some task planners of interest to them for illustrations of these components.

Problem Description   Each problem type is briefly defined and described. Descriptions may include information about prevalence, etiology, maintaining causes, subtypes, and consequences, depending on what information is available and applicable and can be succinctly stated.

To enable ready location, we opted for a listing of problems in practitioner-friendly terminology rather than for a more conceptually elegant scheme. In some cases problems have been identified by the kind of program (e.g., foster care) or setting (e.g., schools) in which they occur. We use the more generic term "couple" to refer to marital problems. The subject index should be of help in locating problems that the user docs not find in the place expected.

Literature   References to literature on the problem and associated interventions are cited here. Included are sources that amplify the tasks contained in the planner as well as more general references. Where available, syntheses of research on interventions relating to the problem, either meta-analyses or research reviews, are cited. There may be citations to additional literature specific to particular aspects of the problem description or tasks elsewhere in the task planner.

Tasks   Tasks for clients and other service providers are displayed. Generally family members are seen as clients, and tasks may be divided among them. Tasks are stated as suggestions directly to the client, although they may contain technical terms that might need to be interpreted or recast when the practitioner presents them. Client characteristics or circumstances that may affect the task are put in brackets, for example, [If mentally ill]. Tasks may be followed by information organized under **Elaboration** or **Practitioner's Role.**

Elaboration   This subheading denotes additional information about the task, which might include its rationale or details about how it can be implemented. Here the reader may also be advised if the task and a given number following it can be logically used in sequential fashion.

By definition clients can work on any of their tasks outside of the counseling session. However, some tasks, as noted, can also be worked on within the session. For example, task 1 under ALCOHOLISM/ADDICTION: ADULT/ADOLESCENT: RELAPSE PREVENTION calls for the client to "design own personal relapse prevention program." Such a task could be begun in the session and worked on between sessions, as is explained in the section below. In fact, some tasks, like this one, are normally begun in the session with the practitioner's help and then carried out independently by the client afterward.

Practitioner's Role   Under this subheading are suggestions about how the practitioner can facilitate the client's implementation of the task. Practitioner's Role is used selectively, primarily to spell out practitioner activities that cannot be assumed from the statement of the client's task. Some tasks are straightforward actions that would not require practitioner assistance to complete. For other tasks, the practitioner's activity may consist of basic intervention methods that users are already familiar with from experience or from a review of Clinical Uses of Task Planners, below. For still other tasks, the appropriate practitioner interventions can be found in the Common Procedures section, which records in one place methods that are used in a variety of tasks. This section can be accessed through italicized terms in the task description. For example, when the task calls for the client to use *contingency management,* the reader can look up that term in Common Procedures. It is assumed that the practitioner will provide the client with essential information on how to use the method. More generally, it is assumed that the practitioner will give the client whatever information is needed about tasks that may require special knowledge to implement.

Clinical Uses of Task Planners

In this section I set forth guidelines for the use of task planners in clinical practice. I assume that users have or are learning elsewhere basic knowledge and skills for helping people with psychosocial problems—for example, the ability to identify and assess problems in their psychological and social contexts, to form therapeutic alliances with clients, and to apply a range of helping methods.

These guidelines draw on over twenty-five years of use of task-centered methods with individuals, families, and groups (Reid and Epstein 1972, 1976; Reid 1978, 1992; Tolson, Reid, and Garvin 1994; see also the Task-Centered Web site at http://www. task-centered.com). The guidelines update key ideas from this body of work and adapt them to the task planners that follow.

Providing a Direction for Intervention

Once a problem has been identified, a task planner can be used to map out a range of tasks that a client might undertake to resolve it. In some cases the **Task Menu** can provide a general direction for intervention, especially if problem-solving, task-centered, cognitive-behavioral, or other action-oriented approaches are used. Tasks that seem to fit the client's problem can be discussed with the client as a way of starting the intervention process. When the task involves technical procedures, e.g., *exposure,* the user may wish to supplement our description of the procedures with cited source material before using the task.

Tasks are generally best introduced in the context of a collaborative relationship (Reid 1992). A possible task that is new to the client may be suggested by the practitioner as "one thing to try," and a rationale for the task may be given. If the client is receptive to the idea, the practitioner and client attempt together to shape the task to the client's own interests, abilities, and circumstances. Such a process is generally empowering for the client; it also gives the client a sense of ownership of the task and helps ensure that the task takes a form that he or she finds suitable.

Augmenting Intervention

Task planners can be used to expand the range of possibilities in an intervention plan. A practitioner may wish to use one or two tasks to supplement a treatment strategy. Tasks can be used in this fashion with virtually any kind of individual or group treatment approach. For example, they can be used to put into action insight gained in the treatment process: the focus of work with Anita in psychodynamic therapy has been her dependence upon her abusive boyfriend. She now feels ready to break off the relationship. The task planner DOMESTIC VIOLENCE: BATTERED WOMEN provides a range of possible actions that might be useful to consider at this point.

Often clients are beset with problems that are not the main focus of treatment but may be exacerbating their difficulties and thus need to be dealt with. Task planners can provide a quick scan of possible initiatives that the client may undertake. Therapy with Holly has been centered on helping her work through feelings surrounding her experiences of having been sexually abused as a child, feelings that seem to be responsible for her current depression as well as other symptoms. However, child visitation issues involving her ex-husband appear to be contributing to her depression. The task planner DIVORCE/SEPARATION: CONFLICT OVER POST-DIVORCE ISSUES might be useful in her case.

Extending Task Planners

Any task planner covers only some of the possible tasks for a given problem. Users may want to add additional tasks or make other changes. Individual task planners can be printed out from the disk accompanying this volume, or changes can be made electronically on the disk itself. Moreover, new task planners can be created for problems not covered. In some agencies, staff have constructed and shared additional task planners in given areas, thus developing a set of planners specific to the problems encountered in their particular agencies. Such planners can serve as vehicles for recording and pooling practice knowledge.

Specific Processes: Work with Individuals

Task planners are used somewhat differently in work with individuals than in multi-client interviews or group treatment situations. Therefore, I will first take up their application in single interviews and will then discuss distinctive elements that come into play when more than one client is present.

The Task Planning and Implementation Sequence   In using task planners, practitioners can employ a set of methods used in task-centered practice: the Task Planning and Implementation Sequence (TPIS). Its purpose is to provide a systematic approach to helping clients select, plan, and carry out tasks. Studies have suggested that the use of TPIS is associated with higher rates of task completion (Reid 1975, 1985, 1997). TPIS is presented here in summary form with adaptations for use with task planners. More detailed discussion of this method may be found in Reid (1992), Tolson, Reid & Garvin (1994) and Tolson (in press). In general, TPIS is designed to be used flexibly—that is, only those steps relevant to the task are applied. Some tasks that may be done largely in the session, such as the client's identifying factors responsible for a problem, may require minimal use of TPIS. More substantial applications involve helping the client prepare for complex tasks to be completed between sessions. The specific steps of TPIS are:

- Task Selection   It is always important to involve the client in task selection through such questions as "What do you think you might be able to do about this problem?" or "Of the things you have tried, what has worked best for you?" Thus task selection should begin with a dialogue in which the client's ideas are elicited. The practitioner tries to build on these ideas and, if needed, suggest others. Task planners can be used in two ways in this process. First, a planner may give shape and direction to the client's idea for a task. Second, a planner may suggest possibilities or details that neither the client nor the practitioner has considered. It may also stimulate thinking about still other tasks. Whatever possibilities it may suggest need to be adapted to the individual case through continued dialogue. The client's contributions normally become a part of the task. The practitioner does not "assign" the task to the client.

- Task Agreement   An agreement between practitioner and client on the client's task—that is, on what he or she is to do—may be reached after alternative possibilities have been sorted out and the best selected. Generally an agreement at this point concerns the global nature of the client's proposed action, not the detail, which is developed subsequently. If the client appears to accept the task, agreement may be delayed until planning (below) has been completed. In any case, the client's agreement to attempt the task should be explicit.

- Planning Specifics of Implementation   Once a task has been selected, the practitioner and client work on a plan to carry it out. Tasks originating from planners normally need to be customized and fleshed out in collaboration with the client. Suppose the task selected is "Participate in self-help programs, such as Narcotics Anonymous (NA) or Alcoholics Anonymous (AA)" from the task planner ALCOHOLISM/ADDICTION: ADULT/ADOLESCENT RELAPSE PREVENTION. An implementation plan would involve determining how such a program might be located, how the client might learn something about it, when he or she would attend the first meeting, and so on. Other task planners may be of help in developing an implementation plan. In the example just cited, the practitioner would probably want to have a look at ALCOHOLISM/ADDICTION: SELF-HELP GROUPS: PROBLEMS IN USING EFFECTIVELY.

  When the task involves out-of-session activity, the plan normally calls for implementation prior to the client's next session. Regardless of the form of the plan, the practitioner attempts to make sure that it has a high probability of at least some success. It is better to err on the side of having the task be too easy than too difficult, since clients need to experience success in their work on their problems. There is empirical evidence to support this position. Successful performance can create a sense of mastery, and self-efficacy beliefs can augment problem-solving efforts (Bandura 1986). For example, if it seemed that the task of attending a self-help meeting had a low probability of being carried out, the task could be revised to simply locating a group and getting information about it.

For the plan to work, it is essential that the client emerge from the discussion with a clear notion of what he or she is to do. Generally an effort is made to spell out details of implementation that are appropriate for the task and fit the client's style and circumstances. For some tasks and some clients a good deal of detail and structure may be called for. For example, if the client is likely to procrastinate about doing the task, it may be important to spell out the time and place where it will be done. For other tasks and clients a minimum of structure and detail may make sense. For example, planning may be more general with a task requiring a good deal of on-the-spot improvisation. In any case, the main action verbs of the task should be clarified, unless they are readily apparent. If the task (from the planner concerning chores) calls for a mother to show approval if her daughter cleans her room, ways of showing approval and what is meant by cleaning the room should be discussed. Finally, the practitioner and client should go over the plan in summary fashion, at the end of the planning process. For complex tasks it is often useful to elicit from the client the essentials of the plan as he or she sees it. The practitioner can then underscore the essential elements or add parts the client has left out. Summarizing the plan gives the practitioner the opportunity to convey to the client the expectation that it will be carried out and that his or her efforts will be reviewed. Writing tasks down, with a copy for the client and another for the practitioner, is another useful technique, especially when tasks are complex or when several task performers are involved.

• Establishing Incentives and Rationale   The practitioner and client develop a rationale or purpose for carrying out the task if it is not already clear. "What might you gain from doing the task?" would be an appropriate question. The practitioner reinforces the client's perception of realistic benefits, or points out positive consequences that the client may not have perceived.

• Anticipating Obstacles   An important practitioner function in task planning is to help the client identify potential obstacles to the task and to shape plans so as to avoid or minimize them. This function is enacted when the practitioner presses for specificity in the task plan. As details of how the tasks are to be done are brought out, possible obstacles can be identified through "what if" questions. For example, suppose the task (drawn from a task planner on alcoholism/addiction) is: "Discuss with partner ways partner can help you stay sober." Among the questions the client can be asked is: "What if your partner starts to lecture you?" More generally the practitioner can ask clients to think of ways that a task might fail (Birchler

& Spinks 1981). Potential obstacles and ways of resolving them can be discussed. If the obstacles appear too formidable, the task can be modified or another developed.

Often the proposed task relates to previous efforts by the client. Consideration of these efforts and how they may have fallen short can provide another means of identifying potential obstacles. For example, a task under consideration for Mrs. S. was to reward her son with praise and approval for completing his homework. Previous discussion of the mother–son relationship had revealed her difficulties in expressing positive sentiments toward the boy. This might be identified as an obstacle.

- Simulation and Guided Practice   The practitioner may model possible task behavior or ask clients to rehearse what they are going to say or do. Modeling and *rehearsal* may be carried out through *role play,* when appropriate. For example, suppose the client's problem is social phobia. The relevant task planner is used, and the task selected is "Incrementally expose yourself to anxiety producing situations." The task could be planned in relation to a specific situation—fear of speaking up in a class the client is attending. The practitioner could take the role of the instructor and the client could rehearse what he or she might say. Or the roles could be reversed, with the social worker modeling what the client might say.

  Guided practice is the performance of the actual (as opposed to simulated) task behavior by the client during the interview; for example, a child may practice reading. Guided practice can also be extended to real-life situations: a practitioner might accompany a client with a fear of going to doctors to a medical clinic.

- Task Review   Reviewing the client's progress on the task, usually at the beginning of the next session, is a vital part of the implementation process. A form for recording task progress and instructions for using it are included in the appendix. If the task has been substantially completed, the client is praised for his or her success. The practitioner and client may formulate another task on the same or a different problem. If the task has not been carried out or has been only partially achieved, the practitioner and client may examine obstacles, devise a different plan for carrying out the task, or apply other task implementation activities. The task may be revised or replaced.

  If the task has not been completed, a major focus of the review will be obstacles the client has encountered in attempting to carry it out—actual obstacles, as opposed to the ones anticipated during the planning process. The practitioner can use whatever interventions are effective in helping the client overcome the obstacles. For instance, the practitioner may help the client modify distorted perceptions or unrealistic expectations interfering with work on the task. Obstacles involving the external system, such as interactions between a child and school personnel or the malfunctioning of welfare bureaucracy, may be addressed and a plan for resolving them developed. Although a broad range of interventions may be brought to bear, they are concentrated on resolving obstacles to the accomplishment of specific tasks. In other words, the obstacle is dealt with only to the extent necessary to enable the client to complete the task.

Specific Processes: Work with Couples and Families

The processes described above also apply to work with couples and families. However, additional methods must be brought into play in interviews with two or more clients present.

Expanded Use of In-Session Activities   Multiple-client interviews provide opportunities for guided practice and other in-session activities (referred to as "session tasks" in previous writings—e.g., Reid 1985, 1992) involving two or more clients in face-to-face interaction. Possibilities include skill-building communication exercises, structured problem-solving activities, and tasks involving exchanges of information or feelings. For example, Val and Mark may do a task in which each paraphrases what the other has just said, as a means of developing their listening skills. The Brown family may engage in a problem-solving task to work out rules concerning curfew. A daughter may tell her mother about her plans to move out of their home.

In work of this sort the practitioner typically structures the activity and then takes an observer/facilitator role as the participants interact with one another. The practitioner may help the participants stay focused, remind them of ground rules (e.g., to avoid bringing up the past), provide praise and corrective feedback (when tasks involve communication or other skills), or make suggestions when participants get stuck, for example in problem-solving tasks.

Such activities give couples and families the opportunity to work on their problems directly in the session, under the practitioner's guidance and in ways the practitioner can structure for maximum therapeutic benefit. They can sometimes lead to immediate solution of problems—for example, when participants reach compromises that resolve conflicts. The activities provide couples and family members with supervised practice in actions that might prove critical in solving problems in their life situations.

Perhaps the single greatest challenge in helping couples and families carry out face-to-face activities is to keep participants interacting with one another rather than attempting to involve the practitioner, for example to secure his or her support. Also, practitioners may intervene prematurely in ways that result in breakdown of client-to-client communication. To become skilled in the use of such activities, practitioners need to be firm in redirecting communications to themselves back to the task participants and to avoid interventions that might end such activities before they have produced full results.

Types of Tasks   Multiple interviews lend themselves to a greater variety of task structures since they facilitate clients' carrying out tasks cooperatively. Two major types of cooperative tasks are shared and reciprocal.

Shared tasks involve a single undertaking carried out cooperatively by two or more clients—e.g., Mrs. George and Debbie will go to the mall together; Harold and Lisa will discuss the possibility of moving to a new apartment. Many of the tasks in the planners designated for couples and parents can take this form.

Shared tasks can be used in a variety of ways: to accomplish practical goals, such as getting homework done; to provide a structure for problem solving and practicing communication skills at home; and to build relationships through mutually enjoyable activities. If they go well, shared tasks tend to promote cohesiveness since they bring participants together in some joint activity. Such tasks can backfire, however, if they result in conflict or if one client feels pressured to participate. In working with enmeshed client systems, that is, those that are already "too cohesive," shared tasks must be used cautiously.

The use of shared tasks can be extended beyond couples and families. The clients' partner in a shared task may be a teacher, homemaker, home health aide, or fellow resident. In such extensions it is important to involve all participants in the task planning.

Reciprocal tasks (behavior exchanges) involve two clients in an exchange of tasks. Harry agrees to initiate at least one conversation a day; in return Susan will go bowling with Harry once a week. Unlike shared tasks, in which participants engage in a common activity, reciprocal tasks specify different activities for each participant and how those activities will be exchanged.

Reciprocal tasks are used primarily to promote positive interaction and to reduce conflict. They usually require a good deal of planning in the session, which can be done by the participants themselves. As Rooney (1981) has commented, reciprocal tasks tend to be "high risk, high gain." Because two participants, usually with a strained relationship, must coordinate an often-intricate exchange, there are many opportunities for things to go wrong. On the other hand, if successful, a reciprocal task can set in motion a cycle of positive interaction leading to rapid progress. Sometimes there is too much conflict (or too little cohesiveness) between participants for reciprocal tasks to be effective. In such situations separate tasks may be indicated.

Reciprocal tasks can also be extended beyond work with couples and families. For example, reciprocal task partners may be teacher and student. Again, both partners should be involved in the planning.

Using Task Planners in Combination   Most couples and families present highly interrelated problems; in fact, separate problems may not even be clearly defined. Consequently, combinations of task planners may be needed. For example, in work with problems of discord in married or cohabitating couples, practitioners might draw on task planners covering the basic "3 Cs"—conflict, communication, and caring. (These are found in couple or family conflict, couple problems: communication, and couple problems: lack of caring or involvement).

Specific Processes: Work with Groups

The use of tasks may be a central feature in work with treatment groups, like task-centered groups (Tolson, Reid & Garvin 1994) or may be ancillary to other models (see, for example, Pomeroy, Rubin, & Walker 1995). In either case, the task planning and implementation activities discussed above can be applied. When TPIS is used in group situations, all members participate. That is, group members suggest ideas for tasks for an individual member, assist in task planning and review and analysis of obstacles, and so on. The process is repeated with each member in turn. In other words, the group, guided by the group leader, serves somewhat the same function as the practitioner in individual treatment, with respect to selection and planning of tasks. Groups also offer abundant opportunities for role playing, guided practice, and other types of in-session tasks.

Task Planners

Alcoholism /Addiction

Adult /Adolescent Relapse Prevention

Substance abuse may be defined by continued use of alcohol or other drugs despite adverse consequences. These consequences for adults or adolescents may include one or more of the following: family or work disruption, health problems, engaging in high-risk behaviors, such as driving while intoxicated, and poor school performance or failure (Barker 1995; American Psychiatric Association 1994). The leading causes of death among youths are accidents and suicides, both of which are highly correlated with substance abuse. Research has suggested that substance abuse now begins at an earlier age than in previous generations, and that in youths, substance abuse progresses into polysubstance abuse more quickly than in adults (Nowinski 1990).

Although it may be helpful in work with substance-abusing clients generally, this task planner is oriented toward those who have made progress in treatment but face risk of relapse. Relapse is defined as the resumption of drug use after a period of abstinence. Generally relapse is accepted as a frequent part of the substance abuse/ recovery process (National Institute on Drug Abuse 1994). In one large-scale study the only predictor of relapse was severity of drug and alcohol use at admission (McLellan, Alterman, & Metzer 1997).

Literature: Catalano et al. (1991, 1999); Collier & Marlatt (1995); Curtis (1989); Fiorentine (1999); Fischer (1992); Kaminer (1994); Marlatt & Gordon (1985); Marlatt & VandenBos (1997); McLellan, Alterman, & Metzer (1997); National Institute on Drug Abuse (1994); Nowinski (1990); Smyth (1998); Vaughn & Long (1999).

Task Menu Person with substance abuse problem

1. Construct a "relapse plan" that includes actions you will take to prevent relapse if one is imminent (Curtis 1989) and actions you will take if a relapse occurs (e.g., inpatient treatment, increasing relapse prevention efforts, or extended residential placement).

Practitioner's Role: Provide information on inpatient and other appropriate treatment programs. Assist the client in identifying appropriate actions to take to prevent relapse or to deal with relapse should it occur. For instance, a distinction between a "lapse" and a "relapse" can be made. A lapse is a single incident of drug use and may or may not result in relapse (i.e., returning to previous levels of substance abuse [NIDA 1994]). Therefore, a lapse may be appropriately addressed by increasing relapse prevention efforts, while relapse may require admission to inpatient treatment.

2. Participate in drug-free recreation activities (e.g., sports, clubs, creative pursuits, hobbies).

Practitioner's Role: Provide the client with information about drug-free programs and activities in the community. Assist client in identifying interests and suggest possible related activities he or she may pursue.

3. Develop a recovery support system, comprised of people who understand your problem and support your abstinence.

Elaboration: *Identify* supportive relationships and maintain regular contact with your support system via phone calls and shared activities (Nowinski 1990).

Practitioner's Role: Assist the client in identifying supportive people in their family, peer group, school, and community. If needed, assist client in finding additional members for the support system by suggesting social opportunities for making friends.

4. Learn and practice refusal skills.

Practitioner's Role: Obtain materials on refusal skills and provide training to the client using such techniques as *role playing.*

5. *Identify triggers* as well as risky situations that might cause a relapse.

Practitioner's Role: Assist the client in identifying high-risk situations that may lead to substance use, as well as relapse triggers he or she may not be aware of (e.g., feelings such as anger, loneliness, fatigue, anxiety; places or activities that remind client of substance use).

6. *Identify* strategies and alternatives to using alcohol or drugs should relapse triggers occur (Curtis 1989).

Practitioner's Role: Provide the client with helpful strategies, as needed. For example, have client notice how he or she is feeling, rather than using substances. If a client is anxious, recommend *slow diaphragmatic breathing* or *applied relaxation.*

7. *Identify* cognitions that have led to relapse in the past and develop alternative cognitions that help you remain free of alcohol and other substances.

Practitioner's Role: Through use of *cognitive restructuring,* help client assess which cognitions led to the relapse, then work to develop alternative cognitions that assist him or her in remaining free of alcohol and other substances. For example, a client might say, "If I go past our old hangout, I might as well go in and talk to my old friends." Work with client to develop alternative cognitions, e.g., "Although I go by the old hangout daily, I know I shouldn't go inside. If passing by it continues to tempt me, I should go another way until I have the ability to resist going in. I should also hang out with my new friends who are cool and avoid substance use."

8. If relapse occurs, *identify* precipitating events, feelings, and triggers and record this information in a *journal*.

   Elaboration: Keeping a *journal* increases awareness and helps prevent future relapses.

   Practitioner's Role: Read client's *journal* and utilize information to help the client prevent a relapse triggered by similar circumstances at a future time. For instance, if client has certain patterns, such as being able to go to a former place or type of party and abstain from substances four or five times, but then relapses after the fifth or sixth visit, then that place or type of party is not safe even though the initial successful visits seem to suggest that it is. The *journal* showing such a pattern suggests the course of action needed to prevent relapse.

9. [if adolescent] *Identify* school- and career-related goals and take action to prepare for the world of work (Kaminer 1994).

   Elaboration: Do any or all of the following: meet with an academic advisor to discuss academic plans, problems, and future goals; learn more about career aspirations by talking to a career counselor; seek out a mentor; obtain a part-time volunteer position; work at a paid career-related job to gain experience to apply toward career goals; look into vocational training; learn how to network.

   Practitioner's Role: Provide referrals to mentoring, vocational training, and job/volunteer programs, as well as career counselors in the community. Teach the client networking skills.

10. Learn and practice communication and *problem-solving* skills.

    Elaboration: Work on communication and *problem-solving* skills with family members and in other relationships. Participate in family or group meetings and social situations to practice using listening skills and "I messages" (Gordon 1976).

    Practitioner's Role: Train client in communication and *problem-solving* skills through role plays and family work. Provide written materials to facilitate understanding.

11. *Identify* stress reduction activities that work for you and utilize them when under stress (e.g., exercise, *progressive relaxation,* meditation).

    Practitioner's Role: Books, such as Reaching New Highs: Alternative Therapies for Drug Addicts (Heggenhougen 1997) and Life After Psychotherapy (Davison 1997) contain information on meditation as well as other topics to help maintain recovery through the reduction of stress.

12. Participate in self-help groups, such as Alcoholics Anonymous (AA), Narcotics Anonymous (NA), or Alateen.

Elaboration: Attend meetings, obtain and work with a sponsor, learn about and utilize coping and relapse prevention strategies suggested by fellow members.

The following information on self-help groups may be useful:

(for adults)

Alcoholics Anonymous, P.O. Box 459, Grand Central Station, New York, NY 10163; (212) 870–3400. Online directory by states enables one to locate an AA group in any given community: http://www. alcoholics-anonymous.org/econtent.html

Rational Recovery Systems, P.O. Box 800, Lotus, CA 95651; (916) 621–4374 or (800) 303–2873. http://rational.org/recovery/

Narcotics Anonymous World Services, Inc., P.O. Box 9999, Van Nuys, CA 91409; (818) 773–9999; FAX: (818) 700–0700. http://www.na.org or mailto:info@wso.com

SMART Recovery, Self-Help Network (Self-Management and Recovery Training). SMART is an abstinence program based on cognitive-behavioral principles, especially those of rational-emotive-behavior therapy. SMART, 24000 Mercantile Rd., Suite 11, Beachwood, OH 44122; (216) 292–0220 (day) or (216) 951–0515; FAX: (216) 831–3776. mailto:srmail1@aol.com or http://www.smartrecovery.org/

(for adolescents)

Alateen International, c/o Al-Anon Family Group Headquarters Inc., 1600 Corporate Landing Parkway, Virginia Beach, VA 23454–56127; (757) 563–1600 or (800) 344–2666. http://www.al-anon.org or http://www.alateen.org

Practitioner's Role: Provide meeting lists, but be aware that some clients are uncomfortable with twelve-step programs for various reasons. If client is an adolescent, he or she may be unable to relate to perceived differences in personal experiences or perspectives when group members are older. Some communities have young people's groups, which would be preferable for an adolescent client under these circumstances. See Alateen above.

13. Discuss with your partner ways he or she can help you stay sober.

Practitioner's Role: Meet with client and partner to develop a plan that the partner can use.

14. Imagine positive aspects of not using and negative aspects of using.

Task Menu Parents or caregivers [if client is an adolescent]

1. *Learn about* adolescent substance abuse, relapse, and relapse prevention strategies and read articles and books about substance abuse recovery, adolescents, and parenting.

Practitioner's Role: Educate parents about adolescent substance abuse, relapse, and relapse prevention strategies. Provide reading materials and suggest relevant books (Nowinski 1990; Hawkins & Catalano 1992) on adolescent substance abuse.

2. Participate in Al-Anon or Families Anonymous program.

   Elaboration: Attend meetings and obtain and work with a sponsor. Practice the coping skills suggested and ask for support from other members.

   The following information may be useful in locating a group:

   Al-Anon: Al-Anon Family Group Headquarters Inc., 1600 Corporate Landing Parkway, Virginia Beach, VA 23454–5612; (757) 563–1600 or (800) 344–2666. http://www.al-anon.org

   Families Anonymous: National: Families Anonymous, P.O. Box 3475, Culver City, CA 90231–3475; (800) 736–9805 or (310) 313–5800. email: http://www.familiesanonymous.org

   Practitioner's Role: Provide meeting lists. Suggest the book <u>Alcohol Problems Among Adolescents</u> (Boyd, Howard, & Zucker, 1995).

3. Work with adolescent to *identify* risky behaviors and together plan reasonable consequences for behaviors.

4. Provide appropriate supervision.

   Practitioner's Role: Educate and provide parents or caregivers with information and strategies for appropriate supervision of an adolescent with a substance abuse problem. The <u>Handbook of Parenting, Volume 4: Applied and Practical Parenting</u> (Bornstein 1995) should prove useful in this task.

5. Whenever possible, keep household drug/alcohol free.

6. Provide transportation to drug-free activities and twelve-step meetings.

7. Assist adolescent with school- and career-related goals, help with decision making, be supportive, and praise efforts to avoid substance use (Kaminer 1994).

8. Work collaboratively with school system to organize a recovery assistance program for adolescents, as an alternative to the drug culture at school; weekend and summer drug-free recreation programs for adolescents, as part of the recovery assistance program.

Patricia Brescia, Lorn Gingerich, Pamela Zettergren

Alcoholism /Addiction

Craving

Craving is a compelling need to drink or use drugs. It is intensified by deprivation and is most intense in the first few months after withdrawal from substance use, although it can occur in early, middle, or late stage recovery (Moore, Eisenberg, & Eisenberg 1992). The phenomenon is believed to have two roots. One is physiological and represents the complex physical reactions to decreasing blood levels of alcohol or other substances. Individuals who are chemically dependent manifest these physical reactions as withdrawal symptoms. Other individuals who may not be dependent regularly appear to experience subtle physiological cues that contribute to the sense of craving for a substance.

The second root of craving is psychological, a learned response that occurs when the individual is exposed to stimuli, both actual and symbolic, and environments associated with substance use. This combination of physiological and psychological cues together define the dimension of craving. With respect to alcohol, Nace (1987) identifies the various manifestations of craving as physical (the individual can taste the beverage and feels thirsty); compulsive (he or she can't think of anything else); cognitive (thoughts center around alcohol); and affective (the individual experiences such dysphoric moods as irritability, depression, anxiety, and resentment). Studies indicate craving can be elicited by emotional states (either positive or negative) or by states of physical discomfort that lead to physiological arousal similar to withdrawal reactions; accelerated heart rate, hyperventilation, tremors, and insomnia may all trigger craving.

Literature: On alcoholism/addiction recovery and treatment, see Estes & Heinemann (1986); Moore, Eisenberg, & Eisenberg (1992). On relapse, see Collier & Marlatt (1995); Rogers & McMillin (1991); Toneatto (1999).

Task Menu
1. *Identify* individuals to talk to when craving occurs.

   Elaboration: The individual could be a friend, sponsor, spouse, practitioner, anyone who could be asked not to leave you alone until the craving passes.
2. *Identify* ways to distract yourself from drinking or substance use or go somewhere where neither drugs nor alcohol are available.
3. Find a self-help meeting about to begin; go directly there and talk about the craving.
4. Tell yourself that cravings will pass.
5. Keep liquor and drugs out of the house.
6. Remember that craving is a normal experience.

   Elaboration: Over time cravings become less intense, less frequent, and shorter in duration.
7. Avoid or change situations that lead to craving.

   Elaboration: *Self-monitoring* of cravings is useful in showing what the pattern of craving is and assists in discovering the types of situation that cause the desire to use substances or alcohol (Estes & Heinemann 1986:292).
8. Avoid people, places, and things associated with drug and alcohol use until they do not automatically produce craving.

Practitioner's Role: Use *role play* to help the client practice avoiding situations that might stimulate craving. Additionally, instruct client in the process of *systematic desensitization.*

9. When cravings for drugs or alcohol do occur, take out and review a letter, written in advance, about how bad things were when you were abusing substances.
10. Use *progressive relaxation* to combat craving.
11. Use *self-reinforcement* after successfully resisting a craving.

Kim Hunter

Alcoholism /Addiction

Irrational Guilt /Shame

Normal guilt provides internal feedback about lack of adherence to your own values and beliefs. Irrational guilt or shame can arise in response to AA's suggested inventory work in the form of feelings such as embarrassment, unworthiness, or disgrace that may be remembered from drinking episodes (Twelve Steps and Twelve Traditions 1952). Irrational guilt can act as motivation for ongoing drinking (Zimberg, Wallace, & Blume 1982).

Literature: Moore, Eisenberg, & Eisenberg (1992); Nowinski & Baker (1992; 1998); Zimberg, Wallace, & Blume (1982); Alcoholics Anonymous (1976); Twelve Steps and Twelve Traditions (1952).

Task Menu
1. *Identify* behaviors, thoughts, and actions that provoke feelings of guilt and shame.
    Elaboration: Tasks 1–4 form a logical sequence.
    Practitioner's Role: Provide feedback to client about the rational/ irrational nature of thoughts and feelings.
2. *Identify* alternative responses to thoughts, feelings, and behaviors through reflection or readings (e.g., Alcoholics Anonymous 76–84; Twelve and Twelve 77–87).
3. *Identify* the possible consequences of continuing to ruminate on these thoughts, feelings, and behaviors (i.e., return to drinking).
    Practitioner's Role: Provide feedback and suggest consequences that the client has not thought of.
4. Record actual incidents of self-blame and remorse.
    Elaboration: Recording these incidents will facilitate the identification of what is triggering the self-blame and remorse.

    Practitioner's Role: Have the client share record in session for feedback. Discuss client's reactions when he or she had feelings of self-blame and remorse.

5. *Learn about* the disease concept or biopsychosocial model of addiction to increase your understanding of alcohol's effects (<u>Alcoholics Anonymous, Twelve Steps and Twelve Traditions</u>). See ALCOHOLISM/ADDICTION: NON-ACCEPTANCE OF CONSEQUENCES, task 2.

    Practitioner's Role: Clarify any concepts that client has questions about.

6. Request that family members and friends be patient and discuss with them the long-term benefits of recovery.

    Practitioner's Role: Have client *identify* and list the long-term benefits for him or her before discussing them with family.

7. Keep an ongoing log of new behaviors and positive growth (while being careful not to minimize or ignore negative behaviors) to help awareness that you are using new ways of relating to others.

    Practitioner's Role: *Role play* new behaviors and discuss alternatives to behaviors that are causing the client discomfort. Offer hope while helping the client to acknowledge responsibility for harms done.

8. Develop and maintain a strong support network.

    Practitioner's Role: Suggest that client discuss feelings of shame and guilt with others who have had similar experiences.

7. Learn the difference between responsibility and accountability for actions.

    Practitioner's Role: Explain to the client that while one is rightly accountable for one's *actions,* one is not responsible for being an alcoholic or other substance abuser and should not feel guilt or shame for having the problem.

Kim Hunter

Alcoholism/Addiction

Low Self-Esteem

Low self-esteem is characterized by a discrepancy between one's ideal self-concept and one's actual self-concept (Turner 1995). Lack of self-esteem typically plagues alcoholics and addicts in active use and in early stages of the change process. Low self-esteem can cause clients to not follow through on treatment or to see themselves as not valuable enough to merit the work necessary to stay free of substances (Urbanska 1991). The treatment literature relating to self-esteem (Kitaj & Frost 1995; Turner 1995; Byres et. al 1990) seems to suggest a significant link between raising self-esteem and successfully treating substance abuse—a connection that may be especially strong for women (see also SELF-ESTEEM, LACK OF).

Literature: On alcoholism/addiction recovery and treatment, see <u>Alcoholics Anonymous</u> (1976); <u>Twelve Steps and Twelve Traditions</u> (1952); Estes & Heinemann (1986); Moore, Eisenberg, & Eisenberg (1992); Nowinski & Baker (1992, 1998); Zimberg, Wallace, & Blume (1987); on self-esteem, see Urbanska (1991).

Task Menu

1. *Identify* values that relate to how you evaluate self-worth and also note what makes you believe that you matter or are important.

   Elaboration: Keep in mind that when a business takes inventory it pays particular attention to good stock items.

2. *Identify* what having character means to you.

   Elaboration: Find dictionary definitions of the following words: honesty, compassion, discipline, industriousness, reverence, perseverance, devotion, forgiveness, kindness, courage, gratitude, grace. Reflect on the relevance of these words to your own character. (Urbanska 1991).

   Practitioner's Role: Discuss with client what having character means and add any additional words you or the client think exemplify the client's character.

3. Learn assertiveness skills.

   Elaboration: It is often useful for individuals with alcohol or other substance abuse problems to become more assertive. Part of this process is becoming aware of feelings and expressing them honestly in an appropriate manner (e.g., being polite when making demands).

   Practitioner's Role: Either use *role play* in individual sessions or refer client to an assertiveness training group (see ASSERTIVENESS, LACK OF).

5. Use *self-reinforcement* on accomplishment of positive goals.

6. Continue to inventory behaviors and review in session ongoing destructive behavior or positive behavioral changes.

   Practitioner's Role: Review behavior and any changes with client. Evaluate whether positive change is being identified, in addition to any continuing self-defeating behaviors.

7. *Identify* and perform a small task for someone else each day.

   Elaboration: Research shows that measures of self-esteem increase when individuals help others (Byers 1990).

8. Begin to make amends for harms done.

   Practitioner's Role: Help the client to accurately assess whether harms are genuine and process with client any negative responses he or she receives when attempting to make amends.

9. *Identify* self-esteem losses associated with mistakes made under the influence of alcohol or other substances.

Practitioner's Role: Help clients *identify* and forgive themselves for past mistakes that happened while under the influence of alcohol or other substances.

10. Commit to a program of change to help increase your self-respect.

Practitioner's Role: Assist client in designing a program to achieve small increments of change, so he or she can feel successful.

11. *Learn about* the disease concept.

Elaboration: See ALCOHOLISM/ADDICTION: NONACCEPTANCE OF CONSE-QUENCES, task 2. Knowing that while one is still accountable for one's actions, one is not responsible for being susceptible to alcohol or other substances (e.g., is not just weak or immoral) can help increase self-esteem.

12. Honor goals and commitments to yourself and others.

Elaboration: Be attentive to making goals realistic and modest.

Practitioner's Role: Discuss what a reasonable or realistic goal is with client.

14. Evaluate values and determine if they are comfortable to live by; work on altering them if needed.

Practitioner's Role: Assist the client in the evaluation and alteration of values, if needed.

15. Ask yourself before acting: "What will I think of myself if I do this?" "Will I respect myself more or less than I did before doing this?" (Moore, Eisenberg, & Eisenberg 1992:335).

16. *Identify* successful activities.

Elaboration: Keep a *journal* of activities or tasks that are successfully completed.

17. Use *self-monitoring* in regard to self-statements.

Practitioner's Role: Instruct client in the use of *self-monitoring* techniques and the importance of correcting negative self-talk. Client can think, "Cancel that thought," when a negative self-statement comes to mind.

Kim Hunter

Alcoholism/Addiction

Nonacceptance of Consequences

Frequently alcoholics and addicts are unable to accept or acknowledge the consequences of their substance abuse. As a result, they may deny the existence of a problem, which complicates their treatment.

Literature: Miller & Rollnick (1991); Moore, Eisenberg, & Eisenberg (1992); Nowinski & Baker (1992, 1998); Rogers & McMillin (1991).

Task Menu

1. Break acceptance into three stages: 1) I have a problem with alcohol or drugs; 2) drinking/using drugs is making life more difficult and causing more problems; 3) as I am unable to limit use, giving up alcohol and substances makes sense.

   Practitioner's Role: Work with the client in a nonjudgmental manner; reiterate the consequences of alcohol and substance abuse that he or she mentions. If client is particularly resistant to accepting that there is a problem, go over with him or her the checklist of what constitutes abuse of or addiction to alcohol or other substances in the DSM-IV (American Psychiatric Association 1994).

2. *Learn about* the consequences of alcoholism/addiction.

   Elaboration: Readings might include: Twelve Steps and Twelve Traditions 21–24; Alcoholics Anonymous 1976; "The Doctor's Opinion," "Bill's Story," "More About Alcoholism," Narcotics Anonymous 1982; "Who Is an Addict?," "Why Are We Here?," "How It Works," Living Sober 1975:7–10.

3. List in chronological order experiences and events that illustrate how your life has gradually become more unmanageable as a consequence of drinking or using other substances.

   Practitioner's Role: Encourage client to look for insights regarding circumstances that bring about substance abuse. Point out connections that the client may have missed.

4. Write a letter to yourself about how bad life became while you were drinking or using substances (attach pictures if available).

   Elaboration: This assists in remembering what a good choice change was, when the natural tendency to idealize or glorify the former lifestyle occurs.

5. Tell the story of your drinking or substance-abusing lifestyle to another recovery group member or to the group as a whole.

6. Make a public commitment to plan for change, i.e., tell family, spouse, friends, employer, etc.

   Elaboration: This is a way to make others and yourself fully aware of your commitment to change and some of the steps that you will be taking. It also allows others to be supportive of your efforts.

Kim Hunter

Alcoholism /Addiction

Partners of Heavy Drinkers

Individuals living with heavy drinkers are likely to experience a variety of problems. It is well documented, for instance, that wives of normal drinkers are much less likely to experience distress and marital conflict than those of heavy drinkers (Finney et al. 1983; O'Farrell & Bircher 1987; Palolino & McGrady 1977). Failure to cope effectively with the problem drinker may result in frustration and lowered self-esteem that leaves individuals more susceptible to psychological damage (Wiseman 1980). A 1993 study by Velleman et al. noted the struggles of partners dealing with heavy users. These individuals oscillated between engaging with the user and disengaging, being tough or soft in their attitude, and choosing to stay or leave.

There has been a trend toward designating the partner deviant (Barber & Gilbertson 1997). These authors suggest that such terms as "codependent" or "co-alcoholic" have been readily accepted, despite lack of consensus as to what they actually mean.

Literature: Barber & Gilbertson (1997) review programs that have been used recently in work with individuals living with heavy drinkers. They identify the empirical support for the approaches discussed and comment on what participants in the programs actually have to gain. They suggest that when a problem drinker refuses to participate in therapy, unilateral interventions are the only options. Thomas et al. (1990) and Thomas, Santa, Bronson, & Oyserman (1987) discuss unilateral family therapy. The membership benefits of Al-Anon are discussed by Keinz, Schwartz, Trench, & Houlihan (1995). See also Garrett et al. (1999).

Task Menu Partner of heavy drinker
  1. Attend Al-Anon meetings.
      Elaboration: Al-Anon is probably the best known and most widespread unilateral approach for partners of heavy drinkers. It is sometimes helpful to keep and review a *journal* of the support group experiences detailing feelings, thoughts, and any discomfort with the experience. To locate Al-Anon groups, contact Al-Anon Family Group Headquarters Inc., 1600 Corporate Landing Parkway, Virginia Beach, VA 23454–56127. (757) 563–1600 or (800) 344–2666. http://www.al-anon.org
      Practitioner's Role: Assist client in determining whether Al-Anon may be useful in his or her situation. Give an outline of what the meetings will generally be like and suggest that the essential dynamic of the Al-Anon meeting is the candid sharing of emotional reactions, experiences, and strategies for coping. Another important feature is the reassurance that comes from others' having successfully dealt with the same situation. The

disease concept of alcohol is stressed, perhaps to alleviate burdens of hostility and guilt.

2. *Learn about* reinforcement training (RT) or use positive reinforcement when your partner is not drinking.

    Elaboration: RT is a program, based in learning theory, developed by Sisson and Azrin (1986) to teach partners of heavy drinkers how to avoid or minimize physical abuse to themselves, encourage sobriety, coax the drinker into treatment, and eventually assist in treatment.

    Practitioner's Role: Introduce the topic of RT to the client. Instruct clients in positive reinforcement and make a list of possible reinforcers that the client is willing to use during times when the drinking partner is abstinent. Instruct the client to make clear that the positive reinforcements occur because the partner is not drinking. Suggest strategies such as expressing positive feelings for the partner, requesting continued sobriety, and scheduling activities the partner enjoys where drinking would be difficult.

3. *Identify* and list times when your partner has inconvenienced or diminished your life by drinking heavily.

    Practitioner's Role: Draw attention to how the partner's drinking is diminishing the client's life. Items listed can include a range of problems from embarrassment in public to physical abuse.

4. Be present at the time of drinking to encourage your partner to eat or consume nonalcoholic beverages, and make your partner aware of the amount he or she is actually drinking.

    Elaboration: Ignore the drinker if he or she becomes intoxicated despite these efforts; leave if abuse becomes a possibility.

5. Hold the drinker fully accountable for his or her behavior and suggest counseling when the drinker recovers.

6. Learn ways to enhance and protect your own life and, if applicable, *identify triggers* that have led to violence in the past.

    Practitioner's Role: Suggest that clients may want to pursue interests outside the home, away from the drinker. Where applicable, have clients reconstruct the sequence of events that typically leads to violence. Have client agree to call police and press charges if violence occurs despite their use of protective behaviors.

7. Use environmental contingencies to control your partner's drinking.

    Elaboration: The objectives in using environmental contingencies are to provide the client with a greater measure of control over his or her life and to place the drinker under escalating pressure to change.

    Practitioner's Role: Instruct client in fundamental objectives. In regard to escalating pressure, provide the nondrinking partner with feedback and information about the change process (e.g., there will be times when situations will be going well, then take a turn for the worse and vice versa). Instruct client that pressure from the environment is required to produce change in drinkers. Have the nondrinking partner complete a battery of instruments that include measures of the drinker's alcohol dependence. Score the instruments immediately and invite the client to comment on the results.

Next, emphasize that the client is not accountable for the partner's drinking. Warn client that this concept will be challenged, especially by the problem drinker, as it is one of the rationalizations for the drinking. The client should also be informed that there is no explicit or implicit reason that the partnership they are in must be preserved, so they are free to end the relationship at any point. Explain the distinction between pressure and nagging or quarreling.

This and other tasks in this planner can be facilitated by use of methods from unilateral family therapy—a four- to six-month program of intensive work with the partner of the problem drinker (Thomas et al. 1987). A clinical assessment identifies the drinker's behaviors and consumption level, in addition to the partner's responses to the drinking. Sessions that follow are geared to assisting the partner in developing positive ways of interacting that aid in rehabilitation of the heavy drinker. The well-being of the nondrinking partner is focused on and efforts to increase independence from the drinker are encouraged. The nondrinking partner is given a chance to discuss emotional problems, such as anger, depression, and stress. Should the heavy drinker's intake not decrease, the partner's well-being becomes the sole focus of the intervention.

8. *Identify* times of high risk for intoxication and then use incompatible activities to curtail opportunities for your partner to drink to excess.

Elaboration: The incompatible activities will give the drinker similar benefits to those identified as the important benefits he or she gets from heavy drinking.

Practitioner's Role: Discuss with the client the benefits the drinker appears to get from heavy drinking and help generate or suggest alternative activities to use to modify drinking behavior (e.g., giving a massage or exercising with partner if stress is a factor for heavy drinking).

9. Do an enabling inventory.

Elaboration: List what you may be doing that unintentionally encourages alcohol or other substance abuse (enabling). For example, do you comply when your alcoholic spouse is hung over and wants you to call in sick for him or her?

10. Select two issues from the enabling inventory and develop detaching responses to use in their places (that do not enable the alcoholic or substance abuser).

Elaboration: For example, a detaching response would be to refuse your spouse's request to call him or her in sick (Nowinski & Baker 1998).

Practitioner's Role: Suggest typical scenarios if client has difficulty identifying enabling responses; also assist in the development of ways to detach by eliciting client's ideas, making suggestions, and conducting *role plays.*

Pamela Zettergren

Alcoholism /Addiction

Self-Help Groups: Problems in Using Effectively

The benefits of participation in self-help groups for substance abusers are well known (Estes & Heinemann 1986). Not all abusers make use of such resources, and many do not use them effectively. Lack of social skills, shyness in groups, reluctance to reveal oneself to others, and unwillingness to accept the religious orientation of many self-help groups are among the reasons. Traditional AA (Alcoholics Anonymous) or NA (Narcotics Anonymous) groups tend to be less effective in helping clients who are both mentally ill *and* chemically addicted (MICA). MICA clients have reported negative experiences of shame, embarrassment, and being ostracized because of their psychiatric symptoms. In addition, AA and NA traditionally insist on complete sobriety, including abstinence from all mind-altering substances. To the mentally ill chemical abuser, this confusing mandate can inspire foregoing prescribed mood-altering medications (Avatar Productions 1989).

Literature: Campbell & Daley (1993); Mental Health Association of New York State (1994); Estes & Heinemann (1986); Miller & Rollnick (1991); Moore, Eisenberg, & Eisenberg (1992); Nowinski & Baker (1998).

Task Menu

1. Locate self-help groups.

   Elaboration: Call a self-help hotline or helpline to get the times and locations of local self-help group meetings. Hotline and helpline numbers may be found under Alcohol Abuse, Drug Abuse, etc. in the white pages of the phone book. (See ALCOHOLISM/ADDICTION: ADULT/ADOLESCENT RELAPSE PREVENTION, task 12 for information about locating groups through national organizations.) Review meeting lists and choose meetings with convenient days, places, and times.

   Practitioner's Role: Assist client in locating groups and encourage attendance.

2. Make an appointment with a self-help group member to go together to your first meeting.

Practitioner's Role: It is more likely that the client will go if he or she makes an appointment in advance with a member. You can facilitate this by making some contacts with active recovery group members yourself so that appointments may be easily made.

3. Read literature on the self-help group you plan to attend—AA (Alcoholics Anonymous), RR (Rational Recovery), SOS (Secular Organizations for Sobriety), NA (Narcotics Anonymous).

   Elaboration: Reading might include: <u>Living Sober</u> (1975); "Getting Active," "Making Use of Telephone Therapy," "Availing Yourself of a Sponsor," <u>Alcoholics Anonymous</u> (1976); "Anonymous Number Three," <u>Narcotics Anonymous</u> (1982).

4. Attend a meeting, raise your hand, and introduce yourself.

   Practitioner's Role: Encourage the client to try several groups until he or she finds one that seems appropriate; for example, there are alternatives to AA, such as Rational Recovery and Secular Organizations for Sobriety, for clients who do not like AA's spiritual aspects.

5. Start a personal recovery *journal* in which you note any AA, NA, or other recovery group meeting attended and include your thoughts about and reactions to the meeting.

6. Become active in the self-help group by making coffee, setting up chairs or putting chairs away after meetings, putting out literature, and greeting people as they enter the room.

7. Ask for phone numbers of other members.

8. Attend different types of meetings (discussion, step, topic, literature review, etc.).

9. Ask in a meeting about sponsorship and how you would go about getting a sponsor.

10. Attend self-help group-sponsored social events or activities (dances, campouts, bowling, golf, softball, conventions, area workshops, and other events).

11. Share your experiences with others.

12. Find out what resources are available through the self-help group.

13. Become familiar with self-help slogans ("Easy does it," "Fake it till you make it," "Turn it over," "One day at a time").

14. Become active in the running and everyday activities of the group—from holding office to designing T-shirts.

15. If not attending meetings, *identify* reasons.

   Elaboration: Stated reasons may represent only the "tip of the iceberg." You may feel unable or unwilling to verbalize issues around attendance.

   Practitioner's Role: While validating and helping to resolve stated problems, encourage the client to explore underlying issues. If obstacles concern difficulties in socialization or public speaking, help client develop skills through *role play* or *social skills training.* If transportation is identified as a problem, help the client to determine and access transportation. Skills-building (e.g., how to ride a bus) may be indicated. See TRAVEL DISABILITY: COGNITIVELY IMPAIRED PEOPLE.

16. If MICA, learn about MICA groups.

Elaboration: It is important to know not only where and how to access MICA self-help groups but also how they are run, what will be expected of members, what the benefits are, etc. Because of mental illness, MICA clients may find it difficult to fit in at AA and NA meetings as their behaviors or appearance may at times seem inappropriate to other members. Information given at such meetings may be confusing (e.g., encouragement to abstain from all drugs, without making the distinction between drugs and medication).

Practitioner's Role: Assist client in locating MICA self-help groups, such as Double-Trouble, Dual Disorders Anonymous, or other twelve-step MICA groups. Next, explain the groups' significance and prepare client to participate by *role playing* what might happen at a typical meeting to help alleviate anxiety. Contact Dual Disorders Anonymous, P.O. Box 681264, Schaumburg, IL 60168–1264; (847) 956–1660.

Dan Cole, Kim Hunter, Diane Austin

Anger Management and Aggression Control

Adult

Anger may be defined as "a strong feeling of displeasure and belligerence" (Steinmetz 1993:24). It is a complex phenomenon in which stimuli are processed at multiple levels, and it may profoundly affect mental and physical health. Anger may be worked out in a way that converts it from a negative response into a positive source of energy for self-improvement. Evaluating anger on a number of dimensions can be useful in making appropriate treatment decisions. Some possible clinical dimensions of anger include justified versus unjustified anger arousal, normative versus maladaptive levels of anger arousal, and anger suppression (Biaggio 1987).

Thoughts affect anger. Cognitive theory postulates that there is an essential link between the way people think, feel, and behave. It is the meaning we assign to events that gives them the power to affect us in a positive or negative way (Deffenbacher 1996). Although anger may be provoked with no cognitive distortions present (such as when someone is being abused), once a person is angry, cognitive distortions may be obvious. Feelings of anger result from a negative activating experience, and are strongly influenced by a belief system. Discovering what beliefs contribute to these negative feelings makes it possible to alter them by examining their unreality and irrationality (Ellis 1977).

Therapeutic interventions are indicated when anger is expressed inappropriately in terms of frequency, intensity, mode of expression, or impact on interpersonal relationships. Inappropriate expression of anger may be seen in patients with personality disorders, substance abuse, post-traumatic stress disorders, or other psychiatric disorders. It is also necessary to determine the social context in which anger occurs. In some instances, treating the family or couple may be more effective in addition to, or rather than, treating the individual. Additionally, cognitive interventions for anger management can be effectively delivered in groups. Group interaction leads to greater demonstrations of automatic negative thoughts and other dysfunctional thought patterns that can then be addressed within the group context. A group of five to ten clients is recommended (Anderson-Malico 1994).

A meta-analysis (research synthesis) of fifty studies found that cognitive-behavioral intervention was consistently effective as a means of helping children and adults with problems of anger control. The average recipient of this intervention showed greater improvement in anger control than 76 percent of untreated subjects (Beck & Fernandez 1998). Most of the tasks below draw from this approach.

Literature: Abernethy (1995); Deffenbacher (1996); Kellner & Tutin (1995); Larkin & Zayfer (1996); Steinmetz (1993); Weisinger (1985).

Task Menu

1. *Learn about* anger.

    Practitioner's Role: Provide reading suggestions, such as <u>Anger</u> (Viscott 1976:80–104), and discuss reading. For women particularly, <u>The Dance of Anger: The Language of Feelings</u> (Lerner 1985) is recommended. Explain cognitive appraisal. Anger management principles include recognizing anger when it starts, deciding how to handle anger, and developing forgiveness and empathy skills (Grogan 1991a,1991b; Smith & Beckner 1993).

2. *Reflect on* expressing anger in a negative manner and blaming others (Sappington 1996; Smith & Beckner 1993).

3. Use *self-monitoring* to bring to consciousness the frequency of your anger (Kellner & Tutin 1995; Wilcox & Dowrick 1992).

    Elaboration: It is possible to positively affect anger by observing its frequency. It is also possible to self-monitor more subtle aspects of anger, such as destructive things one says to oneself that increase anger (counterproductive self-statements) and physiological changes. With practice, you should be able to self-monitor many aspects of anger simultaneously (Weisinger 1985).

    Practitioner's Role: Discuss three essential components of anger: thoughts, bodily responses, and behavior. Give the client a form on which to record data. Tell the client about five specific signals that anger is creating problems: when it is too frequent, is too intense, lasts too long, leads to aggression, disturbs work or relationships (Weisinger 1985).

4. *Identify* and record an event that you are still angry about, or a recent source of anger, and next to it write down how you appraised it. Then, write down an alternative appraisal, for example reflecting the other person's viewpoint (if another person is involved).

5. *Identify* the bodily disturbances that you are aware of when you are angry and begin to use them as a cue (Kellner & Tutin 1995).

6. *Identify* distorted cognitions underlying anger reactions.

   Elaboration: Deffenbacher (1996:51–52) has identified a number of cognitive distortions specific to anger, including overestimating negative events—e.g., unfair treatment; "misattribution," such as ascribing malevolent motives to the actions of another; "dictatorial thinking," or expecting others' actions to conform to rigid rules ("She had no right to do that!"); "inflammatory thinking," labeling another or another's actions in a highly negative way ("He's a scumbag!") with increasing anger in reaction to the labels.

   Practitioner's Role: Help client *identify* dysfunctional thoughts and actions as well as more functional ways of thinking and responding (Kellner & Tutin 1995; Moore, Adams, Elsworth, & Lewis 1997). Use *cognitive restructuring* to help the client modify distorted beliefs underlying anger reactions.

7. Use time out when you are in an anger-provoking situation and fear loss of control.

   Elaboration: The main components of a time out, as developed by Weisinger (1985), are summarized below:

   Leave the situation for one hour. This gives time to cool down.

   Do not drink or take drugs. They will only make matters worse.

   Do something constructively physical, such as walking or cleaning the garage. This will help discharge some of your physical tension.

   After one hour, return to the situation if the person is still there or phone the person and ask if he or she would like to talk. If so, discuss the situation, telling the other what made you feel angry. Ask how he or she felt. This is the beginning of effective anger dialogue. Returning to the situation gives you the opportunity to cope with it and build confidence for handling future provocation.

8. Use *applied relaxation* in anger-provoking situations and *progressive relaxation* at least once a day (Kellner & Tutin 1995; Moore, Adams, Elsworth, & Lewis 1997).

9. List two expectations you have for someone else at whom you have recently become angry. Ask yourself, "Are they realistic?" and "What makes you think so?"

   Practitioner's Role: Teach strategies that help the client decide if expectations are realistic. These might include asking trusted others what they think is realistic, as it may be difficult to be honest with oneself and other people can give feedback as to whether or not one is being too hard, just right, or too easy (Weisinger 1985).

10. Use positive coping *self-verbalizations* (Larkin & Zayfer 1996).

    Elaboration: For example, "I will stay calm and not let this upset me!" For additional examples, see ANGER MANAGEMENT AND AGGRESSION CONTROL: CHILD, task 11.

11. Develop *social skills* that will enable you to better handle provocation.

    Elaboration: Key skills include use of appropriate self-assertion as an alternative to aggressive responses, use of "I messages" (Phillips-Hershey & Kanagy 1996), and communication and conflict management skills (Biloon & Quinn 1996; Smith 1995). See ASSERTIVENESS, LACK OF; COUPLE OR FAMILY CONFLICT; COUPLE PROBLEMS: COMMUNICATION.

    Practitioner's Role: Use *role play* to help client rehearse ways to handle difficult situations. Taking the role of the other, challenge the client with provocative behavior; model appropriate responses by taking the role of the client.

12. *Identify* incidents in which you successfully applied new anger management skills.

    Elaboration: This helps reinforce the idea that you can control your behavior (Sappington 1996).

13. Use *coping imagery* (Larkin & Zayfer 1996).

    Elaboration: While in a relaxed state, imagine how you would handle a situation likely to make you angry. Use skills—coping statements, assertive responses, etc.—learned in other tasks.

14. Use *stress inoculation* methods (Richlin & Sholl 1992; Wilcox & Dowrick 1992).

    Elaboration: Such methods can help prepare you to handle provocative situations.

Patricia Bruno, Pamela Zettergren

Anger Management and Aggression Control

Child

In young children anger and aggression may be vented in tantrums; in older children it may be expressed in swearing, using threatening language, hitting, and destroying property. Factors responsible may include frustration in the immediate environment, reactions to abuse, following examples set by aggressive adults, or perceiving (misperceiving) the intentions of others to be hostile. Anger and resulting aggressive behavior may be reactive (responding directly to events or to the prior behavior of another person) or initiated independent of identifiable external cues.

Literature: Tasks that parents can use in coping with anger in children can be found in the literature on *parent training* and parental skills (see Briesmeister & Schaefer 1998: Polster & Dangel 1984). Tasks for children can be found in literature on juvenile anger management (Taber 1981; Kendall 1991). Some interventions focus on decreasing anger or increasing frustration tolerance and coping skills, some on helping children shift attributions (i.e., to more accurately perceive and evaluate others' intentions and reduce untoward perceptions of harm), or a combination of these depending on the needs of a given child.

A meta-analysis (research synthesis) of fifty studies found that cognitive-behavioral intervention was consistently effective as a means of helping children and adults with problems of anger control. The average recipient of this intervention showed greater improvement in anger control than 76 percent of untreated subjects (Beck & Fernandez 1998). Tasks listed under "Child" draw from this approach.

Task Menu   Parents or caregivers

1. *Identify* contextual factors that provoke the child's anger or aggression (see problem description above) and take steps to remove them or make them less provocative.

    Elaboration: Try to identify a main theme or pattern to the child's aggression to help develop the most appropriate interventions. For example, the aggression may seem to occur mostly when the child is feeling frustrated or because the child routinely presumes others are out to hurt him or her.

2. Help the child understand what alternative behaviors are acceptable and reinforce those behaviors when they occur.

3. Use *contingency management* to encourage nonaggressive behavior.

4. Help the child express sources of anger verbally (when child is beginning to become upset and as an alternative to acting it out).

5. With younger children, use *time out* as the consequence for aggressive behavior.

6. Try to involve child in substitute physical activity.

    Elaboration: A parent or practitioner can create a simple game to involve a child in physical activities. For example, a dice-throwing game can be used in which numbers are assigned different activities. If a child throws a 3, he or she might be asked to run around the block three times; a 4 might mean shooting baskets for a certain amount of time; and so on. The purpose of the task is to create constructive alternatives to expressions of anger, not to provide a "release'" for anger. "Cathartic" activities, such as punching a pillow, are of dubious value in anger control.

7. [for teacher or caregiver] Team child up with a supportive buddy in class or group who can help with reminder cues for successful behavior; reward child and buddy when behavior goals have been met.

Task Menu Child

1. *Identify triggers*—people and situations that prompt anger or aggression as well as physical signs of tension that occur early in the aggressive sequence.

   Practitioner's Role: Teach, in individual or group sessions, about awareness of the physical signs of building anger, and develop with the child simple intervention skills (taking deep breaths, pulling back from a confrontation, counting to self, self-talk such as "take it easy," etc.).

2. *Identify* differences between anger and aggression, and between justified and unjustified anger.

   Practitioner's Role: You may need to explain distinctions between these terms to facilitate the task, but child should then work through differences with examples from his or her own situation.

3. *Identify* alternative explanations for the other person's behavior or statements; practice by reviewing pictures from storybooks or take the role of the other person in role play.

   Practitioner's Role: Make use of board *game* to help facilitate tasks.

4. Develop and use covert *self-verbalizations* to control anger in provocative situations—e.g., sizing up a provocative situation, planning an approach, congratulating yourself if it works.

   Elaboration: Examples of *self-verbalizations:* I can manage the situation; I know how to regulate my anger. If I find myself getting upset, I'll know what to do. Try not to take this too seriously. Easy does it. Remember to keep my sense of humor. This could be a testy situation, but I believe in myself. Stay calm, just continue to relax. As long as I keep my cool, I'm in control. Just roll with the punches, don't get bent out of shape. Think of what I want to get out of this. I don't need to prove myself. I'm not going to let him get to me. For someone to be that irritable, she must be awfully unhappy.

5. Record provoking situations and how you restrained (or did not restrain) yourself from aggressive behavior.

   Practitioner's Role: To make recording more interesting for the child, you and child can construct an "anger thermometer" with a range of temperatures from cool to very hot and with supporting colors and numbers. The child can define what different temperatures mean to him or her and can use the temperatures to record feelings experienced in different situations. Younger children can use a chart, which they can help construct.

6. Refrain from responding aggressively when provoked; use alternative coping responses, e.g. *self-verbalization,* assertive behavior, walking away.

   Practitioner's Role: Involve the child in developing coping responses. Responses can be rehearsed and practiced through *role plays* in session alone or with peers providing gradually increasing provocation. Help child shift from an emphasis on threat in situations to an emphasis on problem solving, and to expand his or her available repertoire of nonaggressive coping measures or "smart moves" to make instead, such as disengaging from the situation, diffusing the situation, asking for help from an adult, or working out a compromise.

Mary Corrigan, Chevelle Jones-Moore, Alice Vanwagner

Anorexia

According to the DSM-IV (APA 1994), anorexia is characterized by deliberate self-starvation, unwillingness to maintain minimal body weight (at least 85 percent of the recommended weight), and a profound distortion of body image such that potentially life-threatening weight loss occurs and engenders stronger efforts to diminish food intake and reduce fat areas of the body. Clients with anorexia are preoccupied with both their bodies and food. Striving for perfection, they derive self-esteem from their ability to assert self-control by curtailing food intake and by adhering to rigorous exercise schedules. Whereas some anorectics lose weight by reducing food intake (restricting type), others may binge and purge (binge eating-purging type). Physical complications from this disorder develop not only from the effects of self-starvation, but also from the means by which anorectics purge: self-induced vomiting and use of laxatives, diuretics, and enemas. Hospitalization may be required to treat the client's physical problems and to initiate a comprehensive treatment plan.

Anorexia is most prevalent among females in late adolescence and young adulthood who live in societies where the internalized ideal female type is thin (Faludi 1991). Peer teasing, acute illness with associated weight loss, or a physically or emotionally strenuous experience, such as summer camp, during which weight is lost are common precipitants for childhood anorexia (Robin, Gilroy, & Dennis 1998). Assessment requires information from the client, family members, significant others, and the primary physician because anorectics tend to minimize or deny the seriousness of their weight loss. Literature on the disorder suggests that effective treatment must be multidimensional and multidisciplinary and administered in a coordinated, holistic manner, as fragmentation between various aspects has been shown to be detrimental to effectiveness (Yager 1994; Zerbe 1992). There is a high degree of comorbidity among anorectics, with many having such additional diagnoses as borderline personality disorder, drug or alcohol abuse, or a major affective disorder (Braun, Sunday, & Halmi 1994; Zerbe 1992).

Literature: Review Schlundt & Johnson (1990) for assessment instruments; Duker & Slade (1988) for diagnosis guidelines; Dare & Eisler (1997) for family therapy. Also see Braun, Sunday, & Halmi (1994); Kennedy & Garfinkel (1992); Minuchin et al. (1975); Robin, Gilroy, & Dennis (1998); Williamson, Cubic & Fuller (1992); Wilson & Fairburn (1993); Yager (1994); Zerbe (1992).

Task Menu Family members

1. *Identify* family dynamics that may contribute to the anorexia.

    Elaboration: Parental overprotectiveness and overcontrol may be evoked by a child's anorexia. The anorectic member may become overly dependent on her parents, while using the illness in making demands on them. This process may mask other family conflicts, such as marital discord, and may lead to enmeshment, or lack of autonomy, among family members. The dynamics may in turn help maintain anorexia. The child's symptoms are reinforced when they help him or her win demands from the parents. Moreover, concentration on the child's illness may prevent other conflicts from emerging; hence the illness begins to serve a function in maintaining family balance (Minuchin et al. 1975, 1978; Robin, Gilroy, & Dennis 1998).

    Practitioner's Role: Help family members reduce overprotectiveness and control of anorectic member. Encourage them to use his or her behavior rather than the illness as a basis for interactions. Assist them in identifying conflicts that may be masked by the focus on the anorexia.

2. Decrease frequency of conversations involving food, body weight, and weight loss.

3. Expect the anorectic to eat at mealtime (parents), a normal family activity (e.g., develop a home-based behavioral weight gain program [Robin, Gilroy, & Dennis 1998]).

    Elaboration: In the early phases of treatment, some parents establish a time limit of 30 minutes per meal, limit food choices, and/or monitor what is eaten, giving the child positive feedback for eating all the food and corrective action for eating only part of it (e.g., no activities or television, only bed rest).

4. Reward anorectic for weight gain or positive attitude change by participating in a *mutually enjoyable activity.*

5. As progress is made with the anorectic's physical condition, shift focus to problem solving, communication, and individuation or growth and autonomy issues.

Task Menu Person with anorexia

1. Keep a diary of the type and amount of food eaten and document periods of exercise, including the times, feelings, thoughts, and situations before, during, and after eating and exercise.

2. Record instances when you decided not to eat, including when the decision was made.

Practitioner's Role: Help the client locate information and educational material about anorexia and the physical and psychological effects of starvation. One nonprofit organization on the Internet is ANRED (http://www.anred.com/ or http://www.anorexia.org/support or http://www.anorexia.org/services/). Maintain regular contact with client's medical doctor.

3. Establish guidelines for quality, quantity, and spacing of meals and eat according to predetermined plans.

   Elaboration: This may diminish the importance of weight and food during treatment.

   Practitioner's Role: Assist client in locating a dietitian.

4. Eat once a week with someone who consumes a normal amount of food for health.

5. Once a week, eat a food that is currently being avoided. If necessary, use *systematic desensitization* to facilitate this process.

6. Gradually eliminate excessive weighing.

7. *Identify* thoughts, feelings, and situations that lead to restrictions of food intake or purging.

   Practitioner's Role: Use *cognitive restructuring* to help the client change beliefs about body size, what is normal food intake, and other cognitive distortions that perpetuate self-starvation (e.g., "Only thin people are lovable," "When I am at lunch, people will see me as a pig if I take more than one bite").

8. Develop alternative strategies to cope with stressful situations (e.g., *progressive relaxation,* attending a support group).

   Practitioner's Role: Assist the client in locating and attending a local eating disorders support group. A group format is helpful to the individual anorectic in that members provide support, encouragement, and understanding. Attending group may also be helpful in giving a forum for emotional expression. The anorectic should aim to learn direct expression of thoughts and feelings, deal with conflict in an open manner, discuss fears surrounding change, and work toward developing independent relationships outside of the family, as many anorectics are socially anxious and tend to isolate themselves.

9. Use *self-reinforcement* when you have eaten a normal amount of food (e.g., "I ate a nutritious lunch and thought about how my body was growing stronger. That is a real improvement in how I think").

Mary Whitaker, Kathryn Baraneckie, Pamela Zettergren

Anxiety

Agoraphobia Without History of Panic Disorder

Agoraphobia appears in the DSM-IV (APA 1994) in two forms. One form is panic disorder with agoraphobia, which is discussed under the task planner on panic disorder. The other form is agoraphobia without history of panic disorder; its central feature is anxiety associated with being in places or situations where leaving may be difficult or embarrassing. People with this form of agoraphobia fear incapacitation or humiliation related to paniclike symptoms, but have never experienced a full panic attack. The feared paniclike symptoms can be any of the thirteen symptoms of a panic attack: 1) sweating; 2) trembling or shaking; 3) palpitations, pounding heart, or accelerated heart rate; 4) feeling of choking; 5) sensations of shortness of breath or smothering; 6) chest pain or discomfort; 7) nausea or abdominal distress; 8) feeling dizzy, unsteady, lightheaded, or faint; 9) depersonalization or derealization (feelings of unreality); 10) fear of going crazy or losing control; 11) fear of dying; 12) paresthesias (tingling sensations or numbness); 13) hot flushes or chills. They may also include incapacitating or embarrassing symptoms such as sudden loss of bladder control or diarrhea; dizziness, then fainting and being left helpless on the ground.

Typically, agoraphobia leads to an avoidance of multiple situations, such as being alone outside the home or by oneself at home, being in crowds, traveling by car or forms of mass transit, being in elevators or on bridges. Those individuals able to expose themselves to the feared situations do so with considerable dread. Generally, the individual needs a companion in order to endure the feared experience. Traveling to work can be almost impossible. Homemaking responsibilities such as grocery shopping or taking children to the doctor's or dentist's office can also be impaired. Women are diagnosed with agoraphobia more often than men. Only anecdotal information is available on the course of agoraphobia without history of panic disorder; however, this information suggests that some individuals suffer for years with considerable impairment (APA 1994).

Meta-analyses and research reviews of controlled studies of interventions for agoraphobia have suggested that *exposure* methods have larger effects than alternatives (Clum et al. 1993; Mattick et al. 1990; DeRubeis & Crits-Christoph 1998). Task 4 below makes use of *exposure* methods.

Literature: Bouman & Emmelkamp (1996); Bourne (1995); Craske, Rapee, & Barlow (1992); Otto & Harrington (1999). A good self-help book is Peurifoy (1995). A useful Web site for information about phobias is the Anxiety Network Homepage (http://www.anxietynetwork.com/contents.html).

Task Menu
1. Involve family members in your efforts to overcome your fears.

    Elaboration: Often family members are unaware of their role in enabling or justifying the dependent behavior and distorted beliefs of vulnerability and helplessness that are frequently cognitive features of agoraphobia (Beck & Emery 1985). Although there is no solid evidence of superior therapeutic results when family members have been incorporated into *exposure*-based treatment programs (Baucom et al. 1998), family involvement can serve to decrease feelings of frustration, sadness, and anger (Beck & Emery 1985).

    Practitioner's Role: Explain benefits and encourage client to involve significant others in treatment.
2. *Identify* situations and experiences through *self-monitoring* and recall that have led to an agoraphobic response.

    Practitioner's Role: Provide clients with a self-monitoring instrument to be used when situations that evoke symptoms occur. The instrument should have a scale to rate the intensity of the symptoms. It can be reviewed in session for greater insight, as well as to develop and record rational responses to the thoughts occurring when experiencing symptoms (Burns & Beck 1978; Rehm & Roeke 1988).
3. Develop and practice using *coping imagery.*

    Practitioner's Role: Instruct client and significant other in the use of *coping imagery.* Have the significant other act as a coach and help with the design of coping images.
4. Begin to practice *exposure* to feared situations.

    Elaboration: Rank order feared situations from most to least stressful. Work from the least stressful situation on your hierarchy to the most anxiety producing. As you expose yourself to situations, use *self-reinforcement* with particular attention to employing coping self-statements (e.g., instruct yourself to remain in the situation, accept feelings, and discount unrealistic beliefs). This will help you identify progress and experience control.

    Practitioner's Role: As *exposure* has been proven highly effective, suggest that client proceed with this intervention. Teach client *self-reinforcement* to make the *exposure* less difficult. Instruct significant others in *exposure* practices. Have them help design and suggest how to apply anxiety-control strategies. Train them to serve as coaches during practice of *exposure* tasks. You may also assist the client in carrying out *exposure* tasks.

    Also, help the client develop a hierarchy of fear-eliciting places and situations, beginning with the one that provokes the least anxiety and ending with the one most feared. Constructing the hierarchy compels the client to name situations that elicit less fear than others. She or he is likely to experience success and self-control more rapidly by overcoming the least threatening feared situation. Next, encourage the client to move up the hierarchy by confronting each situation until the anxiety it produces either can be managed comfortably or is totally eliminated (graduated *exposure*). Consider imaginal *exposure* if client is unable to engage in any form of in-vivo *exposure*.

5. Use *applied relaxation* procedures when experiencing anxiety.

Practitioner's Role: Instruct client in *applied relaxation* techniques or other forms of *relaxation* (e.g., *coping imagery*, meditation, *slow diaphragmatic breathing* exercises). Demonstrate and explain to client that when relaxed, he or she can practice imagining anxiety-provoking scenes of increasing intensity and then use *relaxation* techniques to self-demonstrate coping ability.

6. Use safety signals.

Elaboration: Safety signals are behaviors (e.g., traveling familiar routes), objects, or even individuals that add an element of security for an individual undergoing *exposure.*

7. *Learn about* the side effects of stimulant prescription drugs and over-the-counter medications.

Elaboration: Medications containing amphetamines or epinephrine can cause physiological arousal, making you more susceptible to anxiety, which in turn can make *exposure* and therapy increasingly difficult.

Practitioner's Role: Supply client with information on the major medications that cause physiological arousal. Also advise the client to inform his or her health care professional of the agoraphobia diagnosis, so appropriate medications can be prescribed.

8. Consider psychotropic medications to decrease anxiety.

Elaboration: Should you have a very difficult time undertaking real life *exposure* to phobic situations, you may need medication to enable you to negotiate graded *exposure* to phobias. The benefits of *exposure* are likely to be retained even after medication is discontinued if the dose has been sufficiently low. Note that it is necessary to experience some anxiety during *exposure* for the practice to be effective. Therefore, as an illustration, if Xanax is being prescribed, an appropriate dose would be somewhere between 0.5–1.5 mg. per day. Your practitioner should be aware and inform you of the risk of addiction to medication. Medication is suggested as a temporary complement to therapy (Bourne 1995).

Practitioner's Role: If the client is unable to use any form of *exposure,* including *imaginal exposure,* psychotropic medication might be considered. First assess the client for an addiction disorder. Then assess and discuss with the client the possibility of a referral to a psychiatrist or a physician for medication to reduce, but not to eliminate, the anxiety so graded *exposure* can begin. The discussion with the client should also include possible medication choices and their side effects.

Donna Packard-Mahony, Kathrine Baranackie, Pamela Zettergren

Anxiety

Generalized Anxiety Disorder

> Still thou art blest compared wi' me!
> The present only touches thee:
> But oh! I backward cast my cyc
> On prospects drear!
> An' forward tho' I canna see
> I guess and fear!
> —Robert Burns, "Ode to a Mouse"

Generalized anxiety disorder (GAD) accounts for only about 10 percent of clinical samples with a diagnosis of anxiety, but is among the more common of the anxiety disorders in the general population (Craske, Rapee, & Barlow 1992). The principal characteristic of GAD is persistent and excessive anxiety (worries) related to specific stimuli that are interpreted as threats to self-esteem, safety, or well-being. For example, a person may worry about physical injury, illness, or death afflicting the self or loved ones, about failures to cope, or about being rejected or depreciated by others (Beck & Emery 1985). Feelings of tension, inability to concentrate, and fears of losing control are also common symptoms. The boundaries between people with GAD and those who simply worry a great deal are not clear. For practical purposes the distinction may not be critical.

A meta-analysis (research synthesis) of eleven controlled studies of interventions for GAD suggested that cognitive therapy had larger effects than alternative methods (for example, nondirective or behavioral therapy) (Durham & Allen 1993); also, cognitive therapy had better results than analytic therapy in a recent randomized trial (Durham et al. 1999). Tasks 2–4 are consistent with a cognitive therapy approach. Support has also been found for the efficacy of *applied relaxation* (see task 1).

Literature: Beck & Emery (1985); Brown, O'Leary, & Barlow (1993); Craske, Rapee, & Barlow (1992); DeRubeis & Crits-Christoph (1998); Kendall, Krain, & Treadwell (1999); McLellarn & Rosenzweig (1998).

Task Menu
1. Learn and use *applied relaxation* techniques.
2. Learn to assess more realistically the likelihood of the actual occurrence of threatening events.

    Elaboration: Try to estimate the actual probability of a feared event happening—e.g., a loved one dying in a plane crash on the way home—using available data, your own sense of how often such events happen, etc. Then try to assess how realistic your fear is.

    Practitioner's Role: Use *cognitive restructuring* to help clients become more realistic in their appraisals.
3. To reduce anxiety associated with "catastrophizing," imagine the worst that could happen and focus on how you would cope with the situation.

    Elaboration: The focus on coping responses takes attention away from the amorphous dread of the imagined catastrophe. Also, you may see that the consequences are not as dire as you had imagined.
4. Deliberately bring about events that you are afraid of.

    Elaboration: For example, if you worry persistently about making mistakes at work, deliberately make one. Then evaluate the consequences of your actions (on the assumption that the consequences will be nonexistent or trivial in comparison to what was imagined).
5. *Reflect on* all the times events that you feared would happen did not.
6. Try to reframe an event you are worried about as something that could possibly occur but is not likely to.

    Elaboration: Life is full of risks. You could drop dead in the next minute from a heart attack, for example. But even people with GAD can't worry about everything. Try to think of your worry as one of those thousands of hazards that might conceivably happen. This will help you gain some perspective on your worry.
7. Learn and practice "worry *exposure.*"

    Elaboration: This method makes use of basic *exposure* techniques (Brown, O'Leary, & Barlow 1993). Construct a hierarchy of anxiety-provoking scenes reflecting the worst consequences of your worries. Start the *exposure* with the least distressing. Imagine the occurrence of your worst fears for approximately 25–30 minutes. Then think of as many benign alternatives as you can to the dreadful outcome you had imagined. Next time practice with the next most worrisome scene on your hierarchy.
8. Learn and practice *systematic desensitization.*

    Elaboration: As in worry *exposure* above, you work your way through a hierarchy of anxiety-provoking scenes but use relaxation and coping statements to reduce anxiety.

Anxiety

Medical Condition or Procedure: Hospital Setting

Hospitalized clients frequently experience anxiety over their medical condition or impending medical procedures. The anxiety may be manifested in obsessive worrying, sleeplessness, nausea, headaches, changes in sleeping and eating patterns, tension, etc. It may be aggravated by a sense of helplessness and loss of control over the environment, lack of activity and social interaction, and feelings of isolation. Incomplete knowledge of the medical condition, treatment options, and possible outcomes may also aggravate the problem. Lack of an adequate social support system may be a contributing factor.

An exploration of the client's history of anxiety over health or other issues and how the client has coped with such anxiety may yield clues to understanding the present episode and developing tasks. The practitioner should also be alert to possible client anger or self-blame relating to his or her condition.

Literature: Hudok & Gallo (1994); Kozier, Erb, Blais, & Wilkenson (1995); Peurifoy (1992).

Task Menu

1. *Learn about* medical condition or procedure through reading or getting information from doctors, nurses, or social worker.

    Elaboration: Some people do not want this kind of knowledge because of fears that it will increase their anxiety; others may gain a sense of control and reassurance from it. Nurses are often a valuable source of information. Hospitals frequently have educational resource centers with a wealth of medical literature and videos available for patient and family use. The Merck Manual of Medical Information: Home Edition is a useful source. The Internet can be used to get information from associations that specialize in certain diseases, like the American Cancer Society.

    Practitioner's Role: Provide reading materials, coach client in asking questions, or share their own expertise as well as arrange for appropriate hospital personnel to provide information. Medical staff can be asked for detailed information prior to the procedure. This informs the client of what is to follow and therefore decreases helplessness.

2. Engage in activities to keep your mind occupied—a hobby or other activity that you enjoy and can do in the hospital setting.

Elaboration: You may benefit from music or *relaxation* videos or tapes that can easily be utilized in the hospital setting. Hospitals often have video libraries and portable VCRs available. Friends, visitors, and support networks may be useful at this stage.

3. Use *progressive relaxation.*
4. Talk to someone—e.g., another patient or a volunteer—who has successfully overcome the condition or experienced the procedure, or join a support group if one is available.

   Practitioner's Role: Help the client locate an appropriate person or group, or develop support group.
5. Combat isolation with frequent visits or telephone contacts with family or members of support system.

   Practitioner's Role: Help client mobilize a social support network and work out schedule for contacts or visits.
6. Take anxiety-relieving medication.

   Practitioner's Role: Consult with physician regarding indications for use of medication. [if anxiety relates to procedure] Explore alternative procedure with client or, if indicated, with family, physician, or interdisciplinary treatment team.
7. Utilize simple externalization (focusing on external objects) to provide distraction and redirection.

   Elaboration: Systematic forms of simple externalization help to focus attention away from the self and the fear of escalating symptoms, thereby breaking the cycle of anxiety.

   Practitioner's Role: Instruct the client in methods of externalization, such as counting specks on ceiling tiles, intensively examining designs of nearby objects, recalling the words to songs, counting backward from 100 by 7, etc.
8. Replace negative self-talk with constructive self-statements.

   Elaboration: Positive self-statements help to improve confidence, optimism, hope, and self-esteem, thereby increasing coping mechanisms and fostering a sense of control.

   Practitioner's Role: Assist the client in developing a list of positive self-statements to practice on a regular basis. Instruct client to incorporate these statements into external dialogue, to reduce helplessness and associated anxiety.
9. Use methods of *stress inoculation* to handle medical procedures or other aspects of illness that provoke anxiety.

Kathleen Kaufman, Theresa Seastrom

Anxiety

Obsessive-Compulsive Disorder

Obsessive-Compulsive Disorder (OCD) is an anxiety disorder that affects both adults and children. OCD is characterized by the presence of recurrent obsessions or compulsions or both that are severe enough to be time-consuming (e.g., they take up more than one hour a day), cause marked distress, or interfere with the individual's routine (e.g., social activities, relationships, or occupational functioning). An obsession is a thought, image, urge, or impulse that is intrusive, persistent, and anxiety-provoking (Albano, Knox, & Barlow 1995). A compulsion is a ritualized, repetitive behavior or a mental act (e.g., counting, repeating a rhyme) used to diminish or neutralize the anxiety associated with the obsession or other situations. It should be noted that whereas adult sufferers of OCD recognize that their symptoms are internally produced and senseless at some point over the course of the disorder (Riggs & Foa 1993), children are more likely to perceive their symptoms as ego-syntonic, that is, as natural occurrences (Albano, Knox, & Barlow 1995).

According to the DSM-IV (APA 1994), community studies indicate that OCD is prevalent in about 2.5 percent of the population; slightly more than half of the sufferers are female (Riggs & Foa 1993). There is a sex-based difference in age of onset: it is earlier for males (ages six to fifteen) than for females (ages twenty to twenty-nine). Onset of OCD is usually gradual, and its course in adults ebbs and flows. Stress may exacerbate the symptoms (APA 1994). A critical aspect of assessment is identifying the extent to which people significant to the client may contribute to the occurrence, expression, or maintenance of OCD symptoms.

It should be noted that the diagnosis and assessment of childhood-onset OCD may be more difficult than that of adults. Not only are children secretive about their obsessions and compulsions, but Albano, Knox, and Barlow (1995) also report that their symptom patterns change over time. These writers suggest using parent report measures of OCD symptoms (e.g., diaries), as well as information from other sources (e.g., teachers).

Reviews of research have suggested that methods using *exposure* and response prevention have well-documented efficacy in the treatment of OCD (DeRubeis & Crits-Christoph 1998; Stanley & Averill 1998). Tasks 5 and 6 draw on these methods.

Literature: Albano, Knox, & Barlow (1995); Anderson (1995); Baer & Greist (1997); Foa & Riggs (1993); Garssen (1996); Hoffman (1996); Kozak & Foa (1996); Spencer, Wilens, & Biederman (1995); Stanley (1992); Stanley & Averill (1998); Steketee (1990).

Task Menu
 1. *Learn about* OCD.

   Elaboration: Reading material provided by the practitioner about the nature of OCD and its treatment increases the individual's knowledge and understanding of the disorder. This may ameliorate feelings of fear about "going crazy," and shame associated with symptoms of OCD. Educational material may be especially useful for the parents of a child experiencing symptoms of OCD, because it may illustrate how they unintentionally reinforce the child's obsessive thoughts and compulsive rituals. The material may also enlighten parents on what information the practitioner needs for insight into how to disrupt the patterns the child has developed. Books on OCD include <u>Stop Obsessing: How to Overcome Your Obsessions and Compulsions</u> (Foa et al. 1991) and <u>Brain Lock</u> (Schwartz 1997). An Internet site with further listings is http://home. interhop.net/oocdn/reading.htm
 2. Learn techniques that enable you to tolerate anxiety associated with obsessions or compulsions.

   Elaboration: These techniques are wide ranging and include *slow diaphragmatic breathing, progressive relaxation, stress inoculation, systematic desensitization,* and *self-verbalization,* e.g., "I consciously checked the door to see if it was locked" or "I was mindful of whether I turned off the stove, so I do not need to go back and look at it again."
 3. *Identify triggers* of obsessions, rituals, and discomfort.
 4. Design personalized *exposure* and ritual prevention goals.
 5. Participate in in-session and between-session *exposure,* imagined or in vivo.

   Elaboration: Exposure to symptom-inducing fear triggers affords opportunities to habituate to the concomitant anxiety. For example, a woman who fears germ contamination from others will allow herself to shake hands with them and increase the time between the touch and her compulsive response of hand washing, with the goal of eliminating the hand washing completely.

   Practitioner's Role: Help the client identify between-session *exposure* activities and to participate in some of them. In treating the child with OCD, train the parents in *exposure* techniques. One component of training is making sure that the parents do not attempt to minimize the anxiety that the child must tolerate during *exposure.* This type of training is also beneficial for significant others of adult clients who play an active role in the course of the disorder. Provide encouragement and monitor sessions for sufficient duration and frequency for habituation to occur. For example, Stanley (1992) suggests 10 daily sessions of 2 hours each of intensive *exposure* (flooding), followed by less frequent sessions. In-vivo *exposure* with the practitioner present is usually regarded as preferable in the beginning phase of treatment.

6. Participate in in-session and between-session response prevention.

   Elaboration: Response prevention is the inhibition of the compulsion. In the example noted in task 5, the individual tolerates the anxiety that the handshake induces by using any of the techniques identified in task 2.

7. *Identify* and challenge irrational beliefs associated with OCD.

   Elaboration: Catastrophic thinking or other kinds of irrational beliefs may accompany the symptoms of OCD. These are amenable to *cognitive restructuring.*

8. *Identify* and choose methods of stress relief.

   Elaboration: Use exercise or other recreational activities. Discuss with practitioner or friend an appropriate amount of time to spend doing them (and adhere to the time suggested, so the stress-relieving activities do not become additional compulsive behaviors).

9. Obtain psychiatric consultation to learn about risks and benefits of psychotropic medication.

   Elaboration: If medication is taken, adhere to medication schedule and keep medication management follow-up appointments. Antidepressants have been reported effective for adults and children in helping to manage the symptoms of OCD, especially in more severe cases (Riggs & Foa 1993; Spencer, Wilens, & Biederman 1995).

   Practitioner's Role: If client is prescribed medication, you may need to clarify and provide information about the medication and its side effects, as well as explain how to develop a medication schedule. Often, the client needs to work through negative feelings and beliefs about medication use, as many psychiatric consultations are too brief to adequately cover these topics.

10. Complete relapse prevention training.

    Elaboration: The ebb-and-flow course of OCD increases the likelihood of symptom relapse. Consequently, relapse prevention is a vital component of treatment. The individual should be able to identify the "OCD cycle"—fear cues or trigger, obsessions, elevated anxiety, compulsion, and temporary reduction in anxiety (Albano, Knox, & Barlow 1995) and also to understand that the cyclical nature of OCD serves to increase anxiety over the long term.

    Practitioner's Role: Arrange to contact client for follow-up. Offer booster or maintenance sessions as needed.

Andrea Orrill, Pamela Zettergren

Anxiety

Overanxious Disorder: Child

This is a condition of persistent anxiety, stress, and worry that is triggered by anticipation of future events, memories of past events, or ruminations about the self. Triggers often include the quality of performance or competence at school or in sporting events, but clients may also express excessive worries about punctuality or catastrophic events, such as earthquakes or nuclear war (APA 1994). They may be overly conforming, perfectionistic, and unsure of themselves and need constant reassurance. A certain amount of anxiety and worry is normal in the development of a child; it is often a realistic response to new roles and responsibilities. However, when symptoms become extreme or disabling, or when a child experiences several symptoms over a period of a month or more, they may be a signal of an anxiety disorder. As many as 50 percent of children with anxiety will also suffer from depression. A review of outcome research by Kazdin & Weisz (1998) suggests that cognitive-behavioral treatment is effective with this disorder. The tasks below reflect that approach.

Literature: Barrett et al. (1996); Bell-Dolan (1995); Hamilton (1994); Kearney & Wadiak (1999).

Task Menu Child
1. *Identify* underlying thoughts and beliefs associated with anxiety.
    Practitioner's Role: Provide a positive, accepting, pressure-free environment in which to explore thoughts and beliefs.
2. Learn to use and practice *progressive relaxation* techniques.
3. Use *exposure* to gradually habituate yourself to anxiety-producing situations.
    Practitioner's Role: Gradually reintroduce the anxiety-producing thoughts, people, situations, or events so as to confront the child in a gentle, calm manner (Bell-Dolan 1995). To maximize learning, role model and offer rewards for effort and success.
4. Utilize creative visual imagery.
    Practitioner's Role: Have children write down or draw pictures of each detail of the anxiety-producing event or situation, including where they feel the anxiety in their bodies (e.g., tightness in the stomach or chest, increased body temperature, dry mouth) and imagine what it would be like to let go of the anxiety. Have them visualize the anxiety leaving their bodies.
5. Learn to use *cognitive restructuring* to disrupt the maladaptive cycle of thinking and modify cognitive distortions.
    Elaboration: Link anxiety-elevating cognitions to more positive self-talk. Instead of thinking "I know I'll screw up" or "other kids will think I'm

a dork," think in terms of "people make mistakes, I need to be easier on myself" (Kendall 1992).

Task Menu Parents
6. Assess the severity of your child's anxiety, get the child a physical exam, and consult with service providers to determine need for professional help.
7. Utilize outside resources: Anxiety Disorders Association of America, 6000 Executive Blvd., Dept. A, Rockville, MD 20852; (310) 231–9350. National Institute of Mental Health, 5600 Fishers Lane, Rm. 7C-02, Rockville, MD 20857; toll-free information services for panic and other anxiety disorders, (800) 647–2642.
8. Keep a daily record of the child's anxiety utilizing a self-anchored scale. Ask child to assign a number to their anxiety (1 = I feel calm today with no anxiety, 10 = I am so anxious today I cannot function) to help see antecedent events and to monitor progress.

Jennifer Hescheles

Anxiety

Panic Disorder

The DSM-IV (APA 1994) lists two categories of panic disorder, one without agoraphobia and one with agoraphobia. Both types are characterized by the presence of unexpected, recurrent panic attacks. An individual with agoraphobia has anxiety about being in places or situations where escape may be difficult or embarrassing and help may not be available in case of such an attack. Panic attacks are discrete periods of intense fear or discomfort in which four of the following symptoms develop abruptly and peak within ten minutes: 1) sweating; 2) trembling or shaking; 3) palpitations, pounding heart, or accelerated heart rate; 4) feeling of choking; 5) sensations of shortness of breath or smothering; 6) chest pain or discomfort; 7) nausea or abdominal distress; 8) feeling dizzy, unsteady, lightheaded, or faint; 9) depersonalization or derealization (feelings of unreality); 10) fear of going crazy or losing control; 11) fear of dying; 12) paresthesias (tingling sensations or numbness); 13) hot flushes or chills (APA 1994:395).

In panic disorder there is at least one month of persistent concern about having another panic attack in addition to worry about possible implications or consequences of the significant behavior related to the attack. The symptoms of panic attack are not attributed to a direct physiological or medical condition, and at least two unexpected attacks are required for the diagnosis. If panic disorder (without agoraphobia) is left untreated, the recurrent fear of panic attacks may lead to avoidant behavior. It is common for an individual with panic disorder to additionally develop agoraphobia within the first year (APA 1994).

Research reviewed by DeRubeis & Crits-Christoph (1998) suggests empirical support for the efficacy of *exposure*-based methods as well as *applied relaxation* in the treatment of panic (see tasks 4–6 below).

Literature: American Psychiatric Association (1994); Bouman & Emmelkamp (1996); Craske, Rapee, & Barlow (1992); McNally (1994); Dobson (1988); Freeman, Simon, & Beutler (1989); Meichenbaum (1985); Suinn (1990); Taylor (1999).

Task Menu

1. *Identify* people or situations that seem to trigger or evoke panic.

   Elaboration: Carefully recalling situations where panic attacks have occurred may lead to a conscious awareness of what precedes a panic attack. This can increase the predictability of the attacks and thus lead to a reduction in anxiety, since the attacks will no longer seem inexplicable physical catastrophes. Also, you may be able to modify the triggers and ward off an attack (Bouman & Emmelkamp 1996).

   Practitioner's Role: Have the client, while in a detached emotional state, recall the details, including thoughts, images, and bodily sensations, surrounding situations and people that seem to trigger panic (Craske, Rapee, & Barlow 1992).

2. Keep records of the duration and frequency (including the time of day) of the panic attacks, while also maintaining a stress log or diary to identify feelings, cognitions, situations, people, and physical cues that precipitate an attack.

   Elaboration: Some individuals suffering from panic disorder may have a low tolerance to exercise.

   The main by-product of muscle activity is the lactate level in the blood. It has been discovered that individuals who suffer from panic have an elevated amount of lactate in their bloodstream. During exercise, too much lactate may be produced, which may lead to symptoms of panic (McNally 1994).

   Practitioner's Role: Ask client to log all feelings, cognitions, physical cues, and people present at the time of his or her panic attack (in addition to duration and frequency of the attack) and review the notes and patterns in the next session.

3. When anxiety/panic symptoms are present, attempt to see physiological phenomena, such as rapid breathing or heartbeat, as the result of anxiety rather than as life-threatening symptoms.

   Elaboration: In general, work on recognizing unrealistic fears. This can help take the focus off the panic attack, so the pattern can be interrupted and the attack eliminated or cut short.

Practitioner's Role: Use *cognitive restructuring* to help the client see unrealistic bases of his or her fears. The client can learn that there may be little basis for his or her interpretation of panic symptoms as life threatening. For example, the client may have experience symptoms many times without dire physical consequences (Bouman & Emmelkamp 1996).

4. Experience paniclike anxiety under controlled conditions, which will give you an opportunity to develop ways of coping with it.

    Practitioner's Role: *Exposure* use procedures that induce paniclike sensations reliably—cardiovascular exercise, spinning, hyperventilation—in a graduated format, which often helps decrease clients' panic attacks triggered by physical cues (Craske, Rapee, & Barlow 1992).

5. When experiencing *exposure*, use coping self-statements (e.g., instruct yourself to remain in the situation, accept feelings, and discount unrealistic beliefs).

6. Use *applied relaxation* procedures when experiencing anxiety.

    Practitioner's Role: Instruct client in *applied relaxation* techniques or other forms of *relaxation* (e.g., *coping imagery,* meditation, *slow diaphragmatic breathing* exercises). Demonstrate and explain to client that when relaxed, he or she can practice imagining anxiety-provoking scenes of increasing intensity and then use *relaxation* techniques to self-demonstrate coping ability.

7. Practice *slow diaphragmatic breathing.*

    Elaboration: Some individuals suffering from panic attacks feel as if they cannot get enough air and begin hyperventilating. This results in an intake of too much oxygen and a release of too much carbon dioxide, which in turn causes additional symptoms such as tingling or numbness of body parts, dizziness, lightheadedness, and fainting.

    Practitioner's Role: Help client learn *slow diaphragmatic breathing.*

8. If you have a fear of death, it may be helpful to compile a list of all previous medical documents and tests for reassurance that the panic attack is not physiological in origin and will not result in a heart attack or stroke.

    Practitioner's Role: Refer client to a physician who can provide the needed documentation.

9. In times where there are no symptoms of panic, engage in enjoyable activities and rediscover hobbies enjoyed prior to the onset of the disorder.

    Elaboration: This behavior will increase motivation to work on alleviating the panic disorder, and can be a valuable resource to reassure oneself that a panic attack, not a physical illness, is being experienced.

10. Join a support group for individuals with panic or other types of anxiety disorders or read case studies on other suffering individuals to assist in the recognition that you are not alone.

11. Assert feelings or opinions to your friends and family and suggest that family or significant other attend a therapeutic session.

Elaboration: Sometimes, in addition to the feelings of helplessness associated with the anticipation of panic attacks, a sufferer may be apprehensive about expressing feelings. For instance, *going on an outing may produce panic, especially if in locations where hospitals are distant.* Fear of losing or aggravating friends or family, however, often prevents the individual from voicing concerns.

Practitioner's Role: *Role play* with or model for client assertive behavior in expressing feelings and concerns. Encourage client to have important individuals in his or her life attend sessions or go to their own counseling to help them deal with the client's condition.

Pamela Zettergren, Lisa Guido

Anxiety

Post-Traumatic Stress Disorder (PTSD): Adult

People exposed to traumatic events are at risk of developing post-traumatic stress disorder (PTSD), a syndrome characterized by three distinguishing categories of symptoms: hyperarousal, intrusion, and avoidance/numbing. Physiological changes initiated by the traumatic event present as a chronic state of hyperarousal characterized by a heightened startle response, irritability, explosive anger/rage, difficulty sleeping, and hypervigilance. Intrusion refers to a conscious or unconscious compulsion to remember or relive significant aspects of the traumatic event, generally through recurrent thoughts, memories, dreams, nightmares, flashbacks, and re-enactments of the traumatic theme. These symptoms tend to evoke the overwhelming emotions associated with the original traumatic event. Consequent avoidance of trauma-reminiscent stimuli is often seen in this disorder. Emotional numbing and a vastly diminished capacity to experience pleasurable activities are typical (Herman 1992; Meichenbaum 1994; van der Kolk 1996). Common features include significant difficulty trusting, cognitive distortions, low self-esteem, multiple fears, isolating behaviors, and perceptions of loss of control, which may be compensated for through perfectionism, authoritarianism, and compulsivity. Depression and substance abuse often present as comorbid conditions.

Traumatic events are extraordinary in nature and beyond the victim's normal range of accommodation. Symptoms often represent coping strategies designed to adapt to uniquely terrifying circumstances in which the victim feels powerless and helpless (Herman 1992). Such events are defined in the DSM-IV (APA 1994) as involving actual or threatened profound endangerment to one's own or another's physical integrity or learning of such an event involving a loved one. Many people in the United States are exposed at some point to such events. Severity and duration of traumatic events influence the degree and chronicity of symptom manifestation. Generally symptoms occur within the first three months after the event, although they may be delayed for months or even years. Symptoms may be acute, chronic, delayed, intermittent, or recurrent (Meichenbaum 1994).

Literature: Beck (1976); Bloom (1990); Herman (1992); Howes (1991); Meichenbaum (1994); Rothstein (1991); Sherman (1998); van der Kolk (1996); Vonk & Yegidis (1998); Walker (1994).

Task Menu

1. Develop safety plans if need is identified.

    Elaboration: In addition to external threats such as perpetrator proximity, safety encompasses preventing a broad range of problems including disruption of biorhythms affecting sleep and appetite, self-harming behaviors, impulsive behaviors, and suicidality. It may also entail a perception of safety in the face of overwhelming emotions and loss of control.

    Practitioner's Role: First address safety concerns by supporting the client in identifying threats as well as internal and external danger signals. The next step is to help the client develop a concrete, workable safety plan. The client should be encouraged to rehearse the plan to assure viability and to foster empowerment and a sense of security. Such a plan may represent a totally new conceptual orientation for the client who, despite apparent agreement, may resist. Revisit this area until the client is comfortable, unless there is imminent danger, in which case immediate intervention is necessary (Walker 1994). It is important to offer support and encouragement, as the implementation may occur slowly or in a fragmented manner.

2. *Learn about* PTSD and the recovery process.

    Elaboration: Education is an ongoing process both within and outside of the therapy session. People with PTSD are generally frightened and confused by their symptoms. In addition to providing information, education helps sufferers to feel that their symptoms are "legitimate" and that their responses to traumatic events are "normal."

    Practitioner's Role: Information must be provided within the context of the client's narrative and level of established trust. Use the educational process to reframe and instill hope. Sharing of information must be individualized at a pace that does not overwhelm the client and in a format that is suitable to his or her intellectual capacity. Check frequently the client's understanding of the information and application of it to his or her own situation.

3. Recount the story of the trauma.

    Elaboration: Telling the story integrates traumatic memories into your life story. This is essential for recovery. The unfolding of the narrative is a highly individualized process in terms of both pacing and mode of expression. Significant aspects of traumatic memories are typically not encoded in the normal verbal and linear mode. Although you experience trauma symptoms, memory may be partial or absent. Because traumatic memories are often visual and kinesthetic in nature, nonverbal therapies involving creative expression, such as drawing, painting, and sculpting may help in expressing the memories. Depending on the individual, writing out the story, letter writing, and psychodrama may also be effective tools.

Practitioner's Role: Attention must be paid to the client's ability to cope with the material disclosed. You may need to redirect the focus of sessions at various points in the recovery process to prevent the client from becoming emotionally overwhelmed. Too much disclosure before trust and coping skills are sufficiently established can be counterproductive to treatment. A major component of work with PTSD clients is the development of trust and a sense of safety within the sessions and with the practitioner.

4. Recognize and name symptoms by completing a daily symptom checklist.

Elaboration: Through this task, symptoms are objectified, thereby diminishing the sense that something is intrinsically "wrong" with you.

Practitioner's Role: Supply the checklist and discuss noted symptoms with the client.

5. Identify and develop positive self-soothing techniques.

Elaboration: Most people learn positive methods of self-soothing that help to modulate affect beginning in childhood. People suffering from PTSD need to identify and apply methods that are new or have worked for them in the past (e.g., having a glass of warm milk, wrapping up in a blanket) to help deal effectively with overwhelming emotions and fear. People who suffered repeated childhood trauma may have never learned how to self-soothe and may therefore require additional assistance in understanding and developing these tools.

Practitioner's Role: Assist the client in identifying and using self-soothing actions. Focus discussion on what to use and when to use self-soothing. Check with the client to verify that this is working.

6. Develop skills to cope with tension.

Elaboration: It is important to develop ways to reduce tension to enhance your sense of control and to help modify hyperarousal responses.

Practitioner's Role: Explore various *relaxation* techniques with the client and mutually agree on acceptable techniques, then teach and rehearse them in session. Pay attention to structuring frequency and to monitoring through self-report.

7. Use *exposure* for coping with symptoms (Keane et al. 1992; Sherman 1998).

Practitioner's Role: In using *exposure* the client recounts the traumatic episode in a safe situation—e.g., with a practitioner. Between sessions the client may continue the process through *exposure* to safe stimuli associated with the traumatic event (for example, watching a war film). Care must be taken to avoid excessive *exposure*, which might result in anxiety the person can't control (Sherman 1998).

8. Transform traumatic memories.

   Elaboration: The transformation process necessitates accepting traumatic memories and integrating them, examining and modifying distorted cognitions and dysfunctional beliefs. The goal is to overcome tendencies to avoid reminders of traumatic events (Sherman 1998).

   Practitioner's Role: Facilitate acceptance by validating the client's feelings, reframing his or her self-damaging perceptions, and offering alternate coping strategies. Attention must be given to the symbolic meanings, often expressed through metaphor, that reflect the individual's perception of self in relation to the traumatic event. Traumatic events damage fundamental assumptions about life and distort the client's perception of self and others. This in turn negatively impacts on self-esteem, feelings, and behaviors. Specific treatment strategies such as *cognitive restructuring* can help the client to modify distorted beliefs associated with the painful memories.

9. Learn to control anger.

   Elaboration: People with PTSD often have problems related to anger and rage, regardless of the nature of the trauma. See ANGER MANAGEMENT AND AGGRESSION CONTROL: ADULT.

10. Join a self-help support group.

    Elaboration: Support groups offer a format for normalization and social interaction. They provide an arena for victims of overwhelming stressors such as war, sexual abuse, natural disasters, captivity, and domestic violence to tell their stories and have them witnessed by people who have experienced the same type of stressor. Common difficulties are shared and explored while mutual support is given to the recovery process. Support groups can help to build trust and positive self-esteem.

    Practitioner's Role: Clients should be encouraged to locate local support groups to enhance self-efficacy. Periodic inquiry will disclose the degree to which the client's involvement is sustained and offer a basis for discussion of related issues and experiences.

11. Engage in controlled activities, such as organized wilderness adventures or self-defense training, that challenge the hyperarousal syndrome (Herman 1992).

    Elaboration: This may be suggested only in the later stage of the recovery process. Its purpose is to reconstruct normal physiological responses and to bolster self-esteem by improving your sense of control and confidence.

    Practitioner's Role: Help the client to generalize positive aspects of the experience.

Diane Austin

Anxiety

Post-Traumatic Stress Disorder (PTSD): Child

According to the DSM-IV (APA 1994), post-traumatic stress disorder (PTSD) results from experiencing an extreme trauma, such as an event that involves serious injury or the threat of death, either to oneself or to someone close. The trauma might also include a threat to one's physical integrity, as in the case of sexual abuse.

To meet the diagnostic criteria for PTSD, the child's response to the stressor must also include a display of "disorganized or agitated behavior," and possibly "intense fear, helplessness, or horror" (424). The characteristic symptoms that follow exposure to the stressor can be grouped into three categories: reexperiencing, avoidant, and hyperarousal. These symptoms can present themselves in various ways, including repetitive play, reenactment of the trauma, nightmares, difficulty in concentrating, and physical symptoms such as stomachaches and headaches. In order for a diagnosis of PTSD to be made, the reexperiencing, avoidant, and hyperarousal symptoms must last for more than one month and cause a significant impairment in important areas of functioning.

Although there are studies that support PTSD as a valid diagnosis for children, it is important to realize that not all children who experience traumatic events will develop the full range of symptoms (Lipovsky 1991), and that "the severity, duration, and personal impact" of the event will affect the development of PTSD (Husain & Kashani 1992:112). A child, for example, "may be more likely to develop PTSD if the traumatic event is violent, results in physical harm to the child, or if the child witnesses the injury or death of a significant other" (Lipovsky 1991:43). Although the prevalence of PTSD varies considerably, studies of individuals in at-risk situations have revealed prevalence rates of 3 to 58 percent (APA 1994). There is relatively little controlled research on the effectiveness of interventions for PSTD in children (Sherman 1998).

Literature: Eth & Pynoos (1985); Gil (1991); Johnson (1989); Kearney & Wadiak (1999); Koverola (1995); Landreth, Homeyer, Glover, & Sweeney (1996); Lipovsky (1991); Saylor (1993); Sherman (1998); Terr (1990).

Task Menu Parents or caregivers
1. *Identify* symptoms displayed by the child.

   Elaboration: It may be difficult for children to describe and report their symptoms; therefore, the symptoms can be observed and reported to the practitioner by the parents/caregivers, teachers, and other adults who often see the child.

   Practitioner's Role: Contact individuals, in addition to the parents/caregivers, who may be able to provide information about the child's actions and statements.

2. Provide the child with a safe and supportive environment.

Elaboration: "In order for children to work through a traumatic event, they must be able to symbolically represent or reexperience the event in tolerable doses within a safe and supportive context. Thus, the clinician (and parents/caregivers) must provide the context in which such material can be explored safely without, of course, retraumatizing the child through confronting him with more trauma-based material than he can integrate or process at the moment" (Gillis 1993:167).

Practitioner's Role: To create this safe and supportive environment, educate the child and caregivers about the typical symptoms of and responses to PTSD (see task 3, below). Help the parents/caregivers learn how to communicate with their child about the traumatic event. Also allow the child to discuss and explore the event through the use of play therapy, letter writing, and drawing.

3. Educate the child about the typical symptoms of and responses to PTSD.

Elaboration: Providing information about post-traumatic symptoms and responses may help the child realize that symptoms he or she is experiencing are typical and that other children have had similar reactions to traumatic events (Lipovsky 1991; Gillis 1993). Examples of typical responses can include nightmares, heightened anxiety, and sleeping difficulties (Gillis 1993).

Practitioner's Role: Locate and share information with the parents/caregivers about what types of symptoms and responses to expect from the child (Johnson 1989). Inform the parents/caregivers (and the child, if this information will not be harmful to him or her) about what to expect during the intervention process and what types of behaviors the child may display in response to this process.

4. Learn to cope with your own reactions to the traumatic event.

Elaboration: "Traumatic events evoke not only protective responses from parents, but also feelings of vulnerability, guilt, and sometimes memories of prior traumas" (Gillis 1993:170). Therefore, "a common reaction of parents is to want to avoid discussion of the trauma with their children. This is the opposite of what is helpful to the child. Therefore, it is crucial to attend to the emotional needs of the parents and to overcome their resistance" (Gillis 1993:170).

Practitioner's Role: Help the parents/caregivers express their thoughts and feelings about the event and recognize the needs of the child (Klingman 1993).

Task Menu Child

1. *Identify* the characteristics and nature of the traumatic event.

Elaboration: Knowledge of the characteristics of the event enables the practitioner to create a more thorough assessment to better comprehend your responses to it. Typical information can include: how you and others responded to the event, your perception of how threatening the event was, if you felt that you or significant others would be hurt or killed; and your "level of exposure to the event" (Lipovsky 1991:44).

Practitioner's Role: Provide paper and drawing supplies, puppets, or dolls to a younger child who may not be able to verbally describe the characteristics of the event.

2. *Identify* resources to be used when in need of support.

Elaboration: Develop a list of individuals with whom you are able to talk for support. With the assistance of parents/caregivers and the practitioner, also develop a plan for when and how to contact these individuals. In addition, adults at school (teachers, guidance counselors, and school social workers and psychologists) can be a source of support and part of the treatment process.

Practitioner's Role: Establish effective levels of communication with professionals and with the parents/caregivers.

3. *Identify* and label feelings that are associated with the traumatic event.

Elaboration: Work to experience your full range of feelings (Lipovsky 1991).

Practitioner's Role: Allow the child to safely experience his or her feelings associated with the issues and memories of the event. Also, see **Practitioner's Role** in task 2 above.

4. *Identify* the relationship between feelings and behaviors.

Elaboration: An important step is "to recognize feelings and the expression or behavior which is congruent with those feelings" (Fatout 1993:91). Use index cards or a *journal* to record thoughts, feelings, time, location, surrounding peers, activities, and expectations when experiencing anxiety, helplessness, or other symptoms of PTSD. You can also draw pictures and include them on the cards/*journal* to represent how you are feeling and behaving. In order for the task to be effective, you must be able to identify when feeling stressed or anxious and to implement the strategies appropriately and independently. Therefore, this task may be more appropriate for older children.

Practitioner's Role: Review the index cards or *journal* with the child and establish coping strategies for specific fears or anxieties. Search for any cognitive distortions and use *cognitive restructuring* (see task 10 below) to help the child eliminate the distortions.

5. Utilize *stress inoculation* techniques to manage stress and anxiety.

Elaboration: According to Johnson (1989:101), symptoms of PTSD, "such as intrusive imagery and loss of control," can cause stress and anxiety. Therefore, the use of *stress inoculation* techniques "can be useful in teaching the client to monitor and control trauma-related stress problems" (Johnson 1989:101).

Practitioner's Role: Make any necessary modifications to the *stress in-oculation* techniques so that they are appropriate to the child's skill level.

6. Try to understand the nature and meaning of the traumatic event.

Elaboration: You may misunderstand how the traumatic event happened or assign a dysfunctional or distorted meaning to the event (Gillis 1993). Therefore, it is necessary to explore, challenge, and reframe these distorted thoughts through *cognitive restructuring* or other "modes of communication such as play or drawings" (Lipovsky 1991:48).

7. Learn and implement *progressive relaxation* techniques.

Elaboration: The goal of *progressive relaxation* in this context "is to provide the children with a tool so that they experience anxiety in measured doses that can be controlled without feeling overwhelmed" (Lipovsky 1991:46).

Practitioner's Role: Make any necessary modifications to the *progressive relaxation* techniques so that they are appropriate to the child's skill level.

8. Experience cues (memories, thoughts, and feelings) to the traumatic event in a comfortable manner.

Elaboration: Make sure you have a safe and supportive setting to discuss the traumatic events.

Practitioner's Role: Provide such a setting by allowing the child to discuss and explore the events through the use of play therapy, letter writing, drawing, and storytelling (Lipovsky 1991).

Robert Mattola, Mark Horowitz

Anxiety

Separation Anxiety Disorder

"Separation anxiety disorder (SAD) is one of the most common childhood psychiatric disorders" (Bell-Dolan 1995:217), affecting an estimated 4 percent of children and young adolescents (APA 1994). In order to receive a DSM-IV diagnosis of SAD, for at least four weeks a child must exhibit at least three of the eight symptoms listed: 1) unrealistic worrying that the attachment figure might get harmed or will leave and not return; 2) fear that a catastrophic event (i.e., killing or kidnapping) will separate the child from the attachment figure; 3) persistent reluctance or refusal to go to school or anywhere else due to fear of separation; 4) refusal or reluctance to sleep away from the attachment figure; 5) excessive fear of being home alone without the attachment figure; 6) repeated nightmares involving the theme of separation; 7) complaints of physical problems (i.e., stomachache or nausea) when separation from the attachment figure is anticipated or occurs; 8) excessive distress in anticipation of separation or upon separation (i.e., temper tantrums) (APA 1994). Other criteria include the following: onset must be before the age of 18; the symptoms cannot only occur during a psychotic disorder (i.e., schizophrenia) or pervasive developmental disorder (autism); the anxiety must be developmentally inappropriate as well as excessive; and there must be significant impairment or distress in academic, social, or other important areas of functioning (APA 1994). SAD is seen most often in prepubertal children, with the average age of onset being nine years (Kashani & Orvaschel 1988, 1990; Last et al. 1987). There are three modes in which SAD may be expressed: cognitively, physiologically, and motorically. Treatment needs to be relevant to the modes of expression, the child's developmental and cognitive level, what treatment modes parents agree to (i.e., flooding versus gradual *exposure*), and the context of the larger system (e.g., the child may fear going to school (Bell-Dolan 1995). *Parent training* may be a useful aspect of treatment (Barrett, Dadds, & Rapee 1996; Briesmeister & Schaefer 1998: Hagopian & Slifer 1993). Hagopian and Slifer (1993) state that "although SAD generally has a widespread effect on the child and family, it may be more efficient to focus treatment on the situation in which the separation anxieties are most prominent and disruptive to the child and family"(279). For this purpose *planned activities training* may be apropos (Harrold et al. 1992; Lutzker & Steed 1998).

Literature: Bell-Dolan (1995); Barrett, Dadds, & Rapee (1996); Bernstein & Borchardt (1991); Fischer, Himle, & Thyer (1999); Hamilton (1994); Francis (1992); Hagopian & Slifer (1993); Kearney & Wadiak (1999); Lutzker & Steed (1998).

Task Menu Child

1. Gradually expose yourself to the anxiety-provoking situation (Barrett, Dadds, & Rapee 1996; Bell-Dolan 1995).

    Elaboration: For example, if you are scared to sleep alone, the first move can be to sleep on the floor in your parents' room, move closer to the door, outside the door, and then to your own room (Bell-Dolan 1995). In a situation where you cannot stay in the classroom without a parent, the time in class without a parent should gradually be increased, with proximity and interaction with parent being decreased concurrently (Hagopian & Slifer 1993). During or right after the graduated *exposure* assignment, record anxiety from 0 (not scared at all) to 8 (as scared as I have ever been). Rating of 0 to 3 are considered acceptable levels of anxiety, and progression to the next hierarchy step is allowed (Bell-Dolan 1995). Hagopian and Slifer (1993) recommend meeting the current criterion at least two times, as well as having both child and parent feel comfortable, before proceeding to the next step/criterion. In graduated *exposure* all of the assignments should be in complete agreement among the child, parent, and practitioner. *Imaginal exposure* is another alternative, or it can be used prior to in vivo practice (Thyer 1991). Real life *exposure* appears to be more effective than imaginal approaches, especially with younger children (Morris & Kratochwill 1983). Another option is flooding (Bell-Dolan 1995).

2. Use *self-verbalization* during graduated *exposure* (Barrett, Dadds, & Rapee 1996; Francis 1992).

   Elaboration: Coping *self-verbalization* assists in mastering anxieties. Use *self-verbalization* to reinforce a more realistic appraisal of the situation that is producing the anxiety ("Nothing bad happened last time my mom left me at school, so I bet it won't this time either"). Mastery-oriented coping statements can also be used ("I'm pretty brave; I can do this"). (Bell-Dolan 1995).

3. Learn to use and practice *relaxation* (Barrett, Dadds, & Rapee 1996; Francis 1992; Bernstein & Borchardt 1991).

   Elaboration: Modeling techniques can be used to help show a child how to relax when faced with an anxiety-provoking situation (Hamilton 1994).

4. Keep a behavioral chart to show progress throughout treatment (Hamilton 1994).

Task Menu Parents

1. Get physical exam for child.

   Elaboration: This is to make sure that there are no physical causes contributing to the ailments of which the child complains (Hamilton 1994).

2. Record baseline of avoidant and anxious behaviors.

   Elaboration: A written narrative report should be kept when separation is attempted. Hagopian and Slifer (1993) discuss keeping this baseline for two weeks as well as recording another two weeks of avoidant and anxious episodes where separation was not attempted.

3. Attend parent training courses (Barrett, Dadds, & Rapee 1996).

   Elaboration: Parenting courses include "training the parents in skills for managing the child's anxiety and avoidance, helping parents deal with any anxiety problems they themselves experience, and improving family problem solving" (Barrett, Dadds, & Rapee 1996:334).

4. Reward the child for appropriate behavior (Bell-Dolan 1995; Hagopian & Slifer 1993; Bernstein & Borchardt 1991).

   Elaboration: If the child, for example, remains in his or her seat while the mother leaves the room, the child should receive a small reward (e.g., a sticker). Small rewards can be exchanged for bigger prizes at the end of the week (Hagopian & Slifer 1993).

5. Ignore excessive complaining and anxious behavior, such as inappropriate and excessive crying (Barrett, Dadds, & Rapee 1996; Hagopian & Slifer 1993).

   Elaboration: Parents should respond empathetically and with reassurance the first time a child complains. However, after the first time the parents should tell the child to engage in the coping strategies he or she learned. Then, until the anxious or complaining behaviors cease, the parents should withdraw their attention from the child (Barrett, Dadds, &

Rapee 1996). Parents should provide only minimal attention to child's inquiries about unrealistic worries (e.g., parents' well-being) (Hagopian & Slifer 1993).
6. Help child do *relaxation* exercises.

Practitioner's Role: Provide parents with instructions and modeling techniques to use in *relaxation* activity (Hamilton 1994).

Miranda Koss

Anxiety

Social Phobia

The DSM-IV (APA 1994) defines social phobia as a persistent fear of one or more situations in which the person is exposed to possible scrutiny by others and fears that he or she may act in a way that will be humiliating or embarrassing. Examples of such situations may include public speaking, eating in public, or saying something foolish. Other criteria include: 1) an invariable "immediate anxiety response" when exposed to the particular phobic stimulus; 2) avoidance (or endurance with intense anxiety) of the phobic situation; 3) usually some degree of interference with social activities, occupational activities, and relationships; 4) a recognition that the fear is excessive or unreasonable. "Individuals who are social phobic become pressured and fearful in ordinary social situations in which others show little vestige of fear" (Riskind & Mercier 1994:313). Lifetime prevalence ranges from 3 to 13 percent and appears with about the same frequency in both sexes (APA 1994). There is also a high likelihood the social phobia will coexist with other anxiety disorders (Stein et al. 1990).

Typical forms of treatment include *social skills training, systematic desensitization, exposure, relaxation* techniques, and several types of cognitive-behavioral therapy (Donohue et al. 1994).

Literature: Donohue et al. (1994); Riskind & Mercier (1994); Stein et al. (1990); Wells (1998).

Task Menu
1. Improve *social skills*—for example, conversational skills.
    Elaboration: If you have the requisite skills but are too anxious to perform them in social situations, you may not benefit from *social skills training* (Donahue et al. 1994).
    Practitioner's Role: Make use of methods of *social skills training*.
2. *Identify* and correct (through use of *cognitive restructuring*) maladaptive thoughts giving rise to anxiety.
3. Learn and use *relaxation* methods.

Elaboration: Evidence suggests that while relaxation methods may be better than no treatment, their effects are relatively modest. Such methods may be best used in combination with other tasks.

4. Use positive self-statements to control anxiety.
5. Use distractions to take your mind off anxiety-producing stimuli.
6. Use *exposure* to habituate yourself to anxiety-producing situations.

Elaboration: Client and practitioner can develop a hierarchy of increased *exposure* to threatening situations, starting with a minimal level of *exposure*—e.g., spending only a few minutes at a social gathering. Client starts with tasks at the lowest level of the hierarchy.

Practitioner's Role: You may want to be present in the actual situation to provide on-the-spot assistance and support.

Anxiety

Specific Phobia

The DSM-IV (APA 1994) describes specific phobia (previously called "simple phobia") as the "marked and persistent fear of clearly discernible, circumscribed objects or situations" (405). Whereas adolescents and adults realize that their fears are extreme, children with specific phobias do not. The fear results in avoiding the object or situation; it is of clinical significance when the client experiences distress (e.g., anxiety and its physical symptoms) and her or his usual functioning is disrupted. The DSM-IV identifies types of specific phobias: 1) animal (e.g., snakes, dogs); 2) natural environment (e.g., storms, water); 3) blood injection (seeing blood or witnessing certain medical procedures); 4) situational (e.g., flying/crashing); and 5) other (a fear that is stimulated by cues other than 1–4). Specific phobias affect about 10 percent of the population, and often are the result of childhood fears that are not outgrown. In fact, children's fears are often reinforced by significant adults, resulting in a familial pattern to some types of specific phobias.

Literature: Anthony, Craske, & Barlow (1995) provide self-help books; Bourne (1995); Thyer (1987); Seligman (1990); Davis, Eshelman, & McKay (1995).

Task Menu

1. Learn and use *applied* or *progressive relaxation* techniques.
2. *Learn about* the feared object or situation and correct distorted information.

Elaboration: Phobic reactions may be stimulated by false information, for example, the belief that most snakes are aggressive.

3. Practice *exposure* three to five times weekly.

   Elaboration: *Exposure* has been shown to be the most effective tool for simple phobia. Breaking the fear into small increments makes it more manageable. It is generally helpful to have a support person or clinician with you as you begin *exposure*. For example, a fear of driving on an expressway can be approached by initially driving extremely short distances that are then gradually increased, or by initially driving at times when there is little traffic and then incrementally shifting to times when traffic is heavier.

4. Practice visualizing the phobic situation, through use of *imaginal exposure* (Anthony, Craske, & Barlow 1995).

   Elaboration: *Imaginal exposure* is useful when it is impractical to conduct repeated real life exposures—as with fear of flying—or when fear is so intense that any degree of actual *exposure* is impossible. The procedure is done in two steps. Begin by spending 10 to 15 minutes getting relaxed using *applied* or *progressive relaxation* techniques. Next, visualize the phobic situation until uncomfortable, then switch to *relaxation*. This procedure needs to be practiced daily to be effective. It may be helpful to tape-record instructions and use them at home as a practice aid.

   Practitioner's Role: Use can also be made of *systematic desensitization*, a method similar to *imaginal exposure*.

5. Counter negative self-talk with positive self-statements.

   Elaboration: To increase awareness of the negative self-talk about your fears, keep a *journal* recording distortions (words such as "always," "never," "everyone," etc.) in one column. In the other column counter with rational positive self-statements. As you become aware of the negative self-talk in the phobic situation, try countering it with constructive affirmations.

Kathryn Baranecki

Assertiveness, Lack of

Assertiveness is standing up for one's rights and acting in one's own best interests without undue anxiety, and expressing thoughts, beliefs, and feelings in a straightforward, honest, appropriate way that does not infringe on the rights of others (Rakos 1991). Being unable to assert themselves with others in situations where it is called for leaves many individuals feeling frustrated and inadequate. For most people, learning to be appropriately assertive involves overcoming social anxieties and inhibitions and being proactive in situations where they previously would have behaved in a passive or timid manner (Burke 1989). Successful assertive behavior can not only help a person attain what he or she wants but can also lead to increased self-efficacy (Collier & Marlatt 1995). Moreover, aggressive individuals may gain from learning to assert themselves in a respectful, appropriate manner.

Literature: The literature most relevant to practitioners concerns assertiveness training. Illustrative of the great variety of programs found in this literature are those for drug addicts and alcoholics (Collier & Marlatt 1995; Silverman 1990), for adolescents (Kiselica et al. 1994), for college students with low self-confidence (Foss & Hadfield 1993), for people with severe self-defeating anxiety (Hovland 1995) and social anxiety (Agathon 1994), for physically disabled adults (Glueckauf & Quittner 1992), for mildly mentally retarded people with dual diagnoses of different psychiatric disorders (Nezu, Nezu, & Arean 1991), and for patients with psychiatric illnesses that include schizophrenia, personality disorder, and affective disorders (Brown & Carmichael 1992). Assertiveness training has been suggested as one technique for school counselors to use to help prevent aggression in schools (Studer 1996). It has also been integrated into high school sexuality education curricula with the goal of enhancing students' ability to be assertive in the face of pressure to engage in sexual activity (Duggan-Ali 1992). Learning assertiveness skills to prevent date rape has also been suggested (Parrot 1996).

See also Ballou (1995); Burke (1989); Covey (1989); Foder (1992); Gambrill (1995); Kasl (1989); McLain & Lewis (1994); Rakos (1991).

Task Menu

1. *Identify* and evaluate the situations in which you believe you are under-assertive.

   Elaboration: Tasks 1–3 form a logical sequence.

   Practitioner's Role: Assist clients in identification and evaluation of situations in which they believe that they are underassertive. Explore past choices with clients and help them determine if the fears they have about being assertive are founded in reality. If there were times client was appropriate in behavior, despite not being assertive, point this out (e.g., a situation where assertion is perceived as being disloyal or aggressive by a poorly adjusted supervisor, and could put the client's job in jeopardy, might be a case for restraint until client has an alternative job lined up).

2. Decide what your goal is for a situation.

   Elaboration: Robb (1992) encourages individuals participating in assertiveness training to look out for themselves and to do so based on their long-term best interests (e.g., ask yourself: "What do I feel?" "What do I think?" "What do I really want?" "Can I be assertive politely without suffering consequences I perceive as negative?").

   Practitioner's Role: Explore directly the probable consequences of pursuing or not pursuing what is wanted regardless of the hassles involved (Robb 1992). Also explore the cost of not being assertive in terms of self-esteem or unwanted behaviors (e.g., excessive drinking) and the self-anger that may result.

3. Plan and carry out an appropriately assertive response to the situation.

   Practitioner's Role: Help client practice response through *role play*, paying particular attention to developing phrasing that is assertive but also comfortable for the client.

4. For a full day, listen to your language and to the language of people around you, recording in a notebook how often you use, think, and hear reactive phrases ("If only," "I can't," or "They won't allow that") (Covey 1989).
5. That evening, make another list, changing the reactive responses to pro-active ones (e.g., "If only," "Why not" in place of "I can't" or "They won't allow that").
6. Rehearse uncomfortable situations in private until you believe you are skilled and comfortable enough to behave in an assertive manner in the situations that left you feeling underassertive or angry in the past (Burke 1989).

    Practitioner's Role: Instruct client in using *coping imagery* to assist in this task.
7. Using *exposure,* start engaging in assertive behaviors, beginning with situations that you perceive as slightly uncomfortable to mildly threatening and then expanding to more severely threatening situations (Burke 1989).

    Practitioner's Role: Teach client to use *exposure,* then *role play* the threatening situations with client. If client has trouble thinking of or enacting assertive behaviors, the practitioner may also take on the client's normal role, modeling appropriate assertive responses that client can practice. Additionally, the practitioner may need to model appropriate expression of emotion, while being assertive and teaching the client how to accurately interpret situational cues, use effective decision-making skills, and behave in an acceptable interpersonal manner (Rakos 1991).
8. Attend an assertiveness training group.

    Practitioner's Role: Process experience with the client with special attention to client integrating knowledge from training that was useful and pointing out that some elements of the training may not work for the client as presented, so he or she can discard information that was not relevant or comfortable to use.

Pamela Zettergren, Alison Molea-Lavigne

Attention Deficit / Hyperactivity Disorder

Adult

Attention deficit/hyperactivity disorder (AD/HD) is characterized by inattention, impulsivity, and hyperactivity (Jackson & Farrugia 1997). Basic types are: predominantly inattentive type; predominantly hyperactive-impulsive type; and combined type (DSM-IV, APA 1994). It is likely that the disorder has a neurological basis (Jackson & Farrugia 1997; Anastopoulos 1998).

Although the DSM-IV lists AD/HD as a disorder usually first diagnosed in infancy, childhood, or adolescence, some individuals with AD/HD may not actually be recognized and diagnosed until adulthood. It has been argued that these individuals have found ways to compensate for difficulties in their lives and that many may have been improperly and unsuccessfully treated for mood or anxiety disorders (Jackson & Farrugia 1997). Adults with AD/HD may present with such symptoms as physical and mental restlessness, avoidance of intimacy, failed relationships, impulsivity, disabling distractibility, low self-esteem, and a sense of underachievement. Because several recent studies of AD/HD in adulthood indicate continued or augmented impairment, it is important that mental health professionals accurately understand, identify, diagnose, and effectively treat the adult with AD/HD (Jackson & Farrugia 1997).

Literature: Hallowell (1995); Jackson & Farrugia (1997); Wilens, Spencer, & Biederman (1995); Triolo (1999).

Task Menu
1. Be sure of the diagnosis.

    Elaboration: Make sure you are working with a professional who really understands AD/HD and has excluded related or similar conditions such as anxiety states, agitated depression, hyperthyroidism, manic-depressive illness, or obsessive-compulsive disorder. Accurate diagnosis is critical because of the high rate of comorbidity and problems with differential diagnosis. Therapy with children may be primarily behaviorial; however, adults with AD/HD may need a more cognitively oriented approach. When the adult with AD/HD understands the nature of the disorder, it is easier to deal with the cognitive, emotional, and self-esteem problems that are often inherent.

2. *Learn about* AD/HD.

    Elaboration: Read Hallowell & Ratey (1994) and Hallowell (1995). Talk with professionals and other adults with AD/HD. Perhaps the single most powerful treatment of AD/HD is understanding the disorder (Hallowell 1995). Most adults with AD/HD have suffered years of feeling demoralized, discouraged, and ineffective because of a history of failure in school, work, family, and social domains. The cumulative effect of such a history can be internalization of these negative messages, resulting in an entrenched belief that the situation is unchangeable. The practitioner can point out that the client's symptoms are indeed treatable, giving the client hope and empowerment.

3. Consult with a physician regarding medication.

Elaboration: Pharmacotherapy should be part of a treatment plan in which consideration is given to all aspects of the person's life. Medication should not be used exclusive of other interventions. (Wilens, Spencer, & Biederman 1995).

4. Join a support group or organizations concerned with adult AD/HD such as Children and Adults with Attention Deficit Disorder (CHADD), The National Attention Deficit Disorder Association (AD/HDA), Adult AD/HD Association. See ATTENTION DEFICIT/HYPERACTIVITY DISORDER: CHILD, task 3, for details about contacting support groups.

5. If available, use online services such as America Online's <u>AD/HD support room,</u> CompuServe's <u>GO AD/HD,</u> and Prodigy's adult AD/HD support groups under <u>Support Groups Medical.</u>

6. Subscribe to newsletters: <u>AD/HDendum,</u> a quarterly newsletter, or <u>Attention!,</u> available by joining CHADD; <u>AD/HDult News,</u> published by AD/HDA.

Elaboration: Researchers have found that adults with AD/HD may have serious difficulties in creating and sustaining healthy social and interpersonal relationships because of their problems with inattention, impulse control, all-or-nothing thinking, and disorganized thought patterns that impair their ability to perform socially (Jackson & Farrugia 1997). Many adults with AD/HD have never known another adult with the disorder; therefore, group support and membership in AD/HD organizations decreases their sense of isolation and loneliness.

Practitioner's Role: Provide adult AD/HD resource list.

7. Choose a "coach" to help you.

Elaboration: A coach can be a friend or colleague. It is possible, but risky, for a coach to be a spouse. In therapy with a person with AD/HD, it is usually effective for the practitioner to supply direction and encouragement in the therapy session. Rather than teaching a client how to supply these for him or herself, teaching a client to work with a coach takes into account the inability of the client to focus and organize as efficiently as others (Hallowell 1995).

8. Learn when you are most apt to cease paying attention by timing your attention span.

9. When you miss elements of a conversation, ask whoever is speaking to repeat or clarify what was said and do not feel embarrassed when doing so.

10. In order to avoid overload, break down large or boring tasks into smaller and more manageable tasks.

11. Work on detailed tasks when maximally alert and take rest periods when needed.

12. Create a quiet and organized space for work that is free from environmental distraction.

13. Prioritize attention to activities by making and adhering to a schedule.

  Elaboration: Learning attention management skills will help adults with AD/HD monitor their own behavior and become more productive. These strategies usually take a long time to learn; however, they can be significant. Many times adults with AD/HD are too embarrassed to admit that they were distracted and cover up or mask their inattention.

14. Establish goals and target behaviors, then concentrate on target behaviors one step at a time to reach the goals.

  Elaboration: *Identify* when you unproductively go off track in taking steps to reach goals.

15. Keep a *journal,* use positive *self-verbalization,* and reward yourself for a job well done.

  Elaboration: A combination of self-awareness, self-monitoring, and self-reinforcement has been found effective in improving on-task behaviors in adults with AD/HD (Jackson & Farrugia 1997).

16. *Identify* sources of stress In your life and recognize when they are becoming excessive.

17. Organize the environment by using an appointment planning book, keeping work areas neat, and creating lists of things to do.

18. Minimize distracting stimuli in the environment by turning the phone ringer off, turning the television off, working in a low-traffic area, and finding a specific time of day when the attention span is longest.

  Elaboration: Adults with AD/HD are more likely to create stressful situations for themselves through their inattentive, impulsive, and stimulus-seeking behaviors. In addition, they have been found to overreact to stress. Another reason why daily life seems so much more stressful to adults with AD/HD is their difficulty in blocking out distractions. Adults with AD/HD need to learn to recognize not only when they are essentially creating unneeded stress for themselves, but also when they can reduce and deal more successfully with stress (Jackson & Farrugia 1997).

  Practitioner's Role: Suggest strategies to help clients deal with stress and teach ways to organize the environment.

19. *Identify* common environmental and internal events that lead to frustration and anger.

  Elaboration: Generate a plan for responding to provocation. Develop a self-reinforced contingency plan if you become too angry to deal with the situation. Many adults with AD/HD have low frustration tolerance. This builds into explosive behaviors that can be managed and controlled through anger management techniques. See ANGER MANAGEMENT AND AGGRESSION CONTROL: ADULT.

Patricia Bruno

Attention Deficit/Hyperactivity Disorder

Child

AD/HD is manifested by developmentally inappropriate degrees of inattention, impulsiveness, and hyperactivity. The essential feature of AD/HD is a persistent pattern of inattention or hyperactivity that is more frequent and severe than is typically observed in individuals at a comparable level of development, with clear evidence of interference with developmentally appropriate social, academic, or occupational functioning (APA 1994). According to the DSM-IV (APA 1994), prevalence is 3 to 5 percent in school-age children; typically the disorder is much more frequent in males than in females, with male to female ratios ranging from 4:1 to 9:1. Individuals with AD/HD experience a wide range of behavioral, cognitive, and interpersonal difficulties that significantly interfere with day-to-day functioning and well-being. Parents and teachers may report the child's presenting difficulties in following directions and staying on task, fidgetiness, immaturity, frustration intolerance, temper tantrums, aggressiveness and destructive behavior, impulsivity, and noncompliance (Bernier & Siegel 1994). "AD/HD has an enormous impact on society in terms of stress to families, disruption in schools and structured settings, criminality and financial cost" (Biederman, Newcorn, & Sprick 1991:101). In general, a multimodal approach is indicated, one that includes psychostimulant medication, *contingency-management* training and psychoeducation for the child's parents and teachers, cognitive-behaviorial and play therapy for the child to develop self-esteem and interpersonal problem-solving skills, and family counseling (Anastopoulos 1998).

Literature: Anastopoulos (1998); Barkley (1995, 1996, 1997, 1998); Biederman, Newcorn, & Sprick (1991); Bernier & Siegel (1994); Hoza, Vallano, & Pelham (1995); Silver (1993).

Task Menu Parents
1. Read material on AD/HD such as Bain (1991), Barkley (1995), Fowler (1993), Silver (1993). Consider use of psychostimulant medication at home if child's behavior is seriously disruptive (Silver 1993). [if psychostimulant medication is administered] Monitor the child's behavior and reactions.
2. Consider taking a *parent training* program for parents of children with AD/HD.
   Elaboration: Such programs, which can be carried out in individual or group formats, are most appropriate when the AD/HD child is between the ages of 4 and 12 (Anastopoulos 1998).
3. Join a support group for parents of AD/HD children.
   Elaboration: To locate support groups contact CHADD (Children and Adults with Attention Deficit Disorder), 499 N.W. 70th Avenue, Suite 308, Plantation, FL 33317; (305) 587–3700; to obtain educational resources

contact ADDA (Attention Deficit Disorder Association), P.O. Box 972; Mentor, OH 44061; (800) 487–2282. Online, contact http://www. chadd.org/ or AD-IN (Attention Deficit Information Network), Inc.; 475 Hillside Ave.; Needham, MA 02194–1207; (617) 455–9895 (Tues. and Thurs., 10 A.M.–noon); mailto:adin@qis.net or http://www.capecod.net/ awelles

4. Keep a log or journal of noncompliant behavior to establish baseline and monitor behavior.
5. Use the following methods to control unwanted behavior and to promote desired behavior: *contingency management* or *token economy, time out,* and *self-verbalization.*
6. Establish consistent daily/weekly schedule of activities including household responsibilities, homework, bedtime, and hours of selected television programs.

    Elaboration: This strategy might include utilizing checklists, posting schedules, and putting a clock or timer near the child to help structure time for activities. This can be used to record successful behavior as a part of *token economy.*

7. Encourage parent/teacher communication. The child's school status and modifications should be discussed in detail. Parents should ask about the legal rights of children with AD/HD within the school system; emphasis should be placed on the child being in the least restrictive and most consistent educational environment (Anastopoulos 1998).
8. "Learn to anticipate in what settings child misconduct may arise, e.g., stores, restaurants and visitors to the home, and review with the child a plan to manage the situation before misconduct begins" (Barkley & Murphy 1991).
9. Establish "special time," setting aside time with the child when you must remain as nondirective, supportive, and noncorrective as possible, pointing out the successes of the day in specific terms (Anastopoulos 1998). For example, "you helped set the table for dinner, you didn't throw your toys today."
10. Influence the child's behavioral choices through a four-step process: 1) "Tell the child what behavior is expected in a given situation"; 2) "Tell the child the consequences for doing or not doing what is expected"; 3) "Give the child the opportunity to make a behavioral decision"; 4) "Hold the child accountable for his or her choice by applying a consequence for the unacceptable behavior" (Fowler 1993).
11. Increase positive attending skills and give commands more effectively.

    Elaboration: Only issue commands you intend to follow through on. Commands should take the form of direct statements rather than questions; should be relatively simple; should be issued in the absence of outside distractions, with direct eye contact; should also be repeated back to

you, so as to give you an opportunity to clarify any misunderstanding (Anastopoulos 1998).
12. Use structured play to help the child improve behavior.
    Elaboration: Utilize hands-on resources and *games* for children with AD/HD.
13. Educate the child or adolescent about his or her condition so that he or she can understand past difficulties. "By doing this his self-image and self-esteem can improve" (Silver 1993).
14. Reduce stimuli in the environment when possible (i.e., noise, clutter, number of individuals in a room, and bright colors).
15. Break homework or other work situations into short time periods to encourage completion (Hartmann 1993).
16. Encourage physical activity and creativity as an outlet for extra energy.
17. Maintain positive expectations for the child's behavior rather then expecting failure (i.e., be surprised at the child's failure).
18. Encourage the child to talk about his/her own feelings. Differentiate appropriate from inappropriate behavior; restate the child's feelings to show them you are listening and understand.
Jennifer Hescheles, Susan Camarata

Binge Eating

A binge is defined in the DSM-IV (APA 1994) as eating, in a discrete period of time, an amount of food definitely larger than most people would eat under similar circumstances. The client generally has a sense of being out of control during these episodes and usually consumes the food rapidly in secrecy. Often the individual becomes uncomfortably to painfully full before discontinuing the binge episode. Binge eating may or may not be followed by purging behavior: the misuse of laxatives or diuretics, enemas, or self-induced vomiting. If purging is not used, other inappropriate compensatory behaviors, such as excessive exercise or fasting, may be used to avoid weight gain.

The DSM-IV suggests that binge eating is typically triggered by interpersonal stressors, dysphoric mood states, feelings related to body weight or shape, and access to food or intense hunger following dietary restraint. Behaviors may also be linked to other psychological disturbances, "some of which have been identified as stress, boredom, loneliness; and the binge is a means of releasing the tension caused by stressors" (Morgan 1987:88). Binge eating may reduce dysphoria, but typically an episode is followed by lowered self-esteem, self-deprecating thoughts, and depressed mood. Additionally, binge eating of fatty, highly caloric foods may be a health risk for already overweight or obese individuals.

Literature: Davis, Eshelman, & McKay (1995); Fallon, Katzman, & Wooley

(1994); Kayloe (1993); Kostas (1993); Kris-Etherton & Krummel (1996); Morgan (1987); Reibel (1991); Reiff & Reiff (1992); Saunders (1985); Seligman (1990); Ulene (1995).

Task Menu

1. Keep a food diary, noting food eaten, quantity, time, location, and feelings prior to eating.

    Elaboration: Learning that you eat because of sadness, anger, or boredom as opposed to hunger can, over time, help you gain more control of your food consumption.

    Practitioner's Role: Explain the purpose and importance of the *journal* in both assessment and treatment. Identify potential obstacles to *journaling* with client, and make suggestions for overcoming obstacles. Review *journal* with client to *identify triggers.* Assist client in identification of triggers if client is unable to recognize them.

2. Complete a self-report assessment instrument such as the Binge Eating Scale (Gormally et al. 1982).

    Practitioner's Role: Conduct a clinical interview using a reliable assessment instrument such as the Eating Disorders Inventory-2 (Garner 1991).

3. Contact a registered dietitian with experience in eating disorders and meet to develop an eating plan; continue to participate in follow-up sessions with dietitian at regular intervals (weekly or biweekly).

    Practitioner's Role: Confer with dietician to exchange information and to develop a coordinated approach to work with the client.

4. Follow the eating plan developed with the dietitian.

    Elaboration: Eat three meals spaced throughout the day, including breakfast, plus planned snacks. Eat recommended foods in portion sizes indicated in the eating plan. Plan in advance so appropriate foods are available at meal and snack times. Avoid caffeine, alcohol, sugar, and marijuana, as these stimulate the appetite. Continually review food intake with the dietitian.

5. Learn about healthy versus unhealthy foods, how to read nutritional labels, and low-calorie snacks.

    Elaboration: Learn to think in terms of healthy eating instead of restrictive eating, and that the taste for high-density foods can decrease over time. Utilize the library to locate readings on nutrition.

6. Use delay techniques to either prevent or interrupt the binge cycle.

    Elaboration: Leave the room where food is located. Next ask yourself, "What am I feeling and thinking?" Then decide whether to eat the food you were going to eat. If you choose to eat it, ask yourself if eating a smaller portion will satisfy you or if there is something healthier that is just as appealing as your original food choice. Learn to accept and feel good about the decisions you make. Another delay technique is to wait for 10 minutes before eating the food you crave. Often, after this period of time, the craving will subside. This technique shows you how to be less impulsive with food and that you have options other than bingeing.

7. Use enjoyable alternative behaviors to avoid binge eating, e.g., going for a walk, calling a friend, or eating healthy, low-calorie foods, such as carrots or celery.

8. *Identify* primary or secondary benefits from binge eating.

    Elaboration: Identifying benefits will bring to light motivations for binge eating.

    Practitioner's Role: Help client understand primary and secondary gains.

9. Set short-term behavioral goals for food intake.

    Practitioner's Role: Encourage client to be realistic about progress and accept setbacks as a normal part of the process.

10. Gradually introduce feared foods into the diet.

    Elaboration: Eating foods you consider "unsafe" can trigger a binge early in treatment. Successful exposure to these foods after you have made progress can provide a feeling of confidence and a sense of control over your life.

11. Participate in regular aerobic and strength training exercises (with approval of physician).

    Elaboration: Find exercise that is enjoyable, and do it for the pleasure, stress relief, and health benefits of the experience and not to promote weight loss. Exercise improves mood, body image, and sense of self-control.

12. Measure body weight no more than once every other week.

    Elaboration: Daily weight fluctuations are meaningless in terms of physical well-being. Daily weighing only reinforces self-evaluation based on body weight and shape.

13. Note symptoms that may develop as binge-purge behavior ceases: fluid retention, bloating, gas, constipation, diarrhea, weight fluctuations, sleep disturbances, and increased moodiness or other distressing feelings.

    Elaboration: Such symptoms are normal and temporary, especially since bingeing on food often serves to block out unwanted feelings. The symptoms indicate that you are adjusting to a healthy eating pattern.

    Practitioner's Role: Reassure client that symptoms are normal and temporary.

14. Join a self-help program.

    Elaboration: One program is Overeaters Anonymous, P.O. Box 44020, Rio Rancho, NM 87174–4020; (505) 891–2664 or look in white pages for local number. http://www.overeatersanonymous.org or mail to:overeatr@technet.nm.org. Other groups include Eating Disorders Anonymous; Bulimics/Anorexics Anonymous; Food Addicts Anonymous.

15. Make a list of at least ten things to treat or take good care of yourself that are unrelated to food. Review and update the list periodically.

Reid McCauley

Body Image, Negative (Women)

Internalized cultural messages that women receive can result in the development of a negative body image (Srebnik & Saltzberg 1994), which often correlates with low-ered self-esteem, depression, and eating disorders. There is a tendency to be obsessed with weight and appearance to the extent that it interferes in other life domains (Mintz & Betz 1988). The goal of these tasks is to shift the body ideal from a weight goal to a level of health, comfort, and pleasure that is internal rather than external in its evaluation.

Literature: Brouwers (1990); Jarny (1998); Srebnik & Saltzberg (1994); Thompson et al. (1999).

Task Menu

1. Read psychoeducational material on body image.
   Elaboration: Srebnik & Saltzberg (1994) suggest that bibliotherapy can challenge myths about the accuracy of weight tables, the relationship of weight to an individual's food intake, and the effectiveness and health risks of dieting. Some self-help guides they suggest using in therapy are Kano 1989; Katzman et al. 1986; Orbach 1978; and Freedman 1988.
   Practitioner's Role: Discuss reactions to material with client or group.
   Elaboration: For instance, process any feelings of anger generated from awareness of the feminist perspective (body image as linked to op-pression). Link societal and media influences to body image as expressed in national best-sellers such as <u>Backlash</u> (Faludi 1991). Discuss historical changes in the ideal feminine body (Brouwers 1990).
2. Learn to *identify* maladaptive thoughts associated with body image and correct them through use of *cognitive restructuring.*
   Elaboration: An example of a maladaptive thought might be believing that you deserve to be treated badly because of your body size.
   Practitioner's Role: Use *cognitive restructuring* techniques to help client alter maladaptive thoughts. Ask client to write down or verbalize thoughts regarding body image. For instance, if a client wrote or said, "I deserve to be treated badly because I am fat," the practitioner could ask if the client believed she should treat a friend badly because of how that friend looked. Also confront avoidance behaviors, such as not participat-ing in an activity because of appearance. This can be done through *expo-*

sure exercises, which have clients first discuss and then do the behavior they have avoided (e.g., swimming) to test their assumptions (Srebnik & Saltzberg 1994).

3. Address body image distortion.

   Elaboration: Distortion can be addressed through blind weighing (guessing your weight before being weighed), estimating weight relative to norms, and drawing on paper to compare actual to perceived size and shape (Hutchinson 1985; Miller 1991; Rosen et al. 1989).

4. Develop counterarguments and adaptive restatements surrounding body image.

   Practitioner's Role: Client should participate in developing counterarguments and adaptive statements (e.g., "I have a strong, healthy body," "I feel good about myself, even if my sister thinks that I should be thinner"). Responses can be rehearsed through *role plays* with practitioner or peers. Corrective feedback from other group members can be used as a basis for the client's adaptive self-statements (Rosen et al. 1989).

Pamela Zettergren

Bulimia

The essential diagnostic features of bulimia nervosa, as suggested in the DSM-IV (APA 1994), are binge eating (see BINGE EATING) and inappropriate compensatory methods to prevent weight gain. Such behaviors must occur, on average, at least twice a week for three months. Other features of bulimia nervosa are repeated attempts to lose weight by severely restrictive diets, self-induced vomiting, the use of laxatives, enemas, colonics, diuretics, and excessive exercise (Siegel et al. 1997). Self-evaluation of individuals with bulimia nervosa is characterized as being excessively influenced by weight and body shape. Sufferers may be compelled to purge for two reasons. Some may want to maintain weight even though they have just eaten large quantities of food. An anorectic, however, may eat what is considered a normal amount of food, but need to purge whatever is ingested in order to have continued weight loss.

Obsession with weight loss may be a means of trying to gain acceptance from society. The abnormal behavior is often associated with a constant drive for thinness or desire to maintain current body weight while settling a desire for food. Research conducted by Emerson et al. (1991) suggests that patients with eating disorders experience more distortions in body image than average. Eating disorders are not merely problems with food and weight; rather, they are thought to involve complex psychological factors that need to be identified for successful recovery. Regardless of a person's size, weight fluctuations from dieting and binge cycles are found to be a higher health risk than weight maintenance. Eating disorders can be physically harmful and may even result in death. "Suicide is the most common cause of death among individuals with bulimia nervosa" (Morgan 1987).

In a meta-analysis of 18 experimental tests of intervention for bulimia, Hartmann et al. (1992) found that helping the client understand the link between symptoms and relationships was more effective than intervention lacking this component. In another meta-analysis (19 studies), Whitbread and McGowan (1994) found support for the superiority of cognitive-behavioral interventions over alternative approaches. Robin, Gilroy, and Dennis (1998) review several studies that suggest both interpersonal psychotherapy and cognitive-behavioral therapy are useful for the treatment of bulimia.

Literature: Brownell & Fairburn (1995); Emerson et al. (1991); Fairburn & Wilson (1993); Reiff & Reiff (1992); Robin, Gilroy, & Dennis (1998); Siegel et al. (1997); Williamson, Cubic, & Fuller (1992).

Task Menu

1. If you are not already working with a physician, contact one to assess level of health and obtain a referral to a nutritionist or a registered dietitian with training or experience in eating disorders.

   Elaboration: Bulimia is physically taxing to health. If you are actively purging, electrolyte levels could be abnormal. Weight varies in individuals diagnosed with bulimia nervosa, but if gradual weight gain is necessary, a physician should monitor it and explain thoroughly the complications that might be experienced. Take dietary supplements, particularly vitamins A, D, E, K, and potassium for dehydration. Additionally, if moderate exercise is to be utilized as an outlet to relieve stress, heart function, which may have been affected by the bulimia, should be checked.

   Practitioner's Role: At the initial meeting, explain that bulimia nervosa sometimes causes organ damage, so an assessment of health status is necessary. Also, at this time discuss the possibility of a psychiatric assessment with client, especially if there is evidence of a coexisting psychiatric disorder. Explain to the client that serotonin reuptake inhibitors (SSRIs) (fluxetine, fluvoxamine) have been shown to be effective in the treatment of bulimia and that the FDA has approved Prozac for such treatment. Emphasize that a psychiatrist with training or experience in eating disorders is the best person to prescribe these medications.

2. Keep a daily *journal*.

   Elaboration: Record food intake, time and location of meals, and binge-purge (if applicable) episodes. Note activities and feelings during episodes, as self-knowledge must precede treatment. Understanding triggers of binge-purge episodes such as feelings, time of day, or certain situations assists in developing strategies to eliminate the triggers.

   Practitioner's Role: Explain the purpose and importance of the *journal* in both assessment and treatment. Identify potential obstacles to *journal-*

ing with client, and make suggestions for overcoming obstacles. Review *journal* with client, asking client to *identify triggers.* Assist client in identification of triggers if client is unable to recognize them.

3. *Identify* negative self-statements and dysfunctional cognitions regarding food intake, weight, and body image. Keep a list of negative statements and cognitions and write corresponding positive self-statements and alternative cognitions. Practice using these positive statements.

   Elaboration: Negative self-talk and dysfunctional cognitions reinforce binge-purge behavior. Identifying and altering such statements and cognitions increases sense of self-control, self-esteem, and self-efficacy, thus removing the need for binge-purge behavior (see also BODY IMAGE, NEGATIVE).

   Practitioner's Role: Use *cognitive restructuring* to help client modify dysfunctional beliefs around being overweight. One point to make is that overweight individuals have fewer health problems than individuals who purge.

4. Learn and practice *progressive relaxation.*

   Elaboration: Binge eating often is a reaction to stress and anxiety, and purging is often a means of relieving anxiety following a binge. *Relaxation* techniques can relieve anxiety, making binge-purge behavior unnecessary.

5. Use response prevention to break the binge-purge cycle.

   Elaboration: Eat binge foods until you feel the urge to vomit, but refrain from vomiting. Both anxiety and the urge to vomit usually subside within two hours (Williamson, Cubic, & Fuller 1992).

   Practitioner's Role: Develop with the client a hierarchy of binge foods to be eaten, starting with those that produce the least anxiety. If response prevention is done during a treatment session, help client discuss reactions to eating the food and examine distorted cognitions.

6. Use temptation *exposure* (Williamson, Cubic, & Fuller 1992).

   Elaboration: Tempt yourself with binge foods but do not eat them.

   Practitioner's Role: If done in session, reinforce verbally client's success in refraining from eating.

7. Develop healthy eating practices as an alternative to binge eating.

   Elaboration: See BINGE EATING for information on healthy eating practices.

8. Identify factors, such as low self-esteem, depression, or a negative body image, that might be contributing to your bulimia.

   Elaboration: Once factors have been identified, see relevant task planner, e.g., *self-esteem, lack of; depression; negative body image* to develop possible solutions.

9. *Identify* connections between your symptoms and interpersonal issues that may be triggering them.

   Elaboration: Interpersonal problems may exacerbate tendencies to binge and purge (Hartmann et al. 1992). These can be particularly difficult to address as many children and adolescents with bulimia come from alcoholic, chaotic, disengaged, sexually and physically abusive families (Robin, Gilroy, & Dennis 1998).

Practitioner's Role: Encourage individuation from the family where such issues are involved. Deal with loss reactions involved in letting go of overinvolvement with the family of origin.

10. Attempt to resolve interpersonal role disputes that may be contributing to your symptoms.

    Practitioner's Role: Involve parents and significant others periodically in conjoint and collateral sessions (Robin, Gilroy, & Dennis 1998). See COUPLE OR FAMILY CONFLICT and PARENT-ADOLESCENT CONFLICT.

11. Remedy interpersonal deficits by practicing *social skills.*

12. Participate in a treatment group.

    Elaboration: Group therapy has the benefit of countering the shame that is often associated with bulimia, through the sharing of common experiences. Groups also help counter social isolation, low self-esteem, and difficulty in maintaining meaningful relationships—all part of the interpersonal deficits that are the most common problem of binge eaters (Wilfley, Grilo, & Rodin 1997).

Bruce Parker, Nancy Brinch, Lisa Guido

Caregiving: Burden on One Family Member

Even under the best circumstances, caregiving is a physically and emotionally demanding task. When it becomes the primary responsibility of one family member it can be overwhelming. The responsibilities impact family life, leisure time, work life, personal finances, and in some cases physical and mental health. Emotional burdens of caregivers include grief, anger, anxiety, guilt, depression, embarrassment, and altered family dynamics (Mellins, Blum, Boyd-Davis, & Gatz 1993; National Alliance for Caregiving 1997). As the care recipient declines and providing care becomes more involved, the situation tends to become increasingly tense for the care provider. One study of caregiving daughters showed that having responsibilities in addition to caregiving, specifically those of worker and mother, was clearly associated with feelings of overload. However, resentment in the caregiving role was highest for those who had fewer roles apart from eldercare, especially when they had to quit work to provide care and they did not have a partner to talk with. Life satisfaction was higher for partnered and working caregivers (Murphy et al. 1997).

Primary caregivers frequently state that they need time for themselves, though many do not utilize services. Service utilization rates were lowest among Asian caregivers. Blacks and Hispanics were more likely than whites or Asians to cite caregiving as a financial hardship (NAC 1997). A nonwhite caregiver is more likely to be an adult child, friend, or other family member rather than a spouse. Nonwhite individuals also report lower levels of caregiver stress, burden, and depression and endorse more strongly held beliefs about filial support. Nonwhite caregivers use prayer, faith, or religion as coping mechanisms (Connell & Gibson 1997).

In one study (Cotrell 1996), home respite was found to be greatly preferred over daycare by spouses whether or not they had used respite services. The majority of spouses saw overnight family care as appropriate only for emergencies, while adult children saw overnight care as appropriate for social and recreational activities. Adult children who resided with the care recipient reported employment and caregiver stress and their resulting exasperation as an impetus for utilizing services.

Studies of interventions for caregiver burden suggest that individual intervention may be more effective than group intervention (Knight et al. 1993; Toseland & Smith 1990).

Literature: Clark & Rakowski (1983); Connell & Gibson (1997); Cotrell (1996); Gendron. Poitras, Dastoor, & Perodeau (1996); Mellins, Blum, Boyd-Davis & Gatz (1993); Murphy et al. (1997); National Alliance for Caregiving (1997); Toseland et al. (1990); Zarit & Edwards (1996).

Task Menu
1. Communicate the problem of being overburdened to other family members.
2. *Identify* better ways to balance caregiving role with other family members.
3. Designate other responsible caregivers.
   Elaboration: Asserting oneself is particularly important in unbalanced caregiving relationships (Gendron, Poitras, Dastoor, & Perodeau 1996).
4. Split caregiving tasks among family members.
   Practitioner's Role: Prepare the client for the increased tension and conflict that will likely result from this task. Have client remind family members that this situation, if handled with a positive attitude, can result in increased closeness, social support, and time spent together among them (Mellins, Blum, Boyd-Davis, & Gatz 1993).
5. Set up a family care plan, including who will be responsible for what type of assistance, and establish a process of monitoring the situation to ensure the needs of the care recipient are being met.
6. Discuss as a family (including the care recipient) the possibility of requesting outside services, including respite care.
   Elaboration: Two types of respite currently exist, short term and long term. Short-term respite may consist of having a person come into the home and watch the elder or temporary placement outside of the home in a structured setting, such as adult daycare (Mace & Rabin 1991). Short-term respite may last from one hour to a whole day. Respite has been found to increase caregiver attitudes, decrease caregiver stress, and minimize de-

pression and health and relationship problems (Cox 1997). Respite has also been found to decrease the probability of long-term care placement (Cox 1997). In addition, in respite the elder can spend time with others, make friends, increase social behaviors, enhance feelings of self-esteem and self-worth, and increase independence from caregivers (Cotterill 1997). Long-term respite most often is a structured setting in which the elder can stay for a number of days at a time, usually two days to a week (Mace 1991). Long-term respite offers the caregiver an opportunity to rejuvenate him- or herself. Respite of any length improves caregiver attitudes and feelings of well-being and enhances ability to care for loved ones (Cox 1997). Places that may offer long-term respite include hospitals, nursing homes, and foster homes; also, family or friends may be able to care for the elder for an extended period of time.

7. If relevant, designate family members to investigate services available and arrange for an initial contact.
8. Discuss as a family (including the care recipient) the possibility of placement in long-term care.
9. If relevant, designate family members to investigate long-term care facilities and arrange initial contact.
10. Explore ways to recover personal time.

    Elaboration: Set aside blocks of personal time in which caregiving responsibility is covered by someone else (family member, adult daycare, respite care).

Matthias Naleppa, Holly Hokanson

Child Abuse: Parental Anger and Stress Management

Parents vary in their ability to tolerate their children's difficult behavior. Those at risk of abusing need help to deal with the stress and anger that arises from parenting. Bloomquist (1996) suggests that there is a cycle that perpetuates itself. Children exhibiting behavior problems create stress for parents, which in turn leads to disruption of parenting. This then results in further discord and additional behavior problems in children. Anything that alleviates parental stress or anger is potentially useful in breaking this downward spiral. Additionally, conditions outside the children's behavior that add to parental stress need to be ameliorated, such as lack of social supports, personal stressors, and marital discord. When left ineffectively moderated, these factors lead to greater incidents of neglect and physical abuse for children. Parents may be unable to provide for their children's needs unless they manage their own stress and personal problems first (Veltkamp & Miller 1994). A meta-analysis (research synthesis) of 25 controlled studies of interventions for problems of parental anger and abuse toward children suggested that social learning-educational programs had larger effects than psychodynamically based programs (Videka-Sherman 1989). Most of the tasks below are of the former kind.

Literature: Bloomquist (1996); Frick (1994); Nugent (1991); Shapiro (1995); Whiteman, Fanshel, & Grundy (1987); Veltkamp and Miller (1994); Videka-Sherman (1991); Webster-Stratton & Hancock (1998).

Task Menu

1. *Learn about* sources of children's behavior you find anger-provoking.

    Elaboration: Realizing that your children's needs—e.g., fatigue, hunger, or frustration—may be causing their negative behavior will allow you to attribute less negative meaning to situations you formerly interpreted as provocative. Also, better knowledge of your children's developmental level will help you develop more realistic expectations. Knowing your children aren't trying to be difficult will generally arouse less anger than if you believe the children are misbehaving on purpose.

    Practitioner's Role: Teach parents about children's needs and developmental levels. Stress realistic expectations for children. In cases where children have emotional or behavior disorders or other developmental challenges, such as learning disabilities, remind parents that age is not an indicator of what the child is capable of.

2. Participate in *parent training.*

    Practitioner's Role: *Parent training* has been found to be an effective intervention for abusing parents (Videka-Sherman 1991). Refer the client to a *parent training* program or make use of parent training protocols in work with client (see for example Webster-Stratton & Hancock [1998]). Many of the tasks in this planner reflect the content of such programs. In teaching parenting skills, use in-session tasks involving parent and child. For example, model a clear parental command to child in *role play* with child, then have parent practice command in her role play with child.

3. Use *coping imagery* and *progressive relaxation* to promote relaxation responses.

    Elaboration: Anger and stress provoke physiological responses that often lead to impulsive action. Having techniques to use when those responses are aroused can lessen pressure to act.

    Practitioner's Role: Suggest that the client envision individuals around whom they would control their behavior, no matter how emotionally aroused (e.g., a boss, someone they fear, etc.) and substitute that image for their children when angered or stressed to the point of arousal.

4. Use *problem-solving* methods with your children.

    Elaboration: *Problem-solving* methods will help you generate effective behavioral alternatives to disciplining or dealing with your children in ways that society considers abusive.

Practitioner's Role: Make use of *problem-solving training* manuals to help parents learn skills (Webster-Stratton & Hancock 1998).

5. Use the triple-column technique developed by Burns (1980).

Elaboration: This technique has been used in dealing with anger in family situations (Nugent 1991). Create three columns on a piece of paper. In the first column, write down automatic thoughts that you have when your children or partner behave in ways that create feelings of distress, anger, or anxiety in you. Next, list the cognitive distortions that characterize your automatic thoughts. In the last column, write down a rational response (e.g., one free of errors in thinking) that replaces the cognitive distortion.

6. Use a *contingency management* system to help control children's behavior.

Elaboration: Decreasing children's aversive behavior will decrease provocation and angry responses.

7. Anticipate and plan for difficult, anger-provoking situations with the children.

Elaboration: Make use of methods of *planned activities training.*

8. Engage in *mutually enjoyable activities* with children.

Elaboration: Such activity—e.g., playing, watching TV together—can strengthen the positive side of the relationship.

Practitioner's Role: Use in-session tasks to demonstrate nonconflictual play activities (Webster-Stratton & Hancock 1998).

9. Develop a social support network.

Practitioner's Role: Suggest that the client enlist the support of family members, neighbors, or religious organizations. Support groups designed to assist parents feeling overwhelmed or isolated include WITS END and Parents Anonymous (see OPPOSITIONAL DEFIANT DISORDER, task 7 for contact information). Help the parent connect with a relative or friend that he or she can contact when under stress with children.

10. Utilize community services that provide respite child care for parents having difficulties with their children.

Practitioner's Role: Refer client to community services by providing a list of phone numbers from a local community services handbook.

Amy Lynn Sciangula

Child Neglect

Child neglect, an act of omission, is the most common form of child maltreatment reported to public child protective services (DePanfilis 1996). Child neglect occurs when "a parent or caregiver responsible for a child under the age of eighteen, either deliberately or by chronic disregard, permits the child to experience avoidable suffering or fails to provide one or more of the ingredients generally deemed essential for developing a person's physical, intellectual, social and emotional capacities" (Gaudin, Wodarski, Arkinson, & Avery 1990–1991:101).

Rose and Meezan (1996) identify nine components of child neglect: 1) inadequate supervision; 2) inadequate food; 3) inadequate shelter; 4) inadequate emotional care; 5) inadequate clothing; 6) exposure to unwholesome circumstances; 7) inadequate medical care; 8) exploitation; and 9) inadequate education.

Children exposed to prolonged neglect may experience developmental delays. Socio-behavioral and emotional disorders, including low self-esteem and attachment problems, are also common consequences (Wolfe & Wekerle 1993; Wolfe 1993). Child placement has been a traditional solution for child neglect (Holliday & Cronin 1990). Recently more attention has been given to interventions aimed at keeping children in the home (DePanfilis 1996). Interventions can focus on the children and parents as individuals or on the family as a unit. When the children are not removed, interventions may be directed at helping parents develop and carry out tasks that will enable them to improve their child care in respect to any of the nine components listed above. *Parent training* or *planned activities training* may also be used. Direct work with children can be guided by task planners for the specific problems they present.

Literature: Mattaini, McGowan, & Williams (1996): Wolfe (1993); Gaudin, Wodarski, Arkinson, & Avery (1990–1991); Holliday & Cronin (1990); Howing, Wodarski, Gaudin, & Kurtz (1989); Daro (1988). For a review of 21 intervention studies, see Wolfe and Wekerle (1993). For a review of social support assessment and intervention models, see DePanfilis (1996). For case examples, see Campbell (1997). For an article on cultural variations in perception of child neglect, see Rose and Meezan (1996). Outcomes of family preservation programs designed to help abusing and neglectful families in their own homes are reviewed in Fraser, Nelson, and Rivard (1997).

Task Menu Parents

1. *Identify* how you may not be providing adequate care for your children.
   Elaboration: The nine components above may provide guidance for this task.
2. *Identify* factors leading to the inadequate care.
3. Take steps to correct deficits and factors identified in tasks 1 and 2.
   Elaboration: Steps should result in tasks specific to the causes and nature of inadequate care. For example, if neglect consists of leaving children alone at night to go out with friends (inadequate supervision), tasks might include developing a suitable child care plan or satisfying needs for companionship, etc., in other ways.
4. Learn basic problem-solving skills and apply them to situations that could lead to neglect (Howing, Wodarski, Gaudin, & Kurtz 1989; Daro 1988).

Elaboration: Neglectful parents may use avoidant methods to handle problems within the family and may lack basic problem-solving skills (Wolfe 1993).

Practitioner's Role: Methods of *problem-solving training* may be used, preferably in home visits, to help parents learn skills in resolving situations contributing to neglect. Twenty-four-hour telephone availability may be indicated (Wolfe 1993; Howing, Wodarski, Gaudin, & Kurtz 1989).

5. Learn and apply verbal communication skills (DePanfilis 1996; Wolfe 1993; Holliday & Cronin 1990; Gaudin, Wodarski, Arkinson, & Avery 1990–1991).

    Elaboration: Neglectful parents tend to have poor verbal communication/interpersonal skills, which can lead to social incompetence in children and negative interactions and conflict within the family. Good interpersonal/verbal skills can help parents meet the demands of a situation and provide positive outcomes (Wolfe 1993).

6. Learn and apply parenting skills (DePanfilis 1996; Holliday & Cronin 1990; Gaudin, Wodarski, Arkinson, & Avery 1990–1991).

    Elaboration: This includes learning to empathize with your children; tracking children's behavior; reinforcing prosocial behavior; understanding needs of children; having age-appropriate expectations; and using nonphysical methods of discipline, such as *time out* and withdrawing of privileges (DePanfilis 1996; Gaudin, Wodarski, Arkinson, & Avery 1990–1991; Howing, Wodarski, Gaudin, & Kurtz 1989).

    Practitioner's Role: Use *parent training* or *planned activities training* methods or refer to a parent training program. In direct work with client, use modeling of appropriate responses, preferably in interactions with the client's children.

7. Establish specific events, such as bedtime or a television show, as occasions for attending to your children (Mattaini, McGowan, & Williams 1996).

8. Learn and apply household management skills (Gaudin, Wodarski, Arkinson, & Avery 1990–1991; Holliday & Cronin 1990; Daro 1988).

    Elaboration: Examples include budgeting, cleaning, meal planning (DePanfilis 1996).

9. Learn and apply *stress inoculation* techniques.

10. Develop *social skills* and increase social interaction (DePanfilis 1996; Gaudin, Wodarski, Arkinson, & Avery 1990–1991; Daro 1988).

    Elaboration: This includes joining a support group if available, such as Parents Anonymous (Howing, Wodarski, Gaudin, & Kurtz 1989; Daro 1988) (see OPPOSITIONAL DEFIANT DISORDER, task 7 for contact information on Parents Anonymous). Neglectful families lack strong support networks, are socially isolated, and lack social skills (Wolfe & Wekerle 1993; Gaudin, Wodarski, Arkinson, & Avery 1990–1991). Groups provide parents with the opportunity to share coping strategies and receive peer support and feedback (Howing, Wodarski, Gaudin, & Kurtz 1989). Social support interventions for neglectful parents promote parental competencies and behaviors that will increase their ability to nurture children successfully and help alleviate stress (DePanfilis 1996).

11. Obtain resources needed to correct neglectful situations.

   Elaboration: Many families in which there is neglect suffer from a lack of resources, such as housing, food, clothing, medical services, legal assistance, transportation, and respite care (Howing, Wodarski, Gaudin, & Kurtz 1989).

   Practitioner's Role: Help link the family with appropriate agencies and community resources, such as food pantries, subsidized housing and day-care programs, and respite care (Wolfe 1993; Gaudin, Wodarski, Arkinson, & Avery 1990–1991; Holliday & Cronin 1990; Golan 1978).

12. Reduce family conflict that may be contributing to neglect (Gaudin, Wodarski, Arkinson, & Avery 1990–1991).

   Elaboration: Common problems in neglectful families include marital discord, coercive family interactions, and a history of violence (Wolfe and Wekerle 1993).

Miranda Koss

Conduct Disorder

Conduct disorder is a diagnosis given children or adolescents who exhibit persistent antisocial behavior, such as fighting, stealing, and destructiveness, usually resulting in conflicts with authority figures and involvement with the juvenile justice system (APA 1994). Typically such children are regarded as unmanageable by significant others. Kazin (1995) estimates that 2–6 percent of children exhibit the problem. Conduct disorder is extremely common among juvenile delinquents. One study revealed that 90 percent of juvenile offenders were diagnosed with conduct disorder (Wierson et al. 1992). Children who exhibit conduct disorder behaviors are also at risk for school failure, membership in deviant peer groups, and becoming adult criminals.

Conduct disorder is an undercontrolled behavior disorder first diagnosed in childhood or adolescence. It encompasses a wide variety of behaviors that can be subtyped as socialized or undersocialized. The "socialized" form consists of adolescent antisocial acts carried out in a peer group context, such as truancy, group stealing, and gang membership, and primarily involves delinquent activities. Youth regarded as "undersocialized" usually display behavioral excesses that are more physically and verbally aggressive, including noncompliance, intrusiveness, lack of self-control, and impaired interpersonal relations (Quay 1986). Both subtypes comprise behavior patterns that violate social norms and the basic rights of others and also include hostility to others, aggression, and willingness to break rules (Rutherford & Nelson 1995).

Conduct disorder is often comorbid with attention deficit/hyperactivity disorder and rarely occurs without another behavior disorder. Those diagnosed with both conduct disorder and oppositional defiant disorder also will likely meet criteria for attention deficit/hyperactivity disorder (Braswell & Bloomquist 1991; Sommers-Flanagan 1998).

Diagnosing conduct disorder can be tricky, as the information sources necessary to help distinguish it from other childhood behavior disruptions are not consistently credible. Self-reports from a possibly deceitful child or adolescent client may be unreliable. Parents who provide inadequate supervision may not be aware of a child's antisocial behaviors, and teachers may be misinformed of the extent or nature of client misbehaviors (Sommers-Flanagan 1998).

There is agreement that treatment for conduct disorder should also include treatment of any related disorder, e.g., depression or substance abuse/dependence. Practitioners should also consider social, cultural, situational, or environmental factors that may be exacerbating the child's symptoms (Sommers-Flanagan 1998). Often conduct disorder behaviors coincide with physical/sexual abuse, homelessness, immigration, and family conflict. An effective method of family treatment for conduct disorders may be found in Henggeler & Borduin (1990).

Meta-analyses of largely controlled studies of interventions for delinquents (most of whom could be classified as conduct disorders) have produced the following results. Programs containing cognitive components (for example, problem solving, negotiation skills training, rational emotive therapy, role playing, modeling, or cognitive-behavioral therapy) had larger effects than programs lacking such components (Izzo & Ross 1990). More structured and focused interventions (for example, behavioral, skills-oriented) produced larger effects than less structured and focused interventions (for example, counseling); multimodel interventions had larger effects than unimodal interventions (Lipsey 1992). Programs coded a priori as "appropriate" (for example, behavioral and nonbehavioral) using structured interventions had larger effects than "inappropriate" programs (for example, nondirective relationship-dependent counseling or unstructured psychodynamic counseling; milieu and group approaches with emphasis on within-group communication) (Andrews et al. 1990). The tasks below are consistent with these conclusions.

Literature: Henggeler & Borduin (1990); Kazdin (1995); Matthys (1997); Rutherford & Nelson (1995); Sommers-Flanagan (1998).

Task Menu Parents

1. Learn methods of helping your child increase prosocial behaviors and decrease antisocial behaviors.

     Elaboration: Use *contingency contracting, contingency management,* or a *token economy* in a systematic effort to reinforce positive behavior and discourage negative behavior. Make clear the consequences that will follow the child's noncompliance (Rutherford & Nelson 1995).

Practitioner's Role: Make use of methods of *parent training,* including *planned activities training.* Help the parent and child together identify target behaviors and rewards. Evaluate the program during regular sessions and use encouragement and positive reinforcement for successes (Matthys 1997). Consider use of *parent* and *planned activities training,* and other methods of work with parents and children, within the context of multisystemic family therapy (Henggeler & Borduin l990).

2. Present a united front to the child.

   Elaboration: Avoid alliances—e.g., one parent siding with the child against the other—that might reward child's antisocial behavior.
3. Resolve conflicts between partners that may make it difficult to present a united front to the child or that might lead to dysfunctional alliances.
4. Develop rules for family and child's behavior through negotiation with child (see FAMILY DYSFUNCTION: LACK OF RULES).

Task Menu Child or adolescent
1. Learn and apply a systematic problem-solving approach to situations that might get you into difficulty.

   Practitioner's Role: Make use of methods of *problem-solving training.*
2. Learn and apply skills in effective communication to handle peer pressure, to control anger, and to interact with authority figures.

   Practitioner's Role: Make use of methods of *social skill training.* Anger control programs developed for aggressive and violent children include: *stress inoculation* (Meichenbaum 1985), Adolescent Anger Control (Feindler & Ecton 1986), Aggression Replacement Training (Rutherford & Nelson 1995). See also ANGER MANAGEMENT AND AGGRESSION CONTROL: CHILD.
3. Learn to redirect attention away from hostile social cues.

   Practitioner's Role: Help client identify equally plausible explanations for others' actions that he or she has regarded as hostile.
4. Make a list of behaviors and attitudes that might help you diminish conflict with authority figures.

   Practitioner's Role: Help the client learn inhibitory *self-verbalizations,* e.g., "Stop, think! What can I do?" to mitigate impulsive responses (Matthys 1997).
5. Learn appropriate behavior and coping skills through interaction with prosocial peers.

   Practitioner's Role: Use activity groups in which conduct disordered children are mixed with prosocial peers (Feldman, Caplinger, & Wodarski 1983).

6. Join a recreational program that engages in activities such as wilderness survival or sports.

   Elaboration: These activities help the child develop a sense of worth and responsibility (Wierson et al. 1992).

7. Make a list of events where your own actions resulted in negative consequences.

   Practitioner's Role: Explore with client reasons for blaming others for his or her own actions and give positive feedback for accepting responsibility.

8. Volunteer for an organized community project.

   Elaboration: Observing adult or peer models actively engaging in prosocial behaviors can reinforce at two phases—when observing the model and when performing the act (Rutherford & Nelson 1995).

Karen Duckett

Couple or Family Conflict

Conflict is the common denominator of most difficulties in couple or family relationships. Many problems are expressed directly in terms of conflict: between marital partners, parents and children, and siblings. Problems expressed indirectly, such as poor communication or lack of intimacy, may not be discussed because the couple or family members are in disagreement about how these aspects of their relationship should play out. Moreover, conflict may not necessarily be overt; one partner may suffer the other's behavior in silence. In most cases the resolution of such hidden conflicts requires that they be brought to the surface. See also COUPLE PROBLEMS: COMMUNICATION and COUPLE PROBLEMS: LACK OF CARING OR INVOLVEMENT.

Literature: Baucom et al. (1996); Berg-Cross (1997); Hecker & Deacon (1998); Jacobson & Christensen (1996); Jacobson & Margolin (1978); Reid (1992); Sheras et al. (1998); Weiss & Halford (1996).

Task Menu

1. Define conflict in a clear and specific way.

   Elaboration: Tasks 1–5 form a logical sequence. In-session work on the tasks involves face-to-face problem-solving communication by clients with the practitioner serving as a facilitator or coach.

   Practitioner's Role: Prior to the task, help clients identify their conflict in general terms. Introduce certain ground rules to be followed for this and subsequent tasks. The following are the more commonly used: Participants should focus on the problem itself and solutions for it rather than on each other's personal qualities. In the case of disagreement, participants should attempt to make some concessions, that is, they should be prepared to accept something less than (or different from) their conception of the ideal solution to the problem. Participants should try to see positive elements in each other's proposals, acknowledge the positives, and try to build on them. Each participant should offer to take some constructive action to help resolve the conflict. Problem behaviors or possible problem-solving actions should be spelled out as specifically as possible.

2. Reveal to one another your points of view, motivations, rationales, and expectations concerning the issue.

    Elaboration: This may involve extensive and free-ranging self-revelations if the issue is pervasive or deep-set. Revelations should be expressed in ways that respect the feelings of your partner.

3. Generate alternative ways for resolving conflict.

    Elaboration: One approach is to use brainstorming (Osborne 1963), in which participants are asked to generate numerous alternatives without initially considering quality. Then the most promising alternative is selected. While brainstorming often produces creative solutions and adds humor to the process, it may not be the best choice for all circumstances. In many situations there may be only two or three viable alternatives, which are quickly recognized. It may be more productive to pursue these often complex alternatives in depth than to spawn a number of possibilities that may be off the mark.

    Practitioner's Role: When clients are unable to generate alternative solutions acceptable to one another, suggest one or more possibilities. Also draw on your own expert knowledge or clinical experience to offer possible solutions that may not have occurred to clients.

4. Offer concessions and exchanges to resolve conflict.

    Practitioner's Role: Unless they do so on their own, ask clients in turn to indicate concessions or exchanges they would be willing to make to reach a solution. A concession involves the client's giving up a previous demand. An exchange is an offer to do something for something in return—a concession or another behavior. If concessions or exchanges are offered but an impasse continues, use what has been offered to develop and propose a solution for the clients to consider. Also, you may conduct individual caucuses with each client alone to explore their position and the kind of concessions or exchanges he or she is willing to make.

5. Plan implementation of the solution agreed upon.

    Elaboration: Most solutions (including many that may appear to be relatively straightforward) require some planning, which can be done as a between-session task you agree to carry out.

6. Plan and carry out a *mutually enjoyable activity.*

Elaboration: This task is designed to promote alleviation of conflict indirectly by strengthening your relationship.

7. *Identify* cognitive distortions or unrealistic beliefs that may be exacerbating the conflict and correct them through use of *cognitive restructuring.*

Elaboration: For example, Hal thinks Betty should prepare dinner after they both get home from work since to do so is part of the "woman's role." Her reluctance to take sole responsibility for this chore is a source of conflict. After critical examination, Hal concludes that his expectation is unrealistic and agrees that they should work together to prepare the evening meal.

Practitioner's Role: Help clients identify and examine beliefs through Socratic dialogues or in the context of in-session communication tasks or reenactments of past interactions. For example, a *role play* reenactment between Hal and Betty (in the example above) of a quarrel about preparing dinner might have revealed the basis of Hal's expectations.

Couple Problems

Communication

A range of difficulties between partners can be related to expressing themselves to each other, including quarrelling, underdisclosing, overdisclosing, lack of clarity, overblaming, sidetracking, mind-reading, and defensiveness. Often major differences in values, interests, personality styles, and other traits may underlie communication problems. However, viewing such differences as communication problems may still offer a useful way of framing issues as a basis for intervention. See also COUPLE OR FAMILY CONFLICT and COUPLE PROBLEMS: LACK OF CARING OR INVOLVEMENT.

Literature: Berg-Cross (1997); Gordon (1970); Gottman (1993, 1994); Jacobson & Margolin (1979); Reid (1992); Weiss & Halford (1996).

Task Menu

1. Use paraphrasing to develop listening skills.

Elaboration: While discussing an issue, each partner paraphrases what the other has just said before responding (Jacobson and Margolin 1979). For example, when Alice finishes her response, Mark summarizes (without editorializing) what Alice has just said before responding to her communication. Alice listens to his response and paraphrases it in return.

Practitioner's Role: Couples learn these and the other communication skills that follow through in-session activities in which the practitioner helps the partners select a real issue they want to work out. However, the issue should not be so toxic that the couple is not able to satisfactorily complete the task.

2. Express dissatisfactions with each other in as nonthreatening a manner as possible.

   Elaboration: The skill here is in stating something undesirable in the other person in a manner that conveys your feelings and perceptions but that minimizes their angry or defensive reactions. Beginning statements in the first person ("I statements"), followed by a specific indication of what you are upset about and an illustrative example, is a good way of disclosing problems (Gordon 1970). Also use situational rather than dispositional attributions (Berg-Cross 1997). Situational attributions explain another's behavior in terms of momentary states or environmental pressures—e.g., "I think you forgot because you had a lot on your mind." In dispositional attributions the other's behavior is explained in terms of personality characteristics—e.g, "I think you forgot because you are thoughtless." The latter are more likely to provoke angry defensive reactions.

3. Use *problem-solving* communication skills.

   Practitioner's Role: Help couple learn essential skills: to state the problem by beginning with something positive, to be specific, to avoid derogatory terms and overgeneralizations, to express feelings, to admit to their own role in the problem, to deal with one problem at a time, to offer compromises, to be neutral rather than negative, and to focus on solutions (Jacobson & Margolin 1979).

4. Self-disclose in a mutually satisfying fashion.

   Elaboration: Issues may concern a partner's inability to self-disclose, with the result that the other feels deprived of necessary information or generally "shut out" of the partner's life, or a partner's self-disclosing in a way that the other sees as excessive and burdensome.

   Practitioner's Role: Help the couple to identify cues that can be used to let the underdisclosing partner know that more disclosure is desired (or less for a partner who overdiscloses). The couple can practice using cues in an in-session exercise.

5. Communicate with your partner in a validating manner (Gottman 1994).

   Elaboration: "Validation stresses responding to the emotional state of the [other] and can be expressed by apologizing, complimenting, acknowledging feelings of the [other] and taking responsibility for making the other person upset or worried" (Berg-Cross 1997:233).

6. Agree to disengage—e.g., one or both leave the room—when quarrelling begins to reach "name calling" stage.

   Elaboration: Identify cues or signals to let each other know when a disengagement is advisable.

7. Set aside a certain amount of time each day (or a certain time on specific days of the week) to practice communication skills, to discuss meaningful issues, or simply to have an enjoyable conversation.

Couple Problems

Lack of Caring or Involvement

One or both partners complain of a lack of caring or involvement between them. There may be concern about lack of common interests or activities or about distance in the relationship. The complaints may be intertwined with problems of conflict, communication difficulties, or other issues related to couple discord. They may arise in response to a specific event such as an extramarital relationship.

Intimacy and closeness may also vary over the course of a relationship (Ingersoll-Dayton, Campbell, Kurokawa, & Saito 1996). This seems to happen most often with mid- to later life couples (Mares & Fitzpatrick 1995; Qualls 1993). It may be normal for romantic forms of love to decline as the relationship ages, even though other forms of love stay constant (Tucker & Aron 1993). As passionate love has been correlated with marital satisfaction, even when cultural differences and different marital expectations are factored in (Contreras, Hendrick, & Hendrick 1996), therapeutic interventions that attempt to reawaken passion may be in order for older "cooled-off" relationships. See also COUPLE PROBLEMS: COMMUNICATION and COUPLE OR FAMILY CONFLICT.

Literature: Berg-Cross (1997); Clements, Cordova, Markman, & Laurenceau (1997); Dattilio (1998); Falloon (1988); Jacobson & Gurman (1995); Reid (1985); Stuart (1980); Weiss & Halford (1996); White (1996). Literature specific to infidelity: Glass & Wright (1997).

Task Menu
1. Plan and carry out a *mutually enjoyable activity.*

   Elaboration: Specify when and where it is to occur and how it is to be done. Possibilities for an activity might be things you enjoyed doing together in the past (e.g., during courtship). The activity should be seen as fun by both partners. Discuss how each would like the other to act during planned activity; also discuss things that may go wrong with your plan and what could be done to prevent them.

   Practitioner's Role: Structure an in-session task in which clients plan an activity. Such in-session planning, *rehearsal,* and practice applies to the remaining tasks.

2. Select and carry out activities that would please or express caring for each other (Dattilio, Epstein, & Baucom 1998; Stuart l980; Weiss & Halford 1996).

   Elaboration: Agree to exchange pleasing or caring actions. Each partner lists things that he or she would find pleasing or see as an expression of caring. Each then selects a number of these behaviors from the other's list and agrees to do one or more of them during the week. Alternatively, each partner can generate a list of activities that he or she would see as pleasing or demonstrating caring for the other and agree to carry out certain ones. This method of "self-directed change" (Weiss & Halford 1996) avoids such issues as which partner should initiate the process of change.

3. Have daily debriefing conversations (Berg-Cross 1997).

    Elaboration: In debriefing conversations, partners discuss events of their day. Such conversations provide a vehicle for sharing experiences and feelings and developing intimacy.

4. Discuss with each other your mutual expectations and then what each of you can do to meet them.

    Elaboration: Emphasize what each of you can do to meet the other's expectations. Avoid criticizing the other's beliefs.

5. Tell each other what you most value about the other.

6. *Identify* and correct (through use of *cognitive restructuring*) distorted beliefs that interfere with caring and involvement.

    Elaboration: This process can be begun through dialogue around issues. For example, Joan may think that Bob ignores her at parties because of lack of caring. In discussing the issue, Joan learns that Bob's attention to others is motivated by his desire to cultivate business contacts. In regard to another issue, Bob may think that Joan's reading at breakfast is a way of ignoring him. When they discuss it, he learns that it is a lifelong habit she has always enjoyed and is likely to indulge in regardless of breakfast partner.

Michael Kirby, Pamela Zettergren

Date Abuse: Female Victims

Though date abuse can be physical, verbal, emotional, or sexual (Silverstein 1994), this task planner is directed toward physical date abuse. "Physical date abuse is any bodily contact that hurts the other person, including hitting, punching, shoving, grabbing, beating, kicking, biting, choking, throwing things, pulling hair, and using a weapon. Physical abuse does not have to leave a mark" (Silverstein 1994:10). Sugarman and Hotaling (1989) have suggested that almost four out of ten women report experiencing violence at least once in the course of a particular dating relationship. In a study of 631 students from three high schools in the Midwest, Bergman (1992) found that one in four females reported severe violence (physical or sexual) in high school dating relationships. However, experiencing violence with a dating partner does not necessarily lead to the dissolution of the relationship (Rosen & Stith 1993). Studies have indicated that between 41 and 79 percent of victims of abusive dating continue to be involved with the abuser (Bergman 1992; Rosen & Stith 1993). Many young women may remain in abusive relationships because they "base much of their self-esteem and self-evaluation on their ability to retain a boyfriend, no matter what his behavior. This leaves adolescent girls at high risk of accepting abusive behavior" (Jaffe et al. 1992:131). Abusive dating relationships may impair a woman's self-worth and emotional and psychological well-being. According to Graham and Rawlings (1991), effects of being involved in an abusive dating relationship include: anger and resentment, lowered self-esteem, homicidal and suicidal ideation, isolation from friends and family, distrust of men and intimate relationships, shame, and loss in productivity at work or at school (Rosen & Stith 1993).

Literature: Books on dating violence include: Levy & Giggans (1995); Levy (1991); Levy (1993); McShane (1988); Pirog-Good & Stets (1989); Rue (1989); Silverstein (1994). Articles include: Bergman (1992); Jaffe et al. (1992); Nightingale & Morrissette (1993); Rosen & Stith (1993).

Task Menu

1. Develop a safety plan (Rosen & Stith 1993).

   Practitioner's Role: Help the client recognize and prepare for the likelihood of later violent acts by helping her identify the sequence of interactions that precedes violent incidents. Help plan how she can get away before or when the violence erupts (Rosen & Stith 1993).

2. Join a support group (Levy 1991).

   Elaboration: Talking with other young women who have had similar experiences is empowering and will help you avoid feeling stigmatized (Levy 1991).

3. *Learn about* violence against women (Rosen & Stith 1993).

   Elaboration: Include characteristics of abusers (Hamberger & Hastings 1991), the battered woman syndrome (Walker 1984), and the cycle of violence (Walker 1979); continuums of abuse: sexual, physical, and emotional (NiCarthy 1991); and the differences between nurturing, romantic, and abusive love (NiCarthy 1991).

4. *Learn about* how abuse affects women (Sousa 1991; NiCarthy 1991; Levy 1991).

   Elaboration: Since teens are inexperienced and generally feel a need to conform, they may adhere to traditional sex roles for men and women, in which men are dominant in relationships. Some men interpret this to include the right to reinforce their power over women with violence (Sousa 1991).

   Practitioner's Role: Let the client know she is not alone. However, make sure to let the young woman know abuse is not acceptable or proper (Rosen & Stith 1993).

5. *Learn about* how violence is escalated (Rosen & Stith 1993).

   Elaboration: It is common for young women to hit back or even hit first when they are angry. However, their own use of violence tends to escalate their partners' use of violence (Rosen & Stith 1993).

Practitioner's Role: Help the client see the dangers of retaliatory or mutual violence. Encourage the use of other ways to deal with anger that do not covertly or overtly support partner's expression of anger. Use words like "violence" to make it difficult for the client to minimize the abuse. Also help the client understand that violence has a tendency to become more severe over time (Rosen & Stith 1993).

6. Understand the discrepancy between your partner's actions and intentions (Rosen & Stith 1993).

Practitioner's Role: Help the client understand that when her partner apologizes he is usually genuinely sorry. However, being sorry does not equal his changing his behaviors or discontinuing the abuse. He probably will continue the abusive behavior until or unless he learns new ways to cope with anger (Rosen & Stith 1993).

7. Work through unrealistic fantasies about the relationship (Rosen & Stith 1993).

8. *Reflect on* the option of leaving your partner.

Practitioner's Role: Help the client see that there is more than one option. She can stay with him or leave him. Empower her to see she is not stuck with him. If she is not ready to leave, you can work on a pretend scenario with her about the steps she could take to leave.

9. Develop new activities, creating your own space and time that is not with him (Rosen & Stith 1993).

10. Reestablish severed relationships (Rosen & Stith 1993).

Elaboration: It is common for young women who are in abusive relationships to become isolated from family and friends. They are forbidden by their partner to have other relationships or embarrassed by bruises, or their friends get tired of hearing about the problems.

Miranda Koss

Depression

Adult

A major depressive episode is typified by both a depressed mood over which the individual has no control and a constellation of motor, neurovegetative, and cognitive symptoms that constitute a common psychiatric disorder. Major depression is not only frequently disabling, but also highly correlated with suicidal behavior (Ivanoff & Riedel 1995). The individual with a clinically significant depression has sustained negative views of the self, of current experiences, and of the future, and these views are products of the enduring cognitive patterns that determine how the individual organizes experiences of the self and the environment (Beck et al. 1979; Craighead,

Evans, & Robinson 1994). The cognitive patterns are maintained by thinking that excludes contrary alternatives (e.g., use of global versus specific explanations of bad events) (Peterson & Seligman 1984).

The DSM-IV (APA 1994) states that a depressive episode is characterized by a period of at least two weeks of either depressed mood or the loss of interest or pleasure in nearly all activities, such that the individual experiences great subjective distress or impairment in interpersonal, social, and occupational functioning. Symptoms of depression include marked changes in weight or appetite; changes in sleep; changes in sexual activity; psychomotor agitation or retardation; decreased energy; feelings of worthlessness or guilt; difficulty concentrating; and preoccupation with death or suicide.

According to Kessler et al. (1994), approximately 13 percent of women and 8 percent of men in the United States experience a major depressive episode each year. Moreover, about 21 percent of women and 13 percent of men suffer one or more episodes over the course of their lifetimes. Kaplan et al. (1994) observe that women are twice as likely as men to experience major depression. Hypotheses for the sex-based difference in prevalence include hormonal differences, the consequences of childbirth, and social role differences. Kaplan et al. (1994) also point out that race does not have an impact on the prevalence rates of major depression; however, underdiagnoses or misdiagnoses occur when the race or culture of the diagnostician is different from that of the client.

The etiology of major depression is unclear and very likely results from an as-yet-unknown interaction among biological, psychosocial, and genetic factors. Biological factors include neurotransmitter abnormalities (a target of many antidepressant medications); psychosocial factors include the extent of psychopathology in the client's family, which may affect her or his rate of recovery, and the loss of a spouse or partner (Kaplan et al. 1994).

Assessment of major depression includes obtaining a history of prior depressive episodes and the extent and severity of current symptoms. Particular attention should be given to the stressors that may have precipitated the depression or that may be maintaining it.

Observation of the client is also pertinent. Kaplan et al. (1994) report that the "classic" presentation of a depressed individual includes a "stooped posture, no spontaneous movements, and a downcast, averted gaze" (532). Finally, objective rating scales, such as the Beck Depression Inventory (Beck 1978) may be used.

The concept of depression is broadly applied to various disorders that do not meet the criteria of major depression. These include minor depression, brief recurrent depressive disorder, dysthymia, and sub-threshold depression (Badger & Rand 1998). The task planners below apply to all forms of depression.

Meta-analyses and research reviews of controlled studies of interventions for depression provide support for cognitive-behavioral, cognitive, interpersonal, psychodynamic, and drug therapies but have not established that one of these methods is superior to any other (DeRubeis & Crits-Christoph 1998; Dobson 1989; Robinson et al. 1990).

Literature: Akiskal & Cassano (1997) sets out an overview of chronic depressions and their clinical management; for a cognitive approach to depression see Beck et al. (1979) and Thase (1996). Badger & Rand (1998) provide an overview of diagnostic considerations. Barker (1993) offers a self-help guide to managing depression. Cornes (1990) presents the interpersonal model for treating depression. Craighead, Evans, & Robins (1992) discuss cognitive-behavioral treatment of depression: see Libassi (1995). Nezu, Nezu, & Perri (1989) present a problem-solving approach. O'Connor (1997), a clinician who himself has struggled with depression, provides a useful resource for both practitioners and clients.

Task Menu

1. Consult with psychiatrist to assess need for antidepressant medication.

   Practitioner's Role: If psychotropic medication is prescribed for the client, educate her or him about the role of the medication vis-à-vis depression (Libassi 1995). Assist client in monitoring the effectiveness of the medication, as well as unwanted side effects (Libassi 1995).

   Advocate for the client with the physician and others (e.g., multidisciplinary treatment team) in relation to factors that have an impact on the client's compliance with the medication schedule and the effectiveness of the medication (e.g., nutrition, supportiveness of other people significant to the client) (Libassi 1995). Collaborate with other professionals—e.g., provide psychosocial information gleaned from the client and people significant to her or him (Libassi 1995).

2. *Identify* modifiable factors, especially stressors, that might be causing or aggravating your depession.

3. Select a stressor that you think you can change and take at least one step to change it.

4. *Identify* resources and coping mechanisms that can be utilized to alleviate your depression.

   Elaboration: Develop a task that makes use of one of these resources or coping mechanisms. For example, if discussing your problems with a particular person has helped in the past, try to arrange to have a conversation with this person.

5. Keep track of things you enjoy and accomplish.

   Elaboration: A depressed person may downplay pleasurable or successful activities. In any case it is helpful to determine what is or is not being enjoyed or accomplished.

   Practitioner's Role: A tool for recording is the Weekly Activity Schedule (Beck et al. 1979), in which the client records his or her activities and rates the sense or pleasure or mastery associated with them.

6. Undertake an activity that results in mastery or pleasure.

   Elaboration: Depressed people are often convinced that they can do nothing right, that whatever action they undertake will wind up as a failure, or they may see little that they do as bringing them any pleasure.

Practitioner's Role: To challenge these expectations, use graded tasks likely to lead to a successful or pleasurable outcome (Sacco & Beck 1985). A goal suggested by the client is selected. A series of tasks, graduated from easy to difficult, is set up to bring about step-by-step progress toward the goal. The goal itself may be a relatively simple accomplishment, such as a home improvement project or joining a social group. However, attainment of the goal itself is secondary to the main purpose of providing the client with a successful or enjoyable experience. The grading of the task permits repeated successes as well as adjustments if difficulties are encountered (Reid 1992).

7. Increase your social activities.

Elaboration: Withdrawal from social contacts is a common feature of depression. Simple tasks, such as attending a church event, may provide ways to begin to enhance your social life.

8. *Identify* thoughts and beliefs that may add to your depression.

Elaboration: A person prone to depression tends to have an unrealistically negative view of self, the external world, and the future (Beck 1967; Sacco & Beck 1985). Distortions toward the negative are maintained by errors in processing information (see *cognitive restructuring*). With a depression-prone individual, these errors overemphasize the negative. Thus, negative details about a situation are focused upon, the significant negative events are magnified and overgeneralized, events are given a negative twist and personalized, and black-or-white thinking usually favors the black side (Reid 1992).

Practitioner's Role: Useful client self-monitoring tools are the Daily Record of Negative Automatic Thoughts and the Daily Record of Dysfunctional Thoughts (Sacco & Beck 1985). With the aid of such client self-recording, help the client *identify* cognitive distortions (e.g., personalization, dichotomous thinking) that may add to his or her depression. Using *cognitive restructuring,* help the client correct these distortions and generate rational responses to events and situations.

9. *Identify* beliefs and assumptions that underlie depression.

Practitioner's Role: Help client extract from automatic thoughts and affective responses to situations the assumptions by which she or he organizes experiences. For example, Leonard may believe that he is basically unattractive to women. Thus he avoids initiating relationships with members of the opposite sex, a factor in his depression. Use *cognitive restructuring* to help client examine and challenge such assumptions and to replace them with more rational appraisals.

10. Learn *social skills* to improve interpersonal relationships, including assertion and conversational skills.

Practitioner's Role: Help client identify and learn appropriate social skills using methods of *social skills training* (Craighead, Evans, & Robins 1992).

11. Set realistic, attainable goals.

    Elaboration: Depressed people often attempt to attain perfectionistic goals or standards; failing to live up to these expectations can aggravate depression.

12. *Identify* "messages" from important figures in the past that may be contributing to depression and attempt to act in ways that would modify these messages.

    Elaboration: For example, Joan may have received the message from her parents that "you need to give in to get along," which has contributed to a pattern of submissive behavior, leading to feelings of self-contempt and resentment at others. Acting in a more appropriately assertive way could increase her self-esteem and lead to more satisfying interpersonal relations (Jensen 1994).

    Practitioner's Role: Help the client identify such messages, including their dysfunctional components, and plan corrective tasks.

13. *Identify* role disputes and role transitions that may be contributing to depression (Cornes 1990).

    Elaboration: Interpersonal role disputes (e.g., conflict with marital partner or employer) and role transitions (e.g., loss of job) can lead to depreciated self-esteem and demoralization and hence can be factors in depression.

    Practitioner's Role: Help client carry out the identification process, develop understanding of the problem, and devise a plan of response. For example, the client may have to mourn the loss of a cherished role before he or she can replace it. (Other task planners may relate to role problems. See, for example, COUPLE PROBLEMS: COMMUNICATION and PARENT-ADOLESCENT CONFLICT: PROBLEM SOLVING.)

14. *Identify* difficulties in establishing satisfactory interpersonal relationships, attempt to understand factors contributing to these relationships, and take steps to resolve them.

    Elaboration: Interpersonal deficits, with related problems such as loneliness and unstable relationships, can lead to depression (Cornes 1990).

    Practitioner's Role: Help the client carry out processes of identification and development of understanding; help client develop tasks to improve interpersonal relationships.

15. Express your feelings.

    Elaboration: "Depression is an effort to avoid feeling" (O'Connor 1997). It is better to experience painful feelings than to ward them off. Try to express them to others who will be accepting and provide you with support.

Kathyrn Baraneckie

Depression

Child

Children express depression in ways similar to adults, depending on where they are developmentally. Common emotional signs are sadness, feelings of loss, apathy, irritability, and loneliness (Brown 1996; Psychiatric Star Team 1996; Zimmerman 1988). Cognitive symptoms may be poor self-concept, negative expectations of the future, and an inability to concentrate. Depressed children often express low motivation and have a lack of interest in activities (PST 1996; Zimmerman 1988). They appear to be withdrawn and do not want to become involved in any situation. Often their appetite is poor, they have sleep disturbances, and they are lacking energy. Along with the depression come behaviors that negatively impact on the child. As many children do not have a sophisticated vocabulary to express how they are feeling verbally, they exhibit many of their strong emotions through negative behaviors (Brown 1996). Depressed children can be self-destructive or accident prone, express their anger inappropriately, and act out (Zimmerman 1988). School absences are common, as well as weak academic records (PST 1996). These behaviors may cause others to treat the child as if he or she were a troublemaker, which only supports the child's disparaging view of him- or herself.

Family history of depression increases the likelihood of an episode of depression occurring in childhood. A child has a greater chance of experiencing depression if his or her parent has a history of depression or a history of any mental illness (Fleming & Offord 1991). Major life events, positive or negative, can also affect a child's risk of depression. The most common events are family disruptions, especially parental divorce or the death of a parent (Fleming et al. 1991; Jaffe-Ruiz 1984). Other known risks for psychological adjustment problems in children are low socioeconomic status, being an oppressed minority, history of neglect or abuse, large family size, parental absence, rigid parenting, maternal anxiety, a developmental disability, parental alcohol or substance abuse, and parental disinterest (Birmaher et al. 1996; Seifer, Sameroff, Baldwin, & Baldwin 1992; Zimmerman 1988).

Literature: Birmaher et al. (1996); Fleming & Offord (1993); Hansen, Heckt, & Futa (1998).

Task Menu   Parents
1. Arrange for a visit to the pediatrician to evaluate the child's physical health.
2. Arrange for the child's visit to a child psychiatrist to assess if psychotropic medication is needed.

    Practitioner's Role: If medication is prescribed, teach the parents about it. Instruct them about the importance of following the medication regime and why the child was prescribed the medication.

3. Monitor the child's behaviors in the home and in social situations.

   Practitioner's Role: Educate parents about the importance of being able to identify behaviors that may be expressions of the child's depression. Sometimes a child's behavior may be angry and violent because the child is unable to articulate how he or she is feeling. Parents need to be made aware that when a child misbehaves, it may be due to the depression. Positively reinforce the parents' progress with the child (Dowling 1988).

4. Provide the child with positive feedback.

   Practitioner's Role: Educate the parents about when and how to reinforce positive behavior in the child. Identify situations that would be appropriate to positively reinforce the child's behavior.

5. Maintain expectations of the child's participation in family activities and completion of household chores (Dowling 1988).

Task Menu Child

1. Monitor daily activities and feelings about each day (Allen-Meares 1987; Reynolds 1987).

   Elaboration: Monitor yourself in a *journal* or notebook. Write about the day's events and if you experienced any good or bad feelings. If unable to write, draw pictures (Allen-Meares 1987).

2. Plan and carry out activities.

   Elaboration: Keeping active leaves less time to focus on negative feelings. Choosing your own activities provides a sense of independence and control.

   Practitioner's Role: Direct the child to positive activities in which he or she can participate. Encourage child to participate in activities where he or she will experience success (Dowling 1988).

3. Learn positive self-talk and be able to identify sad feelings.

   Elaboration: Acquire skills that provide you with the ability to identify your own irrational thoughts and to modify those thoughts (Dowling 1988). If you believe that no one likes you, learn to say "I am liked." Learn appropriate problem-solving techniques and alternative ways of processing information.

   Practitioner's Role: Help the child to focus on changing negative thoughts and feelings.

4. Learn and practice *progressive relaxation* techniques (Dowling 1988).

   Elaboration: Learn to know when you are feeling stressed or tense and then use relaxation to dispel those uncomfortable feelings.

5. Acquire *social skills* so interpersonal relationships can be improved (Epstein & Cullinan 1986).

   Practitioner's Role: Practice for situations where the child may have difficulty functioning with present coping methods. This includes providing modeling, self-management techniques, rehearsing, and feedback (Epstein

& Cullinan 1986). Child will participate in *role play* with practitioner to practice learned skills. Model new behaviors that will give examples of more appropriate coping styles.

Stacey Kolomer

Developmentally Disabled

Elderly Parents

In the recent past, having a developmental disability meant a relatively short life expectancy (Ansello & Eustis 1992). Hence, caregivers of developmentally disabled people did not have to worry about permanency planning issues. However, today the number of adults with developmental disabilities is steadily growing (Ferreira de Mello & Mann 1995) due to decreased mortality rates, the use of antibiotics, improved population health status, and the aging of the baby boom generation (Smith, Tobin, & Fullmer 1995). "Now, in numbers without precedent, adults with lifelong developmental disabilities are surviving into old age, and in many instances outliving their parents [or caregivers]" (Ansello & Eustis 1992:3). Thus, caregivers must now plan for the future of their developmentally disabled child, when they will no longer be around or able to continue parenting.

Literature: Relevant articles and books include: Anello & Eustis (1992); Heller & Factor (1991); Janicki et al. (1996); Kaufman, Adams Jr., & Campbell (1991); McClenny (1996); Roberto (1993); Smith & Tobin (1989); Smith, Tobin, & Fullmer (1995); Seltzer (1992); Smith, Majeski, Smith, & Tobin (1993). An article to help social workers examine their own views and roles with these families is McCallion & Tobin (1995). Articles addressing cultural issues when working with these families include Heller & Factor (1988) and McCallion, Janicki, & Grant-Griffin (1996).

Task Menu Parents or caregivers
1. *Identify* needs and wants in regard to permanency planning.
   Practitioner's Role: In cases where the client does not know where to begin, provide a general overview of typical needs. According to Smith & Tobin (1989), successful permanency planning consists of three important components: legal protection, financial security, and residential arrangements.
2. Prioritize the identified needs.
   Practitioner's Role: Let the client understand that what he or she is going through is normal and that there are many others in the same position. Emotional support might be needed throughout the process; the practitioner should address this. Suggest support groups for the client and the

child if they are available in the area. Another suggestion, if available in the area and a group setting is not desirable, is single support from another parent in the same situation.

3. Attend a support group for aging caregivers.

   Elaboration: The groups may be psychoeducational or solely for emotional support.

4. Make a decision about whether to involve other members of the family in the decision-making process on permanency planning issues.

   Elaboration: A typical caregiver is an older woman, often a widow, in her mid- to late 70s (Janicki 1996), who may have cognitive or physical deficits. She may want the assistance of another family member who is close to the child. Accomplishing the tasks relating to housing, financial, and legal planning can be worked on in any order—most preferably in the order of importance to the caregiver.

5. Contact your agency of choice for case management services.

   Practitioner's Role: Provide resource information on how to obtain a case manager, whom to contact, and what to expect when the client contacts the office. Explore if there is a central registry in the county or state. Placing the child on a central registry list will establish eligibility as well as cut down on future paperwork. It is important to be familiar with rules and regulations in your area pertaining to this task as well as the tasks to follow, since they might be different depending on location. Additionally, for this and other tasks, establish with client whether assistance is needed (including completing all paperwork). Due to the age of the caregiver, you might be much more involved in assisting the client than you would be with other age groups.

6. Make necessary residential plans.

   Elaboration: Become familiar with different residential planning options that are available in your area, through developmental disabilities networks, aging service networks (Smith & Tobin 1989), and private, nonprofit agencies. Depending on the intellectual level of your child, there are different residential options, for example independent living and group homes.

   Practitioner's Role: Suggest having the child go along to look at the housing options, to get the child accustomed to the fact that the caregiver is not always going to be around, as well as to involve the child in making some decisions about his or her future (this depends on the functional level of the child).

7. Make necessary legal/financial plans: creating a special needs trust, writing a will, naming a health care proxy, creating guardianship, developing a health care plan (including applying for Medicaid, Medicare, Social Security disability, Supplemental Security Income, food stamps).

Practitioner's Role: Work with client to prioritize the financial / legal issues and work on the most important ones first.

8. Make necessary plans to deal with other issues pertaining to the child's future, such as transportation and vocational rehabilitation.
9. Identify personal needs and wants.

Elaboration: You have needs of your own. For example, while your child is still living at home, you may need respite services.

Miranda Koss

Developmentally Disabled

Need for Supported Employment

The need to help people with developmental disabilities or mental retardation find gainful employment in their communities was brought to the forefront of advocates' agendas in the mid-1980s, as a combined need for empowerment and financial independence was acknowledged by practitioners in the many fields interacting with this population. Moving a developmentally disabled person into the community in an employee capacity can be facilitated through various avenues, including sheltered workshops, supported employment, job coaching/shadowing, and natural supports within employment settings.

Sheltered workshops are highly structured training grounds for people with special needs. Jobs are contracted out from local agencies to the workshop, and the workshop participants fulfill the usually low-level duties, such as filling boxes with Styrofoam peanuts, collating papers, etc. The work is paid for on a piece-by-piece basis.

Supported employment is employment in the community within an agency that has a structured program intended to employ people with developmental disabilities. Training and supervision is tailored to the needs of the individual and is often under the auspices of a social service agency.

Job coaching/shadowing is a program in which a developmentally disabled person is helped by an agency-affiliated person to transition into the work force. Job coaches/shadows are available to help developmentally disabled people in many work settings, such as grocery stores, fast-food restaurants, etc.

Natural supports in employment settings are outgrowths of the job coach/shadow rubric. Supports within the work setting by fellow workers can be ever more effective and comprehensive in helping the developmentally disabled person learn how to navigate the working world.

Literature: Butterworth, Whitney, & Shaw (1997); Christian & Poling (1997); Garff & Storey (1998); Olney & Kuper (1998); Wehman & Parent (1996).

Task Menu

1. *Learn about* sheltered workshops available in your area.

    Elaboration: Sheltered workshops can help you learn skills while earning money. You will also make connections for future employment. Resource guides are available through local or state agencies, such as the Office for Mental Retardation and Developmental Disabilities in New York.

    Practitioner's Role: If the client is cognitively disabled, you may need to help her or him find sheltered employment opportunities in the area or associated with your agency.

2. *Examine* employment areas that interest you.

    Elaboration: There are many tests available to explore what kind of work you would be best suited for. You can also make a list of your skills, likes, dislikes, future ambitions, etc., and assess what kinds of jobs would be to your liking.

    Practitioner's Role: You can aid in this review of interests by helping the client make a list similar to what is described above, as well as by administering simple tests or checklists that can guide the search for employment.

3. *Learn about* vocational rehabilitation / habilitation services in your area.

    Elaboration: Vocational agencies can help you learn new skills, find jobs, and link with area programs for people with developmental disabilities. In New York the state agency is the Vocational and Educational Services for Individuals with Disabilities (VESID). Similar offices can be found in most states.

4. *Learn about* self-management techniques to aid with hygiene.

    Elaboration: One expectation in a work environment is that all employees be clean and presentable to the public. Self-management techniques can help you to learn routines and rituals that will help you look professional and presentable on the job (Garff & Storey 1998).

    Practitioner's Role: Help the client to come up with daily routines and checklists to reinforce proper hygiene.

5. Fill out applications at local grocery stores, fast-food restaurants, etc.

    Practitioner's Role: If necessary, help the client to obtain and fill out applications.

6. Contact a local agency to find out if they have a job coach/shadow program.

    Elaboration: Many agencies offer job coaching/shadowing programs for those who qualify. You may have to show documentation of your disability or insurance coverage (private or Medicaid) to participate in the program.

7. Contact local and state agencies for employment resources and programs.

    Elaboration: See tasks 1 and 3 above. Resources online:

    VESID (New York State). http://web.nysed.gov/vesid/vesid.html

    ddConnections: outlines various types of employment programs available. http://www.ddconnections.org/voc.htm

LOGAN: helps link people with developmental disabilities with employment opportunities. http://www.logancenter.org/employmentservices.cfm
8. Shadow a friend or relative at his or her work site.

Elaboration: With the permission of your friend or relative's employer, go to work with your friend or relative to see what the work environment is like and if his or her field of employment interests you.
9. File your resume with an employment agency.

Elaboration: Many employment agencies are looking for people to fill temporary and permanent positions. Once you file your resume or application with an agency, they will contact you when a job opening matches your abilities.

Practitioner's Role: Help advocate on the client's part when working with the employment agency.

James Golden

Discharge Plan, Need for

Adolescents Leaving Residential Institutions

Discharge from residential placement is a critical period in an adolescent's treatment (Durrant 1993). Often mandatory clients do not follow through on their aftercare programs and relapse into preplacement behaviors. This is especially true with conduct disordered clients, who often show minimal improvement upon discharge but may improve over the long term (Pyne 1985; Wells 1993; Brown 1994). As conduct disordered youth often suffer from a myriad of comorbid disorders, especially substance abuse, the task planners for their specific problems should also be consulted in the discharge process.

Involvement of the family is imperative. Family dysfunction is often manifested in the child or adolescent's acting out. Pyne (1985) noted marked family disharmony among 70 percent of his study group, and many studies show a strong correlation between family functioning, involvement in the patient's treatment, and successful outcome (Pfeiffer 1990; Force 1985; Brown 1994).

An aftercare plan should specify the services the adolescent is to receive during the transition from residential care to living at home, who is to provide them, and the processes of referral. The plan should include attention to the client's school performance. How well the child does in school, both academically and behaviorally, has been found to be a good predictor of outcome (Force 1985; Kowitt 1989).

Literature: Brown, Myers, & Mott (1994); Durrant (1993); Force & Sebree (1985); Kowitt et al. (1989); Pfeiffer & Strzelecki (1990); Pyne, Morrison, & Ainsworth (1985); Wells & Faragher (1993).

Task Menu Adolescents and parents (while in residential setting)

1. *Identify* successes in the program and how these changes will translate into home life.

   Elaboration: Tasks 1–4 can be completed as *journaling* homework and discussed at the next session.

2. *Identify* possible and probable causes of problem behavior at home.

   Practitioner's Role: Meet with client and family to review progress and anticipate future obstacles. Ideally, there should be at least three joint sessions with the parents and the adolescent in the last month before discharge, with one of these sessions occurring on discharge day. During sessions, help family and adolescent negotiate rules the family will follow when he or she is home on pass. Help them focus on how home will be different from what it was prior to placement when he or she returns.

3. *Identify* strengths and interests that promote positive behavior at home.

4. *Identify* home support structures, i.e., helping agencies and individuals.

5. Become involved with practitioner in writing final discharge reports, recommendations, and referrals.

6. Develop a plan for home pass.

   Elaboration: Identify necessary appointments—e.g., with aftercare services—for the next home pass and make the appointments from the practitioner's office. *Identify* issues to talk about with parents and others.

   Practitioner's Role: Arrange for home passes with frequency and length contingent upon teenager's behavior in the residence and at home. Home passes should become much more frequent and of longer duration as discharge nears.

7. Examine feelings about returning home.

Task Menu Adolescents and parents (when on home pass)

1. Make contact with home support organizations—e.g., aftercare service, Alcoholics Anonymous.

   Practitioner's Role: Facilitate initial client contacts with outside agencies and helping organizations, including school. Meet with family members to discuss issues identified in task 7 above.

2. Practice new living skills—e.g., saying no to old "friends" who want to involve you in using substances.

3. Participate in previously identified positive lifestyle choices (work out in a gym, go to a concert, for a walk, to a movie, etc.).

4. "Hang out" with a friend who won't get you into trouble.

   Elaboration: If you don't have such a friend, try to make one.

5. Take an active part in at least one family activity each week.

Russell Gray, Laura Tyce

Discharge Plan, Need for

Alcoholism /Addiction, Mental Illness

Discharge planning is an important part of the overall treatment for clients in inpatient settings (e.g., the frail elderly, the mentally ill, substance abusers). Effective discharge planning entails organizing aftercare services that meet the needs of discharged patients. How well a client continues to do after hospitalization is often dependent on his or her plans for discharge. Clients need to be assessed for cognitive impairments (Cummings & Cockerham 1997), functional limitations, psychiatric symptomatology (Clark & Travis 1994) or psychological impairments, dangerous behaviors, socially unacceptable behaviors, and relationship problems (Kazarian, McCabe, & Joseph 1997). Their housing needs, entitlements, daily activities, history of drug abuse, criminality, potential for violence, past treatment noncompliance, and the type (if applicable) of diagnoses and psychiatric treatment resources needed should also be assessed (Cohen, Gantt, & Sainz 1997).

Discharge planning is particularly important for clients diagnosed as mentally ill and chemically dependent, as post-treatment environment predicts outcomes more strongly than treatment environment across a range of inpatient and residential alcohol treatment programs (Moos et al. 1990). Vaillant's (1966, 1983) longitudinal research demonstrates that recovery usually occurs over years, so what happens to the client in the aftercare phase of an intensive inpatient treatment program takes on particular importance. Inadequacies in available resources for discharge planning are illustrated by homeless individuals who have double or triple disorders, e.g., schizophrenic substance abusers (Walters & Neugeboren 1995). According to Kazarian, McCabe, and Joseph (1997), successful planning for community-based mental health services includes the following essential elements: a protected hospital environment, treatment augmentation in psychosocial rehabilitation programming, and the availability of supports and services in the community. In discharge planning, what kind of programs are needed must also be considered (a full or partial day program, ongoing case management, nutritional or medical services, etc.). Care should be taken to avoid duplication of aftercare services, and discharge planning should be meaningful to clients. For example, lifestyle (e.g., does the client drive, live alone?) should be considered. If necessary, a client's support systems should be utilized to anticipate potential adverse effects of certain plans (Bushy 1994). In general, good discharge planning includes identifying, organizing, and evaluating whatever information is available and relevant in order to determine the appropriate course of action for a given client.

Literature: Drake et al. (1993); Drake, Noordsy, & Ackerson (1995); Olfson & Walkup 1997; Osher & Kofoed (1989); Ries & Ellingson (1990).

Task Menu
1. *Identify* aftercare options.

Practitioner's Role: Generally, inpatient treatment and discharge is conducted by treatment teams during case review with one practitioner assigned as case manager. Discuss with other team members their assessment of the client and identify client needs. For instance: Will client need to be on medication? Does the client have legal obligations? What is the client's financial situation? Does the client have insurance, Medicaid, Supplemental Security Income (SSI), Supplemental Security Income for Disabled (SSD) or some other way of paying for aftercare treatment? Next, solicit suggestions and discuss ideas for possible aftercare services for client with team members and referring agent (often when a client is referred to a particular type of treatment the referring agent expects to have a say in the client's ultimate outcome). Does the client need a halfway house or will community outpatient services be enough?

The next step after deciding placement is to coordinate with the referring agent possible resources that are close to client. For example, in the case of substance abuse, are there Alcoholics Anonymous (AA) or Narcotics Anonymous (NA) groups geographically near the client? In the case of mental illness, are psychiatrists readily available to prescribe medications for the client? Is a hospital accessible if the client needs one? This step is followed by exploring what each resource has to offer. For instance, how many days a week and hours each day is a possible outpatient program? What is the staff-to-client ratio at the halfway house?

Follow that with developing several plans combining resources, so there will be alternatives. Then if the client refuses a plan, such as halfway house placement, the practitioner might have another, such as an intensive outpatient program combined with attending AA or NA group meetings, as an alternative discharge option.

Finally, collaborate with other team members in setting the discharge date.

2. *Identify* pros and cons of each plan.

Practitioner's Role: Discuss benefits and liabilities of each option with the client, keeping in mind the risk of relapse. It may be necessary to point out that a restricted environment, such as a halfway house, may be advisable as a means of avoiding relapse.

3. *Identify* benefits of attending aftercare treatment and taking medications (if applicable).

Practitioner's Role: Discuss what has happened to clients who have not continued to take medications and attend their aftercare programming. See MEDICAL OR OTHER TREATMENT: NONADHERENCE TO.

4. Contact appropriate agencies and do intakes (if necessary) or visit.

Elaboration: For example, you may need to do an intake with a halfway house or want to visit a facility.

Practitioner's Role: Dial phone numbers (if necessary). Be emotionally supportive of clients by sitting with them while they make calls for intakes and follow-up appointments. *Role play* what the client will say or do. Use this as an opportunity to model problem-solving skills. Have client use *self-reinforcement* to reward him- or herself for successful interactions. Use *social skills training* (if necessary). Intervene if client becomes confused, agitated, or emotionally upset.

5. *Identify* any anxieties you are experiencing regarding departure.

   Practitioner's Role: Discuss appointments and any anxiety client has regarding departure from inpatient treatment.

6. Involve partners and family members in developing the plan.

   Elaboration: Family members frequently can provide information that will affect discharge planning, and often can take responsibility for coordinating the plan (Olfson & Walkup 1997).

Russell Gray, Pamela Zettergren

Discharge Plan, Need for

Hospital Patients

All hospital patients require some level of discharge planning. For many, this is achieved by themselves or in conjunction with their families and physician/nurse. A large number, however, require the assistance of a social worker because of the complex interaction of their medical needs with social, emotional, and psychological issues. The philosophy of social work discharge planning is to promote patient self-determination by acknowledging the risk sharing inherent in client-focused goals. Tasks are developed that integrate planning and care to secure the greatest independence for the client. Specific objectives might include prevention of unnecessary hospitalization or inappropriate use of residential care. Discharge planning is often done by a team consisting of a social worker, a physician, and other health professionals. The task planner below assumes a single practitioner.

Literature: Abramson (1990); Abramson et al. (1993); Clemens (1995); Feather (1993); Kadushin & Kulys (1994); Showers et al. (1995).

Task Menu
1. Identify your own goals for discharge and those of family members, if different.

   Practitioner's Role: Identify physician's goals for discharge, if different from client's and family's. Evaluate and document: client's present functional status; functional status/living situation prior to admission; progress on case to date; original plan of care; changes in plan of care. If indicated, help the client negotiate differences in discharge objectives with family and physician. Joint meetings with family members and physician may be called for.

2. *Identify* obstacles to achieving the discharge goal.

   Elaboration: These might include physical and psychological health; family; financial, insurance, and legal issues.

   Practitioner's Role: Raise possible obstacles that client has not identified.

3. Develop a plan for resolving identified obstacles.

   Practitioner's Role: Assist the client in developing plan; help him or her anticipate long-term care needs. Make suggestions for referrals to agencies that may help with financial, legal, or other problems. Arrange for referrals if necessary; directly assist with complex medical or psychiatric follow-up.

4. Finalize the discharge plan.

   Practitioner's Role: Help client formulate and carry out discharge plan. Help coordinate efforts of all those involved in caregiving.

Paul Copp

Divorce/Separation

Child's Adjustment to

Over a quarter of the children in the United States can be expected to experience a parental divorce. Considerable research has shown that this can have deleterious effects on the child's adjustment and development in such areas as academic achievement, peer relationships, and self-esteem. Significant stressors include experiencing conflict between parents, emotional turmoil of the custodial parent, disruption of the relationship with the noncustodial parent, parent dating and remarriage, and economic hardship (Kalter & Schreier 1994).

Literature: Guides to interventions with children can be found in Buchanan et al. (1996); Hetherington et al. (1995); Kalter & Schreier (1994); Lamb et al. (1996); Portes et al. (1991).

Task Menu Parents

1. Tell the child about the separation or divorce in a way that places responsibility on you and reassures the child of your love.

2. Develop a custody plan that facilitates the continuing involvement of both parents in the children's lives (Hetherington et al. 1995) and that provides adequate financial support to the custodial parent.

   Elaboration: The Department of Social Services may be of assistance if the separating spouse is unwilling to provide child support.

Practitioner's Role: Use *mediation* to help parents work out the plan.
3. Give the child a necessary outlet to heal from the emotional pain.

Elaboration: Provide "external support systems" (Portes et al. 1991) for the child to openly express his or her feelings, whether an adult mentor, a counselor, or a support group.

Practitioner's Role: Make a referral to the school social worker or psychologist if the child's schoolwork seems to be affected.
4. Avoid criticizing ex-spouse in the child's presence or fighting in front of the child.
5. Develop a support system for yourself to help you cope, without relying on your child for emotional support—e.g., join a support group, such as Parents Without Partners, 401 N. Michigan Ave., Chicago, IL 60611–4267; (800) 637–7974. http://www.parentswithoutpartners.org/ email to: frhlpheart@aol
6. Read self-help books on adjustment to divorce for both parents and children—e.g., Adler & Archambault (1990); for parents—Divorce Book for Parents: Helping Your Children Cope with Divorce and Its Aftermath (Lansky 1989) and Growing Up with Divorce: Helping Your Child Avoid Immediate and Later Emotional Problems (Kalter 1990).
7. Have the child maintain consistent visitation with the noncustodial parent.

Elaboration: In cases of violence or sexual abuse, appropriate adjustments to this task may be necessary.
8. Help the child accept that the parents will not be reuniting.

Elaboration: Provide reality to discourage fantasy and the child's efforts to reunite you. Provide comfort and assistance in helping the child cope with issues of loss, loneliness, grief, and a sense of powerlessness.
9. Help the child express anger verbally and understand the difference between destructive and constructive anger.

Elaboration: Discuss underlying feelings expressed as anger (fear, hurt, rejection) and provide support and comfort.
10. Discuss internal conflicts with the child, such as the struggle to preserve his or her allegiance to both parents.
11. Work on postdivorce issues, making use of *mediation* as needed. (See DIVORCE/SEPARATION: CONFLICT OVER POSTDIVORCE ISSUES).
12. Attempt to maintain consistent standards and expectations in both homes.
13. Take steps to maintain the child's relationships with family, extended family, and friends.

Task Menu Child
1. Avoid self-blame for the divorce.

Elaboration: Often children feel that the divorce was caused by a single event, such as a major fight, for which they may blame themselves.

Practitioner's Role: Help children recognize self-blame, if present, and to see that the divorce is their parents' responsibility.

2. Disengage from parental conflict.

Elaboration: Often children attempt to intercede in parental conflict, especially in the predivorce stage.

Practitioner's Role: Help the child understand the need to intercede but also the futility of such action.

3. Resolve feelings of loss of the "missing" parent (if the noncustodial parent does not maintain regular contact).

Practitioner's Role: Encourage the child to communicate feelings to the custodial parent and to initiate contact with the "missing parent," while validating and normalizing feelings of loss; help the child write a letter to the missing parent; use play or art therapy techniques to help younger children express feelings about loss.

4. Read about divorce and stepfamilies. (See **Literature** and task 7.)
5. Attend a treatment group for children of divorce.

Karen Duckett, Jennifer Hescheles

Divorce/Separation

Conflict Over Postdivorce Issues

The processes of separation and divorce challenge the adult's sense of self and ability to maintain personal balance. Reduced support from the lost partner and changes in living arrangements further strain the ability to continue to parent. Separation and divorce also commonly challenge the children emotionally, developmentally, and psychologically for a period of two years or more postdivorce. Some sources of stress for children include open hostility between separated or divorced parents, feeling responsible or blaming themselves for the parental problems, feeling caught in the middle of parental conflicts, and feeling pressured to choose between parents. "The task for parents is to isolate the anger they legitimately feel as hurt and rejected spouses, so that it minimally disrupts the alliance that is possible for them to maintain as parents. Even when they are in conflict over other matters, cooperation in childrearing is linked with healthier adjustment among children" (Luster & Okagaki 1993:103). See also DIVORCE/SEPARATION: CHILD'S ADJUSTMENT TO.

High conflict between parents before, during, and after the divorce is associated with behavioral disruptions in toddlers, school-aged children, and adolescents (Fauber et al. 1990) and is a powerful predictor of negative outcomes for all involved, including parents and their children (Hetherington, Cox, & Cox 1979; Johnston & Campbell 1988; Johnston et al. 1991). Empirical research consistently supports the hypothesis that continuing problems among children of divorce are specifically related to interparental conflict and not the divorce itself (Braver et al. 1992).

Forehand et al.'s (1994) longitudinal research provides strong evidence that among all variables studied, including the divorce itself, current conflict between divorced parents is most related to adolescents' external and internal problems. Their study revealed that current parental conflict was correlated with poor adolescent functioning during the first three years after a divorce, the time period during which the family system needs to restabilize (Carter & McGoldrick 1989). Other researchers have proposed that the relationship between postdivorce conflict and adolescent incompetence can be explained by the modeling effects of resolving problems poorly, parenting disruptions, and the anxiety generated by stress, which affects all family members (Grych & Fincham 1990; Fauber et al. 1990).

When divorced parents are overinvested in discord, they cannot adequately fulfill their parental roles of meeting the emotional needs of their children (Burroughs et al. 1997). As postdivorce conflict escalates, parents can become increasingly absorbed in battles over custody, visitation, child support, etc. Parents who perceive a lack of control around these issues are more likely to feel "noncontrol distress" and engage in unnecessary conflict (Braver et al. 1992). Family systems theorists posit that at times children's misbehavior becomes a mechanism to divert the parents from their conflict. Scapegoating can damage the child-parent relationship as well as intensify the child's behavioral problems (Fauber et al. 1990). After divorce, parent-child relationships can become strained for several reasons. However, if custody/visitation conflicts persist, children may become vulnerable to behavioral and cognitive difficulties.

Literature: Braver et al. (1991, 1992); Burroughs et al. (1997); Carter & McGoldrick (1989, 1993); Saposnek (1983); Schutz et al. (1989). Donahue (1996) presents a task-centered mediation model for divorced and separated couples with custody and visitation conflicts.

Task Menu

1. Accept that some amount of conflict will occur as part of the processes of separation and divorce despite the best intentions of all parties, and arrange specific outlets for its expression that do not involve the children.

   Elaboration: *Identify* available adult supports and how they will be used. This can help reduce the inappropriate involvement of children as confidantes and also reduce the parental isolation that can otherwise fuel conflicts.

2. *Learn about* the common effects of separation and divorce on children (both at the current ages of the involved children and at the developmental stages likely for them next).

   Elaboration: This task may be addressed in individual or family sessions, through a group for separating/divorcing parents in general, or in conjunction with a children's group. Bibliotherapy can be a helpful adjunct (e.g., <u>Dinosaurs Divorce</u> [Brown 1986], a book for parents and children; Ricci 1997; Ware 1982).

3. Learn what adults can do that best helps children deal with separation and divorce.

    Elaboration: This includes preventing conflict where possible, as well as addressing conflicts constructively when they do arise.

4. Develop a plan for custody, visitation, and support that is acceptable to both of you.

    Elaboration: Pay attention to such issues as which parent the children will spend Christmas with, children's birthdays and other special days, transportation arrangements, and payment for special expenses. Try to work out the basics of the plan prior to involvement with lawyers. With older children a family discussion may be useful in developing a plan.

5. Agree as parents what will be communicated to the children about the nature and logistics of the separation and divorce, and how you will do this; inform appropriate adult family members and ask for their cooperation.

6. Keep in mind developmental needs of your children in discussing visitation and custody arrangements.

    Elaboration: For instance, young children do not really grasp days of the week or times of day, and are commonly stressed by not being sure where to go after school. Parental cooperation to provide the consistency in routine and surroundings essential to children's sense of safety is very important.

7. Recognize signs of communication breakdown (confiding more in children, putting down the other parent or his or her family, erratic or shifting visitations, relaying messages through the children, etc.), and act to contain the conflict by instead directly contacting the other parent, or involving an objective third party (whether a counselor or mediator).

8. Negotiate conflicts around custody, visitation, and other issues with each other.

    Practitioner's Role: Serve as mediator, facilitating constructive face-to-face discussions when appropriate (Donahue 1996).

9. Reexamine present life stressors so as to reduce or eliminate those that compromise well-being and add to stress.

    Elaboration: Many newly divorced mothers are overburdened with economic hardship and isolation, and feel unhappy, frustrated, anxious, incompetent, imprisoned, and distressed. Working mothers may suffer from task overload (Carter & McGoldrick 1993). A rational review of self-imposed obligations to decide whether they should be continued may be useful if responsibilities have become too burdensome and cause tension.

10. Learn how to be a good role model by resolving conflicts rationally, maturely, and effectively.

    Elaboration: While parents should refrain from conflict with ex-spouses while children are present, at times it may not be practical to avoid discussions altogether. When children witness their parents solving problems effectively, they are more likely to duplicate that behavior.

11. Locate a co-parenting program in your area.

> **Elaboration:** Many family court systems and social service and mental health agencies conduct such programs from time to time.

Mary Corrigan, Cheryl Hilsman, Karen Duckett

Domestic Violence

Adjustment of Children to

Every child exposed to family violence, e.g., wife abuse, is affected differently. However, there are some common behaviors and characteristics of children who live in violent households. Externalizing behavior problems include misbehaving, aggression, uncooperativeness, and acting out (Carlson 1996; Frey-Angel 1989; Davis & Carlson 1987; Fantuzzo et al. 1991). Internalizing behavior problems include anxiety, depression, introversion, and withdrawal. Both kinds of behavior may be elevated in children exposed to domestic violence as compared to those who have not been exposed (Carlson 1996; Frey-Angel 1989; Christopoulos et al. 1987; Davis and Carlson 1987; Fantuzzo et al. 1991). These children may also have problems with eating or sleeping (Carlson 1996; Frey-Angel 1989) as well as a poor self-concept (Rosebaum & O'Leary 1981).

Relevant articles include Frey-Angel (1989); Grusznski et al. (1988); O'Keefe (1996); Raggs (1991); Smith & Berthelsen (1996); Wilson et al. (1989). Relevant books include Wilson (1997). Numerous catalogues have *games* that practitioners can use to help children express their feelings.

Task Menu Child
1. Create a safety plan (Raggs 1991).

> **Elaboration:** The intricacy of the safety plan depends on the age of the child. For example, for a preschooler, a safety plan might consist of leaving the area where the violence is occurring and seeking shelter. For a school-age child, the plan can include dialing 911 and identifying sources of help (Raggs 1991).

2. Enroll in a support group for children exposed to violence (if available).

> **Elaboration:** According to Frey-Angel (1989), "the most effective way to expose the children to different behaviors or ideas is in a group setting" (99). A "group setting allows for generalizing the problem by letting the children know that others are going through similar experiences with their own parents" (100).

3. *Learn about* different types of violence, including family violence (Wilson et al. 1989).

Elaboration: The main focus here is not solely on family violence, but on getting started thinking about many different types of violence in this society, such as violence on television; parents hitting parents or children; children hitting peers, siblings, or parents (Wilson et al. 1989).

Practitioner's Role: Make available some markers or crayons and paper to help children express what they think of as violence.

4. Identify and express feelings about witnessed violence at home (Wilson et al. 1989; Grusznski et al. 1988).

Practitioner's Role: There are card and board *games* available to use with children to help them express their feelings.

5. Learn about healthy and unhealthy ways of dealing with anger. (Wilson et al. 1989; Grusznski et al. 1988).

Elaboration: Children exposed to family violence may have problems with their own aggression. Examples of healthy ways to express anger include learning to verbally communicate your anger without becoming violent or giving yourself a *time out.* See ANGER MANAGEMENT AND AGGRESSION CONTROL.

6. Recognize who you are and are not responsible for in regard to your parents' fighting. Learn not to blame yourself (Wilson et al. 1989; Grusznski et al. 1988).

Practitioner's Role: Many children blame themselves for actions that go on in their households. This can lead to poor self-concept (Frey-Angel 1989). Grusznski et al. (1988) suggest making up a song or chant that repeats the statement: "It's not my fault" (425). Be sure not to make the child feel she or he has to choose between parents (who is good, who is bad). Help the child separate the abusers' actions from the abuser.

7. Maintain or increase positive social contacts (Wilson et al. 1989).

Elaboration: It is common for children to isolate themselves in an attempt to make sure they keep the family secret (Grusznski et al. 1988).

Practitioner's Role: It is important to attempt to counter the isolating behaviors by encouraging children to use a social support network when they are upset. Such a support system could include extended family, friends, and after-school programs (Wilson et al. 1989).

Miranda Koss

Domestic Violence

Battered Women

Within the past two decades, a good deal of attention has been given to the problem of women who are physically abused by their husbands or male partners (Webb 1992;

Grusznski, Brink, & Edleson 1988). According to Stark and Flitcraft (1988), a fifth to a quarter of all women have been abused at least once by their male partners. About 22 to 35 percent of women who receive treatment in emergency rooms of hospitals are there for injuries related to ongoing abuse (Randall 1990). Statistics from the Bureau of Justice Statistics National Crime Victimization Survey estimate that 29 percent of all violent crimes against women by single offenders were initiated by an intimate partner (Bachman & Saltzman 1995). Women experiencing abuse often feel confused, frustrated, frightened, helpless, hopeless, depressed, angry, downtrodden, and worthless (Webb 1992; Schumaker 1985; Walker 1978). Mistaken beliefs (cognitive distortions) about themselves and others interfere with the women's ability to behave in a self-sustaining manner (Webb 1992). This contributes to difficulty in breaking away from the abusive relationship. Battered women seeking to free themselves must struggle with a combination of emotional and practical issues. These take different forms depending on the nature of the relationship with the batterer.

Literature: Carlson (1997); Petretic-Jackson & Jackson (1996); Dutton (1992); Webb (1992); Wilson (1997).

Task Menu

1. Gain perspective on your situation by relating your experience of abuse to others'.

    Practitioner's Role: An abused woman should be encouraged to "tell her story" to people she trusts who would respond supportively, including the practitioner (Davis & Srinvasan 1995; Dutton 1992; Petretic-Jackson & Jackson 1996). This helps her gain perspective and prioritize her issues (Petretic-Jackson & Jackson 1996).

2. *Identify* past efforts to control or stop abuse (Carlson 1997).

    Elaboration: Taking inventory of past attempts to leave the relationship or control violence and assessing the extent to which these efforts have proved effective are important in evaluating what future steps to take (Carlson 1997).

3. *Identify* reasons/beliefs that you have for continuing the relationship (Dutton 1992).

    Elaboration: Look at cognitive distortions about yourself and others. Webb (1992) suggests using a diary to write down these beliefs.

    Practitioner's Role: Instruct and encourage client to use *self-monitoring* to evaluate and record behavior.

4. *Identify* other concurrent stressors.

    Elaboration: Assess what other issues might affect your future decisions and your ability to mobilize resources to address the abuse (Petretic-Jackson & Jackson 1996).

5. Develop a safety plan (Carlson 1997).

    Elaboration: A safety plan may include a number of components, depending on whether you plan to leave your partner—knowing where to go in case of danger, arranging for transportation to get out, having necessary items prepared in one place (for example, ID, medication, birth certificates, Social Security card, driver's license), changing locks on your residence, obtaining an order of protection, securing an electronic necklace that can be used to summon police if in danger, notifying employers whom to call if you are absent, and arranging for safe care of children. Petretic-Jackson and Jackson (1996) suggest rehearsing mental-escape drills in session and then doing a "walk through" at home when the abuser is not there.

6. [if planning to leave batterer] Develop a plan for self-sufficiency in terms of income and shelter, including putting money aside prior to leaving.

    Practitioner's Role: Explore resources as indicated—e.g., shelters, support groups, special counseling programs, legal aid.

7. [if planning to leave batterer] Anticipate the need to grieve the loss of the relationship and consider supports that may help with this process.

8. [if planning to leave batterer] Reinforce the break-off by doing other new things symbolic of starting a "new life"—getting a new hairstyle, joining a group, etc.

9. [if planning to leave batterer] Make use of help and support that might be provided by friends and family.

10. [if planning to leave batterer] If you have children and your partner is the father, work out a plan for custody and visitation.

11. [if planning to leave batterer] Develop a plan for starting new relationships.

12. [if planning to leave batterer] Consider circumstances in which you might be tempted to resume the relationship and devise ways of coping with these circumstances.

13. *Learn about* causes, dynamics, effects of battering, and services available.

    Elaboration: It is important to learn the nature of domestic violence and its effects, how women's historical oppression in society impacts on this problem, what services are available in the community, and common emotion, physical, and behavioral aftereffects. (This can help in "normalizing.") In particular, it is important to learn about the cycle of abuse—abuse followed by contrition and reconciliation, then further abuse—and how it applies to your situation (Carlson 1997; Petretic-Jackson & Jackson 1996; Dutton 1992). A useful book for victims of domestic violence is Wilson (1997).

14. Enhance coping strategies and modify cognitive distortions (Carlson 1997; Petretic-Jackson & Jackson 1996).

    Elaboration: Look at previous coping strategies and create a new repertoire of coping efforts. Modifying cognitive distortions includes modification of distorted and maladaptive beliefs, such as the belief that you can control your partner's violence or that he will start keeping his oft-broken promises never to hit you again. Consider modifying behaviors that are dysfunctional (e.g., being overly dependent emotionally or economically on the abuser). Cognitive-behavioral techniques that could be used include *cognitive restructuring, stress inoculation,* and coaching (Carlson 1997; Webb 1992).

14. Enhance problem-solving and decision-making skills (Carlson 1997).

Elaboration: This includes realizing that you have the right to make choices for yourself, and that you have alternatives and options (Carlson 1997). See *problem-solving training.*

15. Reduce isolation and increase social support (Carlson 1997; Petretic-Jackson & Jackson 1996).

Elaboration: Many women who are in abusive situations become socially isolated (Neilsen, Endo, & Ellington 1992). It is important to increase *social skills* and social support while reducing isolation, as they are important coping resources. The support of women who were formerly in abusive relationships and have been able to achieve violence-free lifestyles is very valuable (Carlson 1997, 1996; Brown & Dickey 1992).

Practitioner's Role: To help increase social support, you can encourage the client to attend battered women's support groups and reconnect (mobilize) with family and friends (Davis & Strinivasan 1994; Dutton 1992).

Miranda Koss

Domestic Violence

Battered Women: Asian

Current preventive and treatment strategies for violence against women fail to take into consideration victims' racial or cultural backgrounds because they are intended for white women (Ho 1990). Interventions should focus on cultural contexts that empower women and utilize cultural resources as a source of support and assistance. When working with Asian battered women it is essential to keep in mind the importance of the family, and that the individual represents the entire family (Kim 1995). Any mistakes or wrongs done by the individual are seen as representative of the family.

Realizing the stigma and the public embarrassment associated with going outside the family circle for help is of paramount concern to practitioners assisting clients of Asian cultures. Another important factor in assessing Asian women is awareness that they tend to internalize their frustration against male dominance by developing symptoms of depression or psychosomatic illness.

Violence in the Asian community arises out of frustration and misdirected anger: anger at poverty, discrimination, powerlessness, and the oppression that most minority groups experience living in the United States. Violence against women can also be attributed to the subordinate position of women in a male-dominated society, and the cultural adjustment problems in immigrant families (Ho 1990). Asian women must raise these issues in their own community so that healing can take place in cultural context.

Literature: Berg & Miller (1992); Ho (1990); Kim (1995); Rhee (1997).

Task Menu

1. Don't hide or deny domestic violence problems to avoid shaming yourself or your husband in the eyes of the community.

    Elaboration: Acknowledging that you are a victim of violence can help prevent future violence.

2. Think of violence against women as a social and legal problem.

    Practitioner's Role: Encourage clients to explore social explanations for the problem; discuss the dynamics of violence against women.

3. Don't take responsibility for the abuse and blame yourself.

    Practitioner's Role: Explore the client's feelings in this regard and validate her experience by empathizing and acknowledging the abusive behavior she reports. Be mindful of the deep-rooted sense of family loyalty and that the client may feel disloyal in reporting a batterer to authorities. Losing face brings on a great deal of shame and guilt. Practitioners need to keep in mind that many Asian men and traditional leaders will claim that such violence is not a problem in their community.

4. Protect the children from the destructive influence of witnessing or experiencing violence.

    Elaboration: Keep your responsibility to your children in mind as you plan to take action to stop the violence.

    Practitioner's Role: Be prepared to discuss how children are affected by family violence (Davis & Carlson 1987).

5. Participate in a support or treatment group.

    Elaboration: A group experience can help break down your sense of isolation and fear of rejection. A group consisting of just Asian women would be particularly helpful. A mutual contract of confidentiality among group members is very important.

6. Develop a support system outside the family.

    Elaboration: Social isolation of battered women can be part of both the causes and the consequences of abuse. Community elders or spiritual leaders who are supportive of women's well-being can help by intervening in cases of domestic violence. Social services need to develop culturally sensitive shelters and staff.

7. Don't minimize your strengths and coping abilities.

    Practitioner's Role: Practitioner needs to ask clients how they cope with their problems in order to empower them with their strengths (Berg & Miller 1992).

8. Obtain information about a telephone hotline.

    Elaboration: Telephone services can be very helpful if you have a strong fear of losing face. In addition, they provide confidential crisis intervention services (Rhee 1997).

9. *Learn about* what types of services are available, where, and how to access them.

10. *Learn about* legal aspects of domestic violence. See also DOMESTIC VIOLENCE: BATTERED WOMEN.

Malsuk Yoo

Domestic Violence

Male Batterers

Deschner (1984) defines battering as a "series of physically injurious attacks on an intimate or family member that form part of a repeated, habitual pattern" (2). A broader definition of battering includes other physical actions: slapping, kicking, threatening and/or using a knife or gun, beating up, hitting with an object or swinging and missing, pushing or shoving, throwing things, biting (Straus et al. 1980). Using the broader definition, an incident rate of battering is estimated at 25 percent, while using the stringent definition gives an estimate of 2–4 percent of the population. This translates into at least one out of every fifty couples (Deschner et al. 1986).

In addition to the problem that battering is a criminal offense, abusive men suffer from many other issues. Men who batter tend to have underdeveloped communication skills that are inadequate to mitigate emotions (Gondolf 1985). Consequently, these men are prone to outbursts to relieve fears and tensions or thwart the perceived cause of their problems: their female partner (Gondolf 1985). Most men who batter their partners tend to suffer from low self-esteem and depression (Neidig et al. 1986; Rouse 1984). Dewhurst, Moore, and Alfano (1992) suggest that in addition to depression, hostility toward women is a significant factor for males who sexually and physically assault women or their spouses. In men who suffer from low self-esteem, hurt and fear are converted into anger, then aggression (Saunders 1984). These men are generally seen as shy and nonassertive (Rosenbaum & O'Leary 1981) and believe in rigidly defined gender roles, in which the man must have power and control over himself and others (Gondolf 1985). Though these are all important issues to address, the top priority is to eliminate the violence (Neidig et al. 1985).

Literature: Articles that discuss how to work with the men individually or in groups include Saunders & Hanusa (1986); Gondolf (1985); Saunders (1984); Edleson, Miller, Stone, & Chapman (1985); Wallace & Nosko (1993); Schubmehl (1991); Bryant (1994). Articles relating to work with couples (but that can be modified to work only with the batterer) are Neidig et al. (1985) and Deschner et al. (1986). Articles on the evaluation and effectiveness of program for men include Edleson & Syers (1990, 1991); and Edleson & Grusznski (1988). Articles that address psychological types of male batterers include Orr & Guzie (1995) and Ornduff, Kelsey, & O'Leary (1995).

Task Menu

1. Accept personal responsibility for violent behavior (Neidig et al. 1985; Wodarski 1987).
2. Contract for commitment to change (Neidig et al. 1985; Wodarski 1987).

    Practitioner's Role: Assist the client in constructing a contract that includes steps toward changing his behaviors. Remember that these steps must be seen by the client as manageable.

3. Utilize time out to help control violent tendencies (Deschner et al. 1986; Neidig et al. 1985).

    Elaboration: Time out means leaving a situation if you feel you are getting upset, then attempting to calm down and reevaluate the situation. Only return to discuss the issue when you have calmed down (Deschner et al. 1986). See ANGER MANAGEMENT AND AGGRESSION CONTROL: ADULT, task 7.

    Practitioner's Role: Explain the value of taking time out. As many batterers are seemingly stuck in an adolescent or a younger phase of development, this can be a beneficial device for them.

4. Learn to recognize physical indications—for example, tone of voice, muscle tightness, abrupt gestures—as signs that your emotions are heightening in a way that could lead to violence if some coping behavior (e.g., *slow diaphragmatic breathing,* going for a walk to cool down, etc.) is not implemented to interrupt the process (Gondolf 1985).

    Practitioner's Role: Discuss with client that violence is the outcome of a series of sequential steps, rather than a random or sudden isolated event (Neidig et al. 1985).

5. Keep an anger log (Wodarski 1987) and engage in *self-monitoring* behavior.

    Elaboration: Recording information about any incidents in which anger is experienced will assist in identifying what triggers outbursts of anger.

    Practitioner's Role: Discuss with client the experiences (the goal would be to *identify triggers*) that took place before the outbursts of anger. Also process the emotions before, during, and after the event. Explain and instruct the client in *self-monitoring* behavior.

6. Use *systematic desensitization* to deal with triggers.

7. *Identify* negative self-talk (*self-verbalization*) and correct through use of *cognitive restructuring* (Neidig et al. 1985; Deschner et al. 1986; Saunders & Hanusa 1986).

    Elaboration: This includes revising self-talk, changing the assumptions that undermine your attitudes, and learning how to control the anger that follows self-talk (Wodarski 1987). An example of negative self-talk is, "I cannot believe she is doing stuff to piss me off like this. I will teach her to mess with me." Examples of constructive self-talk: "I need to remember what she is doing is not personal and stick with the issue at hand," and "As long as I keep cool, I really am in control of the situation" (Saunders 1984).

Practitioner's Role: Explain self-talk with the goal of assisting the client in understanding how it can lead to anger and violence. *Role play* inner monologue (Saunders 1984).

8. Learn to be appropriately assertive and not aggressive (Deschner et al. 1986; Saunders & Hanusa 1986).

    Elaboration: Learning how to behave in an assertive manner will satisfy the need to express yourself effectively but nonviolently. Assertiveness training includes: learning how to cope with criticism, developing the ability to make requests and assertively say no, and learning how to empathize with another's feelings while expressing your own (Saunders 1984).

    Practitioner's Role: Make definitions clear between assertive, nonassertive, and aggressive behaviors using modeling, coaching, and *rehearsal* as needed (Saunders 1984). Consult task planner on assertiveness.

9. Learn relaxation/stress reduction techniques (Saunders & Hanusa 1986; Deschner et al. 1986)—e.g., *progressive relaxation, stress inoculation.*

10. Develop alternatives to using violence as a means of communication and enhance problem-solving skills by taking part in *problem-solving training* (Deschner et al. 1986; Neidig et al. 1985).

    Practitioner's Role: Discuss *problem-solving training* with client and introduce the following communications skills: listening, validation, feeling talk, positive expression, negative feeling expression, request making (Neidig et al. 1985).

11. Read psychoeducational material on the personal and social roots of violence.

    Practitioner's Role: Discuss the material with the client and how aggressiveness may be part of male social conditioning. This can help reduce shame, which is counterproductive to improvement in controlling violent behavior (Wallace & Nosko 1993).

12. Explore and work on the need to control (Gondolf 1985).

    Elaboration: Your need to control may be too great if, for example, you find that she needs to work late, then become angry and violent with her when she comes home because she did not make dinner for you. Other good examples exist, such as not letting your wife go out with friends, isolating her from friends and family, calling her from work to make sure she is at home, etc.

    Practitioner's Role: Discuss with client how his need for control has caused conflict and frustration in his life. Suggest ways that he can let go of that control (e. g., the serenity prayer or the essence of it, which is the suggestion that you can only control your own self fully).

13. Control consumption of substances, such as alcohol, that alter and affect behavior.

    Practitioner's Role: Discuss with the client how substance use tends to coexist with battering behavior, and also consult task planners on alcohol / addiction.

14. Plan and take part in activities that help increase self-respect (Gentry & Eaddy 1980).

    Elaboration: Low self-esteem or self-respect is considered to be characteristic of men who batter.

    Practitioner's Role: Discuss with client how increasing self-respect could benefit his overall sense of well-being and help reduce or eliminate the urge to batter. Also consult SELF-ESTEEM: LACK OF.

15. Participate in a self-help group, such as Batterers Anonymous, Dr. Jerry Goffman, 1850 N. Riverside Ave., Suite 220, Rialto, CA 92376; (909) 355–1100 [leave message and return address]. mailto:jmgoff@genesis network.net)

Miranda Koss

Elder Abuse

Elder abuse encompasses a wide range of problems including violence, neglect, and financial exploitation. The client is frequently a frail elderly person, but this is not always the case (Seaver 1996). Although descriptions of elder abuse contain common elements, there is no single, consistent definition (Sanchez 1996). Cases of elder abuse, as understood from a family systems approach, cast the abused elder as the identified client and the abuse as a result of family dynamics and the environmental press on both the caregiver and the client. This conception suggests that the dynamics and pressures responsible be identified and addressed. For caregivers, task planners on anger and stress management may also be useful. Some tasks for elder abuse assume that the elderly individual is competent. Other tasks assume that he or she is cognitively impaired.

Financial exploitation, in the elder abuse literature, often falls under the same umbrella as physical abuse and neglect. It may be referred to as material, financial, economic, or fiduciary abuse (e.g., theft, extortion, or blocking access to resources). There are wide cultural variances as to what are normal family financial interactions; screening instruments for financial exploitation that may be valid from the white, middle-class perspective may not work well in minority communities (Sanchez 1996). Elders are not likely to report abuse; at least 70 percent of reported cases come from third-party observers (Berliner 1999).

Literature: Filinson & Ingman (1989); Kingston & Reay (1996); Kosberg (1983); Krummel (1996); Miller & Veltkamp (1998). A particularly useful article that provides a framework for identifying older people subject to financial abuse is Wilber & Reynolds (1996).

Task Menu Elders and caregivers
1. *Identify* elements of abuse.
    Practitioner's Role: Be aware of the mandated filing requirements if you determine abuse to exist. Make your clients aware of your responsibilities in this area; explain what constitutes verbal, emotional, psychological, physical, sexual, and financial abuse, then assist clients in identifying abuse.
2. List separately assets owned or controlled by each of you.
    Elaboration: Assets can be utilized for various changes (e.g., living arrangements, legal assistance, hiring individuals outside the family to assist with activities of daily living, grocery shopping, etc.). A separate listing may be necessary to determine whether financial abuse is actually taking place.
3. *Identify* agencies that may offer help.
    Practitioner's Role: Be aware of the formal and informal resources that are available and be ready to refer clients to them. A local Office of the Aging may be helpful. Also, if needed, go with the client or caregiver to the appropriate agency, such as a Social Security office, public or mental health clinic, local hospital, or legal services office.
4. Contact and visit support groups in your area.
    Practitioner's Role: Communicate that the clients' problems are not unique and suggest both elder and caregiver visit support groups that have members with problems similar to their own (e.g., senior support groups and caregiver support groups).
5. *Identify* the nature and sources of conflict.
6. *Learn about* role reversal, and reframe it as role reformation.
    Elaboration: Adults caring for elderly parents can often interpret the situation as a role reversal in which they are now parenting the parent. This can lead to resentment in both parties, as well as feelings of shame, guilt, and frustration. Reframing the situation as a role reformation helps to reflect the changing roles you both play, while also respecting the parent-child relationship that existed prior to the child assuming the caregiver role (Krummel 1996).
    Practitioner's Role: Normalize the situation as a natural process.
7. *Learn about* how the aging process may affect the elder's capacities.
    Elaboration: Caregivers need to adjust their expectations in relation to the elder's physical and mental capacities.
8. Try to resolve conflict through face-to-face negotiation.
    Practitioner's Role: Make use of the task planner on COUPLE OR FAMILY CONFLICT.
9. *Learn about* nonviolent coping behaviors.
    Elaboration: People can become so angry that they see no coping mechanisms available other than verbal or physical violence. Rage and

frustration can incapacitate the person and lead them to react in violent and hurtful ways.

Practitioner's Role: Teach the caregiver alternative coping methods such as *progressive relaxation* techniques, calmly discussing the situation with the elder, and taking a respite period from caregiving. See CAREGIVING: BURDEN ON ONE FAMILY MEMBER; ANGER MANAGEMENT AND AGGRESSION CONTROL: ADULT.

10. Begin giving each other emotional support or encouragement on a daily basis.
11. *Identify* conflicts or crises that you think may occur and come up with ideas about how they can be handled.
12. *Identify* the possible activities—such as visits to senior centers, churches, or other community settings; out-of-house activities for caregiver—and resources that might alleviate stress, such as home care or overnight care with friends or family, use of volunteers and homemaker services (meals and housekeeping), or neighbors.

    Elaboration: Both elder and caregiver need to enlist all possible help available from family members, friends, and neighbors, volunteers, homemaker services. Caregivers may be able to trade duties with other caregivers.
13. Discuss with your caregiver/elder things they may want to do out of the house and encourage them to pursue these activities.
14. Investigate long-term care facilities and discuss as a family the desirability and possibility of placement in long-term care.

Task Menu Concerned relatives, friends, neighbors who suspect elder abuse
1. Discuss with elders current conditions in their lives to get an understanding of what may be occurring and to assess their degree of cognitive functioning.

    Elaboration: Is the elder's memory, judgment, or reasoning impaired? How is his or her mobility, energy level, ability to read or write? Are there vision or hearing problems? Is the elder emotionally vulnerable and seeking others to help cope with loneliness, bereavement, or loss of self-esteem from illness, such as a stroke or dementia? All these are factors that may leave elders vulnerable to abuse, particularly financial abuse (Wilber & Reynolds 1996).
2. Discuss the elder (if comfortable doing so) with the caregiver to determine if there are any suspicious attitudes on his or her part or if some other helping individual may be suspected of taking advantage of the elder.

    Elaboration: In the relationship between the elder and the person suspected of abuse, is the suspect a family member who is no longer following previous norms of exchange or reciprocity (indications may be either a suddenly improved or a deteriorating relationship)? Is the suspect a friend or neighbor, and if so, who initiated the relationship? Is it long-standing, or has the original basis of the relationship changed over time? Is the individual in a position of professional trust and subject to ethical standards that prohibit conflict of interest? Or is it a fiduciary relationship (e.g., one that requires the caregiver to ensure that the elder's best interest is pursued) based on the trust or written instructions, such as power of attorney, of the elder? (Wilber & Reynolds 1996).

3. If there is reason to suspect some form of abuse, contact proper authorities (Office of Aging or an abuse hotline).

Bruce Parker, Pamela Zettergren, James Golden

Elder African Americans: Need for Services

Elderly African Americans are in "double jeopardy": they face the dual difficulties of being black and old, experiencing both negative attitudes and economic and social hardships because of their status as members of minority and marginalized groups. Taylor and Chatters (1988) stress that elderly blacks are a lot worse off than aged whites on a variety of indicators, including income level, educational attainment, and occupational status. For these reasons, it may be difficult for elderly African Americans to obtain the services they need.

In order to engage elderly African Americans in a quest for service, the practitioner must understand the particular values of their culture—those that define the accepted roles of elderly people in their community—as well as recognize their heterogeneity.

Literature: Readings for working with elderly African Americans may be found in Belgrave, Wyle, & Chio (1993); Carlton-LaNey (1991); Coke & Twaite (1995); Mitchell, Mathews, & Griffin (1997); Ralston (1993); Taylor, Chatters, & Spence (1993).

Task Menu

1. *Identify* and verbalize specific needs.

Practitioner's Role: At first glance to a practitioner of another ethnic background it may appear that elderly African Americans have an abundance of needs, which may leave the practitioner feeling overwhelmed. However, further examination should reveal that they have many strengths. They have stories to tell about how they endured and survived despite the odds. It is important to let them reminisce and to help them recall their strengths, among which may be support that has been, or could be, provided by the extended family.

Look at each individual client and his or her reality; do not assume the black elderly have had universal experiences. Provide brochures that show different ethnic groups represented on the covers. Address the perception that the services are designed for whites only. Attempt to decrease the level of distrust for people "unlike" them by demonstrating an interest to learn from and assist them.

2. Develop a plan to obtain needed services.

Practitioner's Role: Training majority-culture providers and recruiting minority-culture providers are two important paths to cultural competence in service delivery. Practitioners would be better prepared if they understood related customs and beliefs of their clients of other cultures. For example, it is important for providers to know that in some cultures, such as Haitian, people are reluctant to talk to strangers about their health.

Contact the service provider to set up an initial appointment while the client is in session. Reassure the client that the agency offers a friendly environment and wants to help. Provide transportation if needed and accompany the elderly person on his or her first visit if necessary.

To increase the likelihood of utilization, locate services as close as possible to where the client lives. Try to raise awareness about services listed in church newsletters and on posters at community centers, housing projects, and beauty shops. Use the church as a central place for services: self-help screenings, hot meals/food, outreach to isolated individuals, informal meetings on eldercare, etc.

Be mindful that the elderly African American may be skeptical about government motives and may not trust agencies from outside the community. (This population recalls the Tuskegee experiments and the role that the government played in them.) Train people in the community to provide services and greater opportunity for the aged to use services offered by someone "like" them.

3. *Identify* thoughts, feelings, and situations that lead to restrictions on using services.

Practitioner's Role: In work with the individual client, explore possible experiences with discrimination or fears of discrimination that might impede use of services. At a macro level, focus on lobbying to increase federal and state funding to support the capacity of indigenous organizations— e.g., churches—to provide outreach to black elderly in need of services. Promote elder leadership by training members of the community to become their own grassroots advocacy group.

Lunida Gresham

Encopresis

According to the DSM-IV (APA 1994) there are four essential criteria for a child to receive a diagnosis of encopresis: 1) the child repeatedly passes feces in places that are not appropriate, for example on the floor or in clothing; 2) the soiling happens for at least three months, once a month; 3) the child is at least four years old (children with developmental delays must have a mental age of four); 4) the fecal incontinence is not directly caused by a medical condition (except through a mechanism involving constipation) or the direct physiological effect of a substance like a laxative. This is called functional encopresis (Mellon & Houtt 1995).

Additionally, the DSM-IV identifies two subtypes: with constipation and overflow incontinence and without constipation and overflow incontinence. Most often encopresis is involuntary but it can be intentional. The latter subtype is usually associated with the presence of conduct disorder or oppositional defiant disorder, or may be due to anal masturbation (APA 1994). The American Psychiatric Association (1994) estimates that approximately 1 percent of five-year-olds have encopresis. It is more common in boys than in girls: the ratio is 3.4:1 (Boon & Singh 1991).

Additional classifications within encopresis are: retentive vs. nonretentive (Boon & Singh 1991), primary vs. secondary (APA 1994), and continuous vs. noncontinuous (Anthony 1957). In most cases encopresis is caused by chronic constipation (Poulton & Torrens 1996). Over time, the large intestines (colon and rectum) fill with hard stool and get stretched out of shape. Soft stool then "leaks" around the hard-formed feces in the colon (Borowitz 1996; Applied Medical Informatics 1996). Initially the leakage is small, and most parents assume that their child is not wiping well. However, as time passes, the intestines stretch more and more and the amount that leaks increases to a whole bowel movement in their underpants—what parents call accidents. Children generally do not feel the leaking—it just happens (Poulton & Torrens 1996). It is not done out of spite or because the child is lazy.

Other causes for encopresis are problems during toilet training; emotional or family problems; physical illnesses (e.g. Hirschprung's disease); and physical disabilities that make it hard for a youngster to wipe him or herself (American Academy of Child & Adolescent Psychiatry 1996). Children who cannot control their bowel movements are often avoided by adults and made fun of by their peers. This can cause them to feel badly about themselves; they may suffer from low self-esteem, guilt, and shame (AMI 1996). Early treatment can help prevent this. According to Levine (1975), approximately 80 percent of children who are encopretic are the retentive type. Hence, this task planner will concentrate on retentive encopresis.

Literature: American Academy of Child & Adolescent Psychiatry (1996); Applied Medical Informatics (1996); Boon & Singh (1991); Butler & Campise (1998); Borowitz (1996); Mellon & Houtt (1995); Poulton & Torrens (1996); Schaefer (1995).

Task Menu Parents

1. *Learn about* encopresis, the possible causes, and treatment (Stark et al. 1990).

   Elaboration: Parents need to understand that there is no overnight cure for encopresis and that they need to be patient (Poulton & Torrens 1996; AACAP 1996). Successful treatment typically takes from six to twelve weeks (Poulton & Torrens 1996).

2. View encopresis as a physical and behavioral issue, not as an act of spite or laziness (Poulton & Torrens 1996).

Elaboration: It is important not to tease or blame the child about his or her soiling problem—not only for the success of treatment but also for the psychological well-being of the child (Poulton & Torrens 1996; AMI 1996).

3. Get a physical exam for the child (Poulton & Torrens 1996; AACAP 1996).

Elaboration: It is important to rule out physical causes for the encopresis (Boon & Singh 1991). A full physical exam should be conducted, included a rectal examination (Mellon & Houtt 1995). There are eight conditions from which retentive encopresis must be differentiated: hypothyroidism, a pelvic mass, Hirschprung's disease (or aganglionic megacolon), chronic medications, rectal or anal stenosis, postsurgical stricture of the rectum or anus, anterior displacement of the anus, and chronic anal fissure or perianal dermatitis (Schmitt 1984). An abdominal x-ray can confirm that there is impacted stool in the colon since that is a sign of encopresis (Boon & Singh 1991; AMI 1996).

4. Work out a treatment program together with the child.

Elaboration: This includes creating a regular toileting schedule, providing the child with high-fiber foods and plenty of liquids, making sure the child exercises, supervising the child while he or she cleans underpants and body (Poulton & Torrens 1996; AMI 1996; Estes). Throughout the procedure, should refrain from using anger, support the child, and refrain from discouragement or criticism (AMI 1996).

5. Use positive reinforcement with the child for sitting on the toilet, defecating in the toilet, and having clean underwear (Mellon & Houtt 1995; Boon & Singh 1991; Schaefer 1995).

Elaboration: Praise as well as tangible rewards are advised. Children can be weaned off the rewards. For example, supply the child with toys that can be used only when sitting on the toilet (Butler & Campise 1998).

6. Praise the child for any success (Butler & Campise 1998).

Task Menu Child

1. *Learn about* encopresis.

Practitioner's Role: It is important to let the child know that others have the same problem and that the child is not bad. Address the shame and guilt that are associated with encopresis.

2. Get colon and rectum cleaned out with enemas, suppositories, or laxative (Poulton & Torrens 1996; Mellon & Houtt 1995; Boon & Singh 1991).

3. Use stool softener daily (Boon & Singh 1991).

Elaboration: A mild laxative (i.e., milk of magnesia, mineral oil) can be used with a stool softener (Poulton & Torrens 1996; Boon & Singh 1991; Stark 1990). Slowly wean off the laxative and stool softener.

4. Follow a regular toileting schedule.

Elaboration: The goal of having a schedule is to establish a regular pattern of toileting. This is not a punishment for fecal incontinence; rather, it should be viewed as a bowel muscle-building program (Boon & Singh 1991). Sit on the toilet for 10–15 minutes after each meal and before bedtime to try to make a bowel movement (Poulton & Torrens 1996).

5. Practice Valsalva maneuver (Poulton & Torrens 1996).

Elaboration: Hold your breath while tightening your abdominal muscles and bearing down to make a bowel movement (Poulton & Torrens 1996).

6. Eat foods high in fiber, drink plenty of liquids, and exercise daily (Poulton & Torrens 1996).

Elaboration: For example, eat fruits, vegetables, and whole grain products. Fiber foods, liquids, and exercise will help make the stool softer and keep bowel movements regular, as well as minimize discomfort (AMI 1996; Poulton & Torrens 1996).

7. Clean your underpants after soiling and clean yourself (AMI 1996; Schaefer 1995).

Elaboration: Learn to take responsibility for your actions.

Miranda S.G. Koss

Enuresis: Nocturnal

Enuresis is a general term that refers to uncontrolled, accidental, or involuntary discharge of urine (Mellon & Houtt 1995; Schaefer 1995). For a formal diagnosis from the DSM-IV (APA 1994), a child must be five years old. For enuresis to be clinically significant, wetting episodes must occur twice a week for at least three consecutive months, or produce a considerable amount of distress or impairment in academic, social, or other important areas of the child's functioning. The enuresis also cannot be due to a medical condition.

Diurnal enuresis occurs when a child wets him- or herself during the day. Nocturnal enuresis, on which this task planner focuses, occurs when the child wets him- or herself at night. Children can also wet themselves both during the day and at night. When this occurs, it is easier to treat nocturnal enuresis. In about half of the cases, when nocturnal wetting remits, so does the daytime wetting (Schaefer 1995). Enuresis declines with age (Mellon & Houtt 1995; Schaefer 1995); according to Schmitt (1991), from 20 percent of children at age five to 3 percent at age twelve. There are numerous theories and etiological hypotheses regarding possible underlying causes. However, none has been conclusively proven or adequate to explain the problem (Mellon & Houtt 1995; Schaefer 1995). Some theories are: psychological factors (emotional disturbance), toilet training practices, heredity, small bladder, urinary tract infection, and slow maturation (Schaefer 1995). Stromgren and Thomsen (1990), cited in Mellon and Houtt (1995) state that continuous bed-wetting has been associated with problems in social and emotional adjustment.

Literature: Arnold (1997); Butler & Campise (1998); Knell (1995); Maizels, Rosenbaum, & Keating (1997); Mack (1989); Mellon & Houtt (1995); Schaefer (1995); Schmitt (1991).

Task Menu Parents

1. *Learn about* enuresis, the possible causes, and the different types of urine alarm systems.

    Elaboration: The oldest form of alarm is the bell and pad conditioning method. More modern and portable systems include Palco Wet Stop and the Nytone enuretic alarm (attaches to wrist). Information on where to purchase these items is at the end of this task planner. Self-help books include Arnold (1997) and Maizels, Rosenbaum, & Keating (1997).

    Practitioner's Role: Give parents realistic expectations. they should be informed that the average time for success is eight to twelve weeks; some children remit immediately, but others can take over seven months (Schaefer 1995). Children who wet more frequently and those who are multiple wetters take longer to stop wetting the bed (Mellon & Houtt 1995).

2. View enuresis as a deficit of physical learning and not a purposeful act or laziness of the child (Mellon & Houtt 1995).

    Elaboration: Some parents see the bed-wetting as a problem that their child should be able to control, and punish the child when he or she does not. The Tolerance for Enuresis Scale, by Morgan and Young (1975), can be administered to the parents. Seeing bed-wetting as a deficit of physical learning can promote the needed supportive family environment to begin treatment (Mellon & Houtt 1995).

3. Protect the bed from urine (Schmitt 1991).

    Elaboration: Have your child wear thick underwear to bed in addition to pajamas. Place a plastic mattress cover over the mattress to protect it from urine odor (Schmitt 1991).

4. Get a physical exam for the child (Mellon & Houtt 1995).

    Elaboration: A physical exam should definitely include a urinalysis to check for a urinary tract infection that may be causing the enuresis. Ideally, it should also include a sonogram of the kidneys and bladder to check for diseases that might be causing the incontinence (Mellon & Houtt 1995).

5. Purchase urine alarm system and work out the basic treatment program together with the child (Mellon & Houtt 1995).

    Elaboration: This includes helping the child keep a record of dry and wet nights and the size of the spot, making sure the child is fully awake after a wetting episode, helping him or her with retention and overlearning

(Mellon & Houtt 1995), encouraging the child to postpone urination during the day, responding gently to wet nights and positively to dry nights (Schmitt 1991). Investigate Enuresis Support and Information Group (ESIG).

Dr. Tom (http://www.healthy.net:80/home/askdrtom.tomfaq/bw.htm) lists a number of resources to access through the Internet: To subscribe to the Enuresis Support and Information Group (ESIG), send the following command in the body of an e-mail message to LISTSERV@sjuvm.stjohns.EDU: SUB ENURESIS yourfirstname yourlastname. To receive a list of files in the archives, send the following command to the same address: INDEX ENURESIS. If you have any questions about the list, send a message to the list owner, Eric Fricker, at the following address: enuresis-request@sjuvm.stjohns.edu.

Enuresis alarms can be ordered from:

Nytone Alarm: Nytone Medical Products, 2424 South 900 West, Salt Lake City, UT 84119; (801) 973–4090.

Porty Pager Silent Alarm: Ideas for Living, 1285 N. Cedarbrook, Boulder, CO 80304; (800) 497–6573. http://www.w2.com:80/docs2/n/nytonedescr.html

Wet-Stop Alarm: Palco Laboratories, 8030 Soquel Avenue, Santa Cruz, CA 95062; (800) 346–4881.

Enuresis Treatment Centers, 33900 West 8 Mile Road—Suite 171, Farmington Hills, MI 48335; (800) DRYBED4; in MI, 1(800) DRYBED1. help@drybed.com

Call or e-mail for information.

6. Reward the child for dry nights.

Elaboration: The rewards can be praise, money, an object, or a combination.

Task Menu Child

1. Help implement urine alarm treatment.

Elaboration: To be a full participant in eliminating your own enuresis, construct a help chart of when you wet the bed. The chart should include columns for wet nights, dry nights, the size of the wet spot, and whether or not you awaken spontaneously to go to the bathroom (Mellon & Houtt 1995).

Before you go to bed every night: lie on your bed with your eyes closed; pretend it is the middle of the night; pretend your bladder is full and it is starting to hurt; pretend it is trying to wake you up by saying to get up before it is too late. You should get out of bed, run to the bathroom, and empty your bladder like you would if it were actually the middle of the night. Then you need to remind yourself to get up like that during the night. You should understand that the goal is not to hold it in for morning, but to get up and urinate one or more times every night (Schmitt 1991).

2. Shut off the alarm when it goes off.

   Elaboration: You are to shut off the alarm. Newer models are worn on the body and are turned off by removing the alarm from the underwear and drying the probe that is urine sensitive (Mellon & Houtt 1995).

3. Clean up after each accident (Mellon & Houtt 1995, Schmitt).

   Elaboration: No matter how big of a spot there is on the bed, you should go through the entire procedure of remaking the bed and changing pajamas (Mellon & Houtt 1995).

4. Learn retention control (Schaefer 1995; Mellon & Houtt 1995; Schmitt 1991).

   Elaboration: Postpone urination during the day for up to 45 minutes (Mellon & Houtt 1995). This helps stretch your bladder. Retaining urine "during the day can help the bladder wait at night until you can get out of deep sleep and wake up" (Schmitt 1991).

5. Overlearn how to retain water (Mellon & Houtt 1995).

   Elaboration: Once you have kept your bed dry, gradually increase the amount of water intake before bedtime. At night the maximum you should drink is two ounces plus one ounce for each year. For example, if you are eight years old, your goal will be to retain ten ounces. You begin to overlearn by drinking four ounces fifteen minutes before bedtime. If you remain dry for two consecutive nights, increase the amount by two ounces. If you wet the bed, keep on the same amount of water until you remain dry for five consecutive nights. Increase the amount to the maximum. Overlearning ceases when you reach fourteen consecutive dry nights at the maximum amount (Mellon & Houtt 1995).

Miranda Koss

Family Dysfunction: Lack of Rules

Lack of rules for controlling behavior of family members is most frequently an issue when difficulties involve parent-child interactions, especially in single-parent families. Expectations and guidelines regarding children's behavior may be unclear; what rules exist may be inconsistently enforced.

Literature: Epstein & Schlesinger (1996); O'Gorman (1993); Minuchin (1974); Reid (1985); Reid & Donovan (1990).

Task Menu Parents and children

1. *Identify* situations for which rules are needed.

   Practitioner's Role: If rule-making is done in the session, ask family members in turn to suggest situations, or family members can do this themselves in an in-session task. The tasks following can also be done by family members conversing with one another in the session, with you as facilitator.

2. For an identified situation, propose a rule.

Elaboration: Rules can be proposed by parents or children. Alternatively, the family can come up with possible rules by brainstorming. Family members then discuss proposals and develop rules all will accept. If parents are in conflict over rules for children or if the parental coalition is weak or lacking power, parents may do tasks 1 and 2 without children present. If the problem involves undesirable child behavior, the child may propose a rule as if he or she were a parent. If the goal is to increase a particular parent's involvement in family decision making, that parent can be asked to suggest rules or to negotiate rules with children. If the problem involves sibling conflict, siblings may negotiate rules themselves (see SIBLING CONFLICT). If the parent is single and needs to be empowered vis-à-vis her children, the parent may propose rules with the children reacting. Or parents and children may negotiate the rules, with the practitioner supporting the parent.

3. Implement rules worked out in session or in home conferences.

Elaboration: Devices include posting rules on the refrigerator, using *contingency management* and *contingency contracting* to facilitate child compliance.

4. Review how well the rules are being implemented and make necessary modifications.

Fire Setting: Child

It is common for children to be fascinated with fire. Inadvertent fire setting through play is not unusual. It is clear, however, that some youngsters are pathological fire setters (Meeks 1979). There are different levels of risk of future fire settings, ranging from low to high. Sakheim, Osborn, and Abrams (1991) classify four levels of risk by degree of motivation. Minor-risk fire setters are those who set fires accidentally or out of curiosity (Adler et al. 1994). At moderate risk for future fire setting are those who set fires as a cry for help. The emotional needs of these children have not been recognized or addressed. At definite risk for future fire setting are children who are usually antisocial, rebellious, and chronically angry. They use fire as a tool in a power struggle with an adult authority whom they perceive as punitive, rejecting, or depriving. They experience little or no guilt (Sakheim, Osborn, & Abrams 1991). These two groups are not fire players but fire setters: "firesetting usually involves the systematic gathering of flammable materials with the fire being directed at a clearly defined target, either person or property, with anger or revenge as the most commonly reported motives" (Adler et al. 1994:1195). Those who are at extreme risk of future fire setting fall into two categories: 1) those who become aroused or excited by lighting and watching fires; and 2) those who are psychotic, usually paranoid and lacking in judgment and insight (Sakheim, Osborn, & Abrams 1991). See also the DSM-IV (APA 1994). This task planner will focus on moderate- and definite-risk children.

Of 20,000 individuals arrested for arson in 1990, 47 percent were younger than eighteen years of age (Raines & Foy 1994). This statistic makes arson the crime with the highest percentage of involvement of juveniles. Fire setters are likely to have experienced abuse or neglect, to have social problems, and to do poorly in school (Raines & Foy 1994). Other characteristics include anger at parents, difficulty in verbalizing anger, and use of fire to gain power over adults (Sakheim, Osborn, & Abrams 1991).

Literature: Adler et al. (1994); DeSalvatore & Hornstein (1991); Raines & Foy (1994); Sakheim, Osborn, & Abrams (1991).

Task Menu Child

1. *Identify* feelings and what evokes them.

   Practitioner's Role: The types of feelings that should be elicited are fear, guilt, loneliness, sadness, and anger. It is helpful for the child to visualize a day when he or she set a fire to identify these feelings. The intensity of the feelings could also be discussed (Raines & Foy 1994).

2. *Identify* how anger is expressed.

   Elaboration: Over time, fire setters often learn to express their intense anger indirectly. Direct expressions may have resulted in punishment or rejection (Sakheim, Osborn, & Abrams 1991).

3. Graph experiences that led up to an instance of fire setting (Adler et al. 1994).

   Elaboration: Plot the events on the horizontal axis and the intensity of feelings in different colors on the vertical axis. The purpose is to synthesize tasks 1 and 2, so you can recognize the emotional antecedents of the fire setting. This can then help you learn alternative ways to respond to similar events in the future (Adler et al. 1994).

4. Keep an anger log.

   Elaboration: Keep a log of incidents that evoke anger, to help you learn to identify how anger is evoked and how you tend to deal with it.

5. Learn to express anger in more appropriate ways.

   Practitioner's Role: There are numerous ways to help children learn how to express their anger, for example, assertiveness training, modeling, role playing, and *games* (Walsh & Rosen 1979). See also ANGER MANAGEMENT AND AGGRESSION CONTROL; CHILD; ASSERTIVENESS, LACK OF.

6. Obtain a "Smokey the Bear" packet.

   Elaboration: The "Smokey the Bear" packet includes a folder, forest ranger handbook, pen, ruler, pencil, note pad, emblem, book markers, junior forest ranger handbook, and words to a song about Smokey. It can be obtained from the U.S. Department of Agriculture or from a state's forest department (DeSalvatore & Hornstein 1991). This program is important to use with fire setters. Smokey the Bear represents a symbolic ideal. Many fire setters feel bad, whereas Smokey represents something "good" or "right." Emulating Smokey is a way of becoming good (DeSalvatore & Hornstein 1991).

7. Learn about the dangers of fire as well as fire safety and prevention (DeSalvatore & Hornstein 1991; Adler et al. 1994).

   Elaboration: Learn to start and put fires out in a safe manner and in a controlled environment, so you will be rewarded for your actions. Putting out fires is not easy, but they can be controlled and put out (Dalton, Haslett, & Daul 1986). This symbol of your anger and negative feelings can be controlled; "negative feelings could also be realistically dealt with" (Dalton, Haslett, & Daul 1986:716).

8. Graduate from the Smokey the Bear program and become a junior fire ranger (DeSalvatore & Hornstein 1991).

   Elaboration: At graduation you must: 1) demonstrate a level of competency in how to start a safe fire, how to extinguish a fire, etc.; 2) take an exam (written or verbal depending on age); and 3) take a practical exam where you can demonstrate proper fire behavior. Then you will take the "Smokey the Bear" oath and receive a badge, posters about prevention of forest fires, and a membership card. In a ceremony, you will be declared a "Junior Forest Ranger" (DeSalvatore & Hornstein 1991).

Task Menu Parents

1. Implement fire safety and preventative measures in your household (Hunt et al. 1990).

   Elaboration: Make sure you have smoke detectors and a fire extinguisher in your house. Teach family members how to use the fire extinguisher. Make fire-setting materials inaccessible. Create more structure and routine in the household and increase parental supervision. Inform the child of the consequences of fire setting (Hunt et al. 1990).

2. Help the child create and put out fires in a safe manner, and reward him or her for doing so (Adler et al. 1994; DeSalvatore & Hornstein 1991).

   Elaboration: Repetitive fire setting under strict supervision, with practitioner or parent, is done in an attempt to satiate the child's wish to start fires (Adler et al. 1994). Learn to use negative consequences (withdrawal of privileges) in the event of future fire setting (Adler et al. 1994).

3. Help the child express anger in an appropriate way. See ANGER MANAGEMENT AND AGGRESSION CONTROL: CHILD.

Miranda Koss

Foster Care: Child's Emotional Reaction to Separation from Parent(s)

Separation from parents can evoke feelings that include abandonment, guilt, anger, hurt, grief, sadness, low self-esteem, and being "unlovable." As a result, the child may exhibit behavior problems such as tantrums, lashing out, anxiety, depressed mood, multiple crying episodes, nightmares, or withdrawal. The behavior may present school-related difficulties such as not doing assignments and homework or disruptive acts.

Literature: Tasks for practitioners, children, and caregivers can be found in literature on coping skills for children (Cantos et al. 1996; Fanshel et al. 1990; Forman 1993; Mellor 1995), on treatment of children of divorce (Hodges 1986), and on treatment of childhood problems (Schroeder & Gordon 1991).

Task Menu Parents or caregivers
1. Help the child express verbally feelings about separation from the parent(s).
2. When the child exhibits negative behaviors, inquire if they are reactions to feelings related to the separation.
3. Provide positive feedback or reinforcement when the child successfully expresses feelings verbally.
4. Help the child understand that the separation was not because of something he or she did.
    Elaboration: Discuss openly (as developmentally appropriate) the reasons for the separation (Schroeder & Gordon 1991).
5. Assess your own feelings about the child's parent(s) and try to avoid discussing negative perceptions of the parent(s) with the child.
6. Help the child construct a life-story book.
    Elaboration: Adult and child fill an album with photos, greeting cards, documents, and written descriptions of memories. Movies, videos, and audiotapes should be included.
7. Help the child maintain a routine, providing consistent rules and structure.
    Practitioner's Role: Caregivers often feel for the child and want to make the child's stay with them as unstressful as possible. The result may be a lack of rule setting or enforcement. Practitioner should explore this issue with the caregiver and support the caregiver in setting limits.
8. Help the child maintain contact with the parent(s) through letter writing, phone calls, and/or visitation.

Task Menu Child
1. Maintain a log to identify possible feelings and thoughts about separation from your parent(s) and your present situation.

Practitioner's Role: Help the child develop an emotional vocabulary. Use play therapy to elicit the child's feelings regarding the separation.

2. Use *self-verbalization* techniques to decrease stress related to emotional pain and interrupt problem behaviors (Forman 1993).

3. Select a small object (e.g., a photograph, a toy given by your parents) that you can keep with you to help remember them).

4. Talk with an adult (caregiver, teacher, practitioner, etc.) when you are experiencing emotional pain. See also ANXIETY: SEPARATION ANXIETY DISORDER.

Jonathan Caspi, Marsha Descartes

Frail Elderly

Alzheimer's Disease: Spouse and Family Adjustment

The DSM-IV describes dementia as "characterized by the development of multiple cognitive deficits" that include impairment in memory (APA 1994:133). Alzheimer's disease is the major cause of dementia in the elderly, making up about 50 percent of all cases. In fact, some estimates rate late-onset Alzheimer's disease as affecting almost half of the population of the United States eighty-five years and older (Carstensen et al. 1996). The course of Alzheimer's type dementia tends to be slowly progressive. In the early stages, memory loss is prominent. The ability to learn new material is impaired, and there is a decline from the previous level of functioning. Individuals may lose items like their keys or wallet, become lost in unfamiliar places, or leave food cooking on the stove. Some show increased irritability or other personality changes. As the dementia progresses, it becomes more evident that individuals are forgetting previously learned material. They can become lost in familiar neighborhoods or have trouble shopping or paying bills. Aphasia, apraxia, and agnosia (e.g., further cognitive deficits) may develop after several years. In the later stages an individual may forget his or her schooling, occupation, birthday, family members (even spouse and children), and eventually even his or her own name. Gait or other motor disturbances can develop. End stage Alzheimer's disease may result in the inability to maintain basic hygiene and personal care, self-feeding, and even language skills. Victims may eventually be reduced to a vegetable state, becoming mute and bedridden.

Throughout the course of Alzheimer's disease, some individuals may also experience delirium, delusions, or depressed mood in combination with the dementia. The fears, stressors, and losses involved for the family and spouses of the victims are enormous. The average duration of the disease from onset until death may range up to ten years or longer. The realities of day-to-day caregiving and planning needs for the individual with Alzheimer's disease become increasingly burdensome for the spouse and family as the condition progresses.

Literature: American Psychiatric Association (1994); Brechling (1993); Carstensen et al. (1996); Janicki & Dalton (1999); Katzman (1987); Tobin (1999); Toseland & McCallion (1998).

Task Menu Family or caregivers

1. Secure information from physicians and other experts regarding a provisional diagnosis to rule out other causes of dementia and to assess the competency of the patient, stage of disease, etc.

    Practitioner's Role: Assist health care professionals in making a provisional diagnosis.

2. Provide support, nurturing, and assurances regarding provision of care to the patient.

    Practitioner's Role: Provide counseling for spouse and family in order to facilitate their adjustment to the changes taking place in the individual with Alzheimer's disease.

3. If the patient is in the first stage of Alzheimer's, assist him or her with careful execution of advance directives for personal, financial, social, and medical needs.

    Elaboration: Obtain legal advice, as needed. In the very early stages of dementia, people with Alzheimer's disease are usually capable of understanding the devastating implications of their illness and may be willing to review their personal health and financial commitments in anticipation of their future incapacity. Furthermore, someone in the early stage of dementia who is confused or disoriented in time and place may still be capable of making choices and expressing preferences about many aspects of his or her health care (Brechling 1993).

    Practitioner's Role: Be able to respond to families' questions about advance directives, legal resources, etc. Lack of information from social workers and other human service personnel regarding advance directives is commonplace and a disservice to the client (Brechling 1993).

4. File for guardianship (or conservatorship in some states) if the patient is in an advanced stage of dementia and has not utilized advance directives.

5. Read <u>The 36-Hour Day</u> (Mace & Robins 1991).

    Elaboration: This book gives a realistic outlook of what managing an individual with Alzheimer's disease entails.

6. Join a support or stress management group.

    Elaboration: This is particularly important if you are a female, in a deteriorating state of physical health, or limited in financial resources. Generally, these variables are associated with depression in caregivers (Tobin 1999).

7. If the condition is advanced, discuss options for behavioral management of the patient with physician.

    Elaboration: Small doses of neuroleptics are sometimes sufficient to ameliorate disturbances such as severe depression, agitation, aggressiveness, and paranoia. The medications may, however, produce extrapyramidal side effects and marked psychomotor retardation (Katzman 1987), so you may want to consider behavior modification techniques instead.

Practitioner's Role: Practice or demonstrate through *role play* the techniques of *progressive relaxation* and *coping imagery* to the victim's spouse and family. Such techniques may be used to assist the family in behavior modification of an individual with Alzheimer's disease or as aids for the family in stress reduction or effective communication among themselves. Additionally, help the spouse and family to *identify triggers* that prompt agitation in the individual with Alzheimer's disease, so they may be avoided when possible.

8. Discuss living arrangements and plan for long-term care needs (e.g., home care, pain management) as the disease progresses..

    Elaboration: If you are considering institutionalization, research the financial costs and quality and comprehensiveness of care of potential settings (some nursing homes will refuse to accept patients with behavior problems). Make site visits as necessary. See FRAIL ELDERLY: RELOCATION.

    Practitioner's Role: Help the family understand that individuals with Alzheimer's disease may change what they say they want over time. The family will then have to decide whether to honor what was requested originally, when the person was him- or herself, or to abide by the new requests. For example, a person may say that once they become incontinent they wish to go to a nursing home, as they do not want to be a burden on the family, but because Alzheimer's disease has a way of infantilizing victims, by the time they are incontinent they may beg the family not to send them away, not understanding, as they once did, the implications of their condition on the family's functioning.

9. Improve the quality of the patient's physical environment.

    Elaboration: It is important to create an environment that is nonthreatening and predictable by using night lights, clocks, calendars, etc. (Tobin 1999). Additionally, in the early stages of Alzheimer's disease an ordered environment helps the patient externally organize what he or she once internally organized.

10. Read Tobin (1991), focusing on sections referring to "preservation of self."

    Elaboration: This is helpful in allowing the individual with Alzheimer's disease to maintain as much of his or her dignity as is possible under the circumstances.

11. Continue to treat the patient as you always have.

    Elaboration: This reinforces the "preservation of self" for the patient. Simple pleasures seem to facilitate adaptation, when care is taken by spouses and other family members to relate to victims of Alzheimer's in essentially the same way they always have (Tobin 1999).

12. Identify meanings of patient behavior, particularly in the middle to late stages, to assist the patient in retaining a sense of self.

Elaboration: Bizarre behavior often has meaning for the patient, who is striving for preservation of self. Once this principle is understood, families are able to interpret bizarre behavior as the patient's effort to continue his or her identity. It is then easier for them to tolerate, or perhaps encourage, aberrant behaviors (see Tobin 1999 for examples).

13. Consider respite or daycare programming.
14. Consider hospice care if the victim is in the end stage of Alzheimer's.

Practitioner's Role: Initiate referral to a hospice program. Provide counseling to spouse and family for anticipatory grief and loss issues. Discuss the possibility of continued counseling with family and spouse for grief and loss following the death of the victim.

Tammy Rucigay

Frail Elderly

Relocation

Aged people often have to relocate from one living environment to another where they can receive more care, such as an adult home or nursing home. Moving from one residential home to another can cause a great deal of stress and negative consequences, for example, increased mortality and decreased physical and mental capabilities (Danermark & Ekstroem 1990). Moves are often out of the realm of the patient's control, compounding the problem. The term "transfer trauma" is frequently used to describe the difficulties associated with moving elderly individuals. Using a preparation program as suggested in the literature, offering options, and providing seniors with a sense of control helps alleviate these concerns.

Literature: Blasinsky (1998); Danermark & Ekstroem (1990); McCallion & Toseland (1995); Soares & Rose (1994).

Task Menu
1. Ask questions about the new facility and discuss options with practitioner.
   Practitioner's Role: Provide options for the elderly person whenever possible, and act as liaison between him or her and staff at other facilities.
2. If a choice of facilities is provided, list the pros and cons of each, discuss with family/responsible party, and make a decision.
   Practitioner's Role: Assist in decision making by educating the resident and family members about services available at other facilities.
3. Speak with a practitioner at the new facility and request a tour.
   Practitioner's Role: Provide telephone number or telephone use, and accompany the resident on tour, if desired.

4. Visit the new facility or review a site plan or map to familiarize yourself with new surroundings and staff.

   Practitioner's Role: Familiarize the resident with the new setting by facilitating site visits, or reviewing the layout visually by map. Accompany the resident on a site visit when possible, and introduce him or her to staff and activities offered. Educate the resident about the location of the facility (distance from present location and family members).

5. *Identify* concerns or fears.

   Practitioner's Role: *Identify* and correct misconceptions about the move. Prepare the resident emotionally for the move via counseling, and offer such services to family members.

6. Seek out special services for the elderly and for caregivers.

   Practitioner's Role: Link clients and families to special services and address psychosocial barriers to the acceptance of such services. For example, discuss losses, vulnerabilities, defenses, and dependency issues.

7. *Identify* the impact of the relocation.

   Practitioner's Role: Discuss the impact of the relocation with client and family or previous caregiver.

8. Attend support groups, workshops, social and recreational groups.

   Practitioner's Role: Offer information on mutual support groups, psychoeducational workshops, social and recreational groups, and service and advocacy groups (McCallion & Toseland 1995).

9. Make requests for a room or roommate, if possible.

   Practitioner's Role: Work with a social worker from the new facility to create a smooth transition.

10. Decide on the preferred mode of transportation to the new facility (e.g., ambulance, family car, company van).

    Practitioner's Role: Arrange for transportation, as desired by resident.

11. Set a time aside to say farewell to other residents and staff members.

    Practitioner's Role: Assist the resident with packing belongings and saying good-byes to other residents and staff members. Provide follow-up visit if possible.

Maura A. Barrett, Jennifer Hescheles

Frail Elderly

Resident Adjustment to Nursing Home Placement

Placement in a nursing home can be a traumatic experience for older adults or disabled individuals. Many view moving to a nursing home as the end of the line. Emotionally, it is a difficult time for clients as they are separated from home, familiar surroundings, family, and friends. Each individual has to deal with change of residence, daily routine, and support network, in addition to health issues. The placement decision is usually made only after all other alternatives have been exhausted. Caregivers are unable to continue their involvement or the condition of the person has deteriorated and now presents greater needs than the family can address. This decision involves feelings of guilt, grief, and loss for all the parties involved. It is one of the most difficult decisions for families and is often associated with significant family conflict and distress.

Goodness of fit between the motivational style of the resident and the nursing home is important—a self-determined style fits well with nursing homes that allow freedom and choice, while less self-determined individuals may do better in more constrained environments (O'Connor & Vallerand 1994). In one study, white elderly seemed to need a sense of independence more than minority elderly, but this was not tested with cognitively impaired residents (Abrams 1994). Negative consequences have been associated with placement—e.g., increased mortality and decreased psychological wellness (Tobin 1991).

Adjustment to nursing home life can take many months, and even longer. The degree of change in the environment is correlated with psychological stress. The resident usually is concerned about how much control over his or her life will be lost at placement, and particularly about control over events surrounding death (Mikhail 1992). The resident often questions the meaning of life and sometimes loses the human spirit (Starck 1992). Much of the literature surrounding adjustment to nursing home placement focuses primarily on family member transition. However, group work with newly admitted residents provides the opportunity for them to become familiar with and receive support from others who are experiencing similar difficulties. Hence, involvement in such groups can help new residents better adjust to the nursing home.

Literature: Crose (1990); Dye & Erber (1981); Grossmann & Weiner (1988); Harris (1997); Lewton (1990); Porter & Clinton (1992); Taft & Nerhke (1990); Timko & Moos (1989); Tobin (1991); Yoder, Nelson, & Smith (1989).

Task Menu Resident
1. Attend a group for new residents.

    Elaboration: Begin to form new support networks with other residents and staff.

    Practitioner's Role: Organize a group for new residents to assist them in their adjustment to the home. Schedule seven group sessions, meeting twice weekly, for three and a half weeks. Limit group size to seven. Larger group sizes tend to increase hearing difficulties and lessen attention span. Establish meeting time and place, and provide materials. Track new residents and invite them to participate. Introduce the resident to other residents and staff. Facilitate group involvement by offering support, empathy, and assistance in problem solving. Provide follow-up visits to the resident after the final group session.

2. At the first group session, introduce yourself and explain how you came to reside in the nursing home.

   Practitioner's Role: Set a time limit for each resident to speak so that all may have their turn.

3. Bring to the group your own experiences and problems with placement for discussion.

   Elaboration: Discuss what the change means for you. Express feelings surrounding the change of residence, change of routine, loss of cognitive or physical abilities, etc. Use a *self-monitoring* diary to keep track of situations, people, and events that you wish to discuss or remember.

   Practitioner's Role: Facilitate discussion of the meaning of the placement for the resident. Focus on these issues during the second, third, and fourth sessions.

4. Listen empathically and offer support to others.

   Practitioner's Role: Discourage individual residents from monopolizing the discussion. Redirect discussion when necessary.

5. Identify some of your own strengths and coping abilities with respect to the placement process and bring to the group for discussion.

   Practitioner's Role: Allow sufficient time for each individual to recognize his or her own strengths, and offer insights if the resident is unable to express his or her thoughts. Use *cognitive restructuring* if the resident does not see any strengths. Provide support and encouragement. Do, however, continue to encourage each resident to voice their opinion (fifth and sixth sessions).

5. Bring to the group your own ideas for solving problems discussed at previous sessions and share them with other group members.

   Practitioner's Role: Organize ideas on a large chalkboard or overhead to facilitate understanding. Condense ideas generated throughout previous sessions via chalkboard or overhead and encourage residents to voice their concerns to nursing home staff when difficulties arise. Offer ideas on how to utilize these strategies in the future when faced with problems within the nursing home. Model or *role play* problem-solving skills (fifth and sixth sessions).

6. *Identify* previously enjoyed recreations, hobbies, and activities.

   Practitioner's Role: Explore past interests with the resident to ensure a good fit between the person and the environment.

7. Join activities in the nursing home that seem to fit with your interests.

8. Become a member of the residents' council to have input about programming, care, services, etc.

   Practitioner's Role: Encourage the resident to use as much choice as he or she has. Experiencing so many changes and losses, in addition to having many decisions made for him or her, the resident needs to be in control of as much as possible in order to maintain dignity and self-esteem (Tobin 1991).

9. Discuss feelings and thoughts about your situation with family.
10. Use *progressive relaxation* or meditation when situations or people are upsetting and there is nothing you can do about it.

Elaboration: Sometimes other residents are impaired in ways that you may find distressing. If possible, go to another section of the nursing home when such residents are in close proximity.

Practitioner's Role: Discuss using some variation of the adult form of *time out.*

Task Menu Family

1. Establish a visiting schedule.

Elaboration: This is particularly important when the family member is first placed in the nursing home and is making the adjustment.
2. Establish an open, honest relationship with staff.

Practitioner's Role: Maintain contact with the family to discuss placement issues and concerns and to provide support.
3. Listen attentively and empathetically when the resident expresses thoughts and feelings about placement.
4. Encourage the resident to become involved in the nursing home.
5. If possible, bring nursing home resident out on day trips.
6. Address questions and concerns to a social worker or other appropriate staff member (e.g., head nurse, physician, etc.).
7. Treat all staff members courteously.

Elaboration: Nursing home work is often low paying for many staff members. Speaking kindly to them may help ensure that your family member is treated well.

Maura Barrett

Gambling, Compulsive

One of the most disruptive problems to individual well-being and family harmony is problem gambling (Walker 1992). In order for gambling to be considered pathological, an irresistible, recurring single-minded impulse must be present as the basic driving force. Often compulsive gamblers are not highly motivated to change, making treatment of the problem an even greater challenge than the treatment of alcoholism (Das 1990). Moreover, the problem is becoming more serious as legalized forms of gambling continue to grow.

Literature: Texts that suggest treatment strategies for problem gambling include Galski (1987); L'Abate, Farrar, & Serritella (1991); Schneider & Irons (1997); Walker (1992); a study of the effects of opportunity on gambling may be found in Campbell & Lister (1999).

Task Menu

1. *Identify* predisposing factors.

    Elaboration: Hypo-arousal (underarousal) and hyperarousal (over-arousal) are thought to be predisposing factors to problem gambling. Determining which way the arousal level is aberrant affects some of the treatment choices. The overaroused may require lessons in such topics as relaxation training, systematic desensitization, meditation, and the regular use of exercise, while the underaroused may need assistance in finding sources of stimulation and challenge. Taking a course, getting vocational assessment and guidance, or becoming involved in hobbies or sports might be useful for the underaroused individual (L'Abate, Farrar, & Serritella 1991; Galski 1987).

    Practitioner's Role: Assist the client in determining whether he or she has an aberrant level of arousal. If this is the case, make suggestions as to what can be done to find a balance. Then, suggest sources for acquiring the proper skills or training.

2. *Identify* and correct (through use of *cognitive restructuring*) erroneous assumptions about actual odds, the concept of randomness, and the established laws of chance and probability.

3. Practice using *progressive relaxation,* instead of giving in to the urge to gamble.

4. Learn to associate unpleasant states such as being in debt or being criticized by family members with gambling.

5. Substitute alternative activities for gambling.

    Practitioner's Role: Discuss with client what activities he or she finds appealing enough to substitute for gambling.

6. Attend Gambler's Anonymous (GA). The Internet address is http://www.gamblersanonymous.org/about.html.

    Practitioner's Role: Discuss benefits of having a nongambling environment and companions and suggest that the client give GA a try.

7. Understand the abstinence violation effect (Donnell 1984).

    Practitioner's Role: Explain that this effect is the mistaken assumption that one slip into gambling means full-blown relapse. Clients should be reassured that if such a slip occurs, they can still stop gambling.

Pamela Zettergren

Gays, Lesbians, and Bisexuals: Identity Formation in Adolescence

Adolescence is recognized as a difficult, yet vital and complex period of growth, when the primary task is to formulate one's own identity (Dempsey 1994; Jackson & Sullivan 1994; Cates 1987). Part of identity formation is determining sexual preference; it is usually during adolescence that homosexual identification becomes evident (Cates 1987). Gay, lesbian, and bisexual youth "perceive themselves as different from the majority of their peers," and for them "adolescence is even more traumatic" (Dempsey 1994:161). Morrow (1993:655) states more strongly, "Gay and lesbian adolescents are a socially oppressed group discriminated against by a heterosexist and homophobic society." Due to lack of positive role models, lack of education about sexuality, and institutionalized homophobia, few locales exist for homosexual and bisexual youth to express themselves. It is difficult for such youth to "establish and maintain a sense of self-esteem and positive identity" (Sullivan & Schneider 1987:15). "In the early phases of becoming aware of and accepting their non-mainstream sexual orientation, gay and lesbian adolescents are likely to feel embarrassed and bewildered that they are different from the majority of their peers" (Morrow 1993:658). Herdt (1989) has identified four factors that have consequences for gay, lesbian, and bisexual youth: 1) their invisibility; 2) family and friends assuming them to be defective; 3) the stigmatization that accompanies being deviant; and 4) people assuming that all gays and lesbians are alike.

Gay, lesbian, and bisexual teenagers may internalize homophobia (Remafedi 1990), which can present itself as feelings of being evil, feeling inferior, and lacking social value and self-worth (Gonsiorek 1988); shame, depression, guilt, self-destructiveness and self-defeating behavior (Remafedi 1990; Sullivan & Schneider 1987). The stress of hiding one's sexual orientation and of social stigmatization leads to emotional, social, and cognitive isolation, strong feelings of hopelessness, depression, low self-esteem, loneliness, and worthlessness (Mallon 1994). Therefore, identity synthesis (Cass 1979), integrating sexual preference into the rest of their identity, can be a very difficult process for gay, lesbian, and bisexual youth (Sullivan & Schneider 1987). Often they are at risk for anxiety disorders and depression; gay and lesbian youth are two to three times more likely to attempt suicide than their heterosexual peers and may comprise 30 percent of suicides among teens annually (Kruks 1991). Gay, lesbian, and bisexual youth face rejection, isolation, verbal harassment, and physical violence at home, in school, and in religious institutions.

Literature: Berzon (1992); Cates (1987); D'Augelli (1996); Dempsey (1994); Gay Yellow Pages (1993); Gonsioreck (1988); Herdt (1989); Hetrick & Martin (1987); Jackson & Sullivan (1994); Kournay (1987); Martin & Hetrick (1988); Mallon (1994); Sullivan & Schneider (1987). Literature written for gay, lesbian, and bisexual youth includes Alyson (1991); Frick (1983); Heron (1983); Miranda (1993).

Task Menu

1. Seek out material on being a gay, lesbian, or bisexual teenager (Kelley & Byrne 1992; Mallon 1994).

   Elaboration: Young people traditionally do not receive ample education about human sexuality, in particular alternative lifestyles. They are denied access to accurate and comprehensive information (Dempsey 1994). According to Mallon (1994), such material can help abolish myths and stereotypes. Read literature about homosexuality; scan the Internet in an effort to connect with others that are enduring similar experiences; watch gay films and listen to gay music (Kauffer 1996). For suggested readings, see **Literature** above.

2. *Identify* personal values regarding homosexuality.

   Elaboration: *Identify* how homophobia affects the way people view gays, lesbians, and bisexuals, as well as the impact it has on self-perception. Use a *journal* to record the process. Discuss the topic of internalized homophobia.

   Practitioner's Role: Have the client question personal beliefs and assumptions about being homosexual and encourage him or her to develop a personal belief system. Also, examine your own beliefs about homosexuality and heterosexuality (Morrow 1993). It is very important for a practitioner to evaluate his or her own feelings of homophobia and to develop an understanding of homosexuality and become familiar with the culture.

3. *Identify* common negative stereotypes about homosexuality.

   Elaboration: List negative stereotypes and counter them with positive aspects of homosexual identity.

   Practitioner's Role: Work with the client to dispel negative stereotypes. Encourage him or her to take pride in his or her personal sexual orientation.

4. *Identify* negative self-statements regarding sexual orientation and replace with positive self-statements.

   Elaboration: Each time a negative thought about homosexuality occurs, counter it with positive thoughts or phrases.

   Practitioner's Role: Encourage the client to identity his or her strengths. Point out positive aspects of the client's personality and behavior, and that an individual is made up of many parts—sexual orientation is just one. Additionally, monitor client's mental status; be aware of the youth's level of depression and anxiety, and possible suicidal ideation (Kruks 1991).

5. *Identify* where you see yourself in the "coming out" process.

   Elaboration: Four psychological stages of the coming out process are: 1) first awareness that you may not be heterosexual; 2) testing or exploration; 3) identity acceptance; 4) identity integration. Many individuals questioning their sexual orientation will seek counseling during stages 1 or

2. The goal of successful therapy is to move through the stages to the point of identity integration (Dempsey 1994).

> **Practitioner's Role:** It is very important to let the client know that it is okay to be gay, lesbian, or bisexual and also okay to be confused (Mallon 1994).

6. Begin to identify yourself (to yourself) as gay, lesbian, or bisexual.

> **Elaboration:** Try to accept yourself as you are, even though you may have experienced rejection and oppression from others because of your sexual orientation. *Identify* your positive feelings about being gay, lesbian, or bisexual. Negative feelings will impair general self-esteem and may also lead to self-defeating behaviors (Sullivan & Schneider 1987).

> **Practitioner's Role:** Help clients understand and clarify their feelings about their sexual orientation (Mallon 1994).

7. Join a support group (if available) (Mallon 1994).

> **Elaboration:** This will help you realize that you are not alone. Being part of a group helps destigmatize people (Mallon 1994). Your support network can include peers, classmates, family members, and community activities. By becoming involved with others who are respectful, accepting, and supportive, you will feel better about yourself.

8. *Identify* health and social risks of different sexual orientations.

> **Elaboration:** Risks include HIV and AIDS, drug and alcohol abuse, psychological dysfunction, becoming a victim of sexual abuse and violence. These health and social risks may not be directly related to homosexual or bisexual identity, but rather a consequence of the hatred an individual with a nonmainstream sexual orientation directly experiences or a result of the internalization of such hatred (Dempsey 1994).

9. Join social groups for gay, lesbian, and bisexual adolescents (if available).

> **Elaboration:** You may find social groups in schools, gay and lesbian community centers, etc.

> **Practitioner's Role:** Using community resource guides, assist the client in locating resources available to gay, lesbian, and bisexual youth, including books, magazines, local support groups, and centers for gay and lesbian youth.

10. *Reflect on* the idea of "coming out of the closet" and to whom (parents, family, friends).

> **Practitioner's Role:** If the client wants to disclose to parents or others, *role play* the event. Discuss possible outcomes and reactions of others. Decide on an appropriate time and place for the coming out process. Advocate on behalf of your client, particularly in settings where he or she experiences oppression due to his or her sexual orientation. In addition, prepare the client for possible rejection, as there is potential for alienation from peers at a developmentally sensitive time when peer relations are of pri-

mary importance. In the case of rejection, discuss who would provide a safe, supportive, and nurturing environment in which the client could express thoughts and feelings.

Miranda Koss and Kristen Zacek

Grief and Loss

Normal grief reactions consist of emotional cognitive and behavioral responses to the loss of a loved one. They are usually resolved within a matter of months, although may continue for a year or so. "Complicated" grief reactions can vary from the normal in a number of ways. Four types can be distinguished: 1) chronic grief, in which the bereaved grieves for an excessive length of time (often years) and is unable to move through the mourning process; 2) delayed grief, in which reactions to the loss are delayed—the grief may be triggered later by another event, and at that time the reaction may be excessive; 3) exaggerated grief, in which the bereaved is overwhelmed and may develop psychiatric disorders such as clinical depression, anxiety, PTSD, or substance abuse; 4) masked grief, in which the bereaved does not experience grief directly—e.g., grief may be expressed through psychosomatic complaints (Rando 1993; Worden 1991). Although the tasks below can be used in response to normal grief reactions, they are oriented to the needs of clients suffering from more complicated forms of grief.
   Literature: Artelt & Thyer (1998); Rando (1993); Worden (1991).

Task Menu
1. [if the death is not accepted] Begin to actively mourn the death by confirming its reality and acknowledging that the deceased is never coming back.
   Elaboration: This reality must be experienced on both intellectual and emotional levels. Denial of the death delays grieving, but in some cases may be protective. It may help to recount the events surrounding the death, repeatedly, until the loss is accepted.
2. *Identify*, recognize, and express the emotions and pain of grief.
   Elaboration: Unexpressed emotion can lead to pathology. You may experience physical, social, behavioral, psychological pain by allowing an array of emotions to surface, both positive and negative. Identify what you are feeling and verbally express these feelings. Nonverbal expression can be achieved through writing, music, or artwork.
3. Recall memories of the deceased.
   Elaboration: Review both positive and negative memories. It may help to talk about the deceased, write letters, or create a memory book.

4. Use *exposure* to resolve chronic grief (Artelt & Thyer 1998).
   Elaboration: *Exposure* in this context involves exercises in which one experiences for sustained periods mildly distressing stimuli associated with the deceased person—e.g., reminiscences, photos, visiting the grave. Continue *exposure* until distress is experienced and decreases (Artelt & Thyer 1998).
   Practitioner's Role: Help the client use *exposure* through methods of guided mourning (Artelt & Thyer 1998).
5. Acquire new living skills, pursue activities, and develop relationships to promote independence.
   Practitioner's Role: (for all tasks) Use empathic listening, *coping imagery, role play*, the "empty chair" technique (in which the client talks to an empty chair as if it were occupied by the deceased), and *cognitive restructuring* to help the client with the grieving process.
6. [if grief is anticipatory, e.g., loved one has been diagnosed with terminal illness] Help each other work through feelings about the impending death and loss through discussion.
   Elaboration: It is important not to dwell excessively on death / loss issues. Once some resolution has been achieved, try to enjoy the present and preserve pleasurable routines as long as possible. If there is hope for a miracle cure, indulge yourself in it and don't worry about being "in denial." As the end nears, reminisce about satisfactions in the relationship.

Ellen Dziengelski, Carla Sofka

Grief and Loss

Child's Loss of a Loved One

Children may be confronted with death at a very young age. In our culture, children's feelings about death have often been overlooked (Mann 1994). Some individuals question whether children are able to grieve, but as Ketchel (1986) states, "anyone who is old enough to feel is old enough to grieve." Mishne (1992) comments that children have a very sophisticated ability to grieve over loved ones. Their young age and cognitive level require that interventions be shaped specifically to their needs.
   Literature: Ketchel (1986); Mann (1994); Mishne (1992); Wolfelt (1996).

Task Menu Child
1. Create a memory box.
   Elaboration: Fill the box with reminders of your deceased loved one (Mann 1994). The box can be presented to the practitioner for discussion or to other children with similar experience of loss in a group format.

2. Draw a picture of yourself with the person who died and the rest of the family. Then state your feelings based on the picture that has been drawn.

   Elaboration: Art therapy has been shown to be successful with young children for eliciting feelings that cannot be expressed verbally. Similar exercises using other art mediums, such as clay, can also be tried.

3. Complete a list of what you know and don't know about your deceased loved one (Krown, Buirsky, & Buirsky 1994).

   Practitioner's Role: The list can be used to educate the child about death and what has happened to the deceased person. Help the child eliminate magical and/or destructive thinking—children may think that their own negative thoughts toward a loved one caused them to die. Also help the child express feelings of rage associated with the loss. Mishne (1992) indicates that rage is children's most common reaction to death of a parent.

Task Menu Parents and family

1. Discuss the loss with the child.

   Practitioner's Role: Help identify systems of support for the child regarding grief issues. Facilitate meaningful and accurate conversation about the death between the family and the child (Bertman 1984). Educate parents about child's grief.

2. If indicated, reassure the child that he or she is not to blame for the death of the loved one.

Ellen Dziengelski, Carla Sofka

Grief and Loss

Loss of a Child/Sibling

Families are unique environments in which all members share in love, caring, stress, anger, turmoil, and unfortunately grief. One of the hardest things for a family unit to survive is the loss of a child. In order to do so, remaining family must gain gradual and painful acceptance and accommodation (Leon 1990).

As a child develops, so does his or her relationship to other family members; this may have significant impact on how each person reacts to the death. Members will grieve according to circumstances and feelings related to their relationship with the deceased. It is important to remember that parents will react as caregivers, those responsible for the life of the child (Rando 1993). Siblings, on the other hand, will react according to age. This may include magical thinking (the belief that the deceased will return, as if they are hiding) or the fear that they may die also (Papdantou & Papadatos 1991).

Tasks for the family should center around working together to acknowledge the death. The family should reach a level of comfort in speaking about their feelings related to the death and the deceased. It is important to assist parents in their own grieving as well as in coping with their other childrens' grief (Rando 1993). Monitoring of feelings of resentment, frustration, and idealization by both parents and siblings is key to moving through the grieving process.

Literature: Dane (1990); Leon (1990); Papdantou & Papadatos (1991); Rando (1993).

Task Menu Family as a whole
1. Acknowledge and express feelings related to the death.

   Elaboration: Family members may express their feelings to one another or record them in a family *journal* that they can share (Rando 1993; Dane 1990).

   Practitioner's Role: Help the family talk openly about the death and validate the magnitude of their loss (Dane 1990). Help family acknowledge the loved one's absence and continued presence in their memories.

Task Menu Parents
1. Maintain a normal routine to the extent possible (Dane 1990).

   Elaboration: It is helpful to take a respite from grief and to try to enjoy things as you have in the past.
2. Help your remaining children to deal with the loss of their sibling.

   Practitioner's Role: Use *role play* to help the couple rehearse their communications with the remaining children. They should be encouraged to share the feelings they experienced in the role play.
3. Join a self-help group for bereaved parents, such as Compassionate Friends, (630) 990–0010 for information about local chapters; http://connections.oklahoman.net/cfriends/main.html.

Task Menu Children
1. *Identify* what you think of when you think of death.

   Practitioner's Role: This allows the child to show his or her conceptualization and understanding of death to the helper and parents if they are present.
2. List questions you would like answered.

   Elaboration: The questions have no boundaries as long as they are related to loss.

   Practitioner's Role: The parents should try to answer some in session and the remaining ones at home. Answering questions will prompt the child to ask more. Advise the parents of this task prior to the session and encourage them to be as honest and direct as possible and as is appropriate. The children should be commended for their participation in such a difficult task.

3. Talk about any specific fears or reactions you may have because of the death.

Elaboration: This may include trouble sleeping, nightmares, trouble concentrating, etc.

4. With your parents, identify things that you believe they can do to help you.

Practitioner's Role: Encourage the parents to be open and realistic in their helping. Again the children should be praised for sharing.

5. Identify thoughts, both positive and negative, about your sibling (Rando 1993).

Practitioner's Role: This allows the child to incorporate a realistic view into his or her memory. Explain that it is normal for sisters and brothers to have good feelings and bad feelings toward each other. This task may alleviate guilt by bringing negative feelings to the surface and identifying other areas for work.

6. *Identify* at least one activity you would like to resume or start as a family.

Elaboration: This fosters return to normalcy and encourages the family to spend time together not related to grieving.

Jeanne Kavanaugh, Carla Sofka

Hispanic Families: Intergenerational Conflict

Although the structure of Hispanic families varies according to ethnic group—Puerto Rican, Mexican, etc.—the groups have, of course, a common ancestor, the Spanish family, and there are sufficient commonalities among them to permit some generalizations. The Hispanic family is hierarchically organized, with the father in charge; he assumes primary responsibility for the well-being of its members. Ideally, the Hispanic father is to provide for the family while the wife tends to the daily household chores and raising the children. Children are expected to be obedient and respect authority. They must also adhere to cultural norms, such as respecting elders and not bringing shame to the family by discussing family problems outside of the home. Parents exercise a good deal of control over their children, especially their daughters.

Many problems can arise in Hispanic immigrant families when their adolescent children become acculturated to the norms of the United States and begin to eschew their parent's customs and values. Hispanic immigrant children may begin to test authority, explore alternative gender roles, and engage in many of the opportunities their American peers have available to them. This can strain the parent-adolescent relationship. Many immigrant parents cannot understand some of the responses and behaviors their children exhibit once the children begin to assimilate with their peers. This intergenerational conflict can be seen in both first- and second-generation immigrant families.

Literature: Curtis (1990); Falicov (1998); Galan (1985); Gil, Vega, & Dimas (1994); Gonzalez (1990); Hardy & MacMahon (1981); Hines et al. (1992); Millan & Chan (1991); Smart & Smart (1995); Stavans (1995); Zambrana (1995).

Task Menu Parents

1. Involve all family members, if possible, in discussions of issues relating to the children's behavior.

   Elaboration: The father may be reluctant to engage in such discussions in a counseling session because of discomfort in discussing private affairs, acknowledging problems and emotions, and having his actions open for criticism.

   Practitioner's Role: Attempt to draw the father in by emphasizing the strengths of his actions and culture and empathizing with the difficulty of acculturation. Identify reluctance not as defiance, but as a reflection of different values. Here and elsewhere emphasize that differences in values do not suggest that one set is better than the other.

2. *Identify* areas in which your cultural norms and values are being challenged by your adolescent's actions.

   Elaboration: It is important to specifically identify what is bothering you, rather than simply referring to behaviors as disrespectful, inappropriate, etc. Then you can more easily engage in a meaningful discussion about the behaviors.

3. *Learn about* American culture.

   Elaboration: This will help you to understand the impact your adolescent's peers and environmental surroundings are having on his or her behavior. You may come to see that what you once viewed as deviant is quite normal among American teens.

   Practitioner's Role: Learn about Hispanic family structure, values, and norms. Books, such as The Hispanic Condition (Stavans 1995), outline the various obstacles, cultural, social, and psychological, that Hispanic Americans must negotiate in the United States.

4. *Improve* communication with the adolescent.

   Elaboration: Your adolescent may be more proficient in English than your native language and dialect. This may cause communication difficulties, which lead to frustration and an inability to solve problems. You might enroll in an English language course to enhance your language proficiency. Also your adolescent may help teach you English.

5. *Teach* your child about your culture.

Elaboration: Your adolescent may be a first- or second-generation immigrant with little knowledge of your culture or history, who therefore has trouble understanding your feelings about his or her actions.

6. Find fellow Hispanic American and American adult parents to speak with.

    Elaboration: Having friends to confide in concerning your parenting troubles can help relieve some of the stress as well as allow you to get feedback from parents in similar situations as yours.

7. *Role play* a hypothetical situation that would normally cause conflict.

    Elaboration: Attempt to resolve the conflict without arguing and with a mutually agreeable solution. Each family member should attempt to *identify* aspects of the conflict relating to cultural values. Choose a problem you have not already experienced. This will help you to clearly discuss it without reflecting on the anger, sadness, etc. you might have felt when you were actually in that situation.

8. Try to resolve an actual conflict that relates to cultural values.

    Elaboration: Be aware of and sensitive to one another's value positions. Search for compromises. For example, Rosa, age twelve, wants to go to the mall with her girlfriends. Her parents object, saying she is too young to go without parental supervision. A compromise might be that the mother accompanies Rosa to the mall and lets Rosa go with her friends while she does some shopping. Then she and Rosa meet and return home. See PARENT-ADOLESCENT CONFLICT.

9. *Learn about* communication and *problem-solving* skills (Curtis 1989).

    Elaboration: Use family and other relationships to work on communication and *problem-solving* skills. Participate in family meetings to practice using listening skills and "I messages" (Gordon 1976).

    Practitioner's Role: Train clients in communication and *problem-solving* skills through role plays and family work on problems in the session.

Task Menu Adolescent

1. *Learn about* your parents' culture.

    Elaboration: Understanding your parents' history and culture will help you to understand their views about your behavior and to communicate more effectively with them.

2. Find fellow Hispanic American, as well as American, peers to share your story with.

    Elaboration: Confiding in those who are of the same heritage, as well as those who represent the culture to which you are now assimilating, can help you to see that the conflicts you have with your parents are quite normal. You can also learn what others your age have done to improve the situation with their parents.

James Golden, Blanca Ramos

HIV: Reducing Risk of Contracting Virus

HIV (human immunodeficiency virus) is the virus that causes AIDS (acquired immunodeficiency syndrome). HIV can be passed from one person to another through sexual contact, sharing intravenous needles, contaminated blood products, and bodily fluids: blood, semen, and breast milk. Occupational exposure of health care workers to HIV through needle-stick injuries, mucous membrane exposure, or contact with broken skin may also result in transmission of HIV. Reducing the risk for HIV involves behavioral changes in sexual activities and drug use, and acquiring information on risk-reduction techniques. Among adolescents, these techniques include acquisition and use of *social skills* in situations involving sex and drugs and perception of peer support in safe sex practices (Schinke, Forgey, & Orlandi 1996).

Literature: Mueller et al. (1998) review group programs for adolescents aimed at HIV prevention. Schinke, Forgey, & Orlandi (1996) review factors relating to sexual behavior of teenagers and discuss implications for contracting sexually transmitted diseases. Centers for Disease Control (Atlanta, Ga.) provides up-to-date literature on HIV prevention and treatment; see for example Centers for Disease Control (1998); Knox & Sparks (1998) is an edited collection of papers on HIV treatment and prevention for community mental health workers.

Task Menu
1. *Learn about* HIV and how it is transmitted.
2. Assess your level of risk.
    Elaboration: Determine what risk behaviors you are currently engaging in (e.g., unprotected sex, injected drug use).
    Practitioner's Role: Identify whether the client is aware of having engaged in high-risk activities and explore in detail current and past risky behaviors. Help the client to think through what safer sex would be like for him or her. Discuss what behaviors would have to change.
3. Explore the possibility of engaging in a mutually monogamous intimate relationship.
4. Develop negotiation and other *social skills* to avoid unsafe sexual encounters.
    Elaboration: Learn and practice how to request that your sexual partner use a condom, how to refuse sexual encounters that may be unsafe, and how to refuse substance use that might lead to unsafe sex.
    Practitioner's Role: Help the client learn and practice necessary refusal and other *social skills*. In individual treatment use *role play* with the client. In group treatment use *role plays* involving group members. It may be

necessary to determine barriers to client's acceptance and routine utilization of HIV prevention and risk-reduction skills (Purcell et al. 1998; Rotheram-Borum et al. 1998; Charkin et al. 1997). Help client identify dysfunctional beliefs underlying risky behavior (e.g., "I am one of those people who doesn't get infections") and use cognitive restructuring to help change them.

5. Use protective latex barriers during each sexual encounter.

    Elaboration: Use latex barriers *only:* condoms and spermicide containing nonoxynol-9, dental dams for oral sex.

6. Explore alternative forms of intimacy that do not involve sexual intercourse.

7. Use universal precautions in hospital and health care settings.

    Elaboration: Prevent mucous membrane exposure when in contact with blood or other bodily fluids of any patient anticipated to be HIV positive. Use gloves, masks, protective eyewear or face shields, gowns or aprons. Wash hands with antibacterial soap.

8. Do not share injected drug paraphernalia; use only clean needles for injecting drugs.

    Elaboration: Clean drug injection needles or "works" by drawing bleach through the needle several times, then rinse with water by drawing through the needle several times.

9. Do not have sex with many different partners, with someone who has had many different partners, or with someone who uses intravenous drugs.

10. Do not have unprotected sex with someone you do not know well or with someone you suspect could be infected.

11. [if engaging in risky behavior or possibly exposed to the virus] Consult a HIV prevention specialist or HIV test counselor.

    Elaboration: HIV counseling and testing typically requires at least two visits, an initial visit for pretest counseling and a blood draw and a follow-up visit for post-test counseling and receipt of HIV test results. Clients will need support in their decision making and during the waiting period between visits. Anyone thought to have sustained occupational or accidental exposure to HIV should be medically evaluated as soon as possible to determine if postexposure prophylaxis treatment is needed (Centers for Disease Control 1998).

    Practitioner's Role: Provide the client with specific agency referral information, phone numbers, and use of phone if desired, and transport or accompany client on agency visit. Discuss client's concerns or fears about learning about his or her HIV status. *Identify* potential barriers to client receiving HIV counseling and testing services.

Charles Lobosco, Denise Jeremiah

Homeless: Need for Shelter and Employment

Nationwide estimates of the number of homeless individuals in the United States vary, but the most frequently cited figure is 2 million (Morse 1992). The federal government estimates there are up to 600,000 homeless at any given time (Burt & Cohen 1988). The majority are male; however, a growing number of women are being counted (Johnson & Cnaan 1995). Homeless individuals are a heterogeneous group with one common characteristic—the lack of a permanent address. The majority of homeless people are not suffering from severe mental illness, but the Federal Task Force on Homelessness and Severe Mental Illness estimates that approximately one third have such an illness (1992). The Task Force notes that the mental and emotional disorders experienced by these individuals include schizophrenia, schizoaffective disorders, mood disorders, and severe personality disorders. Demographically, most homeless people are young (eighteen to forty-five years of age). Ethnic minorities are over-represented (Johnson & Cnaan 1995).

Another condition that the homeless share is unemployment. Many homeless people suffer from addictions, mental illness, and other disabilities that keep them from attaining and maintaining permanent employment; but far more are able-bodied people eager to find employment. Unfortunately, most have very few marketable skills, a scattered work history, and no employment resources (phone, address, etc.) (Liebow 1993). Many of them are also suffering from low self-esteem and high levels of stress. The only practical way to break the cycle of homelessness and unemployment for these individuals is to provide them with the job training, life skills, and employment resources necessary to obtain a stable, well-paying job (Jahiel 1992). The Stewart B. McKinney Act of 1987 has provided more than $10 million a year for job training and placement programs throughout the United States designed specifically for homeless people.

Literature: Belcher & Ephross (1989); Brown & Ziefert (1990); Burt & Cohen (1988); Cohen (1989); Cohen & Burt (1990); Dail & Koshes (1992); First, Rife, & Toomey (1994); Hoff et al. 1992; Jahiel (1992); Interagency Council on the Homeless (1992); Johnson & Cnaan (1995); Lam & Rosenhack (1999); Liebow (1993); Morse (1992); New York State Department of Labor and Training (1996); Rite et al.(1991); Robertson & Greenblatt (1992).

Task Menu

1. Apply for social services and emergency shelter.

   Practitioner's Role: The client may have a sense of hopelessness and shame. Thus you may need to assist him or her in identifying needs such as shelter, laundry service, and transportation. Some people may avoid "asking for too much," thinking that they are undeserving or that they may be rejected.

If the client is a woman, it is important to investigate the possibility of domestic violence playing a role in her homelessness. Moreover, she may be experiencing sexual abuse or harassment on the streets and in the shelter environment. If so, she may need information and assistance regarding safe shelter and legal protection.

Have a list available of resources for health care, shelter, financial aid, legal aid, employment and job training, and housing. This should include sleep-off stations, drug and alcohol services, abused women's shelters and services, immigrant services, and self-help groups such as Alcoholics and Narcotics Anonymous. Know the eligibility requirements, rules and regulations, and staffing of the various resources. Matching client needs and wishes with the appropriate resources is vital. For example, some shelters require religious service attendance, which the client may find objectionable. Rural areas may require creative solutions. For example, you may need to find individual landlords or boarding house operators willing to provide temporary housing, while waiting for the client's public assistance to come through.

2. Obtain documents (Social Security card, picture I.D., etc.) that the client may need to secure job or assistance, enter a training program, etc.

   Elaboration: Many individuals who move frequently or are in and out of shelters lose these important documents. It is not uncommon for the documents to have been missing for years, because the individuals are unsure how to replace them or lack the resources to do so.

3. Compose a resume.

   Practitioner's Role: Obtain a booklet of sample resumes, and provide the client with copies of resumes that would accentuate their strengths; assist client in preparing resume.

4. Practice interviewing skills.

   Practitioner's Role: Use *role plays* to help the client prepare for job interviews and build self-confidence.

5. Use *stress inoculation* to help prepare for job stressors and to deal with current life situations.

6. Secure appropriate clothing for job interviews, employment, or training program.

   Elaboration: Many homeless people do not have clothing appropriate for job interviews or employment; their clothes have been lost, stolen, or simply worn out over a period of years.

   Practitioner's Role: Locate and familiarize yourself with all local clothing pantries.

7. Apply for job or training program.

   Practitioner's Role: Familiarize yourself with social services, the shelter system, and job training programs in the area so that you can make an appropriate referral. Help the client complete a work and educational history, including vocational training; specify reasons for leaving past employment and note if client has a disability. Make an assessment of the client's skills. If referral to job placement or training program is indicated, assist the client in completing necessary paperwork/applications and in contacting the referral source to set up the initial appointment. See also MENTALLY ILL: HOMELESS; UNEMPLOYMENT.

Isabel Rose

Immigration: Acquisition of Life Skills in New Culture

Recently arrived immigrants often experience a series of hardships associated with migration and acculturation to a new cultural system. They may have numerous social needs and require help finding health care, mental health care, and schools; family and children's service agencies; and community-based organizations.

In work with immigrant clients, it is essential to consider issues related to acculturation, the change that occurs as a result of cultural contact (Kaplan & Marks 1990). Difficulties may arise as immigrants encounter the new symbols, language, and behavioral norms and values of American society (Rogler 1991).

All immigrants experience problems reconciling their previous cultural experiences (language; vocation; education; recreation; social, interpersonal, and familial relationships) with the cultural forms of their new countries (Hulewat 1996). The number and complexity of the problems experienced by an individual immigrant are influenced by factors such as age, facility with the language of the new country, social support network, educational background, earning capacity, and the congruence of values between the country of birth and the new country (Tran & Wright 1986).

According to Golan (1981), the extent to which the immigrant adjusts to the new culture (and vice versa) is a product of the immigrant's level within each of six life skill domains: income management, health, housing, education, recreational activities, and citizenship. Value system differences between the original culture and the current one also affect adaptation (Brown 1991; Cheung 1989). Ben (1995) suggests that the support system of the family is the main agent for adjustment to a new culture.

Literature: Readings for working with immigrants facing acculturation dilemmas may be found in Cheung (1989); Ben (1995); Brown (1991); Chriswick (1993); Falicov (1998); Fuller (1995); Hulewat (1996); Lum (1996); Ryan (1992).

Task Menu
1. *Identify* needs and concerns relating to acculturation.

   Practitioner's Role: Immigrant clients will find it easier to articulate their needs and concerns to practitioners who acknowledge and respect the central role culture has in their lives. Introducing cultural themes into

the dialogue will help increase the clients' level of comfort while simultaneously decreasing their anxiety. Demonstrate a genuine interest in discussing cultural issues; begin by focusing on general, noncontroversial topics such as food, clothing, and sports. Do not assume the recently arrived
immigrant is completely unfamiliar with American culture. Recognize the
individuality of each client; avoid making stereotypical generalizations that
may not apply equally to all members of the client's ethnic group. Universal, cross-cultural nonverbal communication symbols are particularly useful to convey friendliness, respect, and warmth.

2. *Identify* and verbalize cultural differences.

   Elaboration: Immigrants often experience cultural dilemmas stemming
   from mismatches in value systems. These may be perceived as a challenge
   or a threat, depending on the individual. By exploring potential cultural
   differences, you can recognize values that contradict your own. Frame
   cultural differences positively: highlight strengths of your own and others'
   values when differences cause a dilemma.

   Practitioner's Role: Introduce potentially value-laden issues—e.g.,
   gender roles—and share your own views respectfully. Reassure the client
   that you respect differences among people. Be aware of your own values
   and make nonjudgmental comparisons; keep in mind that other ways are
   not better or worse, just different.

3. *Identify* preferred responses to cultural dilemmas.

   Elaboration: Immigrants may respond to cultural dilemmas using a
   variety of coping strategies, ranging from full resistance to new values,
   norms, and methods to complete acceptance. A number of combinations
   in between integrate elements of both cultures. Coping strategies may also
   vary significantly not only among members of a given immigrant group,
   but also among individuals within a single household. See HISPANIC FAMI-
   LIES: INTERGENERATIONAL CONFLICT.

   Practitioner's Role: Familiarize yourself with the various types of responses identified in the literature; share this knowledge with clients, emphasizing the practical implications for their lives. Facilitate client awareness by exploring the benefits of learning new ways (e.g., acquiring necessary instruments to navigate the system) and the continued advantages
   of the old ways (e.g., serving as a source of strength and support). Be mindful of your personal biases and remain neutral. Above all, respect clients'
   views, which usually reflect their own reality.

4. *Identify* cultural dilemmas underlying your problem.

   Elaboration: Problems you have may be associated with cultural
   dilemmas, an awareness of which may help you formulate effective solutions. By identifying their cultural context, you can see that the problems
   is transitional and typical of the acculturation process.

Practitioner's Role: Help clients articulate their cultural beliefs as they relate to the problems and respectfully ask questions about relevant feelings, thoughts, and frustrations. Tentatively pose the problems as part of cultural adaptation. View culture as fluid and dynamic, maintaining a flexible attitude toward its role in the therapeutic process. Be prepared to recognize the presence of multiple influences in a client's life beyond those that relate specifically to culture.

5. *Identify* problem-solving strategies.

Practitioner's Role: Problem-solving strategies may focus on decreasing cultural conflicts. Generally, these should be consistent with the client's preferred response to cultural dilemmas. In some cases, you may wish to generate alternatives to help clients negotiate compromises between new and prior value systems. For example, you may propose an approach that allows the client to alternate between the two cultures without having to choose between them. Work collaboratively with the client; brainstorm for creative solutions. Help client realize that there are multiple ways of effectively achieving the same goal. Offer nonbiased opinions and suggestions. Review your own opinions about cultural diversity and acculturation; be careful not to lose sight of the client's individual adaptational needs.

6. Locate and attend an English as a second language (ESL) class.

Elaboration: Learning English has been found to have economic benefits for immigrants (Chriswick 1993).

7. Obtain or maintain a living situation and make arrangements to finance basic food, clothing, and shelter needs.

Elaboration: "Financing" needs may include obtaining paid employment, accessing the social service program benefits available in your state, and sharing expenses with other family members or friends. Having an occupation has also been found to be important for maintaining self-esteem (Chriswick 1993).

8. Learn where basic services (e.g., medical, legal, dental) in the community can be obtained.

Practitioner's Role: Use a community resource guide to help provide information and direction to the individual client. Also, plan experiential activities that enhance skills acquisition; e.g., have the client work out all phases of a train travel plan during a meeting.

9. Locate and enroll in an educational program.

Elaboration: "Educational" programs may include GED classes, postsecondary educational or vocational training, apprenticeships, and preparation for equivalency examinations.

10. Develop a means and a schedule of household maintenance; e.g., establishing and using bank accounts, locating ethnic food stores, and finding places of worship.

11. Establish an informal support network to get help and advice about the new culture and its norms, as well as to maintain desired connections to the previous culture.

12. Obtain information about your permanent residency status and its benefits or limitations.

13. *Identify* misgivings or other negative reactions related to relocation.

> **Elaboration:** Golan (1981) defines immigration as a transition that demands leaving all that is familiar (the past) and results in a grief response. Symptoms may include depression and anxiety, somatic complaints, and casting the previous home in an unrealistically favorable light.

> **Practitioner's Role:** Assist the client in reviewing the reasons for immigration (e.g., determine whether or not immigration was voluntary; use *cognitive restructuring* to help the client perceive her or his past and current situations more realistically). Educate the client about the grief response to immigration.

Blanca Ramos, Kathyrn Baraneckie

Impulsivity: Child

Impulsivity is characterized at the cognitive level by a lack of consideration of alternative solutions to novel problems or ambiguous situations, leading to rapid responses that prove incorrect. At the behavioral level, impulsive children are not able to inhibit undesirable verbalizations or actions (Kendall & Braswell 1993). According to the DSM-IV (APA 1994), behavioral indices of impulsivity include not waiting one's turn in a group, responding before a question has been posed completely, being accident prone, and placing oneself in dangerous situations (e.g., darting into a busy street to retrieve a ball).

Impulsivity in children is not a discrete diagnostic category. It has been associated with elevated levels of lead in the blood, and it is a feature of attention deficit/hyperactivity disorder (Keenan 1996; APA 1994). Kendall and Brasell (1993) note that although impulsivity is not a symptom of oppositional defiant disorder, conduct disorder, or learning disabilities, children with these disorders are often characterized as impulsive: they evidence poor judgment in focused, self-directed tasks and in social interactions, especially those that are emotion laden. Both familial stress and parenting style have been associated with children's inability to self-regulate.

Accurate assessment of impulsive children is paramount not only because the nature of the construct itself is difficult to define, but also because these children differ in their capacity for aggression, level of hyperactivity, self-esteem, willingness to be compliant, etc. (Kendall & Braswell 1993; Baer & Nietzel 1991). Assessment should be diverse, including behavior rating scales completed by parents (e.g., Conners Parent Rating Scale, Conners 1969) and teachers (e.g., Self-Control Rating Scale, Kendall & Wilcox 1979); child and parent interviews (Meichenbaum 1977); and analogue situations (e.g., use of one-way mirrors to observe parent-child interaction in a problem-solving task) (Kendall & Braswell, 1993). See also ATTENTION DEFICIT/ HYPERACTIVITY DISORDER: CHILD.

A meta-analysis by Baer & Nietzel (1991) of thirty-six outcome studies suggests that cognitive-behavioral intervention is effective in treating impulsivity in children. The tasks and practitioner activities described below are consistent with that kind of approach.

Literature: Baer & Nietzel (1991); Kendall & Braswell (1993); Meichenbaum (1977); Milich & Kramer (1984).

Task Menu Child
1. Learn to solve problems or negotiate ambiguous situations successfully.

   Practitioner's Role: Model in detail for the child the stages of problem solving and articulate out loud what you are thinking and why, as well as what does not work and why (Meichenbaum 1977). Encourage the child to describe each step of the problem-solving process in her or his own words. Complement the child's *self-verbalization* with imagery, e.g., showing the child a stop sign or a picture of a turtle. Discussing the implications of the image may help the child to evoke it when a problem arises.

   Include error making and correction in the problem-solving demonstration not only to show that making mistakes is to be expected, but also to model the cognition and behaviors that correct erroneous responses. Assist the child in constructing coping self-statements (e.g., "Oh oh, I made a mistake. I need to go a little slower next time"). Complement the problem-solving training with positive reinforcement to encourage the child's step-by-step self-talk or successful problem solving (e.g., saying "Slow down" when he or she is stymied about which step to take next; withholding rewards when the child answers without considering alternatives).

   As Kendall and Braswell (1993) emphasize, the child's ability successfully to use overt or covert verbal instruction to manage impulsivity depends on the level of his or her cognitive development. Structured problem-solving training is usually not helpful for a child younger than age seven.

   An older child especially may be self-conscious about self-talking out loud in front of you or others. If so, ask the child to describe his or her problem-solving thoughts and behaviors during each step of the process.

   You may want to use a variety of activities for problem-solving training: connect-the-dots worksheets, number or letter series completion, commercial board *games*, etc. Because game playing is a natural activity for children, the training is more likely to generalize interpersonal and task problem-solving learning to extra-session environments (Kendall & Braswell 1993).

Your modeling of problem solving should not be limited to formal training; it is particularly beneficial in general interactions with the child. For example, you may model slowing down (taking a deep breath) and making statements such as: "What do I need to do first?"

2. If you begin by talking to yourself out loud, learn to talk to yourself so that no one else can hear.

   Practitioner's Role: Model the steps to enable the transition from overt to covert self-talk.

3. Apply *problem-solving* skills in different situations.

   Practitioner's Role: Help the child and parent(s) *identify* problems or situations in which the child's responses are impulsive. Child-specific scenarios can be constructed for *role play* during problem-solving training (e.g., another child at school calls the client's mother a nasty name). It is especially important to help the child label accurately and cope with the feelings that accompany impulsive responses.

4. Learn and use *relaxation* techniques.

   Practitioner's Role: Help the child learn *relaxation* techniques (e.g., *applied* and *progressive relaxation*) that may be used in a variety of contexts.

   Use of *relaxation* techniques may be linked to the imagery that the child uses to complement his or her *self-verbalization*. For example, envisioning a turtle may remind the child both to relax and to start problem solving.

Task Menu Parents

1. Learn *problem-solving* skills to use with the child on a daily basis.

   Elaboration: The parents' ability to master problem-solving skills is especially important when the impulsive child is younger than age seven. For the younger child, the parent(s) are substitute problem solvers and provide external regulation of impulsive behavior.

   Practitioner's Role: Model in detail for the parent(s) the stages of problem solving and articulate out loud what you are thinking and why, as well as what does not work and why (Meichenbaum 1977).

   Parent(s) working as your co-instructors of problem-solving skills afford the child more opportunities for practice and encourage generalization of the skills, especially when parent(s) are encouraged to *model* problem solving at home, including self-instruction (*self-verbalization*). Meichenbaum (1977) points out, however, that the instructing parent(s) may be overly critical of their child. Consequently, you should use in-session rehearsal of the skills with the parent(s) and other techniques (e.g., videotapes). If the problem-solving skills training is offered in a group, the parent(s) might *rehearse* the skills with another child.

2. *Identify* situations or conditions that may contribute to the child's impulsivity.

Practitioner's Role: Assist the parent(s) in identifying and changing situations that may precipitate or exacerbate the child's impulsivity (e.g., being with certain peers, low teacher-to-student ratio in school classrooms).

3. Complete *parent training.*

Practitioner's Role: Facilitate referrals to community-based training sessions. If none is available, provide education and counseling separately to the parent(s).

As noted earlier, parenting style is a critical component of the child's capacity to be less impulsive. *Problem-solving* training that targets the child should be complemented not only by parallel training for the parent(s), but also by a parenting style including flexible use of rewards and punishments, age- and developmentally appropriate expectations of the child, etc.

4. Inform others significant to the child (e.g., teacher) of the components of *self-verbalization,* encourage its use outside of the family, and monitor the results.

Practitioner's Role: Collaborate with the parent(s) and other significant adults (e.g., explain how self-talk can be adapted to specific settings such as the child's lunchroom, glean child-specific scenarios for use in session role play).

5. Praise the child for displaying self-control in provocative situations.

Kathryn Baraneckie

Incarceration (Jail): Adjustment to

Individuals are incarcerated in county jails for the fulfillment of criminal sentences of up to one year in duration. In addition, jails are used as pretrial detention centers, where inmates await arraignment or other dispositions of their cases, for periods of up to ninety days. In addition to the extreme conditions of deprivation and punishment of life in jail, inmates often endure a great deal of uncertainty and delay in the legal process. Information is not easy to procure; it is certainly rarely offered. Most jails house smaller female populations than male, and provide relatively few services or programs. The inmates need support and reinforcement for coping with day-to-day existence; jail time magnifies the pathologies underlying criminal behavior.

Literature: Gilligan (1996); New York State Department of Corrections (1994); Severson (1994).

Task Menu

1. *Identify* and elaborate feelings surrounding your arrest and incarceration.

Practitioner's Role: Inform the inmate that your contact may be arbitrarily terminated if he or she is released or removed to another facility.

Educate the inmate about the system as much as is practicable; arrange for medications review with prison health or mental health staff, if necessary; serve as an advocate within the legal system; treat each session as if were the last; summarize progress at each session.

2. *Identify* exacerbating behaviors and their triggers based upon feelings identified in task 1.

3. [if depressed or having suicidal ideation] *Identify* reasons for depression or ideation.

   Practitioner's Role: Determine if the client is depressed or suicidal. If either is the case, help identify reasons. If suicide is a serious danger, arrange for the inmate to be closely supervised. Review need for medications with psychiatrist. See SUICIDE PREVENTION.

4. Select and engage in a constructive activity.

   Practitioner's Role: Contract with the inmate to engage in an activity of his or her choice. (Because of circumstances of jail, choices may include: *journal* writing, exercise, anger management, seeing visitors, positive *self-verbalization*, meditation or other relaxation techniques.)

5. Get involved in group activities such as religious services, GED programs, Alcoholics Anonymous or Narcotics Anonymous (see ALCOHOLISM/ ADDICTION: ADULT/ADOLESCENT RELAPSE PREVENTION).

6. Think about how jail may be a place to begin to identify and think about how to change things about your life that have caused you grief.

Ellen Middleton, Christine Romano

Insomnia

According to Morin, Culbert, and Schwartz (1994), insomnia is among the most frequent complaints brought to the attention of health care practitioners. Chronic insomnia (lasting at least six months) affects 10 to 15 percent of adults (Morin, Culbert, & Schwartz 1994). The average duration for those seeking help at sleep clinics is fourteen years (Lacks & Morin 1992). The prevalence is estimated to be higher among women, older adults, and individuals with medical (e.g., chronic pain) or psychiatric disorders (Morin et al. 1994). Individuals of lower educational or socioeconomic status report poor sleep more frequently. Sleep disruption is even widespread among children.

Insomnia varies in its expression. Symptoms cover a wide range of types, frequencies, daytime consequences (e.g., fatigue, performance and mood decrements), causative factors, and intensities. It can range from mild to severe and be transient, intermittent, or persistent. There are three subcategories based on the time of night when sleep is most disturbed: sleep onset insomnia (trouble initiating sleep), sleep maintenance insomnia (frequent or extended nocturnal waking), and early morning awakening that includes insufficient total sleep time of less than 6½ hours per night. Patterns may shift over time, and many poor sleepers suffer from a combination of these categories. They may also complain of sleep that is light, restless, and inconsistent from night to night (Lacks & Morin 1992).

Persistent insomnia, though generally not life threatening, has its share of negative consequences. Compared with those who sleep well, insomniacs report more health problems and hospitalizations (Kales et al. 1984; Mellinger, Balter, & Uhlenhuth 1985). They also report suffering from anxiety and depression more frequently and are considered to have an increased risk of developing new major depression. They are thought to be more predisposed to drug and alcohol abuse (Ford & Kamerow 1989; Mellinger et al. 1985; Morin & Grambling 1989) Insomniacs earn less pay and fewer promotions (Johnson & Spinweber 1983); their relationships with family, friends, and employers and general sense of well-being all have been shown to suffer (Lacks & Morin 1992). A 1991 Gallup poll even established a link between car accidents and poor sleep (Rosekind 1992).

A meta-analysis (research synthesis) of fifty-nine controlled studies of interventions for insomnia suggested that stimulus control and sleep restriction had more significant effects than alternative methods (for example, sleep hygiene education) (Morin et al. 1994). Tasks 8 and 9 below are consistent with these results.

Literature: Some journal articles that suggest treatment strategies for insomnia include: Bootzin & Perlis (1992); Kupych-Woloshyn, MacFarlane, & Shapiro (1993); Levy et al. (1991); Morin et al. (1993). An overview is provided by Van Brunt, Tiedel, & Lichstein (1996).

Task Menu
1. Keep a daily sleep diary.

    Elaboration: This will assist in determining the actual severity and frequency of the sleep problems. Sleep diaries provide a means of assessing whether interventions are having an effect and monitoring changes in the frequency of the insomnia.

2. *Learn about* factors that might underlie your insomnia.

    Elaboration: Possible causes of insomnia include: (1) physical disorders (chronic pain, gastroesophageal reflux [heartburn], sleep apnea, arthritis, fibromyalgia, cardiac problems, periodic movements during sleep, restless legs); (2) circadian rhythm problems (shift work, jet lag, delayed sleep phase syndrome, advanced sleep phase syndrome); (3) psychological factors (stress, psychopathology, nightmares, inactivity, reinforcement for insomnia); (4) poor sleep environment (noise, ambient temperature, light, sleeping surface, bed partner); (5) poor sleep habits (extended time in bed, naps, irregular schedule, bed as a cue for arousal); (6) use of substances (caffeine, nicotine, alcohol, hypnotics, tranquilizers, prescription medications, other drugs) (Bootzin & Perlis 1992).

    Individuals with insomnia sometimes require lessons in such topics as relaxation training, meditation, and the regular use of exercise. Information on inadequate sleep hygiene (daily activities that interfere with the maintenance of good-quality sleep and daytime alertness) is sometimes necessary.

   Practitioner's Role: Assist the client in determining whether he or she has or is subject to any of the causal factors. If so, assist client in understanding what can be done. Then suggest sources for acquiring the proper skills or training.

3. Consult a physician to determine whether pharmacologic treatments would be beneficial for use in combination with therapy.

   Elaboration: Drugs, such as the benzodiazepines, often have an immediate effect on insomnia and can be used effectively for short-term treatment; however, cognitive-behavioral treatments may be needed to maintain improvement. Long-term drug use can result in increased tolerance and side effects. Moreover, withdrawal from drugs may precipitate "boomerang insomnia" (Van Brunt, Tiedel, & Lichstein 1996).

4. *Identify* expectations of sleep pattern.

   Practitioner's Role: Educate client about sleep and sleep loss. This is especially important with the elderly, as they may not realize that normal changes in sleep patterns occur with increasing age (Monane 1992).

5. Stay awake as long as possible.

   Elaboration: Insomnia can be exacerbated by worrying about whether you will be able to fall asleep. This task will reduce anticipatory anxiety.

   Practitioner's Role: Suggest a paradoxical task—to stay awake as long as possible. Be sure to provide rationales that emphasize benefits to the client, such as using the time to do constructive things.

6. Practice using *progressive relaxation.*

   Elaboration: Relaxation provides a substitute behavior incompatible with cognitions that would interfere with sleep (Bohlin 1973).

7. Use stimulus control instructions.

   Elaboration: Stimulus control instructions are a set of techniques to help establish a consistent sleep-wake pattern, make the bed and bedroom cues for sleep, and reduce the amount of activity that might associate them with other things.

   Practitioner's Role: Give the client instructions to lie down only when sleepy. Have him or her discontinue behaviors such as eating, watching television, and reading in bed, if these behaviors are incompatible with sleep. Have client get up and go to another room if they are unable to fall asleep. Have him or her get up at the same time every day, regardless of the amount of sleep gotten during the night. Prohibit napping.

8. Practice sleep restriction (Van Brunt, Tiedel, & Lichstein 1996)

   Elaboration: Sleep restriction refers to limiting time spent in bed without sleeping. Many individuals with insomnia sleep less than 85 percent of the time they spend in bed.

ole: Have client limit time in bed to the actual number
they normally obtain.
apy to help restore of proper circadian rhythm.
ion: Chronotherapy is a treatment developed to help primar-
cadian rhythm disorders of individuals with delayed sleep phase
ne. This syndrome is characterized by difficulty falling asleep at
, the sleep-wake rhythm is out of phase with the time the individuals
ose to sleep.

Practitioner's Role: Instruct the client to delay bedtime successively by daily increments of three hours until sleep onset coincides with the desired bedtime. Prevent relapse of insomnia by having the client maintain a regular sleep-wake schedule.

10. Use articulatory suppression.

Elaboration: Articulatory suppression works on the assumption that an interruption in the train of unwanted thoughts (i.e., thoughts that are preempting attention and causing arousal) will produce sleep.

Practitioner's Role: Instruct the client in articulatory suppression (i.e., upon going to bed, client should repeat a small set of phonemes, such as nonsense syllables, a proper name that has no emotional significance, the word "the," and so on, at a rate that seems comfortable to him or her— fast enough that thoughts do not intrude, but slow enough that the client is not aroused by the process, for instance three or four repetitions every second, until sleep comes).

11. Practice sleep hygiene (Van Brunt, Tiedel, & Lichstein 1996).

Elaboration: Sleep hygiene guidelines include avoidance before bedtime of certain substances such as caffeine, nicotine, and alcohol as well as use of sleep-promoting conditions such as regular exercise late in the afternoon, use of earplugs to minimize noise, and a light snack before retiring.

Pamela Zettergren

Loneliness

Loneliness is generally characterized by feelings of alienation and separation from others. There is a lack of connectedness or sense of belonging, and the individual is unable to feel that he or she is part of what others are experiencing. Hagerty et al. (1996) found that a sense of belonging is closely related to indicators of both social and psychological functioning, especially in the case of women. Loneliness is generally associated with many forms of mental illness (major depression, schizophrenia, and borderline personality disorder, to name a few). It is also associated with social problems, such as substance abuse, alcoholism, and suicide. Physical diseases can increase the sense of isolation. Loneliness cuts across all social classes and age groups and is common enough in youth to be called a typical experience of adolescence. Deficient *social skills* may be a primary contributor to chronic loneliness during adolescence (Carr & Schellenback 1993). It may also stem from traits such as shyness (Zimbardo 1977).

Literature: Adolescent loneliness is discussed by Carr & Schellenback (1993); Medora & Woodward (1991); Mijuskovic (1986); Page (1991); Pipher (1994); Zimbardo (1977). Page & Cole (1991) write about the connection between loneliness and alcohol. How loneliness factors into borderline personality disorder is discussed in Gold (1996); Gunderson (1996); Richman & Sokolove (1992); Westen et al. (1992). Cognitive-behavioral treatment for social intimacy and loneliness is in McWhirter, Benedict, & Horan (1996). Weeks (1994) discusses loneliness and old age.

Task Menu

1. *Identify* any losses or significant life changes that may be contributing factors to loneliness.

    Elaboration: For instance, have you recently been physically ill? Have you moved? Has someone close to you died (including beloved pets)? Have you changed jobs, leaving behind valued co-workers and friends?

    Practitioner's Role: Suggest that the client mourn or come to terms with any losses, in his or her own time frame, and then take steps to reconnect to the changed social environment.

2. *Identify* people, thoughts, situations, and events that seem to trigger feelings of loneliness (Mijuskovic 1986).

    Elaboration: Use *self-monitoring,* in the form of a diary or chart, to identify times when you feel lonely. Note if anyone is present and where you are. This is useful for determining what you perceive as the specific causes of your loneliness, which can allow you to tailor interventions. This method can also be a useful tool for monitoring progress (Lewinsohn 1991).

3. *Identify* underlying beliefs and assumptions that may contribute to your sense of loneliness.

    Elaboration: For example, the client may assume that since she is quiet, others will not find her to be an enjoyable companion. Therefore, she does not attempt to make overtures to others, creating a self-fulfilling prophecy.

    Practitioner's Role: Help client correct cognitive distortions through *cognitive restructuring.*

4. *Identify* difficulties with starting satisfying interpersonal relationships and take steps to resolve them.

    Elaboration: Shyness and negative thinking or self-talk, in addition to low self-esteem, may contribute to difficulties in starting relationships.

5. Learn *social skills* to improve interpersonal relationships.

   Elaboration: *Social skills* that may be useful include assertiveness (to help you to feel more comfortable introducing yourself to strangers) and conversational skills (to help you feel comfortable with your ability to converse after initiating a conversation).

   Practitioner's Role: Use curriculum for "Friendly Skills Training" in Lewinsohn (1991) and *role play* skills with the client.

6. Create a support network.

   Elaboration: Join a support group. You will learn that you are not as different or alone as you had believed. Taking part in a group can teach empathy and compassion and refocus your attention on others.

7. *Identify* and list activities that are pleasurable, give you a sense of mastery, or embody your ideals or values.

   Elaboration: Although human companionship is sometimes unavailable, individuals can find fulfillment and meaning in activities that relate to their values and ideals. This can sometimes result in a feeling of spiritual connectedness to the world. Examples of such activities include volunteer work, sports, hobbies, creative expression, music, art, and reading. This is also a way to meet individuals with interests similar to your own (Mijuskovic 1986).

8. Read about lonely, socially isolated people who later became strong, accomplished individuals.

   Elaboration: One excellent choice is <u>Smart Girls, Gifted Women</u> by Barbara Kerr, which examines the adolescent years of Marie Curie, Eleanor Roosevelt, Margaret Meade, and other accomplished women (Pipher 1994).

9. Reach out to others by calling a relative or friend at least once a week.

10. Investigate resources for volunteer opportunities and social groups (e.g., programs like COMPEER, which matches patients and volunteers).

11. Consider acquiring a pet if you feel able to love and care for it (Kehoe 1990).

12. Use *coping imagery* when feeling lonely to soothe or comfort yourself.

    Elaboration: Thinking of pleasant times or experiences and imaging the sights, sounds, and smells that go along with them can help alleviate feelings of loneliness, at least temporarily. *Coping imagery* can also be used to alleviate anxiety surrounding going to new places and meeting new people. You can imagine successful conversations and interactions with others as a way to rehearse desired social performance and reduce anxiety by refocusing attention on the details of the social interaction.

13. Use *progressive relaxation* to reduce stress before attending an event where you will be meeting new people.

Patricia MacDonald, Pamela Zettergren

Medical or Other Treatment: Nonadherence to

Traditionally referred to as "noncompliance" with medical or therapeutic advice, nonadherence is defined by Vandereycken and Meerman (1988) as client behavior that does not "coincide with medical or health advice" as a result of the interaction among "the regimen, the clinician, the patient, and the home environment" (186). A leading type of nonadherence, misuse of prescription drugs, has been referred to as a "worldwide epidemic every bit as dangerous and costly as an actual illness" (Zuger 1998:4). Nonadherence comprises a broad range of client behaviors, from dropping out of care precipitately to minor alterations in the treatment regimen. According to Vandereycken and Meerman (1988), it tends to occur when therapeutic requirements conflict with the client's usual behaviors or personal belief system or when the client receives care over a long period of time, as in the case of a chronic substance abuse problem or a mental illness. In long-term care, nonadherence is generally character- ized by a progressive "slippage" from cooperative to noncooperative behavior. One example could be a client having surgery as recommended by his or her physician and then failing to keep scheduled follow-up appointments.

For many disorders, effective treatment outcomes are largely a function of treat- ment compliance (Sperry 1995). For example, elderly individuals with memory loss and other health-related problems may have problems remembering what medica- tions to take and the right intervals between dosages. One study (Lamy 1990) showed that one third of all hospitalizations related to adverse drug effects and half of all reports of fatalities due to inappropriate use of prescription medication involved elderly individuals. Nursing home admissions have also been linked to elderly people's inability to manage medications at home (Hammond & Lambert 1994). Children with asthma or other diseases, such as diabetes or kidney disease, have trouble complying with therapeutic and medical advice (Creer 1993, Delamater 1993).

Psychiatric patients have particular difficulty complying with treatment regi- mens (Sperry 1995). Large proportions of schizophrenic clients, perhaps from a quar- ter to over half, either do not take prescribed medication or take less than the amount prescribed (Meichenbaum & Turk 1987). Failure to take antipsychotic medication as prescribed is perhaps the single most common reason for hospital readmission (Caton 1984, Pristach & Smith 1990). Medications that control psychiatric symptoms may be abandoned by mentally ill clients for a variety of reasons, such as denial of mental illness with its associated stigma, discomfort with medication side effects, and a lack of understanding about the need to continue medications even after psychi- atric symptoms have abated (Campbell & Daley 1993). Thus with many clients, facil- itating adherence to a drug schedule is a key element of treatment. See also SCHIZO- PHRENIA, CHRONIC: SYMPTOM MANAGEMENT.

Literature: Literature relating to treatment adherence includes Casper & Regan (1993); Connelly & Dilonardo (1993); Meichenbaum & Turk (1987). Literature spe- cific to medication compliance among the mentally ill includes Campbell & Daley

(1993); Caton (1984); Massaro, Pepper, & Ryglewicz (1994); Olfson, Hansell, & Boyer (1997); Pristach & Smith (1990); Salzman (1993).

Task Menu

1. Learn about your condition (e.g., mental illness, diabetes, alcoholism) and medication (most effective time to take, dosage, side effects) by asking your physician, pharmacist, psychiatrist, or other type of practitioner for handouts (Sperry 1995).

   Elaboration: A good general resource is The Merck Manual of Medical Information, Home Edition. Another is Rolland (1994). The Internet can be used to get information from associations that specialize in certain diseases—e.g., the American Cancer Society. If you are a mentally ill, chemically addicted client, learn about the interrelationship between your mental disorder and addictive disorder, including the physiological interaction of addictive substances and medications taken concurrently.

   Practitioner's Role: Ensure that the client has an accurate understanding of his or her condition as well as the action and side effects, if any, of prescription and over-the-counter medications, illegal drugs, or other substances (e.g., alcohol). If MICA (mentally ill, chemically addicted), the client should also be helped to understand discrepancies between treatment recommendations for the chemical addiction and treatment recommendations for the mental illness (e.g., abstinence from all mind-altering drugs versus the continued use of antipsychotic medications). This can be accomplished through small psychoeducational groups and through discussion with the practitioner, with or without the assignment of reading materials.

2. *Identify* reasons for nonadherence.

   Elaboration: Reasons may include unpleasant side effects, fear of dependence or long-term harm, forgetfulness, and doubts about the efficacy of the medication.

   Practitioner's Role: Help client correct misconceptions about medication. Consult with a physician when the reasons appear to have a realistic basis.

3. Learn how and continue to monitor condition.

   Elaboration: For conditions such as hypertension and diabetes, learn to take your blood pressure or test your blood sugar. Chart blood pressure, injections, or medications taken.

4. Combine taking medication dosages and prescribed therapeutic activities with daily habits and rituals.

   Elaboration: For example, if you must take medication in the morning on an empty stomach, have the pills beside your bed with an empty glass. Make it part of your morning ritual to fill the glass with water and take your pill immediately. For medication that must be taken with food, time it as part of your meal activity. If relaxation exercises or other recommended treatments are part of your ongoing therapy, pair them with daily habits and rituals in the same manner.

5. Describe signs and outcomes of mental illness relapse and compare them to your experience when not taking medications.

    Elaboration: Use *self-monitoring* of behavior to write descriptions. Later, discuss the descriptions with others to gain insight into the correlation between psychiatric relapse and medication noncompliance, and consequently the importance of taking medications.

6. Develop a list of advantages and disadvantages to taking medications as prescribed.

7. *Identify* how you could reward yourself for adhering to treatment recommendations.

    Practitioner's Role: Some clients have difficulty thinking of what they enjoy, so have a list of alternatives available.

8. Enlist a friend or significant other to help monitor your progress (Sperry 1995).

    Elaboration: It generally works best for the other person to avoid nagging or other punishing behavior.

9. If there is a period of time when adherence is not working, use *self-monitoring* to become aware of what is happening.

10. Discuss with physician or other involved parties if it is possible to clarify, simplify, or tailor your treatment regimen (Sperry 1995).

    Elaboration: For example, make sure that both oral and written directions for medication(s) and treatment(s) are given. Ask if there is any form of the medication that may be taken once daily or by long-lasting injection. If your literacy level is low, you have poor vision, or your dexterity is limited, *identify* and use *problem-solving* skills to find ways to compensate or correct for these limiting factors (Hussey 1991).

    Practitioner's Role: Discuss with the physician or psychiatrist prescribing medications how best to tailor or customize information and schedule to the client's personality style and circumstances.

11. Obtain a compartmentalized pill box to reduce errors in pill taking.

Diane Austen, Pamela Zettergren

Mentally Ill

Homeless

Before the era of deinstitutionalization, most of the mentally ill were confined within the walls of state hospitals or hidden at home with their families. As cruel as this system was, it provided the mentally ill with twenty-four-hour support and supervision, as well as comprehensive services that met most of their basic needs. When deinstitutionalization was implemented, extensive networks were supposed to be set up in communities to maintain these individuals. Unfortunately, the development of services did not keep up with the number of mentally ill being discharged from hospitals (Bassuk 1986). Because many of these people had never lived on their own and were not capable of making independent decisions, they were forced through the cracks in the system and ended up on the streets.

In most communities, residential treatment facilities have since been established. These programs provide the mentally ill with long-term residences and comprehensive case management and ensure that all of their basic needs are met, offering the structure they were used to in the hospital (Cohen 1990). These programs are of critical importance to maintaining the mentally ill in the community and keeping them functioning at the highest level possible. However, before they can be engaged in such programs, they must come in contact with practitioners who can refer them to the right resources. Homeless adults with severe mental illness experience particularly stressful and vulnerable lives on the streets and in shelters. Often they are highly mistrustful of others and harbor multiple fears. When providing assistance to these clients, the practitioner must first work to engage them and develop a sense of trust and mutual respect (Cohen 1989). This task planner is designed to address the common situation that the client is mentally ill, homeless, and has just been in contact with an agency that places homeless individuals.

Literature: Bassuk (1986); Cohen (1990); Lam & Rosenheck (1999); Leshner (1992); Randolph et al. (1997).

Task Menu

1. *Identify* your current needs and how these relate to past psychiatric treatment.

    Elaboration: A thorough assessment is key to providing you with the best treatment options. By finding out about past treatment providers, the practitioner can negotiate the system and access services most expeditiously.

    Practitioner's Role: Thoroughly assess the client's basic needs (e.g., medical, dental). Obtain consent forms so that you can access records from past treatment facilities, and communicate with service providers.

2. Apply for social services and emergency shelter.

    Practitioner's Role: Utilize contacts with social services and the shelter system so that you can make an appropriate referral and help the client negotiate the system. If the client is hesitant, you may need to accompany him or her to the Department of Social Services (DSS) and to the shelter, in order to ensure that client is provided with all of the benefits to which he or she is entitled. Note that admission policies to psychiatric hospitals are very stringent, and it is not usually an option to use them to help stabilize a client. Thus it is necessary to get the client into a temporary shelter to meet basic needs (food, shelter, clothing) and provide a stable environment from which to seek other services. It is often necessary to go through your local Department of Social Services, because that may be the agency that pays for the shelter stay and related medical services and treatment programs.

3. Formulate a crisis plan.

Practitioner's Role: Familiarize yourself with emergency psychiatric services available in the area, and assist the client in drawing up a crisis plan. Inform the shelter staff of the proposed plan, and provide them with the names and numbers of emergency contacts. It is also important to notify local crisis services of the client's history and location. Note that many of the homeless mentally ill either are unfamiliar with the shelter system or have not fared well in previous stays. Staying in a shelter can be a very difficult and extremely stressful experience; lacking ego strength and social skills and having to interact with a large number of strangers can precipitate a crisis for many individuals with mental illness. By putting a plan in place and getting all parties involved, you can help resolve problems more quickly. Work with the shelter staff on identifying the best ways to meet the client's needs and to avoid any crisis situations (see Schutt & Garrett 1992:87–93).

4. If you are not currently involved with a mental health clinic, go to the local clinic for evaluation and admission.

Practitioner's Role: The mental health clinic should be contacted with all relevant information before the client's visit. The practitioner who becomes the client's case manager should also maintain regular contact with the clinic to follow their medication regimen and ensure collaboration. It is important to get clients on medication and into treatment to maximize their functioning and provide stability. To get into a housing program, the client may be required to be under the care of a psychiatrist.

5. If not already on Social Security, obtain an SSI or SSD application and complete the application process.

Practitioner's Role: Locate the local Social Security office, familiarize yourself with application procedures, and obtain copies of the applications. Assist client in filling out the applications, and accompany him or her to the interview. Be aware that most individuals with mental illness are entitled to SSI or SSD benefits, but often do not receive them because the application process includes being examined by doctors, providing documentation of the disability, and following up with appointments. It is important that you help ensure that all of the requirements are met. It is also important that the client file for these benefits, because they provide the health coverage and the increased funds to pay for clinic treatment and for residential programs, most of which require that the client be on SSI or SSD.

6. Obtain and read literature on all residential programs in the area.

Practitioner's Role: Locate relevant residential programs in the area and familiarize yourself with the services offered. Obtain admission applications from each of the programs. Should the client have difficulty comprehending information, discuss the different programs available and how they will provide for the client's needs.

7. Evaluate the offerings of residential programs and decide which meet identified needs.

    Practitioner's Role: Assist the client in evaluating each program, and help him or her decide which program(s) to enter. Take care to involve client as much as possible in the decision making, as it will increase his or her commitment to the program. Visiting the residence and having a meal there might be a part of the client's evaluation.

8. Fill out applications for programs.

    Practitioner's Role: Assist the client in filling out the applications and add any necessary documents (e.g., psychosocial and/or medical records).

9. Contact programs to set up initial interviews.

    Practitioner's Role: Assist the client in making the initial contacts and facilitate any arrangements that need to be made. It is best to do this in session, so that you can answer any questions that the referral source may have.

10. Begin day treatment program participation (see MENTALLY ILL: STRUCTURED DAY ACTIVITIES, NEED FOR.

11. Make a list of the potential benefits and drawbacks of the program(s).

    Practitioner's Role: Work with the client on identifying concerns about the residential program, and address each concern to clear up any misinterpretations. This process can increase the client's commitment to the residential program and make him or her feel more comfortable with it.

12. Attend all follow-up appointments with the residential program.

    Practitioner's Role: If you are the client's case manager, you may need to keep in contact with the residential program so that the staff knows of all appointments and can remind the client. Maintain regular contact after the client is accepted into the residential program. (See also HOMELESS: NEED FOR SHELTER AND EMPLOYMENT.)

Francis McKearin

Mentally Ill

Structured Day Activities, Need for

People suffering from mental disorders typically have histories of psychiatric illness, and either long-term institutionalization or short-term hospitalizations. Their disorders impede their ability to maintain employment, personal relationships, independence, and many activities of daily living. These difficulties are exacerbated by lack of structure and support in their lives (Peterson, Patrick, & Rissmeyer 1990). An institutional setting provides the mentally ill with a complete daily structure and a twenty-four-hour support system, which allows them to maximize their functioning. However, once patients are discharged, they are frequently without social or recreational supports in the community, and end up back in the hospital. Structured activities offered by day treatment programs, psychosocial clubs, and drop-in centers offer the structure that these individuals desperately need (Cohen 1990). These programs and centers provide vocational/educational training, recreational opportunities, and overall life skills training, and give the mentally ill the social support and routines they need to maintain themselves.

Literature: Cunnane, Wyman, Rotermund, & Murray (1995); Cohen (1990); East (1992); Kanter (1985).

Task Menu

1. *Identify* hobbies, vocations, and activities that you find enjoyable or important.

    Elaboration: The tasks in this planner can be done in sequence.

2. Obtain and read literature on all structured day programs in the area.

    Practitioner's Role: Locate relevant day treatment programs, clubhouses, or drop-in centers in the area, and familiarize yourself with the services offered and membership requirements. Obtain admission applications from each of the relevant programs. If client has difficulty comprehending information, discuss the different programs and how they will address the client's needs.

3. Evaluate the offerings of each structured day program, and decide on the program(s) suitable for you.

    Elaboration: Many mentally ill people have had decisions made for them most of their lives, without any input of their own. Involving them as much as possible in decisions about their day programming not only increases their interest and commitment but also enhances the therapeutic relationship between practitioner and client. Having the client visit the program may be helpful.

4. Fill out applications for program(s), or complete the necessary paperwork.

    Practitioner's Role: You will usually need to supply supporting information to the program(s), so it is beneficial to do this in session. After the client has filled out all of the information that he or she can, add the remaining data and get it to the referral source.

5. Contact the referral source to set up initial contact.

    Practitioner's Role: Help the client, in session, call for an initial appointment.

6. Plan for transportation to and from the program.

Practitioner's Role: If the client is tentative about the intake appointment, you or a family member should accompany him or her to the interview for support and encouragement.

7. Make a list of all the potential benefits of the program and all your concerns or potential drawbacks.

Practitioner's Role: It is very important to find out the client's concerns, so that they may be addressed before he or she enters the program. This process will identify areas in which clinical work must be done with the client.

8. After acceptance into the program, arrange for a regular weekly schedule and transportation.

9. Write down your weekly schedule and post in your residence.

Practitioner's Role: After the client is accepted into the program, maintain contact with program personnel and client to ensure that attendance is monitored and treatment goals are being met.

Francis McKearin

Obesity

Obesity is a risk factor for a number of medical conditions, including diabetes, cardiovascular disease, hypertension, osteoarthritis, gall bladder disease, gout, and hypercholesterolemia. Obese people in Western cultures are also stigmatized. The common perception is that they are unattractive and lacking in willpower. Evidence that obese individuals are discriminated against has been documented in medical, educational, and occupational settings.

Obesity is defined in terms of body fat, but it is usually indexed in terms of weight. A weight of more than 20 percent above the average weight for height is associated with higher morbidity and mortality. Abdominal fat is considered a greater health risk than fat distributed on the limbs. This may partly explain the greater health risks of obesity in men, who tend to have central obesity, as opposed to women, who tend to have peripheral obesity (Wardle 1995).

A meta-analysis (research synthesis) of forty-one controlled studies of interventions for child and adolescent obesity suggested that comprehensive behavioral treatment (behavior modification, special diet, and exercise) had larger effects than alternative methods (for example, behavioral treatment with either exercise or diet) (Haddock et al. 1994). See also BINGE EATING.

Literature: Some journal articles that discuss treatment strategies include Eldredge & Agras (1996); Foreyt & Goodrick (1994); Foster & Kendall (1994); Rosen, Orosan, & Reiter (1995); and Wilson (1994). A good overview may be found in Friedman & Brownell (1996). Williamson et al. (1996) discuss lifestyle changes for long-term weight management. Self-help books include Freedman (1988); Kano (1989); and Hirschman & Munter (1995).

Task Menu

1. *Identify* eating patterns.

   Practitioner's Role: Assist the client in determining whether current eating patterns need adjustment. If this is the case, help the client understand what can be done to normalize eating patterns. Suggest sources for acquiring the proper skills or training.

2. *Identify* and correct (through use of *cognitive restructuring*) dysfunctional beliefs about weight and weight control.

   Elaboration: Dysfunctional beliefs might include the notion that you will be rejected by others because you are overweight or that any weight loss you are experiencing is due to the diet you are on, so you won't be able to maintain the loss once you are off the diet.

   Practitioner's Role: Assist the client in focusing on health rather than appearance. Also, point out that self-worth and appearance are not necessarily related. Help the client attribute weight loss to his or her own successful efforts in controlling food intake rather than to a particular diet.

3. Set realistic weight goals.

   Elaboration: Maintain record of weight change.

   Practitioner's Role: Discuss with the client a realistic time frame for meeting certain weight-loss milestones. A reasonable weight might be a more practical goal than an ideal weight (Friedman & Brownell 1996).

4. Practice using *progressive relaxation* when you are stressed but not hungry, instead of giving in to the urge to eat.

5. *Identify triggers* that lead to overeating.

   Practitioner's Role: Have client engage in self-monitoring.

6. Substitute alternative activities for overeating.

   Practitioner's Role: Discuss with the client what activities he or she finds appealing enough to be substituted for overeating. Assist client in beginning to focus on other areas of life and participate in activities unrelated to body size. This is helpful in increasing self-esteem.

7. Slow your rate of food consumption.

   Elaboration: Slowing your rate of consumption has been found to be a factor in weight loss (Friedman & Brownell 1996). For example, try putting down your utensils between bites and build breaks into the meal.

8. Eat only at mealtimes.

   Elaboration: Avoid between-meal snacks, "mindless" eating.

9. Maintain a food diary, recording what you eat and total calories consumed (Friedman & Brownell 1996).

10. Select and adhere to a diet that will help you meet your weight goals.

Elaboration: Consider using a dietary exchange program (Williamson et al. 1996).

11. Begin an exercise program (Williamson et al. 1996).

    Elaboration: A good beginning is to walk at least twenty minutes a day (Williamson et al. 1996).

12. Strive to make lifestyle changes to bring your weight under contol (Friedman & Brownell 1996; Williamson et al. 1996).

    Elaboration: These would include changing eating habits, establishing exercise routines, and developing new interests (Williamson et al. 1996).

13. Enlist support of family members.

    Elaboration: Family members may help by not snacking in your presence, keeping high-calorie snacks out of sight, encouraging you to follow your diet, and participating in your exercise program.

14. Attend Overeater's Anonymous (OA) or some similar organization. Contact Overeater's Anonymous World Service Office, P.O. Box 92870, Los Angeles, CA 90009; (213) 657–6252(3) or The National Center for Overcoming Overeating, P.O. Box 1257, Old Chelsea Station, New York, NY 10113–0920; (212) 875–0442.

    Practitioner's Role: Discuss with the client the benefits of a supportive environment and companions and suggest that he or she give OA or a similar organization a try.

15. Understand the abstinence violation effect (Donnell 1984).

    Practitioner's Role: Explain that the effect is the mistaken assumption that one slip into overeating means a full-blown relapse has occurred. The client should be reassured that if such a slip occurs, he or she can still stop overeating.

16. Practice successfully dealing with situations that have led to excessive food intake.

    Practitioner's Role: Challenge the client with increasingly difficult hypothetical situations. Help the client rehearse how to respond to temptation.

17. Use *self-reinforcement* after dealing successfully with a challenging situation.

Pamela Zettergren

Oppositional Defiant Disorder

The DSM-IV (APA 1994) defines oppositional defiant disorder (ODD) as a reoccurring pattern of negative, unmanageable, rebellious, or defiant behavior toward authority figures. It is characterized by losing temper, arguing with adults, actively defying or refusing to comply with the requests or rules of adults, deliberately doing things that will annoy others, blaming others for one's own mistakes or misbehavior, being touchy or easily annoyed, being angry and resentful or spiteful and vindictive. According to the DSM-IV, a diagnosis of ODD requires that such behaviors occur more frequently than is typical in individuals of comparable developmental levels and lead to significant impairment in social, academic, or occupational functioning. The disorder is more prevalent in males than in females before puberty, but the rates are more equal after puberty. Symptoms are similar in both genders; however, females display more relational aggression whereas boys display more confrontational behavior and overt aggression (Crick 1995).

Literature: Eyberg & Boggs (1998); Horne & Sayger (1990); Lehmann & Dangel (1998); Schroeder & Gordon (1991); Webster-Stratton & Hancock (1998).

Task Menu Parents or caregivers
  1. *Identify* and praise positive behaviors.
      Elaboration: Reinforce positive behavior with praise, tokens, or privileges. Praise immediately, with enthusiasm, and, if possible, with others present; use praise even if the behavior isn't perfect (Webster-Stratton & Hancock 1998).
  2. Master techniques of attending.
      Elaboration: Set aside at least twenty minutes daily to give your child attention. During this time there should be no questioning or teaching. Ignore negative behavior unless it becomes destructive. You can use the time to play with your child; follow the child's lead, don't give too much direction, and encourage problem solving and creativity (Webster-Stratton & Hancock 1998).
  3. Give clear, age-appropriate commands.
      Elaboration: Commands need to be given one at a time; stated in such a way that the child can understand what is expected; within the child's capabilities; and positively stated (e.g., "Please sit down!"), not in the form of questions or suggestions (e.g., "Stop running around!") (Eyberg & Boggs 1998).
  4. Ignore irritating behavior when possible.
      Elaboration: Select behaviors you are able to tolerate when ignoring.
      Practitioner's Role: Explain to the parent(s) that attention may encourage (reinforce) the behavior.
  5. Provide appropriate consequences for noncompliance.
      Elaboration: Allow the child to experience the natural consequences of his or her behavior (e.g., if not ready for school on time, the child misses the bus and then must walk to school). *Time out* and loss of privileges can be used in the absence of natural consequences. When possible, involve the child in choosing consequences.
      Practitioner's Role: Provide in-session *rehearsal* of discipline methods. Aid in anticipating problems that may arise outside of the session.

6. Use *contingency contracting, contingency management,* or a *token economy* to encourage positive behavior and discourage negative behavior.
7. Learn child-rearing methods through *parent training* or *planned activities training.*
8. *Identify* beliefs that may interfere with your parenting (Lehmann & Dangel 1998).

    Elaboration: For example, some parents may believe that harsh punishment, such as grounding for long periods of time, is the best way to correct a child's misbehavior.

    Practitioner's Role: Help client *identify* such beliefs and use *cognitive restructuring* to help modify them.
9. Participate in a support group, such as Parents Anonymous (a professionally facilitated, peer-led group for parents who are having difficulty and would like to learn more effective ways of raising their children). Parents Anonymous, 675 W. Foothill Blvd., #220, Claremont, CA 91711–3416; (909) 621–6184; http://www.parentsanonymous-natl.org

Task Menu Child
1. Learn and practice self-control methods.

    Elaboration: For specific tasks, see ANGER MANAGEMENT AND AGGRESSION CONTROL: CHILD.

Janine Donzelli, Jennifer Hescheles, Ellen Dziengelski

Pain, Chronic: Adjustment to

Chronic pain is usually defined as the experience of physical pain for six months or longer. Kerns and Jacob (1995) estimate that up to a third of all Americans suffer from one of the many forms of chronic pain, such as lower back pain, recurrent headaches, abdominal and chest pain. Economic costs are reported as staggering, as are the costs in human stress and suffering. Frequent concomitant social and clinical factors include marital and family dysfunction, unemployment or underemployment, depression, alcohol and substance abuse (Kerns & Jacob 1995). A sense of meaninglessness, helplessness, or hopelessness is typically the comorbid emotional factor. Many chronic pain sufferers are at high risk for iatrogenic complications from improper therapy, including narcotic addiction and multiple surgeries. The severity and prevalence of chronic pain is a growing concern for all health care professionals.

Research suggests that active coping strategies, such as trying to function despite pain or to ignore it, have better outcomes than passive strategies, such as restricting activities (Turk 1996).

Literature: Champlin (1992); Gatchel & Turk (1996), an edited collection, contains a variety of approaches to pain management; Syrjala & Abrams (1996) and Turk et al. (1983) discuss roles of hypnosis and imagery in controlling pain; Caudill (1995); Davis, Eshelman, & McKay (1995); Kerns & Jacob (1995); Mostofsky & Lomranz (1998); Seligman (1990); Subramanian et al. (1988); Turk (1996).

Task Menu

1. Consider multimodal treatment approaches in order to comprehensively address both physical and psychological components of pain.

    Elaboration: The active involvement of physicians, physical therapists, and others who can evaluate and treat the biomedical aspects of the problem is important, as is input from experts able to focus on the neuropharmacological and psychosocial aspects. An integration of all perspectives is desirable in developing a treatment plan that is effective in reaching your principal goals (Kerns & Casey 1995).

2. Learn and practice using *progressive relaxation* or some form of breathing technique to effectively improve relaxation and concentration.

    Elaboration: *Progressive relaxation* and breathing techniques, such as *slow diaphragmatic breathing,* are useful aids in quieting the mind and reducing tension. They decrease anxiety and the resulting muscle tension and divert attention away from the pain. These techniques can help you obtain needed rest and sleep and strengthen your feeling of self-control, thus diminishing feelings of helplessness. Increased activity may reduce your need for pain medication and improve your mood.

3. *Identify* unwanted thoughts and take steps to change them.

    Elaboration: Negative thoughts, such as "the pain is so bad it will never go away," contribute to the amount of pain experienced (Turk 1996).

    Practitioner's Role: Use *cognitive restructuring* with client, including thought-stopping.

4. Increase feelings of self-efficacy.

    Practitioner's Role: Help the client to gain a sense that he or she can "successfully execute a course of action (perform required behaviors) to produce a desired outcome in a given situation" (Turk 1996:99). This approach has been found to be useful with self-efficacy beliefs concerning headaches, back pain, and rheumatoid arthritis. Encourage the client to work through a series of tasks, each more difficult than the previous, in an attempt to build the appropriate behavioral and coping milieu.

5. Replace negative thoughts with more hopeful ones.

    Elaboration: This alters your appraisal of the situation, including changing the meaning and the emotional experience of the pain. Refer to the Turk et al. (1983) cognitive program, which teaches patients voluntary control of their appraisal of pain. Self-efficacy expectations, such as that you can successfully complete a task (despite pain), can help control pain (Turk 1996).

    Practitioner's Role: Encourage the client to carry out tasks that he or she can accomplish despite the experience of pain.

6. Master meditation techniques.

   Elaboration: Meditation frees the mind of negative thoughts and energy and keeps an individual focused in the present. Meditation should be done for five minutes each day to start, working up to thirty minutes daily.

7. Use *coping imagery* as a means of controlling pain.

   Elaboration: Imagine yourself to be in a pleasant, safe place where you feel relaxed and comfortable. (Use *progressive relaxation* to heighten sense of physical relaxation.) Focus on analgesic images, such as placing ice on the painful area and imagining the ice absorbing the pain (Syrjala & Abrams 1996).

8. Develop and maintain an exercise program (within your physical limitations), and record exercise on a chart.

   Elaboration: Practice three times weekly, for only as long as is comfortable, because exercise in moderation reduces pain, increases stamina, and relieves stress.

   Practitioner's Role: Refer the client to a professional trained in physical therapy.

9. Maintain a balanced diet.

   Elaboration: Poor nutrition may affect pain levels and decrease energy.

   Practitioner's Role: Refer the client to a dietitian or nutritionist.

10. Learn about similarities between patterns of depression and chronic pain (e.g., cognitive distortion, loss of positive reinforcement because of physical limitation, job loss, declining social and recreational activities, increasingly frequent cognitive appraisals of declining well-being, hopelessness regarding the future, and inability to take action).

    Practitioner's Role: Help the client understand that chronic pain is a serious condition and validate the experience of pain.

11. Join a chronic pain support group.

    Elaboration: Group participation facilitates self-esteem through a mutual helping process in which members must use their individual strengths to participate. The act of coming to a group counters the typically passive response to the chronic pain condition. Information on groups can be obtained from the American Chronic Pain Association, P.O. Box 850, Rocklin, CA, 95677–0850; (916) 632–0922.

Paul Copp, James Golden

Parent-Adolescent Conflict

Interpersonal conflict between parents and teenagers is generally considered to be a normal part of adolescent development. However, some conflict may be severe and cause significant distress. This type of interaction has been described by Hall & Rose (1987:3) as "problematic conflict." An empirically based description of the problem has been developed by Hall (1984) with the following identifiable characteristics: 1) insufficient level of positive or supportive communication; 2) excessive negative or defensive communication; 3) poor problem-solving skills, decision making, and planning; 4) lack of negotiation skills, including the inability to clearly state opinions or to give and receive praise and criticism: poor listening and paraphrasing skills (Hall 1984). Clashes in beliefs about family life may be another source of conflict. For example, parents may believe their adolescent should be obedient at all times while the adolescent may think that his or her autonomy should not be interfered with (Robin, Bedway, & Gilroy, 1994). Immigrant parents may hold cultural beliefs that are at odds with those of their "Americanized" offspring. Finally, conflict is often exacerbated by problems of family structure, such as cross-generational coalitions in which one parent supports the teen against the other parent.

Literature: Descriptions of interventions and programs to address parent-adolescent conflict may be found in Barkley, Edwards, & Robin (1999); Diamond & Liddle (1999); Gordon (1976); Greydanus (1991); Hall (1984), (1978); Hall & Rose (1987), and Reid (1992). Robin, Bedway, & Gilroy (1994) provide a very detailed manual for work with adolescents and parents.

Task Menu Parents and adolescents
1. Talk with one another about noncontested topics and extend the length of conversations (Hall 1984).

    Elaboration: "Equalize the ratio of parent and teen talking. (Reduce parent's talking and increase adolescent's.)" (Hall 1984:494).
2. Learn and practice listening skills through paraphrasing.

    Elaboration: While discussing an issue, paraphrase what the other has just said before responding. For example, when Mom finishes her statement, Tom summarizes (without editorializing) what Mom has just said before answering. Mom listens to his response and paraphrases it in return. Use nonverbal cues to show that you are listening—face each other, make eye contact (if culturally appropriate), lean forward, nod, smile, frown, etc.

    Practitioner's Role: Provide reading materials on the topic—for example, Gordon (1976) and Greydanus (1991). Parents and teens can learn these and other communication skills from in-session exercises in which you help them select a real issue they want to work out. However, the issue should not be so "toxic" that the clients are not able to satisfactorily complete the task. Instruct them and provide encouragement and corrective feedback during their attempts to complete it in session.
3. Learn to express dissatisfactions in as nonthreatening a manner as possible.

    Elaboration: The skill here is in stating something undesirable to another person in a manner that conveys your feelings and perceptions but minimizes angry or defensive reactions. Beginning statements in the first person ("I statements") and following them with specific indications of what you are upset about and illustrative examples is a good way of disclosing problems (Gordon 1970).

4. Learn *problem-solving* communication skills.

Elaboration: Set aside time for *problem-solving* sessions. Specify the time of day and the length of the sessions, which should be convenient for all participants (Gordon 1976). Limit the number of problems to be worked on in each session; focus on one per session if possible (Greydanus 1991). If the agenda is long, prioritize. If you are feeling very angry, avoid problem solving until you are calmer (Hall & Rose 1987). Use "complete I-messages," which include: 1) a specific description of the unacceptable behavior; 2) the feeling experienced (as a consequence of the behavior); and 3) the tangible or concrete effect on you (Gordon 1976). Work together to define problems. Criticize the behavior, not the person (Greydanus 1991). Brainstorm solutions without evaluating them; this will help inspire creativity. Try to come up with as many solutions as you can (Hall & Rose 1987). Evaluate them together, and select the one on which you all agree. Implement the solution and then evaluate its effectiveness. If needed, problem solve again. Use additional methods of *problem-solving training.*

Practitioner's Role: See parents and teen together in the session. Structure and facilitate their face-to-face problem-solving communication. Help them learn to state the problem by beginning with something positive, to be specific, to avoid derogatory terms and overgeneralizations, to express feelings, to admit to their own role in the problem, to deal with one problem at a time, to offer compromises, to be neutral rather than negative, and to focus on solutions (Jacobson & Margolin 1979).

5. Check with each other for understanding by asking questions and requesting further explanations whenever needed (Hall 1984).

6. Take turns telling each other (calmly and without interruption) your points of view about an issue (Reid 1992).

7. Do a reverse *role play* in which you exchange roles and present arguments for your positions.

Elaboration: Having the parent take the role of the teen and present arguments from that position, and vice versa, is an excellent way of helping each to better appreciate the other's point of view.

8. *Identify* and challenge "unreasonable beliefs" (Robin, Bedway, & Gilroy 1994).

Elaboration: For example, parents may think that teens should be obedient at all times; teens may think that they should be free to do what they want.

Practitioner's Role: Help parents and teens critically examine such beliefs using *cognitive restructuring.*

9. Plan and carry out at least one *mutually enjoyable activity.*

> **Elaboration:** For some parents and teens, most interactions are conflictual. A mutually enjoyable activity—e.g., going to the movies, watching TV, playing a game—can help restore the positive aspects of the relationship.

Task Menu Parents
1. Recognize strengths and positive behaviors in your adolescent; praise positive efforts to resolve problems and appropriate decisions when he or she makes them (Hall & Rose 1987).
2. Try to present a united front to the adolescent.
3. Avoid siding with the adolescent against your partner.

Patricia Brescia

Parent-Child Conflict: Chores

A frequent source of conflict between parents and children is chores the child is asked to do in the home. Children may fail to do chores because of forgetfulness or distractibility or as part of a more general pattern of opposition to parental authority. They may fail to do them well because of lack of experience and skill. High parental expectations may create performance demands that children cannot realistically meet. Chore problems can create or exacerbate tensions in the parent-child relationship; parents may accuse children of being lazy or irresponsible, and children may complain about being asked to do too much or about being nagged or scolded. Disputes over chores may escalate into larger conflicts as children react to punishments for not doing them.

> **Literature:** Crisafulli (1999); Reid (1992); Webster-Stratton & Herbert (1993); Wielkiewicz (1995) (chapter 9 provides a variety of behavior management examples, guidelines, and parent materials).

Task Menu Parents
1. Tell the child exactly what to do ("Please carry this laundry basket down to the basement and put it on the table by the washing machine").
2. For more complex chores, work with the child in starting the chore or demonstrate the chore to him or her.

> **Elaboration:** If it makes sense, involve the child in planning the chore.
>
> **Practitioner's Role:** Have parent(s) practice asking the child to do the chore through *role play* with the child in session. Practice can include handling obstacles (e.g., when the child doesn't want to interrupt another

activity to do the chore, or when one of the child's friends calls on the phone during the planned chore time).

3. Develop a simple chore list with your child's help (Crisafulli 1999).
4. Check to see that child fully understands the nature of the chore and set a time when the chore is to be done.
5. Remind the child of the chore as its time approaches.
6. Set the number of reminders after the initial request (e.g., three), the time limit for completing the chore, and the consequences if the chore is not done—e.g., withdrawal of privileges.

    Elaboration: Remind the child if the chore is not done; inform him or her of consequences.
7. Acknowledge and praise efforts the child makes toward completion of the chore.
8. Determine if the child has completed the chore and praise him or her if it has been well done.
9. Reward the child for successful completion.
10. Carry out consequences if the chore is not completed.
11. Use *contingency contracting* or *contingency management* to facilitate chore completion.

Task Menu Child

1. Do the chore as agreed; reward yourself if you do.

Mary Corrigan, Kathleen Lepore

Parent-Child Enmeshment

An enmeshed relationship is characterized by lack of clear boundaries, intrusiveness, and overcontrol on the parent's part, which are resented by the child. The parent may do unrequested "favors" for the child, then become angry or depressed when the child does not appreciate them. The child may alternate between dependence and rebellion, and may feel the need to appease the parent. The two may quarrel frequently over issues relating to any of the above.

Green and Werner (1996) suggest that enmeshment and cohesion have become confused in the literature. Enmeshment or overinvolvement is really intrusiveness (including coercive control, separation anxiety, possessiveness or jealousy, emotional reactivity, and projective mystification). Cohesion or closeness and caregiving (including warmth, time together, nurturance, physical intimacy, and consistency) is entirely different.

Literature: Benjamin (1996); Blair (1996); Cheesebrough & Hill (1996); Green & Werner (1996); Reid (1992).

Task Menu Parent(s) and child

1. Discuss the differences between support and intrusiveness and decide where you will draw the line in your relationship.
2. Discuss the ideas of "boundaries" and "autonomy" as applied to your-selves and develop rules for maintaining each.

    Elaboration: The rules here concern what is my space and what is yours (boundaries) and independent action (autonomy).
3. Develop and carry out independent activities with which the other will not interfere.
4. Plan and carry out a *mutually enjoyable activity* in which you respect each other's freedom of action.

Patricia Signor

Racial Discrimination in Workplace

Racial discrimination includes unfair treatment of or denial of normal privileges to people because of their race; failure to treat all people equally when no reasonable distinction can be found between those favored and those not favored. Anger and rage are the most volatile and difficult psychological effects of racial oppression (Hardy et al. 1995).

Literature: Block & Carter (1998); Hardy & Laszloffy (1995); Jackson (1994); Katz (1978).

Task Menu Victim of discrimination

1. Begin monitoring instances of racial discrimination.

    Elaboration: Enlist the help of co-workers who witness the discrimina-tory acts. Collect and record the names, titles, addresses, and phone num-bers of all people alleged to have discriminated against you.
2. Handle instances of racial discrimination informally.

    Elaboration: In lieu of, or prior to, taking formal action, you might try to deal informally with instances of racial discrimination. When they per-sonally experience discrimination, most people tend to respond by ignor-ing it and saying nothing. An alternative response is to confront the dis-criminator in a manner that does not put him or her on the defensive. Try to engage the person in a dialogue that will permit you to voice your con-cerns in a nonaccusatory manner while trying to understand the other's motives and point of view.
3. File an inquiry, complaint, or grievance.

    Elaboration: Make inquiries if you feel aggrieved because of what you perceive as illegal discrimination. The affirmative action office (if your em-ployer has one) is a good place to go. A complaint usually begins with an individual's making an inquiry and then at a later time requesting some assistance beyond consultation. A complaint is can be utilized to clarify the issues, determine a course of action, and possibly work toward a fair and equitable resolution. If no solution is possible, the complainant can move to a more formal grievance procedure for allegations of racial discrimination in the workplace. Usually there is a time frame in which grievances must be filed. Every affirmative action office should have formal procedures for processing grievances.

If your workplace has no affirmative action office, or as an alternative, contact the nearest regional office of the Division of Human Rights and file a complaint. Find out the compliance regulations and filing procedures. Explore whether you will need private counsel. Submit any documentation that supports the allegation made in your complaint. If possible, supply the names, addresses, and phone numbers of any witnesses to the alleged act(s) of discrimination. Doublecheck documentation for accuracy and clarity of information.

Task Menu Those in the workplace concerned about racial discrimination
1. Examine current policies and procedures for dealing with unintentional racial discrimination.
2. Begin a public dialogue regarding racial discrimination.
    Elaboration: This involves all sectors of the workplace over a period of time in numerous contexts—organizational publications, seminars, meetings, etc. The goal is to provide an an opportunity for everyone to explore their own experiences with racial discrimination, to forge a common language, and to create a broad base of organizational support for an overall plan.
3. Create a comprehensive and well-publicized long-term plan.
    Elaboration: Such a plan should include office climate and employee recruitment, hiring, promotion, and retention, in addition to other areas of the organization that might be affected by racial discrimination.
4. Institute an exposure strategy.
    Elaboration: An exposure strategy involves creating situations in which people of different ethnic groups work together. The idea is that the contact will help break down racial barriers.

Motier Haskins, Denise Jeremiah

Rape

Rape, defined as any forced sexual act, is an emotional, physical, and psychological trauma for the victim. It is generally followed by common problems such as fear, mistrust, guilt or shame, anger, self-blame, and feelings of going insane. Another problem a rape victim may experience (when, and if, she or he is able to discuss the traumatic event) is that friends may tire of hearing about the rape. They may think that the victim should be over the event. However, it is not uncommon for the victim to need to talk about the trauma for six months to a year afterward. Parents often feel guilty about the incident and react by becoming overprotective, which creates other problems. A partner may view the aggressive, violent act as a sexual experience and have feelings of anger toward the victim. Effects the victim experiences following the trauma may include mood swings, fear, difficulty sleeping, depression, loss of self-esteem, flashbacks, nightmares, impaired memory, and avoidance of situations that remind her or him of the rape. Female victims frequently come for counseling three to six months after the rape, when the effects have failed to go away and they feel that they can no longer cope. See ANXIETY: POST-TRAUMATIC STRESS DISORDER (PTSD): ADULT.

Literature: Benedict (1994); Cwik (1996); Foa, Rothbaum, & Steketee (1993); Davis, Eshelman, & McKay (1995); Vonk & Yegidis (1998).

Task Menu
1. Discuss the rape and related feelings and problems with others.
   Practitioner's Role: Help the client identify individuals with whom and circumstances where discussion would be useful and appropriate. Facilitate discussion in treatment session.
2. *Identify triggers* that seem to bring on negative emotions or flashbacks.
   Practitioner's Role: Assist the client in identifying situations or experiences that are troubling or problematic.
3. Use *progressive relaxation* and *coping imagery* to deal with anxiety.
4. Control obsessive or unwanted thoughts.
   Elaboration: Obsessive thinking can increase anxiety (e.g., "If I'm alone in my apartment at night, I will be raped again"). It is important to control negative thoughts, as they frequently precede negative or frightening emotions.
   Practitioner's Role: Use *cognitive restructuring* to normalize rape-related fear for the client. Present anxiety on a continuum, so the client understands it can be stopped in the early stages.
5. Use *self-reinforcement* to positively cope with negative emotions, situations, and experiences.
6. Participate in a local support group that deals with the trauma of rape.
   Elaboration: As friends and others may not understand or be comfortable with your need to talk about the rape, it is important to enlist the support of individuals who have had the same experience. In general, individuals who have been in similar situations will understand the amount of time needed to talk about and recover from such a trauma.
7. Use *exposure* to reduce anxiety or other symptoms associated with memories of the assault.

Elaboration: *Exposure* involves activating anxiety by recalling the assault as vividly as possible; it should last long enough, thirty minutes or so, that the anxiety gradually diminishes. You can begin *exposure* in the practitioner's office and continue it at home. In-vivo *exposure* can be used to reduce anxiety about situations associated with the assault—e.g., entering an elevator (Vonk & Yegidis 1998). *Systematic desensitization* is an alternative method.

8. Deal with the legal aspects of the situation.

Elaboration: This might include making a decision about pressing charges, if this has not already been done.

Practitioner's Role: Help the client develop a plan. Explore the client's feelings about involvement with police and the criminal justice system.

Ellen Dziengelski

Runaways: Family Reunification

Often children and teens who run away have been living in families with varying levels of dysfunction. Most feel they are escaping intolerable conditions (Rohr & James 1994). School problems, substance abuse, delinquency, violence, incest, suicidal ideation, or other such problems may be concurrent with running away. Homeless youths seeking help from runaway shelters have been observed to have more school and personal problems, especially family difficulties, than runaways from home who have also sought help from the shelters (Kurtz, Jarvis, & Kurtz 1991). Runaways report more school fights, more days absent, and higher suspension rates than their nonrunaway peers. They also score lower on academic tests, despite no differences in attitude toward school between themselves and nonrunaways. Prior involvement with child protective services suggests that poor school performance is correlated with a stressful home life (Rogers, Segal, & Graham 1994). Treatment of troubled children and adolescents may be most effective when it addresses the family system through family therapy.

This task planner is written with the assumption that the runaway child or adolescent is receiving services at a youth shelter. Trauma experienced while on the street may also need to be addressed. Task planners on various school or alcohol abuse problems, AD/HD, PTSD, self-esteem, family conflict and dysfunction, parent-teen conflict, sexual abuse, transition from residential care to home, anger management, and *stress inoculation* may also be useful resources. As runaway adolescents are not a homogenous group (Sharlin & Mor-Barak 1992; Zide & Cherry 1991), some may not have the possibility of reconciliation with their families (e.g., "thrown out" runaways who were alienated from their families and those "forsaken" for financial reasons). Runaways who cannot reconcile abuse may be unwilling to reunite with their families.

Literature: Research material related to the selected tasks includes Caldwell (1995) and Gavazzi & Blumenkrantz (1991). Rohr & James (1994) offer suggestions for preventing runaway behavior. Other useful sources include Brendler et al. (1991); Coleman (1987); Fishman (1988); Greene & Ringwalt (1996); Post & McCoard (1994); Warren (1996).

Task Menu Youth

1. *Identify* reasons for running away.

    Practitioner's Role: Help the client pinpoint situations that led to his or her leaving home. Also assess client for substance abuse, suicidal ideation or attempts, and physical and sexual abuse, as these problems are noted in the literature as being common among runaway youths (Feitel et al. 1992; Gary, Moorhead, & Warren 1996; Greene & Ringwalt 1996; Kennedy 1991; Kurtz, Kurtz, & Jarvis 1991; Teare, Authier, & Peterson 1994; Teare et al. 1992; Warren, Gary, & Moorhead 1994).

2. Agree to discuss reconciliation with family members (provided that your safety and well-being can be assured).

    Practitioner's Role: Work with the client to assess whether a reconciliation is possible and *role play* likely family/parental responses to the runaway's attempt at reconciliation. If family and client are agreeable, meet separately with parent(s) and other family members to assess their perception of the situation and attitudes toward family counseling.

3. Participate with other family members in a *mutually enjoyable activity*.

    Elaboration: This may disrupt negative patterns of relating and develop positive feelings in relation to each other. Poor communication and fighting are cited among reasons for running away from home (Kufeldt, Durieux, & Nimmo 1992).

4. Participate in *problem-solving training* with other members of your family.

    Practitioner's Role: If family members are continuing to have angry exchanges and appear anxious, teach *progressive relaxation* to the client and his or her family in addition to *problem-solving. Stress inoculation* can also be used to decrease anxiety and stress levels of client and family members.

5. If attending school, participate in a school-related support group for children or teens experiencing difficulties with parents or other problems, such as substance abuse.

    Elaboration: If support groups are not available in school, look for community programs.

    Practitioner's Role: Assist client in finding school or community resources, so he or she will have a social support network in addition to family contact.

6. Learn how to use *coping imagery* to deal with situations you perceive as unpleasant.

    Elaboration: *Coping imagery* serves multiple functions. It can be used to deal with situations perceived as unpleasant at the youth shelter. It can be also be used to decrease anxiety and stress during encounters in therapy with your parent(s) and later at home during the inevitable friction that occurs between all adolescents and parents. It is one alternative coping mechanism to running away.

7. Examine your expectations about your family.

Practitioner's Role: Use *cognitive restructuring* with client to correct unrealistic beliefs or expectations. For instance, many runaways believe that teens from "good" homes have parents like those in the idealized families on television.

8. Participate in *social skills training.*

Elaboration: Learning a range of *social skills* may give runaway and homeless youths in shelters high levels of satisfaction with the program (Teare, Peterson, & Furst 1994). They may never have learned *social skills* at home or from interactions at school. Work to develop such skills as understanding what another person is saying and responding politely to constructive criticism. *Social skills training* can lead to more productive outcomes with peers and adults and help you feel more positive about yourself, enjoying successful and pleasant interactions with others.

Task Menu Parents

1. Determine from the runaway the reasons for leaving home.

Elaboration: In most cases it is useful to clarify the adolescent's exact reasons for running away as a basis for further work.

2. Negotiate new rules for the parent-child relationship.

Elaboration: Research suggests that aggressive, coercive parenting leaves runaways more vulnerable to being victimized when on the streets (Whitebeck & Simons 1990). See PARENT-ADOLESCENT CONFLICT; COUPLE OR FAMILY CONFLICT.

3. Discuss whether you feel disappointed with the runaway.

Elaboration: Runaways often feel they are not "good" family members because their behavior has disappointed their family (Post & McCoard 1994). Clearing the air on this matter can be useful in rebuilding family ties.

4. If there is a family history of substance abuse, consider its impact on the youth.

Elaboration: Research suggests that runaways whose family members have abused substances have twice the incidence of attempted suicide, even after their own substance use is controlled for; this points to a need for suicide prevention efforts for runaways with this risk factor (Greene & Ringwalt 1996).

5. Discuss ways to help the youth develop as an individual.

Elaboration: One hypothesis is that if the family inhibits individuation, the youth may run away from home in order to develop a differentiated self (Crespi & Sabatelli 1993).

6. Focus on the caring aspects of your parent-child relationship.

   Elaboration: Kufeldt (1991) suggests that trying to control a child rather than caring for him or her may cause running away.

7. Discuss with the runaway events of which he or she may be ashamed.

   Elaboration: The runaway may believe he or she deserves whatever has happened to him or her on the street, which may lead to a decreased sense of worthiness to be part of the family unit. These feelings need to be processed so the runaway can become fully reintegrated into the family.

Pamela Zettergren

Schizophrenia, Chronic

Family Involvement

Schizophrenic clients are often young adults still living with their families or dependent on them. Surveys report that from 30 to 50 percent of chronically mentally ill people live with their families, and the great majority have social contact with relatives (Love 1984). As studies of "expressed emotion" have demonstrated (Leff 1989), family dynamics have a critical influence on the course of the schizophrenic's recovery. Expressed emotion, such as overinvolvement, hostility, and criticism, may contribute to relapse; conversely, families can provide important emotional and tangible resources to facilitate recovery. Family involvement is not always possible or indicated and in some cases should be approached with caution. Some families are not available or have given up trying to relate to the client, and intense conflict between client and relatives may preclude conjoint work. Still, some contact with family members is usually advisable, especially when they can serve as resources. When involvement of the whole family seems contraindicated, clients themselves can be asked to suggest which family member(s) might be most helpful to them, and thus which one(s) might be most profitably seen.

   Literature: Anderson, Reiss, & Hogarty (1986) present an empirically validated model for working with families of schizophrenics; Hogarty (1993) reviews research that has tested this model; Penn & Meuser (1996) review similar studies of family treatment. Bernheim & Lehman (1985) and Barrowclough & Tarrien (1998) discuss a variety of methods for working with families where schizophrenia is an issue. The tasks below are drawn largely from the Anderson, Reiss, & Hogarty (1986) model.

Task Menu Parents or caregivers

1. *Learn about* schizophrenia and how you can best cope with a schizophrenic.

   Practitioner's Role: Help the family understand that the schizophrenic person has a serious illness for which they are not to blame. Recognize the difficulty of coping with the illness, but emphasize what the family can do to facilitate recovery. Stress the need to maintain a low-key environment in which the schizophrenic member is given the necessary psychological space to recover at his or her own pace.

2. Avoid as much as possible expressions of criticism or hostility toward the schizophrenic.
3. Try to anticipate episodes of disturbed behavior by observing such signs as agitation, irritability, and argumentativeness.

    Elaboration: If you see these signs, notify your practitioner and take whatever self-protective precautions seem appropriate (Bernheim & Lehman 1985).

4. Attempt to negotiate conflicts with the schizophrenic person.

    Elaboration: Use methods described in *couple or family conflict.*

    Practitioner's Role: Make sure expressions of conflict in the session do not endanger whatever psychological balance the member with schizophrenia has achieved. It is usually best to start with minor disputes as a low-risk test of the entire family's capacity for dealing with conflict.

Task Menu Schizophrenic

1. Make a positive contribution to the life of the family.

    Elaboration: Examples include doing household chores and engaging in social and recreational activities with family members. Note that the withdrawal, inertia, and apathy typically exhibited by schizophrenics are difficult for families to accept. In fact, these are the object of most of the negative criticism expressed by families (Leff 1989).

    Practitioner's Role: Help the family plan such tasks, preferably in family group sessions.

2. Try to control disturbing behavior.

    Elaboration: Examples include bizarre rituals or incoherent and delusional talk. When you cannot suppress such behavior, you may be able to avoid displaying it to family members who might find it upsetting.

Task Menu Family as a whole

1. Develop interests outside the family.

    Elaboration: It is important for the person with schizophrenia as well as other family members to develop interests outside the family. Lack of such interests tends to reinforce the apathy and withdrawal of the schizophrenic and lead to overinvolvement with the family.

2. Participate in a self-help group.

    Elaboration: Some families find membership in self-help groups, such as the National Alliance for the Mentally Ill (NAMI) (http://www.cais.com/vikings/nami/index.html), to be a source of external involvement as well as a way to connect with other families with schizophrenic members.

Such groups can also furnish practical information about local resources and enable family members to channel their concerns about the schizophrenic member into advocacy for the mentally ill.

Schizophrenia, Chronic

Social Skills Deficits

Chronic schizophrenic clients are often vulnerable to psychosocial stressors in a variety of contexts. When released from a psychiatric facility into a residential housing program for the mentally ill within the community, a schizophrenic may be exposed to persistent stress and react unfavorably to others. The new living arrangement will require interactions within the community and with unfamiliar people. Ambiguous situations can be highly anxiety-provoking for this population who are ill-equipped to cope in stressful situations and are at risk for relapse (L'Abate & Milan 1985). Most chronic mental patients share deficiencies in asserting themselves effectively, enjoying leisure and social life, and solving personal problems and conflicts. Practitioners can help most schizophrenic clients improve on these deficiencies (L'Abate & Milan 1986).

Natural support systems help protect against a multitude of physical and emotional problems by helping the individual cope with stress (LaAbate & Milan 1986). However, chronic schizophrenic clients frequently lack the necessary social skills to maintain strong affiliations with others and, in fact, often have pervasive and stigmatizing social deficits that lead to rejection by peers and those with whom they regularly interact. In this sense, social skills have a direct and reciprocal impact on the severity of their symptoms and their ultimate prognosis (Liberman 1989). Many chronic schizophrenics need to relearn ways to manage anxiety, change cognitive sets, and build skills to enhance socially adaptive and functional behaviors.

Tasks that focus on social skills enhancement can strengthen psychobiologically vulnerable individuals against the stressful effects of life events and the challenges of community adjustment. These skills can help them address their affiliation needs and learn positive interactions with peers and others in their environment, which may facilitate forming new social support systems. A *social skills* program for schizophrenic clients should include basic skills to allow them to (re)build social competence. A group environment is a superb training setting, but the practitioner can modify the tasks for individual therapy sessions. The following task menu was adapted from Bellack et al. (1997) and contains basic skills that can help chronic schizophrenics enhance their conversational, conflict management, assertiveness, expressive, friendship, and vocational/work skills. Research shows that training chronically mentally ill patients in assertiveness, communication, and problem-solving skills can reduce the stress they encounter when they annoy others and provoke retaliation (Penn & Mueser 1996).

Literature: Bellack et al. (1997); Kopelowicz et al. (1998); L'Abate & Milan (1986); Liberman (1989); Penn & Mueser (1996).

Task Menu

1. *Learn about* the rationale for enhancing *social skills* and how *social skills* can enrich your quality of life.

   Practitioner's Role: Elicit rationale from the client by asking leading questions about the importance of such skills (e.g., "Why is it helpful to . . . ").

2. Improve conversational skills by practicing starting, maintaining, and ending conversations.

   Elaboration: The ability to converse with others is central to almost every social situation. Many schizophrenics suffer from alogia, an inability to generate conversations. Expressive skills and nonverbal behaviors are important forms of communication and should be included in this task (Bellack et al. 1997).

   Practitioner's Role: Write down the steps of the skill and post them in a prominent location in the room before the session for reference as needed. Demonstrate the skill to the client/group. Identify steps of the skill: Greet the person, give some information or ask a question, judge whether the person is interested in conversing; if so, make a brief statement about how you feel about something. Then end the conversation by first looking away or glancing at your watch; say "I should go now," then say good-bye. Discuss nonverbal responses and expressive behaviors; include in role play as needed.

3. Practice conversational skill in *role play.*

   Practitioner's Role: Develop role plays and specific scenarios before the session. Including modeling of the skill prior to client practice. If teaching *social skills* in a group environment, ask other members to observe which steps of the skill they see the leaders or clients using in the *role play.*

4. Review the *role play* and *identify* whether each step was used, whether it was effective, and why.

   Practitioner's role: Immediately follow role play with positive feedback by identifying what the client(s) did well. If in a group, ask group members "What did you like about the way X performed that skill?" Immediately cut off negative feedback. Avoid vague phrases such as "not bad" or "pretty good." Praise observers for their feedback. Repeat role plays until all members have had an opportunity to perform the skill.

5. Practice the skill with others outside the session.

   Elaboration: Skills transferred from a group/individual session to a naturally occurring situation are more likely to be generalized and become part of your behavioral repertoire (Liberman 1989; Bellack et al. 1997).

Practitioner's Role: Provide the client with homework assignment cards written in clear, simple language. Ask about possible obstacles the client may encounter while practicing the skill (Liberman et al. 1989). Assist him or her in identifying solutions.

6. Enhance conflict management skills by practicing compromising, disagreeing without arguing, and leaving a stressful situation.

   Practitioner's Role: Explain the concepts of compromise and negotiation before teaching this skill. Identify the steps of the skill: Express a viewpoint briefly, listen to another's viewpoint, suggest a compromise, listen to the other's viewpoint. If the client does not agree, say "it's okay to disagree." End the conversation and move on to another topic. If conflict remains, tell the person you will discuss it at another time, then leave the situation. Repeat practitioner roles described in tasks 1–5.

7. Practice assertiveness skills by learning how to refuse requests politely, make complaints, and respond to them. See ASSERTIVENESS, LACK OF.

   Elaboration: Some schizophrenics tend to avoid conflicts; others create them. Assertiveness is one of the most critical skills that you need to avoid exploitation, have your needs met, and reduce the stress associated with negative interactions (Bellack et al. 1997).

   Practitioner's Role: Explain the steps of the skill: Look at the person; speak firmly and calmly. Say exactly what you would like them to do, e.g., "I would really appreciate it if you would do Y." To refuse a request: Tell the person you cannot do what he or she asks by saying, "I'm sorry but I cannot do Z," and give the reason. Explain the steps of making and responding to complaints: Make good eye contact; state your complaint calmly. Be specific in telling the person how he or she might solve the problem. To respond to a complaint: Maintain good eye contact; listen to the complaint while keeping an open mind; calmly repeat what the person said; accept responsibility or use conflict management skills. Repeat practitioner roles described in tasks 1–5.

8. Practice expressing unpleasant or angry feelings in a civil manner.

   Elaboration: Learn to verbalize exactly what the person did to upset you. Be able to identify emotions so that "I statements" can clarify how the interaction made you feel.

   Practitioner's Role: Help generate a list of unpleasant feelings and label their resulting emotional states. Prepare the client/group by helping them identify early warning signs of anger (heart racing, feeling tense, etc.) and explain that these feelings will subside in time. Identify the steps of the skill: Look at the person; speak calmly and firmly. Tell the person what they did to upset you and how it made you feel. Suggest ways in which the person can prevent the situation from occurring again. Repeat practitioner roles described in tasks 1–5. See ANGER MANAGEMENT AND AGGRESSION CONTROL: ADULT.

9. Practice expressing positive feelings and giving others compliments to enhance friendship skills.

   Elaboration: Generate a list of kind, friendly acts others have done and identify incidents where a compliment is appropriate.

   Practitioner's Role: Initiate discussion of how everybody enjoys hearing positive statements and review incidents where others have given the client compliments. Explain the steps of the skill: Maintain good eye contact; tell the person what he or she did that pleased you; tell them how it made you feel. To give compliments, tell the person what you like. Repeat practitioner roles described in tasks 1–5.

10. Practice responding to criticism without hostility.

   Elaboration: Criticism from others can be very disturbing if you are deeply sensitive to ridicule. Many schizophrenics have difficulty accurately perceiving emotional material and thus may detect disapproval though none was intended. When participating in sheltered employment or living in a residential housing program, you may encounter criticism from supervisors or group home personnel. Most chronic schizophrenics have a history of rejection and criticism and may be prone to misinterpreting statements as critical. Discriminating criticism from suggestions or directives is complex (Bellack et al. 1997).

   Practitioner's Role: Review with the client the advantage of clarifying ambiguous statements; encourage him or her to ask the person to restate the message if they are unsure of its content. Explain the steps of the skill: Listen carefully to what is being said without interrupting or getting angry. Repeat what the person said; ask what you can do to rectify the situation. If the statement is ambiguous, ask questions until you understand. It may be helpful to review the steps of task 8 to ensure that the client has a good understanding of how to manage angry or upsetting feelings. Repeat practitioner roles described in tasks 1–5. See also SOCIAL SKILLS TRAINING.

Karen Duckett

Schizophrenia, Chronic

Symptom Management

The treatment of schizophrenia is a long-term, ongoing process, the goal of which is not to cure it but to substantially reduce symptoms while improving the quality of life for patients and those close to them (Bentley 1998). Learning about the illness (e.g., signs of relapse and forms of treatment) and learning strategies for clear communication and problem solving may help manage the course of the illness and reduce rates of relapse. It is important for patients and their families to understand what is happening to them (e.g., the strange and often frightening symptoms such as hallucinations, delusions, fears, and confused thinking that can result in bizarre behaviors).

Because medication plays such a prominent role in the treatment of schizophrenia, patients and their families need to understand how it affects treatment and rehabilitation. While medications are reported to be 70 percent effective, meaning that with appropriate use seven out of ten people will experience a clinically significant improvement in symptoms, only 15 percent of patients with chronic schizophrenia derive optimal benefits—which leaves a sizeable percentage who are not helped at all (Bentley 1998). These patients are described as being treatment resistant or refractory. The remaining 30 to 50 percent are described as partial responders (Brier & Buchanan 1996; Lieberman 1996). Further, most of the gains achieved from "psychopharmacological treatment occur in the acute phase of the illness, which is the first 6 to 8 weeks following onset, with slower, more subtle gains continuing up to 30 weeks" (Bentley 1998:392). Moreover, conventional antipsychotics and the newer "atypical antipsychotics" are much more effective at reducing the symptoms of schizophrenia (e.g., hallucination, delusions, bizarre behavior) than at changing or altering some of the effects, which include lack of energy and motivation, social withdrawal, and flattened affect (Bentley 1998). Estimates of medication noncompliance among individuals diagnosed with schizophrenia range between 50 and 70 percent (Rogers et al. 1998). Treatment strategies that combine emotional support and cognitive-behavioral techniques have been shown to improve medication compliance and help keep patients engaged in treatment (LeCompte & Pelc 1996). This is consistent with Yank (1993) and Hogarty (1993), who report the complementary and additive effects of medication and psychosocial treatments when combined.

The tasks below can be used for individuals who have recently been diagnosed with schizophrenia, and for those who continue to have difficulty with medication management and noncompliance. See also MEDICAL OR OTHER TREATMENT: NON-ADHERENCE TO.

Literature: Treatment guidelines and information about medications and side effects for patients and their families can be found in Francis et al. (1996). Practical strategies for enhancing medication use for clients with schizophrenia can be found in Diamond (1983). An overview of the efficacy of antipsychotic medications and commonly used adjunctive and side effect medications, and a discussion of trends in psychopharmacological research, can be found in Bentley (1998).

Task Menu

1. *Learn about* the nature and treatment of schizophrenia.

    Elaboration: A good general overview for patients and their families can be found in The Journal of Clinical Psychiatry 57 (Supplement 12 B),

"Expert Consensus Treatment Guidelines for Schizophrenia: A Guide for Patients and Families." This information can also be accessed on the EKS website at http://www.psychguides.com. The National Alliance for the Mentally Ill (NAMI), the national umbrella organization for local support and advocacy ([800] 950-6264) can help you locate your state's Alliance for the Mentally Ill (AMI). The National Mental Health Association (NMHA) information center can be reached at (800) 969-6642; http://www.cais.com/vikings/nami/index.html.

2. Establish a relationship with a mental health worker (e.g., therapist, resident counselor, case manager, or advocate) to be an ally in your treatment.

Practitioner's Role: Develop a therapeutic alliance with the client based on trust, warmth, empathy, and a desire to share (Lecompte & Pelc 1996).

3. Enlist the support of family and friends.

Practitioner's Role: Encourage the client's family to attend a psychoeducational family management program or local support group for families and friends. Support groups can be located through NAMI (see task 1).

4. *Learn about* your prescribed medications.

Elaboration: The first acute episode of schizophrenia is typically treated with high-potency antipsychotic medications such as haloperidol (Haldol) or fluphenazine (Prolixin) or the newer antipsychotic medications such as olanzipine (Zyprexa) or clozapine (Clozaril). These medications usually take effect in two to three weeks. Other commonly prescribed medications include sedatives (if the client is extremely agitated or has difficulty sleeping) and anticholinergics, such as Cogentin, for possible side effects. Higher doses of antipsychotic medications are typically lowered (titrated) gradually to achieve a dose low enough to reduce side effects but not so low as to cause a relapse (Francis et al. 1996).

Practitioner's Role: Encourage the client to talk to his or her prescribing psychiatrist or physician about the role and purpose of each medication and possible side effects. A good source of information for the client and layperson is the local pharmacy where they get their prescriptions filled. However, since the typical medication appointment with the treating physician lasts only fifteen to twenty minutes (mainly for a mental status exam and refill of the prescriptions), it is important to ask the doctor to explain the dosage and intended effect of each medication. Clarify when necessary. For clients who are severely impaired (e.g., highly delusional) orwho have difficulty with social interactions and communication, your presence at the appointment provides needed support. Moreover, you can help explain the purpose of each medication and can also give the prescribing doctor important information on apparent efficacy and side effects.

5. *Identify* your expectations and feelings about taking medication.

Elaboration: It is helpful for you and your family to understand what medications can and cannot do. You may have unrealistic expectations and hopes that medication alone will relieve all symptoms and problems (Dziegielewski 1998). Stigma, both real and perceived, may shape feelings about taking or not taking medication. Rogers et al. (1998) provide detailed descriptions of how patients ascribe a variety of meanings to their medication.

Practitioner's Role: Help clients explore their expectations and feelings about taking long-term medication for their illness in a neutral, nonjudgmental, and supportive way. Responses may vary widely among clients and may include denial of even having a mental illness, psychotic thoughts (e.g., "it's poison"), stigma about having a mental illness and having to take medications, or fears about possible side effects.

6. Explore the benefits and the costs of taking medication in terms of your life goals and plans.

Elaboration: Many people take medication because it alleviates or reduces disturbing symptoms (Rogers et al. 1998). Others may take medication for reasons that have more to do with coercion, social control, or feelings of obligation, such as pressure from families or mental health care providers, or to avoid letting significant others down (Rogers et al. 1998). For those who avoid taking medication, the negative side effects (e.g., fatigue, restlessness, lack of motivation, weight gain, dizziness or fainting, blurred vision, shakes, nervousness, slurred speech or loss of concentration) are not worth the social or clinical gains.

Practitioner's Role: Help the client formulate or articulate meaningful goals and objectives (e.g., "I want my own apartment," "I want to get a job," "I want to have a girlfriend/boyfriend") and weigh the costs and benefits of taking medication in terms of those goals. Elicit and discuss realistic and complementary strategies (e.g., attendance at a psychosocial club or vocational rehabilitation) that can help the client achieve his or her goals. Continue to encourage medication compliance.

7. Learn to *identify* early warning signs of a relapse.

Elaboration: Every individual tends to have his or her own "signature" signs that warn of a coming episode. For example, some people may become increasingly suspicious, worry that other people are talking about them, or become more irritable or more withdrawn before an acute episode (Francis et al. 1996).

Practitioner's Role: Explore this with the client. For example, ask, "When you're feeling okay, what is it like for you to go to work, the store, day treatment program, shopping, etc.?" Then ask them to describe or write what these activities are like when they are feeling symptomatic.

Speak to family members and other providers to further identify and elaborate on prodromal (early warning) signs.

8. *Identify* coping strategies that you already use.

Elaboration: Common coping strategies include listening to music or the radio, talking to other people, exercise, walking, relaxation, meditation, prayer or religion, smoking cigarettes, alcohol, self-medication with other drugs (over-the-counter or street drugs). These methods can control symptoms and often control or ameliorate some of the adverse effects of prescribed medications (Rogers et al. 1998). Obviously, some of these strategies may be problematic.

Practitioner's Role: This exploration with the client may uncover more information about unwanted side effects of the prescribed medications. Reinforce constructive strategies and encourage open discussion with the prescribing psychiatrist. This may result in changes in the time of day a medication is to be taken, an increase or decrease in dosage, or a medication change. This approach allows the client to take and maintain control of the process in a structured way.

9. Practice using identified coping strategies in real-life situations.

Practitioner's Role: Explore what works in different situations and encourage the client to continue to experiment and learn.

10. Develop a crisis plan.

Elaboration: The plan should cover what needs to be done if a relapse occurs. Involve family members or significant others, if possible.

Jennifer Shulaner

School Problems

Anger/Aggression Management

A child may have excessive amounts of anger or inadequate control over expression of that anger (e.g., explosive temper or tantrums), or may express that anger by acting out in ways that are harmful to others. Expression of the anger may be verbal or physical or both, is often perceived as aggression by its recipients, and alienates teachers and peers. Anger can be viewed as a stress reaction that includes physical, cognitive, and behavioral aspects best addressed in combination. A comprehensive anger/aggression management approach will increase a child's awareness of the physical signs of developing anger, shift key faulty cognitions (such as inaccurate perceptions of others' intent to harm him or her), and increase ability to solve problems and generate appropriate alternative behaviors across settings.

Literature: Feindler & Guttman (1994) present a group program for anger control training. Possible causes of school violence and its prevention are discussed in Studer (1996).

Task Menu Parents and teacher
1. *Identify* the ABCs of angry/aggressive behaviors (antecedents, behaviors, and consequences) in key settings (e.g., classroom, lunch, playground, home).

   Practitioner's Role: Be as specific and objective as possible, avoiding critical labels and generalizations such as "always." Bring to the clients' attention that there is always a cognition before the behavior happens. *Parent training* provides a comprehensive explanation of ABCs and additional techniques for parents to use.
2. *Identify* strengths, realistic new target behaviors, and appropriate rewards for the child.
3. Provide regular, predictable, and nonconfrontational time for the child to communicate with you one-to-one, such as "the five minutes" technique (Donovan & McIntyre 1990:102–105).

   Elaboration for parents: "The five minutes" are sacrosanct and set aside daily for the child to communicate (respectfully) to you, while you simply listen attentively. The technique emphasizes the importance of the process, the fulfillment of the commitment between parent and child, and the child feeling heard as even more important than the content of what he or she says. This technique tends to reduce pressure on the child and in the parent/child relationship.
4. Encourage the child to share, weekly, the behavioral goals she or he has set for anger and aggression management.

   Elaboration: This is designed to support the child's efforts to change and help provide appropriate reminders and encouragement.
5. *Identify* situational triggers and modify situations, where possible and appropriate, to help prevent anger and aggression. Give clear, specific instructions about goal behavior to the child.

   Elaboration for teacher: Consider with the child his or her teaming up with a supportive buddy in class who can give reminder cues for successful behavior. *Identify* a special activity or treat (e.g., extra computer time, stickers) for the child/team when behavior goals have been met.

   Practitioner's Role: Have parent(s) and teacher encourage the child's *self-monitoring* and *self-reinforcement* behavior. Explain these techniques to parent(s) and teacher or work directly with child.
6. Help the child develop an awareness of physical signs of building anger and impending aggression.

Practitioner's Role: Instruct parent(s) and teacher about awareness of the physical signs of anger and help them develop with the child simple intervention skills (taking deep breaths, using *progressive relaxation,* pulling back from a confrontation, counting to self, self-talk such as "take it easy," etc.).

7. Help the child shift from an emphasis on threat in situations to an emphasis on problem solving.

Elaboration: Help the child expand the available repertoire of non-aggressive coping measures or "smart moves" he or she can make instead of being aggressive (disengaging from the situation, asking for help from an adult, working out a compromise, etc.). Have child come up with the longest possible list of "smart moves."

8. Consciously and consistently reward the child's success in self-management of behavior with praise and other reinforcers, as appropriate.

Elaboration: Take every opportunity to identify the child as successful in managing his or her own behavior. Consider child as subsequent helpmate to others.

Practitioner's Role: Instruct parent(s) and teacher in use of *contingency management.*

9. Use *time out* if the child is unable to control angry or aggressive behavior him- or herself.

Task Menu Child

1. *Identify* and modify cognitive distortions about anger and aggression.

Practitioner's Role: Help the child explore perceptions and attributions that usually lead to anger. Use modified "Hassle Log" (Feindler & Guttman 1994) or similar worksheets for homework. Use *cognitive restructuring* and follow with brainstorming of alternative responses, or use creative *role play* with peers.

For remaining tasks see ANGER MANAGEMENT AND AGGRESSION CONTROL: CHILD, tasks 8–13.

Mary Corrigan

School Problems

Disruptive Classroom Behavior

Acting out in school is a common problem for students. Sometimes it is motivated by the need for attention, unlike other disorders with similar symptoms (Saxena

1992). As a rule, disruptive behavior falls under four dimensions measured by the Sutter-Eyberg Student Behavior Inventory (SESBI), a teacher rating scale (Burns, Walsh, & Owen 1995): overt aggression toward others, emotional-oppositional behavior, attentional difficulties, and covert disruptive behavior. Various techniques are used to discourage disruptiveness and motivate students to learn self-control. Refer to task planners on *school problems: anger/aggression management* and *attention deficit/hyperactivity disorder: child* if these problems are considered the sources of disruptive classroom behavior.

Literature: Brigham, Bakken, Scruggs, & Mastropieri (1992); Leach & Tan (1996); and Rogers (1994) all discuss disruptive classroom behavior and suggest tasks to use to curtail it.

Task Menu Teachers

1. By observing the child in the classroom, determine the nature and extent of the problem, factors relating to it, and what can be done about it.

   Elaboration: For example, help the child *problem solve* when he or she becomes agitated.

   Practitioner's Role: Instruct the teacher in *problem-solving training* and help *identify triggers* of the child's negative behavior.

2. Reward the child (e.g., verbal reinforcement, smiley faces, stars) for not engaging in negative behavior for a specified period of time.

   Practitioner's Role: Instruct the teacher in *response cost system, contingency management,* and *token economy.*

3. Provide parents with feedback regarding the child's behavior through *school-home notes* (daily "report cards" sent to parents about aspects of a child's problems, sometimes called "home notes") (Reid 1992; Kelley 1990).

   Elaboration: Note that when dealing with older (secondary school) children, research suggests a negative letter is an effective means of increasing on-task behavior (Leach & Tan 1996).

4. Spend time in class helping the child stay focused on tasks, using reminders, gentle restraint, or soft reprimands if the child starts to become disruptive.

   Elaboration: A soft reprimand is one that only the child can hear (O'Leary 1984).

5. Use *time out* as needed.

Task Menu Parents

1. Advise the teacher if the child is under stress that may cause acting out at school.

   Elaboration: For example, marital discord may contribute to school behavior problems (Reid & Crisafulli 1990).

2. Reward the child for good days reported in *school-home notes*.
3. *Role play* in family meetings how the child can handle provocative situations in class (e.g., the parent can take the role of teacher or student in *role play*).

   Practitioner's Role: Demonstrate use of *role play* in a treatment session and participate by taking the role of the child (in which you can model appropriate behavior).

Task Menu Child

1. Work on your ability to stop engaging in a specific negative behavior—e.g., interrupting other children.

   Practitioner's Role: Help the child *identify* negative behavior.
2. Use *problem-solving training* to decide how to prevent negative behavior and record the results.

   Elaboration: For example, request that your teacher change your seat to increase distance from provoking peers, and work on ignoring them. Additionally, keep a *journal* of provocation and your responses to it.

   Practitioner's Role: Discuss the *journal* and responses to provocation in session.
3. Practice responding to provocative situations through *role plays* with parents, teachers, or peers.

   Practitioner's Role: Instruct the child in *problem-solving training, self-monitoring,* and *self-verbalization* to make the task easier. Also, help child *identify triggers* to negative behavior. Have a joint session with client and "antagonist(s)" if negative behavior appears to be the result of interaction with other children.
4. Use *self-reinforcement* when you have had a good day (morning, hour, etc.).
5. Select (with the help of your teacher) a well-behaving peer who can sit nearby and give reminders when you start to become disruptive.
6. Learn and work on using appropriate *social skills.*

Nam Soon Huh, Pamela Viggiani, Allen Neursinger

School Problems

Home Stimulation and Reinforcement, Lack of

A child may be falling behind in school largely because the home environment does not provide the stimulation and reinforcement necessary for him or her to develop and retain age-appropriate skills. The family may have priorities or values that are not conducive to learning. For example, a single parent may have to work long hours and leave the child with older siblings or baby-sitters who are unwilling to help with homework. These individuals may also be unwilling to carry on anything more than minimal conversations with the child. Other chores may compete for the child's time with the parent(s)—cooking dinner, doing laundry, etc. Exhaustion or emotional difficulties, as in the case of divorce, may affect the attention given to the child. Some families do not value educational achievement or feel an education is very important. Some parents spend inordinate amounts of time on the telephone, watching television, and visiting with adult friends, which leaves limited time to devote to stimulating their child's growth.

Literature: Kurtz & Barth (1989) discuss parental involvement and the mounting evidence that suggests it helps children perform better in school. Other research related to parental involvement can be found in Griffith (1996). Impact of parenting practices and style relative to children's achievement can be found in Paulson (1994) and Steinberg et al. (1992).

Task Menu

1. *Identify* possible ways to increase home stimulation and reinforcement of your child's learning.

   Practitioner's Role: Assist parents in the identification process. Explain the kinds of things they can do to increase home stimulation and reinforcement.

2. Meet with the child's teacher to discuss specifics of the need for home stimulation.

   Practitioner's Role: Mediate, if necessary, between parent(s) and teacher.

3. Request that the teacher prepare materials to use at home with the child.

   Elaboration: Request items that the child would enjoy and that would also stimulate learning.

4. Use materials with the child at home.

   Elaboration: Consult the teacher in the specific use of materials, in addition to when and how long to use them. Use *school-home notes.*

5. Enlist the efforts of other caregivers to stimulate the child academically.

6. Provide other home stimulation.

   Elaboration: For example, put *Sesame Street* on the television, display the alphabet in large letters, borrow books from the library and read them to the child, have the child read to you, play *games* involving word and number skills, set aside a small block of time to devote to discussing the child's day and verbally praising his or her activities.

7. Engage in a *mutually enjoyable activity* with child.

Elaboration: Activity can be used to stimulate and motivate a child's learning—e.g., a trip to the zoo, a board *game.*

Leanne Wood

School Problems

Homework

Not completing homework is a frequent contributing cause of poor academic performance and failure. Among factors responsible for lack of homework completion are low student interest in academic subjects, student perception that assignments are too difficult, lack of an appropriate place at home for study, and absence of parental supervision and support.

Literature: Gajria & Salend (1995); Galloway & Sheridan (1994); Loitz & Kratochwill (1995); Moore & Waguespack (1994); Olympia, Sheridan, Jenson, & Andrews (1994); Reynolds & Gutkin (1999); Skinner (1998).

Task Menu Child
1. Set a weekly goal that addresses a small part of the academic problem.
   Elaboration: Partializing academic problems may help you focus on specific aspects and avoid feeling overwhelmed by their magnitude. For example, you can set a goal of completing a certain percentage of homework in a specific subject in a particular interval of time. This will be a definite improvement if you have not been doing any homework.
   Practitioner's Role: You, the parent(s), and the teacher can offer positive reinforcement for the child's attainment of a weekly goal. The reinforcement can be verbal (e.g., praise) or material (e.g., stickers, treats).
2. Locate a "homework buddy" who can help you complete your homework.
   Elaboration: The "homework buddy" should be a peer with adequate academic skills to facilitate your studying.
3. Have your teachers initial your assignment book and completed assignments and share this with parent(s).
   Elaboration: By using the teacher's initials to verify what homework assignments are and which ones are completed, you can keep track of how well you are doing and keep your parents informed about your progress. Your teacher can also grade homework, indicate areas that need to be improved, etc. See *school-home notes.*
4. Spend an agreed-on amount of time on homework each night.
   Elaboration: Use self-recording, evaluation, and graphing to chart progress (Trammel, Schloss, & Alper 1994).

Practitioner's Role: Explain *self-monitoring* procedures to the child.

Task Menu Parents
1. Set a time with your child each night for doing homework.
   Elaboration: Make sure that the child has an adequate place to do homework, free of distractions by siblings, TV, etc.
2. Check assignment book to determine what homework needs to be done.
3. Express interest in the child's homework and offer to help with it.
4. Reward the child for satisfactorily completed homework.
5. Obtain a tutor to help the child if he or she is too far behind to be able to complete homework alone.

Task Menu Teacher
1. Observe the child doing homework.
   Elaboration: Observing the student in a homework setting (e.g., study hall) can give some insight into how the child spends his or her homework time and allow you to see if the child uses the time efficiently.
2. Offer three minutes' early dismissal from class for students who complete homework.
   Elaboration: A study by Schellenberg, Skok, and McLaughlin (1991) found this to be effective with students (senior high).
3. Give the child immediate feedback on homework performance.

Scott O'Leary

School Problems

In-School Work

A child may have trouble motivating him- or herself to do in-school work as requested by the teacher. This may be caused by inability to focus due to excessive interest in the behavior of peers, disinterest in the topic of study, immaturity, etc.

   Literature: Anhalt et al. (1998); DuPaul & Hoff (1998); Heward & Orlansky (1988).

Task Menu Teacher
1. Identify and eliminate potential interference within the classroom environment.
   Elaboration: This may include moving the child away from distractions or closer to you or to resource materials.

2. Reward the child with stars, smiley faces, etc. contingent upon completion of assigned work.

   Practitioner's Role: If needed, educate the teacher on the use of *contingency management.*

3. Send *school-home notes* with the child, indicating progress in completing in-class assignments.

Task Menu Parents

1. Reward the child contingent on completion of in-class work reported in *school-home notes.*

   Practitioner's Role: Educate parent(s) on *contingency management* and suggest participation in a *mutually enjoyable activity* as one way of rewarding the child.

Task Menu Child

1. Use *self-verbalization* while doing in-school work.

2. Record assignments completed in the designated subjects and reward yourself, contingent on the completion of an agreed-on number of assignments.

   Practitioner's Role: Educate the child in *self-reinforcement.*

Allen Neursinger, Linda Maloney

School Problems

Peer Conflict

Six common types of conflict reported in schools are physical aggression or fighting; playground disputes; access or possession disputes; turn-taking disputes; put-downs or insults; academic-work disputes (Johnson et al. 1994). "Low-investment" disputes are usually brief and low or absent in emotional intensity, and do not require intervention, whereas "high investment" disputes are longer-lasting, more complex, emotionally charged, and affect student performance and peer relationships without intervention (Johnson et al. 1994). "Coping effectively with conflict . . . involves managing the emotion present in the situation and then using a negotiation or problem-solving process to work out a mutually acceptable solution to any differences" (Katz & Lawyer 1993:37).

Literature: Crockenberg & Lourie (1996); Caplan, Bennetto, & Weissberg (1991); Chung & Asher (1996); Kinoshita, Saito, & Matsunaga (1993); Laursen, Hartup, & Koplas (1996); Maccoby (1996); Roecker, Dubow, & Donaldson (1996).

Task Menu Teacher
1. Intervene, if possible, before the conflict begins to escalate.
2. Determine whether the conflict was isolated and self-limiting and is now essentially over or if further intervention is necessary (due to intensity or to likelihood of recurrence). If the latter is the case, refer students to an appropriate resource—e.g., school social worker or guidance counselor.

Task Menu Child
1. In higher-intensity conflicts, agree to have a third party help resolve the conflict and lay ground rules appropriate to the setting and circumstances.
    Elaboration: The mediator can be either a peer or a professional. The person mediating is not a judge and will not decide the conflict, but will work to help you come up with a solution that you can agree upon. Each person will get to tell his or her side of the story, in turn; each person will listen without interrupting, and reflect back his or her understanding of the other's perspective until agreement is reached; each agrees to work in good faith to come up with a solution. (Or, if you agree, the process can be akin to binding arbitration, and the mediator will impose a solution if you don't come to an agreement yourselves.)
2. Generate possible alternative solutions by brainstorming or other methods.
    Practitioner's Role: [as mediator] Emphasis is on voluntary, participant-generated solutions. Facilitate this by drawing out the perspective of each participant, making suggestions only as needed to encourage their ability to problem solve. See COUPLE OR FAMILY CONFLICT.
3. Discuss and evaluate alternative ways of resolving conflict, including the pros and cons of each.
    Practitioner's Role: Provide factual information about applicable rules in the school and help the children identify the consequences of each type of decision. Highlight areas of common or similar ground; reinforce signs of active listening and good faith.
4. Select a solution that you both can live with and agree to carry it out.
5. Agree to reconvene with each other, and with the mediator if necessary, to repeat the conflict resolution process as needed.
    Practitioner's Role: If the children are seen individually before mediation or between mediation sessions, *role play* possible reactions or attitudes that may come up when they get together. Instruct the children in the use of *problem-solving* methods and *self-reinforcement* (to self-reward for successfully avoiding conflict).
6. Agree to advise others that the conflict has been resolved.
    Practitioner's Role: Suggest that the principal consider setting up a formal peer mediation program and training a cadre of peer-nominated students as mediators.

Mary Corrigan

School Problems

School Phobia

There are two forms of school refusal: school truancy (see SCHOOL PROBLEMS: TRUANCY) and school phobia (Atkinson, Quarrington, & Cyr 1985; Thyer & Sowers-Hoag 1986; Levine 1984). Four characteristics distinguish school phobia from school truancy: truants are generally doing poorly in school, whereas school phobic children, up to the time of the onset of the disorder, usually are average or above-average students; the school phobic child stays home, while the truant avoids home; truancy is usually characterized by intermittent absence, whereas the school phobic child can remain absent up to months at a time; and the parents of truants are generally unaware of their children's absence, while the parents of school phobic children are well aware of the problem (Thyer & Sowers-Hoag 1986:87).

School phobia generally results from avoidance of anxiety-producing or aversive situations at school or difficulty in separating from a parent (Lee & Miltenberger 1996). As a part of their reaction, school phobics often express somatic complaints or display somatic conditions that may include sleep disorders, enuresis, trembling, screaming, crying, sweating, and vomiting (Thyer et al. 1986; Barth 1984).

Literature: Atkinson, Quarrington, & Cyr (1985); Berry & Lizardi (1985); Blagg (1987); Kennedy (1995); Kearney & Roblek (1998); Lee and Miltenberger (1996); Levine (1984); March (1995); Thyer & Sowers-Hoag (1986). Blagg compares and contrasts psychodynamic, behavioral, and mixed treatment approaches for school phobia. The book includes descriptions of the nature and etiology of school phobia, methods of intervention, and clinical examples, as well as an extensive nineteen-page reproducible form that can be used to observe and record a student's attendance and other relevant behaviors and events of school, social, and family life. Kearney & Roblek (1998) present a parent training approach to school refusal, including both school phobia and truancy.

Task Menu Parents or caregivers
1. *Identify* any medical or physical problems that may interfere with the child's ability to attend school (Blagg 1987).
   Practitioner's Role: Encourage the parents/caregivers to obtain a medical assessment from the family's primary physician as a first step in approaching the issue.
2. *Identify* any patterns or triggers to the child's absences and refusal behaviors.
   Elaboration: The child may be avoiding school because of tests, a certain class, a certain teacher, or teasing by peers, among other reasons. Of-

ten the child may not be able to articulate the bases for his or her fears (Kearney & Roblek 1998).

Practitioner's Role: Help parents recognize the relevance of precipitating events through the assessment process. For this and related purposes you may wish to form a team consisting of parents, teacher(s), child, and relevant others.

3. Develop and implement a monitoring system using a daily log (Blagg 1987).

Elaboration: Observe the child's behaviors, "level of anxiety, depression and general distress" (Lee & Miltenberger 1996:480) at home and record your observations. If the child is able to attend school, there can also be contact between you and teachers, with the teacher(s) using a log to record observations of the child and communicating these observations to you and the practitioner. The teacher(s) can provide information about any difficulties "with other students, school-related activities, places, objects, signs of anxiety and distress or other problems at school" (Lee & Miltenberger 1996:480).

School social workers, psychologist, or counselors can also utilize phone calls and letters home when they notice that a child is missing school.

Practitioner's Role: Help the parents develop a standard form with specific time frames to record observations of the child.

4. Establish routines for getting the child off to school in the morning (Kearney & Roblek 1998).

Elaboration: Get the child up in plenty of time and set up routines with the expectation that he or she will be going to school.

5. If the child refuses to attend school, set up a routine for time at home (Kearney & Roblek 1998).

Elaboration: The routine should involve boring activities and little adult attention to avoid reinforcing school refusal behavior.

6. Establish *contingency management* or *token economy* to reinforce school attendance.

Task Menu Child

1. *Identify* peers who can facilitate your attendance.

Practitioner's Role: Team up the child, when he or she is in school, with another one or two students with regular attendance and base rewards for the group on attendance rates (Barth 1984).

2. *Identify* people, situations, contexts that trigger your avoidance of school.

Elaboration: The child can use index cards or a recording form during school to record thoughts, feelings, time, location, surrounding peers, activities, and expectations when anxious or fearful. He or she can also use a daily *journal* at home to record thoughts and feelings about school. To make recording more interesting, the child can draw pictures and include them on the cards/*journal*.

    Practitioner's Role: Review the cards, form, or *journal* with the child and establish coping strategies for specific fears or anxieties. Also look for any cognitive distortions and use *cognitive restructuring* to help the child eliminate them.

3. Use *role play* at home with parents/caregivers and in session with the practitioner.

    Practitioner's Role: Provide the parents/caregivers with a number of different scenarios to conduct role play exercises at home—e.g., child being teased by a peer.

4. Return to school in incremental steps.

    Elaboration: For example: 1) walk around the school or as close to the school as possible with a parent; 2) enter school during school hours; 3) enter the classroom and attend one class with a parent; 4) attend at least a half day of school without being accompanied by a parent (Morris & Kratochwill 1987; Thyer & Sowers-Hoag 1986).

    Practitioner's Role: Make yourself available to participate in any of the above steps, when necessary.

5. Use *progressive relaxation*.

    Elaboration: This technique is usually reserved for older students or those able to identify when they are feeling stressed or anxious and to implement the strategies appropriately and independently.

6. Use *coping imagery*.

7. [for older children] *Identify* and correct distortions in beliefs regarding school.

    Practitioner's Role: Use methods of *cognitive restructuring* to identify and correct dysfunctional cognitions relating to the child's fears. For example, Jerry may be behind in his homework. He fears that the teacher will shout at him if he returns to school without it done. Your conference with the teacher reveals that this will not be the case.

Robert Mattola

School Problems

Selective Mutism

The essential feature of selective mutism is persistent failure to speak in specific social situations where vocalization is expected, despite speaking in other situations.

Educational or occupational achievement or social communication is impacted negatively. This disturbance must last for at least one month, with the exclusion of the first month of school, when some children are reluctant to speak or are shy. If failure to speak is due solely to lack of knowledge of or comfort with the spoken language, or better accounted for by embarrassment or a communication disorder, such as stuttering (or other disorders, e.g., schizophrenia), selective mutism is not diagnosed.

Children with this disorder often communicate by nodding or shaking their head or other gestures. At times they push or pull to communicate. They may use monosyllabic, short, or monotone utterances, sometimes in an altered voice. Sometimes anxiety disorders (particularly social phobia), mental retardation, extreme psychosocial stressors, or hospitalization are associated with selective mutism. Some cases involve fear of social embarrassment, excessive shyness, withdrawal, social isolation, clinging, compulsive traits, controlling or oppositional behavior, negativism, or temper tantrums, principally at home, as additional features of the disturbance. Selective mutism is slightly more common in females and onset is usually before five years of age. Entry into school often brings it to clinical attention. Generally selective mutism lasts several months, but some cases can persist for years (APA 1994). Research suggests that individuals with persistent selective mutism who present with comorbid anxiety disorders may respond to fluoxetine treatment (Dummit et al. 1996). In school, the child refuses to respond orally in class—to answer the teacher's questions, read aloud, etc.—but his or her verbalization is appropriate in other settings.

Literature: Giddan et al. (1996): Harris (1996); Rossi (1977); Steinhausen & Juzi (1996); Szabo (1996).

Task Menu

1. Establish some form of communication with the practitioner and select a tangible reinforcer for talking.

    Practitioner's Role: See the child individually and stimulate conversation through tangible and verbal reinforcers. Assess whether there are associated features (e.g., social phobia) and address these conditions through use of appropriate task planners. *Social skills training, stress inoculation,* or *systematic desensitization* may also be necessary.

2. Select a few friends from class to form a group.

    Practitioner's Role: Obtain the teacher's permission to allow the children selected to leave class. They should be chosen so that child feels comfortable enough in the group to communicate (e.g., by reading aloud). Use the other children as role models or to help the child talk. The the child is talking comfortably.

Linda Maloney, Pamela Zettergren

School Problems

Truancy

Truancy is defined as chronic, unexcused absences from school or tardiness to the extent that the child's academic performance is adversely affected, resulting in a failure in grade level or in another significant measure of academic performance, e.g., reading or math level (Cimmarusti, James, Simpson, & Wright 1984; Zeismer 1984). Truants are characterized by four broad criteria: they have difficulty in school; they stay away from their homes; they miss school sporadically; and their parents generally are unaware of their behavior (Thyer & Sowers-Hoag 1986). Excessive school nonattendance "has been identified as a major barrier to learning" (Levine 1984). Nonattendance also affects schools, as they may lose attendance-based revenue (Bell, Rosen, & Dynlacht 1994; Barth 1984).

Despite the four criteria described above, truants as a population are heterogeneous, and several authors have proffered multicausal models of truancy (Barth 1984; Cnaan et al. 1989). "Truancy is not the result of a simple causal problem, nor is it simply the act of unexcused school absence. Truancy comprises a whole context of actions. This context involves the interactional relationships of the child, family, and school concerning the issue of chronic unexcused school absence" (Cimmarusti, James, Simpson, & Wright 1984:202). Within the multicausal model, factors such as academic failure, school isolation, school dropouts within the immediate family, level of parents' education, mutual separation between the child and the school personnel, and the child's low self-esteem have been associated with truancy (Cimmarusti et al. 1984; Barth 1984; Allen-Meares 1987; Washington & Welsh 1995). "The child, family, and the school are all involved in creating a context of truancy, and thus, intervention(s) based on a theory that addresses issues of context and relationship will create more options for the practitioner and increase the possibility of successful outcome" (Cimmarusti et al. 1984:210). Therefore, interventions that target the child, the family, and the school are appropriate.

Literature: Allen-Meares (1987); Washington, & Welsh (1995); Atkinson, Quarrington, & Cyr (1985); Barth (1984); Bell, Rosen, & Dynlacht (1994); Berg & Nursten (1996); Berry & Lizardi (1985); Blagg (1987); Cimmarusti, James, Simpson, & Wright (1984); Cnaan & Seltzer (1989); Lee & Miltenberger (1996); Levine (1984); Taylor & Adelman (1990); Waltzer (1984).

Task Menu   Parents or caregivers

1. *Identify* any medical or transportation problems that may interfere with your child's ability to attend school.

    Elaboration: In high-crime areas, you may be hesitant to allow a younger child to walk to school alone.

Practitioner's Role: You may need to encourage the parents/caregivers to obtain a medical assessment from the family's primary physician if a medical problem is suspected. If walking to school alone is a problem, arrange for an older student to serve as a "walking buddy" to accompany the child to school.

2. *Identify* any patterns or *triggers* to your child's absences and refusal behaviors.

Elaboration: The child may be avoiding certain school days due to tests, a certain class, or assignment(s). He or she may also want to avoid conflicts with a teacher(s) or peer(s) at school.

3. *Identify* any changes in your child's environment.

Elaboration: Examine any losses or transitions, especially recent ones, involving the child, family members, or peers.

Practitioner's Role: You may need to help the child and his or her parents/caregivers to recognize the relevance of recent events through in-depth questioning and the assessment process.

4. *Identify* the role(s) played by your child in the home.

Elaboration: Determine if the child is being kept home or feels that he or she needs to remain at home. For example, he or she may provide some type of assistance to the family by caring for siblings.

Practitioner's Role: Help parents to *identify* the ways in which their needs, family organization, etc. might support the child's truancy. Assist the parents in *identifying* and implementing solutions that enable school attendance. For example, if the child is truant because he or she is staying at home to care for younger siblings, assist the parents in locating alternative child care resources.

5. Initiate and develop effective communication with the child's school and *identify* people there who are able to support your efforts to return the child to school.

Elaboration: It is important to feel that you are supported by the school and not being blamed as you work to help your child return. Effective communication can also help you and others involved in the case work cooperatively.

Practitioner's Role: Because truancy has been associated not only with mutual disengagement between the child and school personnel but also with previous familial experience with truancy and dropping out of school, the relationship between the child/family and the school may be poor initially. Therefore, you may want to facilitate the development of a contract between the parents and the school wherein the responsibilities of each party are defined clearly and amenable to monitoring. For example, one school staff member will monitor the child's attendance and provide encouragement, while one parent will call the school regularly to obtain progress reports. Additionally, school personnel should be encouraged to arrange a role for the child at school that capitalizes on his or her strengths and enables re-engagement, e.g., having him or her assist the school nurse during a free period.

You can help establish effective communication between professionals and parents by including both in conferences to discuss strategies to help the child consistently attend school. School social workers, psychologists, or counselors can also use phone calls and letters to the family and to you when they notice that the child is missing school. Encourage the parents to have the child attend school regularly by contacting them on a regular basis, encouraging and praising their efforts, listening to their concerns, and offering them assistance.

6. Use *contingency management* to encourage your child's attendance at school.

Elaboration: Various *contingency management* techniques can be employed. Shaping techniques involve reinforcing gradual improvements in behavior, e.g., rewarding the child for attending school for longer and longer periods of time (Lee & Miltenberger 1996). Extinction techniques involve the "removal of the reinforcers for the undesirable behavior." For example, the parent is "instructed to ignore the child's arguing, complaints, or tantrums in the morning prior to school. If the child is home from school, the parent should avoid providing the child with attention" (Lee et al. 1996:482–483).

Differential reinforcement of alternative behaviors (DRA) involves rewarding the child for performing desirable alternative behaviors so that they will increase and replace the inappropriate behavior. For example, the parent provides "reinforcers when the child gets out of bed, gets dressed, prepares for school, and goes to school in the morning" (Lee et al. 1996:483).

Contingency contracting involves a negotiated contract between an adult and a child covering the possible rewards and punishments that will be used depending on the child's behaviors, including attending or not attending school.

7. Make time daily to discuss school events and review homework with your child.

Elaboration: It is important to provide the child with the opportunity to discuss any thoughts, feelings, and concerns and to offer assistance with schoolwork. In addition to daily discussions, set aside some time during the week to talk about events and examine the student's accomplishments.

Practitioner's Role: Encourage the family to be receptive to the student's making positive and negative comments about school.

Task Menu Child

1. *Identify* people, situations, contexts that trigger your avoidance of school.

Practitioner's Role: Assist the child in *identifying* the reasons for truancy. Then help him or her *identify* and overcome obstacles to regular school attendance.

2. Create a plan that encourages you to attend school every day.

Elaboration: The plan can help you develop a consistent routine of preparing for school, for example, activities to take place the night before: preparing a school snack and lunch, laying out clothes to be worn the next day, setting the alarm clock, etc. This plan can also help you cope with people, situations, and contexts that trigger your avoidance of school.

Practitioner's Role: If you maximize his or her "perceptions of having made a desirable choice" (Taylor & Adelman 1990:230) and make the child an important part of the plan's development, he or she is more likely to participate in the intervention.

3. *Identify* the consequences of truancy.

4. *Identify* personal goals and determine whether or not school attendance will affect your ability to achieve those goals.

Practitioner's Role: Help the child *identify* personal goals and evaluate how they will be affected if he or she continues to be truant.

5. Enlist the help and support of a friend in the effort to attend school.

Elaboration: A friend who regularly attends school can be a source of support and encouragement, for example by phoning you every morning to encourage school attendance.

Robert Mottola

Self-Esteem, Lack of

"Self-esteem is the way one feels about oneself" (Manaster & Corsini 1994:369); it entails self-acceptance, self-trust, and realistic acceptance of strengths and limitations. Self-esteem comprises a sense of accomplishment and mastery, as well as the sense that others recognize one in a positive way leading to appreciation, dignity, and prestige (Manaster & Corsini 1994). Both high and low self-esteem are the result of ongoing self-evaluations, which are cognitive-affective events.

Bendar and Peterson (1995) have suggested that self-esteem is linked to the individual's coping style in the face of anxiety-provoking situations (e.g., psychological threats). Whereas active coping may leads to positive self-appraisals, inability to cope may result in a disparaged personal identity.

Low self-esteem is a factor in several DSM-IV diagnostic categories, such as major depression and anorexia nervosa (APA 1994). "Individuals who do not value or respect themselves lack self-confidence and struggle with a multitude of self-imposed barriers and limitations" (Sheafor & Horejsi 1997:97). Often they engage in self-defeating behaviors and are vulnerable to exploitation and abuse by others. Assessment of self-esteem includes client reports as well as standardized instruments (e.g., Social Self-Esteem Inventory, Lawson 1979; see also Fischer & Corcoran 1994a, 1994b).

Literature: Anshel (1991); Bendar & Peterson (1995); Bourne (1995); Branden (1994); Friedman (1998); Manaster & Corsini; (1994); Kyle (1991); O'Rourke (1990); Overholser (1996); Scheuer & Pedley (1990); Sheafor & Horejsi (1997).

Task Menu

1. *Learn about* self-esteem—e.g., read <u>The Six Pillars of Self-Esteem</u> (Branden 1994).
2. *Identify* approval-seeking behavior and its negative effects.

   Practitioner's Role: Help the client identify approval-seeking behavior in the session, thereby enhancing both his or her ability to self-observe and the effects of experiential learning. Instruct client in *self-monitoring* to facilitate work done outside the session (e.g., time- or situation-based *logs*, *journals*, audiotapes), which may help the client identify her or his coping style and may be especially useful if he or she has initial difficulty verbalizing directly to you approval-seeking behaviors and their effects.
3. *Identify* and label negative self-evaluations (Bednar & Peterson 1995).

   Elaboration: Work done outside the session (e.g., time- or situation-based *logs*, *journals*, audiotapes) may you identify your negative self-evaluations. You should document cognitions, behaviors, and feelings.
4. Confront unrealistic negative self-evaluations; examine the way in which you think and interpret events.

   Elaboration: This task may include in-session *role play* between you and your practitioner, which can help you learn to tolerate successfully or attenuate the anxiety that occurs with negative self-evaluations. Subsequently, tasks may be planned wherein you enter a situation that typically evokes negative self-evaluations.

   Practitioner's Role: Instruct the client in *progressive relaxation* to help relieve anxiety and stress that occurs with negative self-evaluations.
5. Take the necessary steps to build healthy, positive interactions.

   Elaboration: This may require specific skill building (e.g., assertiveness training, *social skills training*) to enhance coping strategies.

   Practitioner's Role: Instruct the client in being assertive in a polite manner, speaking clearly and audibly, using the proper tone of voice and speech content, listening fully to another individual before replying, developing proper posture and eye contact during discourse. Such skills can lead to successful interactions with others, which in turn can enhance self-esteem. Teaching the client to use *self-reinforcement* after successful interactions with others is also useful. For example, the client might say, "He really understood the intent of my message. I am doing a great job of communicating clearly," or "That group usually ignores what most people have to say. My sincere delivery and appropriate eye contact seemed to make them take notice of my viewpoint in a respectful manner."

6. Put negative events in perspective and look at their positive side (Overholser 1996).

    Practitioner's Role: Use *cognitive restructuring* to assist the client in achieving such a perspective. For instance, he or she could exaggerate a failed test that was worth 20 percent of the grade in a course. Characterizing it as one anxious experience with plenty of room for improvement and suggesting a task to improve study skills, such as studying with a successful student, could turn the experience around to one that actually improves future chances of success. These improved skills could lead to an increased sense of mastery or control, hence increased self-esteem.

7. Be realistic in how you attribute problems affecting you.

    Elaboration: People with low self-esteem are often too ready to blame themselves when things go wrong.

8. Try to develop an internal locus of control.

    Practitioner's Role: Guide the client in interpreting his or her successes as being determined by their own efforts, resources, and abilities, allowing a sense of control. "Individuals with low self-esteem tend to feel that their achievements are based on luck, chance or fate and do not feel control in their lives, thereby weakening their confidence in their ability to succeed in the future" (Friedman 1998).

9. Increase frequency of *self-reinforcement.*

    Practitioner's Role: Instruct the client to use self-rewards or self-praise for all successes, no matter how small they might subjectively seem.

10. *Identify* and modify goals and standards that are unrealistic and undermine positive self-evaluation.

    Practitioner's Role: Use *cognitive restructuring* to assist the client in setting achievable goals. Instruct client in how to evaluate what realistic standards actually are for his or her individual temperament and abilities.

11. Take necessary steps to place yourself in situations where you will have an opportunity to discover and develop your abilities (Sheafor & Horejsi 1997). This may include finding a job, volunteering, joining an organization or a club, taking a class, building a friendship, or developing new hobbies and interests.

12. Participate in a support group, personal growth group, or church group where you will be accepted and respected. Learn that you have much in common with others and that everyone has both strengths and limitations (Sheafor & Horejsi 1997). See also DEPRESSION: ADULT.

Kathryn Baraneckie, Pamela Zettergren, Jennifer Hescheles

Sexual Abuse

Adult Survivor: Repressed Memory Retrieval

People who experience traumatic events and are unable to integrate them into their life experience may repress memories of the events as an adaptive mechanism to allow continued routine functioning. This is particularly true of children who, as victims of sexual abuse, lack developmental awareness of sexual issues and the cognitive ability to make sense of complex and often contradictory emotional messages. Repression of memories is a coping mechanism that acts as a buffer, protecting them from having to deal fully with a terrible event or events they are unable to comprehend.

In adulthood, repressed memories often begin to emerge spontaneously or in the context of treatment for other emotional or physical problems (Courtois 1989; Hindman 1989; Sgroi 1989). In at least 25 percent of all cases of child sexual abuse, victims evidence long-term, devastating consequences (Davenport et al. 1994). Accurate recall and effective emotional processing of the abusive incidents are central to recovery from the trauma (Courtois 1989; Paddison 1993). For many survivors the memory recall process is itself traumatizing; it often means "reliving" abusive episodes, the unexpected intrusion of uncontrollable, debilitating flashbacks into normal daily activities, and/or the return of other symptoms associated with coping with the abuse, e.g., sleep disorders, somatic complaints, eating disorders (Paddison 1993; Ganzarain & Buchele 1988). See also *anxiety: post-traumatic stress disorder (ptsd): adult.*

Literature: Courtois (1988); Hindman (1989); Paddison (1993); Hindman (1989); Davenport, Browne, & Palmer (1994); Ganzarain & Buchele (1988); Zlotnick et al. (1996).

Task Menu
1. Learn about the function of repressed memories, particularly as related to experiences of sexual abuse.

   Elaboration: Sexual abuse survivors are generally not well informed about the protective functions of repressed memories. They feel more "normal" when they are educated about development of repressed memories and the relative commonality of this phenomenon among sexual abuse survivors.

   Practitioner's Role: Retrieval of repressed memories is a difficult and emotionally depleting task. Carefully assess the survivor's readiness for this arduous endeavor. Ideally, he or she should have an emotional support network in place and demonstrate willingness and ability to explore issues related to the sexual abuse. Make periodic depression and suicide risk assessments a routine part of the memory retrieval work. Create a therapeutic environment that is empathic and accepting. It is critical that you demonstrate comfort with sexual abuse issues and refrain from appearing shocked by the disclosures.

Your initial role is to educate the survivor about repressed memories from a strength-based perspective, moving slowly and presenting the material in an empathic manner. Overwhelming a survivor with too much emotionally laden information or presenting it in an emotionally neutral manner may heighten the traumatizing effects of memory recovery, strengthen the client's protective defenses, and create barriers to effective treatment.

2. *Identify triggers* for memory retrieval; *identify* "typical" individual retrieval patterns and actively monitor your own processes.

Elaboration: Each individual has a unique memory retrieval process. Some experience flashbacks triggered by environmental cues. Others experience flashbacks spontaneously with no apparent trigger. Still others retrieve memory fragments in dreams or passing thoughts and must actively search for the missing pieces. These experiences can be frightening, especially for survivors who have a history of feeling vulnerable and who consequently need to feel in control in order to feel safe. Understanding your own process reduces anxiety by making retrieval experiences more predictable.

Practitioner's Role: Use the advantages of objectivity and emotional distance from the memories to point out possible triggers and patterns for the survivor's consideration.

3. Develop strategies to deal with the traumatic impact of memory recurrences.

Elaboration: For most survivors, remembering the abuse involves re-experiencing it in visual, auditory, tactile, and other sensate memories. This is usually emotionally exhausting and depleting. The retrieval process must be paced with the individual's ability to withstand the emotional upheaval that accompanies it. Learn methods of controlling the pace of your own process.

Practitioner's Role: You are responsible for the pace of the retrieval process, to assure the survivor's emotional and physical safety as much as possible. You become a trainer and coach for cognitive control. Techniques you choose should match the individual's personality and level of need, and may include thought stopping, *progressive relaxation, self-verbalization,* and distraction. Also support survivors' efforts to generate their own, personal strategies for controlling the pace. Note: In extreme cases the retrieval process may become so overwhelming for the survivor that it is necessary to postpone or to stop the work. Anticipate this possibility and develop a contingency plan with the survivor.

4. Reconstruct critical memories related to the abuse.

Practitioner's Role: Encourage a patient and calm approach to memory retrieval. Pressure and anxiety impede the process. Also assure the survivor that total recall is probably impossible, especially if he or she was a young child when abused. Partial memories are adequate for identifying and resolving issues related to the abuse. Techniques used to stimulate comprehensive memory retrieval include *journaling,* drawing, visualization, review of cues such as photographs, contact with family members or others who shared childhood experiences, visiting past environments. Use caution in stimulating memories lest a survivor become flooded and overwhelmed. Build safety features into strategies for out-of-session retrievals and closely monitor the client's progress. If the retrieval process affects the survivor's ability to adequately function in normal daily activities, a referral for a psychiatric evaluation may be warranted and the possibility of medication considered. Also be careful not to induce the recall of false memories through suggestion, "filling in blanks" for the client, etc.

5. Identify themes emerging from the memories that represent unresolved emotional issues related to the abuse.

    Practitioner's Role: Help survivors identify what about the memories is most troublesome for them. Point out links; suggest patterns and themes related to possible unresolved issues. These become the focus of ongoing work.

6. Integrate recovered memories into your life experience.

    Elaboration: This is the essence of the recovery process; it begins with initial "telling" about the memories and continues until the survivor feels the issues are adequately resolved.

7. Participate in a survivor's group.

    Elaboration: Such a group provides adult victims with a "safe" place to process thoughts and feelings and a support network of understanding peers who can help between sessions. Hearing stories from other victims can also help normalize and give perspective to your own experiences. One group is Survivors of Incest, aself-help twelve-step program for men and women eighteen and older who have been victims of child sexual abuse and want to be survivors. SIA, P.O. Box 21817, Baltimore, MD 21222–6817; (410) 282–3400.

Margaret Ballentine

Sexual Abuse

Child: Difficulty Discussing Abuse and Expressing Associated Feelings

Disclosure and discussion of experiences of sexual abuse are central to the healing process for child victims (Sgroi 1989; Hindman 1989), because a child's telling and retelling of the "story" organizes his or her thinking and helps make sense of the abusive experiences. Effective cognitive and emotional processing of sexual abuse desensitizes the child to traumatic stimuli associated with it and promotes adaptive integration of the experience into the child's life experience (Deblinger, McLeer, & Henry 1989; deYoung & Corbin 1994), thus preventing devastating recurrence of trauma symptoms in adulthood (Courtois 1992; Davenport, Browne, & Palmer 1994). A child victim's ability to discuss abuse may be inhibited by feelings of guilt and shame and further compromised by lack of vocabulary, deficiency in communication skills, and a family culture of closed or distorted communication patterns (Sgroi 1989; Hindman 1989). Ability to discuss the abuse is also related to developmental issues. Young, preverbal children have evidenced symptoms of sexual trauma and later, when they have acquired verbal skills, disclosed congruent memories of sexual abuse consistent with previous symptomotology (Hewitt 1994). Assisting these young victims presents a special challenge for practitioners who most commonly use verbal methods (Marvesti 1989) and must incorporate nonverbal interventions for effective treatment (Webb 1991). See also ANXIETY: POST-TRAUMATIC STRESS DISORDER (PTSD): CHILD.

Literature: Courtois (1992); Deblinger, McLeer, & Henry (1989); deYoung & Corbin (1994); Hindman (1989); Lutzker (1998); Marvesti (1989); Sgroi (1989); Webb (1991).

Task Menu Child
1. Express feelings without losing control over your behavior.
   Elaboration: You may have difficulty controlling behavioral outbursts when expressing powerful emotions. This can be frightening and increase feelings of helplessness and vulnerability.
   Practitioner's Role: Set and enforce appropriate, firm, consistent behavioral limits with the child and encourage development of internal control mechanisms.
2. Learn age-appropriate language for body parts and sexual activities.
   Elaboration: This language must be consistent with the developmental level of the child and the culture of the child's family. Often families have special words for genitals and body functions associated with them.
   Practitioner's Role: Demonstrate comfort in openly discussing sexual issues. Additionally, refrain from appearing shocked upon the child's disclosure of sexual activities, as this may be construed by the child as negative judgment of him- or herself. Anatomically correct dolls and drawings are helpful aids.
3. Learn appropriate labels for distinct emotions.
   Elaboration: Try not to lump emotions together into global good-bad categories. For example, distinguishing and labeling anxiety (worry) as different from sadness is helpful later in treatment when it is important to describe and partialize complex, ambivalent responses to the sexual abuse.

Practitioner's Role: Charts of cartoon characters manifesting various emotions can form the basis of therapeutic activities to acquaint the child with names of emotions. These charts can be used effectively with children through adolescence.

4. *Learn about* the concept of ambivalence.

Elaboration: You may have mixed feelings in response to sexual abuse incidents yet not understand the possibility of having two conflicting emotions simultaneously. Consequently, you may feel something is wrong with your thinking, doubt yourself, and feel inadequate.

Practitioner's Role: Use examples that the child brings to session to illustrate this principle.

5. Draw pictures of yourself, family members, and your family's residence and tell stories about each.

Elaboration: This activity gives practice with creative expression and storytelling not directly related to the abuse. The drawings and stories also have assessment value for the practitioner.

6. Construct stories related to the abuse and communicate them through verbal and nonverbal means.

Elaboration: Choose a way of "telling" that is comfortable. This will vary with respect to level of development, creativity, and interests. You may draw; develop dramas with puppets, dolls or other toys; write a story or tell a story to a tape recorder; tell a story while engaged in other play (such as building with blocks); make up a "story" song; write a poem; etc.

Practitioner's Role: Assist the child in finding comfortable means of expression. Encourage and validate his or her creative expression.

7. Express emotions associated with the stories.

Practitioner's Role: Provide appropriate media (dolls, sand tray, drawing materials) for emotional expression. Carefully monitor the child's escalation of affect to minimize the possibility of trauma. Assure the child's safety in the event of loss of control.

8. When possible, attend a peer group for victims of sexual abuse.

Elaboration: Participating in a group helps reduce social isolation, "normalize" experiences, and detoxify "telling" about the abuse.

Task Menu Parents

1. Recognize the child's emotions in ordinary situations and help him or her to label them appropriately.

Practitioner's Role: Parents may need to be educated to accurately identify emotional cues given by their child, especially nonverbal cues.

2. Openly and appropriately discuss details of the abuse with the child.

Elaboration: Parents may unwittingly respond emotionally to details, which the child may misinterpret as blaming him or her for the behavior.

Practitioner's Role: Beginning these discussions in your presence enables you to model appropriate supportive responses to the child.

3. Set and consistently enforce appropriate behavioral limits for the child so as to avoid negative consequences from emotional expression that may escalate.

   Practitioner's Role: You may need to educate the parent about what limits are developmentally appropriate and realistic for the child, given the circumstances of his or her abusive experiences.
4. Communicate the distinction between emotion and behavior to the child so that he or she is supported in expressing emotions but learns to control negative behaviors in response to those emotions.

Margaret Ballentine, Terry Miller

Sexual Abuse

Child: Lack of Safety in Home and Treatment Environments

Sexually abused children often experience enormous upheaval following disclosure of their experiences. The trauma of the abuse itself is compounded by the intervention of social service and criminal justice systems, throwing families into chaos and leaving the child victim feeling responsible for causing problems, guilty, anxious, and ashamed. Before any meaningful treatment of the child's trauma-related issues can occur, the family situation must be stabilized, the nonoffending parent must create a secure environment in the household for the victim, and the victim must be able to develop a trusting relationship with the practitioner assisting the family (Sgroi 1989; Hindman 1989). Parental support and involvement in the therapeutic process significantly reduces trauma effects for the victim (Wyatt & Mickey 1988; Deblinger, McLeer, & Henry 1990; Sgroi 1989). Dealing with social service and legal systems is frequently confusing and overwhelming in the crisis of disclosure of sexual abuse. The practitioner may need to educate the family about roles of professionals and agencies involved, assist in opening and clarifying communications between systems, and advocate for the child and the family with other agencies.

   Literature: Deblinger, McLeer, & Henry (1990); Hindman (1989); Lutzker (1998); Sgroi (1989).

Task Menu Child
1. Learn which adults you can trust.

   Elaboration: Traumatized children are likely to distrust others, especially adults. In treatment they will be able to disclose fears and feelings of vulnerability only if they are able to trust the practitioner.

   Practitioner's Role: Engage the child in interaction in a manner that minimizes the power differential between you and the child. You may equalize height with him or her by sitting in a lower chair or sitting on the floor. Use language appropriate for the developmental level of the child; additionally, avoid a strongly authoritative stance unless required to help the child control behavior.

2. Experience personal power by making choices.

Elaboration: You may feel vulnerable and powerless, although these feelings are confusing and difficult to understand and articulate. Appropriate use of power and control will become central themes in treatment.

Practitioner's Role: Provide the child with opportunities to exercise his or her own power within the context of a session. For example, the child may choose where you should sit, how play materials are arranged, which activity (media) to engage in (when choice is appropriate), if a parent or other supporting adult should be present.

3. *Identify* changes in the family and your living situation since disclosure.

Elaboration: Initially focusing on concrete environmental issues is less toxic than immediate focus on trauma related specifically to the sexual abuse incidents. This provides the opportunity to develop trust in the therapeutic relationship with the practitioner.

4. Express feelings (including concerns and fears) associated with environmental changes since disclosure.

Elaboration: Evaluate your relationship with the offender and the current status of contact with him or her.

5. *Identify* safety needs related to environmental changes.

6. [with parent(s)] Develop a strategy or strategies to address safety needs.

Elaboration: These strategies will be very case specific and directly connected to your fears. For example, you may need reassurance that you will be protected from chance contact with the offender. You may need the security of a nighttime ritual that could include leaving lights on and checking household locks. An advantage of having parents work *with* the child on developing these strategies is that the parents have the opportunity to demonstrate their ability to protect the child from further abuse, a critical factor in the recovery process. Also, this activity gives both parents and child practice using communication and *problem-solving* skills.

Practitioner's Role: Educate child and parent with regard to steps in problem solving and then model effective problem-solving skills as you assist them in this task.

Task Menu Parents

1. *Learn about* dynamics and effects typical in situations of child sexual abuse.

Practitioner's Role: Educate the parent and normalize aspects of the situation.

2. Evaluate your relationship with the offender.

Elaboration: Children are most often sexually abused by someone closely associated with the family. Nonoffending parents are frequently emotionally attached and otherwise dependent upon the abuser. Disclosure of sexual abuse by the child usually means that the nonoffending parent must choose between the abuser and the child. If the parent is ambivalent or remains loyal to the offender, the safety of the child is in serious jeopardy. Clarifying the position of the nonoffending parent is often a complex, lengthy process. The child may need to reside outside the home until this issue is resolved and the child's safety can be assured.

Practitioner's Role: You may need to maintain a rather authoritative stance during this assessment process. Advocate on behalf of the child's safety and emphasize the importance of the parent's role.

3. State clearly and repeatedly your belief in the child's honesty with respect to disclosure of sexual abuse.

4. Communicate openly and appropriately with the child about the sexual abuse.

Elaboration: Communications in families where sexual abuse occurs are often ineffective. Parents may not know how to listen or interpret nonverbal messages, and may not have age-appropriate language for communicating with the child.

Practitioner's Role: Educate parents regarding effective communication skills and model these in sessions with the parents and the child.

5. Demonstrate your ability to protect the child by assuming appropriate parental roles and modeling effective parenting and problem-solving skills.

Elaboration: Boundaries in families where sexual abuse occurs are often blurred. The child's safety hinges on the ability of the nonoffending parent to assume an appropriate protective role.

Margaret Ballentine, Terry Miller

Sexual Abuse

Child: Maladaptive Behaviors Resulting from Abuse

Child victims of sexual abuse frequently manifest behavioral symptoms (Sgroi 1989; Hindman 1989), many of which are consistent with post-traumatic stress disorder (PTSD) and include: fears manifested in nightmares and other sleep disorders; intense anxiety; bedwetting; withdrawal; obsessive behaviors and hypervigilance; phobic responses to environmental triggers; dissociative episodes; and acting out behaviors such as temper tantrums and inappropriate sexual behavior, e.g., excessive masturbation and sexual victimization of others (Deblinger et al. 1990; Sgroi 1989). Even pre-verbal abused children manifest behavioral responses that must be addressed (Hewitt 1994). Ineffective management of these behaviors by custodial adults (usually parents) often has devastating emotional consequences for victims as they grow to adulthood. Guilt and shame associated with the abuse itself is compounded and reinforced by guilt and blame for "bad" behaviors that are difficult for the child to understand and control (Courtois 1989; Hindman 1989). Treatment of child victims for maladaptive behaviors requires close collaboration between parents and practitioner. The practitioner assists the child in uncovering the connection between the behaviors and the abuse and then helps the family develop strategies to deal constructively with the behaviors (Sgroi 1989; Deblinger et al. 1990). Cognitive-behavioral methods have been effective in reducing behavioral problems for child victims (Deblinger et al. 1990).

Literature: American Psychiatric Association (1994); Courtois (1988); Deblinger, McLeer, & Henry (1989); Hewitt (1994); Hindman (1989); Marvesti (1989); Sgroi (1989).

Task Menu Child

1. *Identify* behaviors that are problematic and the negative consequences associated with each of them.

    Elaboration: You may be confused about the appropriateness of certain behaviors and may not label them as troublesome; you may see them as concerns that grown-ups have.

    Practitioner's Role: In order to prevent a child from internalizing negative feelings of self-worth, it is important for you to demonstrate calm acceptance of the behaviors and assist the child in discovering strategies to avoid negative consequences associated with them. Model appropriate responses to the behaviors for the child as well as for the parent.

2. *Learn about* ways in which your behavior may be related to having been sexually abused.

    Elaboration: Maladaptive behaviors may be viewed as defense mechanisms, efforts to make sense of and to cope with the stress and confusion associated with sexual abuse and its disclosure. You may be unaware of the connection. Making the link between behavior and abuse serves as a way of talking about the abuse somewhat indirectly, a form of gradual *exposure* and desensitization to the trauma.

    Practitioner's Role: Guide the client through this discovery process, educating him or her as needed about dynamics of sexual abuse and typical responses to it, thereby normalizing the child's particular responses. Drawing, *role play,* sand trays and other play therapy methods are helpful in engaging a child in discussion.

3. *Identify* alternate coping strategies to replace or modify maladaptive existing ones.

    Practitioner's Role: Educate the child about appropriate, acceptable limits for behaviors. Depending upon his or her developmental level and motivation, make suggestions about acceptable alternatives. However, it is important to promote the child's sense of empowerment and problem-solving competence, so guard against becoming overly helpful or directive. For example, a highly sexualized child victim may be masturbating on the playground. You may explain to the child that masturbation is not a "bad" thing to do, but it is not an acceptable activity in public. Further, you may suggest that the child choose an alternate, more private, time and place for this behavior. The child is then empowered to generate some specific ideas him- or herself.

4. [with parental collaboration] Implement alternate strategies; evaluate and modify as necessary.

   Elaboration: This process is ongoing until the maladaptive behavior is extinguished. Since behavioral responses to traumatic events, especially sexual abuse, tend to be particularly persistent, many alternatives and modifications may be necessary before the behaviors are reduced to acceptable levels.

   Practitioner's Role: It is important to educate the child and the family about realistic expectations for change. While remaining optimistic, support and reinforce change efforts and encourage client patience and persistence.

5. If possible, attend a peer group of sexual abuse victims.

   Elaboration: Peer group participation normalizes behavioral responses to sexual abuse for child and adolescent victims, and also provides a wealth of ideas for alternative responses, reinforcement of positive change, and opportunities to practice communications and problem-solving skills.

Task Menu Parents

1. *Learn about* the dynamics of sexual abuse and its effects on children.

   Practitioner's Role: Assess the parents' awareness and educate them in areas of knowledge deficiency or misconception.

2. Learn behavioral principles essential for understanding and appropriately responding to the child's maladaptive, sexual abuse-related behaviors.

   Elaboration: Learn to recognize the meaning of a child's behavior as it is associated with the sexual abuse, e.g., a frustration-induced tantrum is likely to be a response to a sense of helplessness and vulnerability brought on by fear of impending failure (frustration at task). You must then address the fear of failure and feelings of vulnerability rather than simply controlling the tantrum.

   Practitioner's Role: Become an educator and guide to demystify the child's behavior.

3. Assist the child and practitioner in the process of identifying problem behaviors, developing alternative behavioral strategies, and implementing those strategies (see tasks 1, 3, and 4 above).

4. Learn and implement effective behavioral management methods.

Elaboration: Practice effective parenting techniques, including setting appropriate limits, consistently reinforcing those limits, maintaining open and clear communication with the child, supporting positive change efforts, and positively reinforcing appropriate behaviors.

Practitioner's Role: Assess the parents' ability to practice effective parenting. In some cases a referral to a *parent training* group may be indicated.

5. Communicate the child's emotional and behavioral needs to the school and other caretaking environments, educating and advocating as necessary.

Practitioner's Role: Assess the parents' capacity to do this and assist in parental skill building as indicated. In some cases, you may have to advocate on the child's behalf and role model for the parents until their skills are adequate for this task.

6. When possible, participate in a parent program.

Elaboration: Since parents of sexually abused children are often socially isolated and lacking in adequate parenting skills, a parent-focused peer group is an excellent adjunct to individual and family work. Ideally this would be a group for parents of sexually abused children. When this is not possible, a *parent training* group or any parent support group can provide opportunities to share frustrations, get support and suggestions from peers, reduce isolation and build *social skills,* and improve overall feelings of adequacy. See ANXIETY: POST-TRAUMATIC STRESS DISORDER (PTSD): ADULT.

Margaret Ballentine

Sexual Abuse

Child: Revictimization

Individuals sexually abused as children appear to be at greater risk of revictimization later in childhood and in adulthood as well. Among female incest victims in a randomly selected sample, Russell (1986) found 82 percent of the women had histories of serious sexual revictimization. Level of long-term traumatic effects of abuse is highly correlated with the number of revictimizations (Davenport, Browne, & Palmer 1994; Russell 1986). Victims are chosen by offenders because they have some vulnerability (naiveté due to developmental level or intellectual impairment, an eagerness to please, need for attention and affection, inability to be assertive, etc.) (Hindman 1989). Addressing these vulnerabilities, establishing appropriate protective measures, and enhancing assertiveness reduce risk of future victimizations (Sgroi 1988; Hindman 1989). Dealing effectively with a child victim of sexual abuse to prevent further abuse minimizes longer-term negative effects. Mobilizing parental resources to monitor safety factors in the child's life and to reinforce learned safety skills is critical (Sgroi 1989).

Literature: Deblinger, McLeer, & Henry (1990); Hindman (1989); Hindman (1985); Kellogg & Hoffman (1997); Sgroi (1989).

Task Menu Child

1. Learn the differences between types of touching—good touch, bad touch, secret touch—as well as the concept of a touching continuum.

   Practitioner's Role: Children may experience sexual abuse as physically pleasant but emotionally confusing. The concept of bad touch does not fit their experience, and secrecy is a major dimension of sexual abuse. Consequently, for many child victims, associating the concept of secret touch with the imperative not to tell is more congruent with their experience. The Very Touching Book (Hindman 1985) is an excellent resource for work with young children. Modifications can be made for use with older children.

2. *Identify* people who can be trusted to listen in each area of daily life (home, daycare, school, etc.).

3. Understand the right to say no, and learn and practice appropriate assertiveness in daily situations.

4. Learn the function of "secrets" in situations of sexual abuse.

5. Identify warning signs of potential abusive behavior of offenders, e.g., giving gifts without reason, playing "secret" games.

6. Imagine possible scenarios and practice protective responses through *role plays.*

   Practitioner's Role: In *role plays,* it can be effective for you to assume the child's role so that the child victim can "correct" the role-played child's mistakes.

7. [with parent] Select and then actively participate in an activity that promotes competence, achievement, and confidence.

   Practitioner's Role: This task empowers the child to pursue an area of interest in which she or he feels comfortable and is likely to participate and succeed. Parental involvement and support are important for assuring the feasibility of implementing the plan. The activity should be age-appropriate and ideally (though not necessarily) include contact with peers under adult supervision.

Task Menu Parents

1. Monitor the child's environment for potential risks; this includes adequately supervising play activities.

2. Minimize the risk of future abuse by removing potential hazards.

   Elaboration: This requires reducing the opportunities for possible offenders to access the child: restricting overnight guests, insisting that the child be accompanied by other children if going someplace with an adult who is not absolutely trusted, not permitting children of different sexes or wide age differences to use the same bed or share a bedroom.

3. Carefully screen and instruct all caregivers about expectations for care.
4. Do not permit the child to be alone in public places.
5. Maintain open communication with the child about his or her fears and general safety issues.
6. Assist the child in practicing appropriate assertive behaviors in daily experiences.

Margaret Ballentine

Sibling Conflict

Fighting, quarrelling, and other forms of conflict among siblings sometimes lead to physical violence. National surveys of family violence (e.g., Gelles & Straus 1988) have found that physical aggression among siblings is many times more common than violence between spouses. Sibling conflict may contribute to conflict with peers and subsequently with spouses and others. Studies have suggested that the quality of parent-child interaction may be predictive of sibling conflict (Johnston & Freeman 1998).

Literature: Felson (1983); Felson & Russo (1988); Johnston & Freeman (1998); Perozynski & Kramer (1999); Reid & Donovan (1990); Steinmetz (1978).

Task Menu Parents
1. *Learn about* sibling conflict.
    Elaboration: A good book for parents is *Raising Cain (and Abel Too)* (McDermott 1980).
2. Apply a consistent set of rules for handling disputes among siblings and for dealing with issues that might provoke sibling conflict.
    Elaboration: Negotiate differences of opinion in how conflicts among your children should be dealt with.
3. Develop procedures to prevent conflict.
    Elaboration: For example, keep lists of whose turn it is to do chores, choose TV programs, etc. (Sloane 1988). Keep a supply of videotapes that the children might like to watch together. Suggest they watch one when things get tense (Johnston & Freeman 1998).
4. Teach children *social skills* for interacting with one another.
    Elaboration: Such skills might include sharing, accepting refusals, and negotiating disputes (Tiedeman & Johnston 1992).
5. Use *contigency management* to prevent and control sibling conflict.
    Elaboration: Give children positive reinforcement for avoiding conflict for agreed-on periods of time as well as for prosocial behavior toward one another. Ignore conflicts that seem aimed at getting your attention.
6. Present a unified front to children in handling disputes.

Practitioner's Role: See the parents together. Use *role play* with parents to practice how they will handle disputes among children.
7. Help children try to talk out conflicts.

Task Menu Siblings
1. *Identify* sources of conflict and work out rules for handling them.
2. Negotiate conflicts when they arise.
    Practitioner's Role: Have siblings negotiate at least one conflict in session (see COUPLE OR FAMILY CONFLICT).
3. Jointly create a list of six to eight things that you agree you should not be allowed to do to each other (Laurie 1998).
4. Make a list of things "I wish my sibling understood about me" (Laurey 1998).
5. Make a list of things that you like about your sibling (Laurey 1998).
    Practitioner's Role: The list (as well as the lists from the preceding tasks) can be done or shared in the session and serve as a basis for discussion among the siblings.
6. Leave the scene rather than fight.
7. Develop and maintain a truce.
    Practitioner's Role: The older sibling may be given responsibility for doing this. Writing out the truce, having siblings sign it, and other rituals may be helpful.

Stress Management

College Students

Stressful situations can be defined as those that threaten or are perceived to threaten a person's well-being or subsequently hinder his or her coping abilities (Weiten 1995). Many college students frequently experience a considerable amount of stress (Altmaier 1983). Stress-inducing factors include difficulties in coping with academic work, lack of routine, worry about interpersonal and financial problems, and strains resulting from combining academic and paid employment.

Literature: Weiten (1995).

Task Menu
1. Create daily routines.
    Practitioner's Role: Help the client establish routines. Discuss how they can help reduce the amount of physical and mental energy expended each day.

2. Practice managing your time and setting priorities.

Practitioner's Role: Help the client schedule blocks of time to study for exams and complete assignments. Help him or her realize how this can avert potentially stressful situations. Rehearse prioritizing based upon the amount of time required to complete assignments as well as their due dates.

3. Designate one day per week as a day of rest.

Practitioner's Role: Help the client make a list of all possible activities that he or she finds relaxing. Discuss the benefits and purpose of such a day.

4. Simplify study sessions and assignments.

Practitioner's Role: Explore with the client different techniques to reduce study sessions and assignments into smaller, manageable parts. Help the client practice more efficient study skills as well as more efficient approaches to completing assignments.

5. Ask for assistance from others.

Practitioner's Role: Discuss with the client how people can be resources. Help him or her make a list of people who would be valuable and reliable sources of assistance. *Role play* with client occasions where he or she will ask for help from others.

6. Recognize that you will not attain perfection in every academic endeavor.

Practitioner's Role: Discuss the client's feelings when perfection is not achieved. Validate those feelings and normalize imperfection.

7. Be sure to get enough sleep and consume enough food to adequately function.

Practitioner's Role: Help the client become aware of the impacts of sleep and food deprivation and recognize that these deprivations can make him or her more vulnerable to stress.

8. Choose nondistracting study environments.

Practitioner's Role: Explore with the client what he or she believes to be distracting. Help identify less distracting study environments.

Brian Friedlander

Stress Management

In the Workplace

Stressful situations can be defined as those that threaten or are perceived to threaten a person's well-being or subsequently hinder his or her coping abilities (Weiten 1995). Major types of stress at the workplace include co-worker or supervisor conflict and job pressure (Weiten 1995).

Literature: Apgar & Nicholson Callahan (1982); Lehrer & Woolfolk (1993); Weiten (1995).

Task Menu Co-worker or supervisor conflict
1. Speak up about petty annoyances while respecting other people's feelings.
   Practitioner's Role: Gather information concerning the activities that annoy the client, then *role play* a hypothetical but possible situation in the workplace, where you demonstrate annoying activities and encourage the client to verbally express his or her discomfort with them.
2. Develop co-worker support networks to help in sharing workloads.
   Practitioner's Role: Help the client to accurately assess his or her co-workers' work habits and assets. Then help client initiate a team-oriented approach with those co-workers he or she finds compatible.
3. Go out to lunch with a co-worker.
4. Develop with co-workers your own brand of happy hour or celebrate birthdays or other events with them as a break in the routine.

Task Menu Job pressure
1. Organize your work by setting priorities.
   Practitioner's Role: Rehearse prioritizing based upon what the client finds to be important.
2. Write down tasks that you have to do.
   Practitioner's Role: Practice making lists with the client. Exercises comparing client memory with client-made lists can be helpful in revealing the benefits of writing down tasks.
3. Do not try to be perfect by doing everything right at all times.
   Practitioner's Role: Discuss with the client his or her feelings and alternatives when perfection is not achieved. Normalize imperfection.
4. Do not try to do two or more things at once.
   Practitioner's Role: Encourage the client to consider occasions when he or she has attempted to complete several tasks at once. If applicable, discuss how such attempts have hindered client's capacity to complete just one of the tasks. Exercises in which you ask the client to complete two or more tasks simultaneously may prove insightful for him or her.
5. Consider occasionally coming in earlier or staying later instead of taking your work home with you.
6. Consider planning the use of uninterrupted blocks of time for big jobs or a collection of smaller jobs.
   Practitioner's Role: Help the client recognize the value of time management instruments such as daily logs, planners, and calendars.
7. Take a ten- or twenty-minute meditation or exercise break during lunchtime.
8. Monitor your work-rest-recreation balance. Make changes as needed.

Practitioner's Role: Assist the client in creating a daily pie chart with the goal of creating an optimal balance of time devoted to work, rest, and recreation.
9. Restrict telephone calls by having them held or by simply closing your door when you are busy or need to concentrate.

Brian Friedlander

Suicide Prevention

There are three categories of suicidal behavior: suicidal ideations that can vary from fleeting thoughts that life is not worth living to an intense delusional preoccupation with self-destruction; attempted suicide, which can vary from suicidal gestures to unsuccessful attempts; and suicide itself.

Depending on the study consulted, suicide is either the eighth or the tenth leading cause of death in the United States. Many individuals at one time or another consider or attempt suicide (Ivanoff & Smyth 1992), and it is increasingly common in many developing countries (Rihmer 1996). Caucasians have a higher rate of suicide than African Americans, and Caucasians sixty-five and older have higher rates than younger people, with males aged eighty to eighty-four having the highest rates. Rates remain relatively constant throughout life for racial minorities, peaking at twenty-five to thirty-four years. Among youths aged fifteen to nineteen, suicide is the second leading cause of death (Ivanoff & Smyth 1992). Suicide rates have increased dramatically for adolescents in the past few decades (Garland & Zigler 1993), by an estimated 300 percent in the last thirty years (Schwartz & Schwartz 1993).

Males commit suicide four times more often than females (Ivanoff & Smyth 1992), perhaps because the methods they select are deadlier—e.g., guns (Isometsa et al. 1994; Lester 1995). Attempted suicides are estimated to be higher by about a three to one ratio for females, compared to males.

Linehan (1981) suggests that four variables in social environments are linked to suicidal behavior. The first is lack of social support, which might be a problem when an individual is retired or unemployed, of immigrant status, shares few characteristics with his or her neighbors, lives alone, or has a hostile or even nonexistent support network (Ivanoff & Smyth 1992). Wandrei (1985) suggests that women who attempt and then succeed at suicide are more isolated than other women and may lack help from service providers. The second risk factor is high negative stress, such as that which accompanies loss or negative life events (e.g., events labeled as distressing or uncontrollable by the client). The third factor is knowledge of others using suicide attempts to solve problems, with a positive outcome. The fourth factor is the expectation of positive consequences for suicidal behavior (for instance, improved family interaction), which could increase the number of attempts and result in suicide.

Environmental settings that may be connected with suicidal vulnerability are mental health and counseling agencies; public assistance or child welfare offices; institutions, such as jails, hospitals, nursing homes, and juvenile detention centers. Personal attitudes and abilities that seem to predict suicide risk include hopelessness, self-negativity, impulsiveness, conceptual disorganization, "all or nothing" thinking, and poor problem-solving performance (Hughes & Neimeyer 1993; Weishaar & Beck 1992). Correlates of increased suicide risk include previous suicide attempts, substance abuse, alcoholism, psychiatric disorders, and physical illness, whether terminal, chronic, or acute. Teenagers who have committed suicide have sometimes had learning disorders or shown signs of antisocial behavior.

Practitioners will encounter clients who have attempted suicide (an intentional, but failed effort to die) or other nonfatal suicidal behaviors, such as suicidal ideation (thinking of suicide), suicide verbalization (talking about suicide), suicide threats (expressing to others that one plans or is preparing to engage in an act of self-harm), and suicide gestures (acts of self-harm where the intention to die is low). Suicidal intent, or how serious a person is about achieving death, is an important factor in choosing an appropriate course of management and intervention (Ivanoff & Smyth 1992).

Literature: Diekstra (1992); Hughes & Neimeyer (1993); Ivanoff & Smyth (1992); Jacobs (1999); Lester (1994); Maris (1995); Overholser (1995); Shankman (1994); Weishaar & Beck (1992). Stillion & McDowell (1991) examine suicide from a life span perspective. Berman & Jobes (1995); Coggan & Norton (1994); Garland & Zigler (1993); Ladame (1992); Meiffren (1993); Schwartz & Schwartz (1993). Spirito & Overholser (1993) focus on adolescent suicide in particular. Felthous (1994) covers jailhouse suicide prevention. Marzuk (1994) discusses suicide and terminal illness. Wasserman (1993) deals with alcohol and suicidal behavior. Henriksson (1993) discusses mental disorders and comorbidity with suicide. Osgood (1991) covers suicide prevention in the elderly.

Task Menu

1. Develop a safety plan, which can be in the form of a verbal or written contract to contact the practitioner, another stipulated service provider, friend, relative, or neighbor when you feel strong urges to harm yourself.

   Elaboration: Identify someone with whom you can talk or who will stay with you until the suicidal crisis is handled.

   Practitioner's Role: After getting a release of information and clearly identifying what situations will require consultation with others, make certain that the designated individuals are likely to be reachable and willing and able to stay with the client until the crisis passes. Find out if they are capable of assessing whether the client can maintain control and willing and able to call emergency services. Discuss who will be included in the safety plan—for example, the city police department, hospital emergency room staff, local mental health crisis line, halfway house staff, or day treatment staff, in addition to the primary practitioner. Each individual needs to have a clear understanding of the role he or she will fill and under optimal circumstances should be involved in the development of the plan.

Additionally, discuss with the client and the individuals involved in the safety plan what kind of situations may require hospitalization, voluntary or involuntary (for instance, when the client has a psychiatric disorder that is linked to increased suicide risk—e.g., delusional disorders, depression, schizophrenia, schizoaffective disorders, panic disorders—and that disorder is in an acute phase, hospitalization may be the best choice). Also, go over negative consequences of hospitalization (e.g., social stigma, potentially unfavorable treatment by staff, and the client's feeling of loss of control) with the chosen individual(s). Should client refuse to agree to a safety plan, suggest a brief voluntary hospitalization as a self-initiated way to help regain control (Ivanoff & Smyth 1992).

2. Make up a "crisis card" (Ivanoff & Smyth 1992).

Elaboration: This is a business-card sized list of phone numbers of your emergency contacts and of coping strategies tailored specifically to help you maintain control. It is meant to be carried at all times.

Practitioner's Role: Make sure that the help listed is accessible and that expectations concerning the client's response to strong suicidal urges are clear.

3. Answer the question, "Who would find you?" (Holman 1997).

Elaboration: This question helps identify salient interpersonal conflicts and social supports. It also suggests directions for reparative and preventive interventions and helps increase awareness of the reality of suicide. Addressing the question helps release emotions and tends to generate a sense of hope.

Practitioner's Role: During assessment determine the client's coping resources and cognitive strengths. Use *cognitive restructuring* to handle cognitive distortions that are contributing to suicidal ideation and behaviors. Identify what changes the client desires and how he or she will recognize that the problem is rectified or different goals of treatment are met. Have the client commit to attending sessions and work actively to meet the goals or resolve the problems jointly agreed on.

4. *Identify triggers* to feeling suicidal.

Elaboration: Use *self-monitoring* by keeping a diary or chart of the times when you feel suicidal. Notice who was with you or whether you were alone, what you were doing and thinking, and where you were.

Practitioner's Role: Ask, "What happens just before you reach a point where you feel like hurting yourself? What thoughts do you have? What causes you to give up or feel hopeless?" Review charts and diary in session.

5. *Identify* important reasons for living, such as supportive others and hopes for the future.

   Elaboration: It is important to have a list to look at when you are feeling suicidal. Memory is thought to be linked to affect, and when you feel negative you may not have access to important positive memories.

   Practitioner's Role: Have the client rehearse the thought, "There are options to suicide, I just can't think of them right now." This can help with possible impulsiveness and may reduce hopelessness (Ivanoff & Smyth 1992).

6. *Identify* if the person, situation, or event that leads to feeling or behaving in a suicidal manner is temporary or permanent.

   Elaboration: Most problems with people, situations, and events have solutions—or at least there are usually ways to get around them. Suicide is a permanent act. Ask yourself, "Is a permanent act called for in this case, or will some other kind of act get the results I want?"

   Practitioner's Role: Adopt and convey to the client a problem-solving set or perspective toward suicidal behavior, as suicidal behavior is considered a maladaptive response to some other problem (Ivanoff & Smyth 1992). This can be done by explaining to the client that the intent they had (to end the pain) was a healthy response, but their choice of how to end it was too drastic. Emphasize that whatever problems the client is experiencing, there are solutions.

7. *Identify* goals that would be achieved if you behaved in a suicidal manner.

   Elaboration: This is a way to identify what is called secondary gain. You may be using suicide in a manipulative fashion modeled from others to accomplish goals that seem impossible otherwise. For instance, if a suicidal gesture mobilizes significant others, it may only be for the short term. Look at a possible outcome: significant others may over time become hostile and withdraw support.

8. *Reflect on* ways to meet these goals without behaving in a suicidal manner.

   Elaboration: Suicidal behavior is considered an inappropriate way to express emotional reactions and needs, so think about alternative solutions that are considered socially appropriate.

   Practitioner's Role: Have the client write out pros and cons of each action taken to meet his or her goals. Model problem-solving skills and behavior to broaden the client's range of felt options. Suggest and help client create alternative solutions to manipulating others with suicidal behavior. Use *role play* in session to help him or her become familiar and comfortable with alternative behaviors.

9. Investigate if medication would be useful for improving your mood or cognitions.

   Practitioner's Role: Establish communication with the prescribing physician to assist in balancing the need for medication with client impulsiveness and the possibility of a lethal self-overdose. Possible solutions would be to discuss with the client the possibility of limiting the number of pills in each prescription or having others store and dispense the medication if the client believes there is a chance of impulsive behavior at some future point.

10. Consider if a partial hospitalization program, substance abuse treatment, family therapy, supportive or supervised housing, emergency food or shelter are needed to control suicidal feelings or behaviors.

11. If you are uncomfortable with or lacking in social skills, work on improving or developing them.

    Practitioner's Role: *Role play* relevant situations that the client identifies as feeling awkward or uncomfortable using principals of *social skills training.* For instance, if the client feels taken advantage of by others and that leads to depression and suicidal ideation, have client practice graciously refusing another's request or demand and then rehearse how to handle the situation if the other person continues to pressure him or her (conflict resolution skills). If introducing him- or herself to others is a problem, role play that and what he or she can discuss after the introduction.

12. Develop social contacts by becoming involved in community activities or support groups.

    Practitioner's Role: Offer suggestions by looking at local community resource references with the client.

13. Ask relatives, friends, or other social contacts for support and attention.

    Elaboration: Individuals who commit suicide are less likely than the general population to ask for support or attention (Ivanoff & Smyth 1992).

14. Schedule activities that you experience as pleasurable.

    Elaboration: Ask yourself, "What do I need to do for myself to get through this situation or event?" and then go ahead and give yourself permission to do it.

15. If you have been diagnosed with a psychiatric disorder that is known in some cases to carry an increased suicide risk (major depression, bipolar disorder, and schizophrenia are among the diagnostic groups at highest risk) and have been feeling depressed or hopeless or behaving in an emotionally isolating way, take steps to reconnect with your practitioner or support group.

    Elaboration: Many suicidal clients leave treatment prematurely with dire consequences, so it is important to return when you begin to have trouble managing suicidal correlates like depression and feeling hopeless.

    Practitioner's Role: In working with suicidal individuals, follow-up letters, phone calls, and home visits are recommended (Berman & Jobes 1994; Ivanoff & Smyth 1992). Litman (1995) suggests low-intensity contact with practitioners for many troubled suicidal individuals, rather than hospitalization.

Malsuk Yoo, Pamela Zettergren

Teen Pregnancy: Prevention of

Pregnancy, birth rates, and abortion among teenage girls are higher in the United States than in any other industrialized Western nation, despite comparable or lower rates of sexual activity (Warren 1992). The birth rate for young teens has been steadily rising, although it may now be leveling off. Both the short- and long-term effects of teenage pregnancy on mother, child, and society are enormous. Pregnant teens are more likely to have low birth weight babies, not to complete high school, and to be single parents. Both the teens and their children are at risk for a whole host of difficulties across life areas.

Teenage years demarcate a time of opportunity and risk, when many behaviors are experimented with and established, including sexual intercourse and use of alcohol and drugs. Because this stage of development is so influential, it is a critical time to address issues of prevention. Providing support to the teen and identifying potential disruptions in lifestyle are useful interventions (Cervera 1993).

Literature: Boyer (1997); Cervera (1993); Moyse-Steinburg (1990); Postrado & Nicholson (1992); Rodriguez & Moore (1995); Warren (1992).

Task Menu
1. Develop an understanding of how early initiation of sexual intercourse is associated with high-risk activities, including ineffective use of contraceptives, multiple partners over a short period of time, high-risk sexual partners, and exposure to sexually transmitted diseases (STDs).
   Practitioner's Role: Assess the teen's status in terms of sexual understanding and presence or absence of sexual activity (current risk of pregnancy and STDs).
2. *Identify* core beliefs, values, and self-efficacy and their relationship to pregnancy prevention.
   Practitioner's Role: Facilitate discussion of the teen's, peers', and family's values regarding sexual activity and pregnancy, and of the relationship between possible pregnancy and life goals. Help the teen project future irreversible consequences of her present behavior.
3. *Identify* a mentor with whom issues of sexuality can be openly and confidentially discussed.
4. Learn to communicate assertively with partners about safe/protected sex.
   Elaboration: Discuss with your partner your refusal to engage in unprotected sex and learn to exit a situation when prevention is not possible.
5. Learn that you have the right to say no and feel confident about it.
   Practitioner's Role: Use assertiveness and *social skills training* to help the teen resist pressure to engage in sex, or refer her to programs that offer such training. Programs such as "Growing Together" and "Will Power/ Won't Power" have been shown to be effective in enabling teens to post-

pone the first experience of sexual intercourse (Postrado & Nicholson 1992).

6. *Learn about* the effects of alcohol and other illicit substances on one's judgment.

7. *Identify* and modify dysfunctional beliefs putting you at risk for pregnancy.

    Elaboration: For example, you may think (magically) that "It won't happen to me."

    Practitioner's Role: Use *cognitive restructuring* to help adolescent develop more realistic beliefs.

8. *Learn about* alternative means of obtaining emotional support and physical closeness.

9. Develop a pregnancy prevention plan.

    Practitioner's Role: Depending on the case, this may emphasize delaying onset of sexual activity, returning to abstinence, or using birth control methods.

10. *Identify* sex education resources.

    Practitioner's Role: Provide or arrange education as needed for the teen (as well as parents or partners, as appropriate) regarding sexuality, pregnancy and pregnancy prevention, and prevention of STDs.

11. *Learn about* safe sex.

    Practitioner's Role: Support healthy sexual behavior. Teach safe sex practices including the use of birth control pills, barrier-method contraceptives (e.g., condoms, diaphragms, and spermicides). Discuss the positive aspects of delaying sexual intercourse. Support securing routine medical care and advice.

12. Join a teen pregnancy prevention group.

    Practitioner's Role: Organize an educational group for teens (if none exists) to provide a safe environment in which to talk about sexuality (Moyse-Steinberg 1990).

Jennifer Hescheles

Travel Disability: Cognitively Impaired People

The capacity to use public transportation is a critical factor in the adaptation of individuals with cognitive impairments resulting (most commonly) from emotional and learning disabilities, mental retardation, brain injury, and mental illness (Zaworski & Horn 1993; Arthur & Passini 1992). In order to participate in the work force, to obtain medical and social services, and for many other reasons, the cognitively impaired need to develop skills in using travel facilities.

Literature: Arthur & Passini (1993); Coburn et al. (1992); Taylor & Taylor (1993, 1996).

Task Menu
1. Learn the cognitive, behavioral, and *social skills* of travel via fixed-route, public transportation in the community.

   Elaboration: Learn about available routes, stops/stations, transfer points, fares, and schedules; proper boarding areas; and how to access the correct vehicle and handle emergencies.

   Practitioner's Role: Assess the client's knowledge and skills in community travel; determine travel competence based on his or her knowledge of the location of various landmarks along the primary travel route. Help the client develop an individualized travel plan by identifying the simplest or most efficient route to a destination based on his or her cognitive map and travel ability; identify and correct distortions in client's cognitive map.
2. Use a map board of the route to be learned to correct faulty cognitions.

   Practitioner's Role: Reinforce correct cognitions.
3. [if in shelter setting] Go on short errands to implement learned travel skills, either on the campus or in the community.

   Practitioner's Role: Provide tokens, tickets, money to facilitate travel; make available a backup crisis intervention system (Taylor & Taylor 1993); locate lost clients in the community through emergency telephone services; enlist bus operators' support in client travel training.

Brennan Taylor

Unemployment

Although the percentage of unemployed people seeking work has declined in recent years, the job environment remains uncertain and many Americans will face job loss one or more times in their working lives (Sales 1995). Individuals experiencing unemployment and their families face more than economic hardship. Many people also suffer from depression, symptoms of bereavement, or a sense of loss of control and alienation due to unwanted unemployment (Macarov 1988). Jobless clients need expeditious assistance in meeting their basic needs as well as support in regaining a sense of control and hope in their lives.

Literature: Borrero (1980); Briar (1987); Burke (1998); Keefe (1984); Macarov (1988); Sales (1995) Turner et al. (1991).

Task Menu
1. *Identify* job or career goals.
2. *Identify* all current available financial resources, including savings, earnings from odd jobs and other household members, cash and in-kind assistance from family and friends.

3. *Identify* all public and private cash and in-kind resources for which you may be eligible, including unemployment insurance, income maintenance assistance, food stamps, utility assistance, Medicaid, and private charitable assistance.
4. Develop a budget covering basic living costs as well as the projected cost of your job search or vocational/education expenses.
5. Assess your employability by listing your knowledge and skills.
6. *Identify* resources for job search assistance.

   Practitioner's Role: Inform the client of available financial, job search, job training, educational, and support group resources. The most helpful employment resources can be accessed through the U.S. Department of Labor, which has local offices throughout the country. Resources available include:

   Unemployment insurance
   Adult training programs
   Dislocated worker programs
   Employment services, including resume preparation, interview skill training, job search resources (newspapers, computerized listings of available jobs, Internet access)
   Special population programs
   Youth training programs, including Job Corps
   Other private for-profit and not-for-profit employment, vocational, educational, and support group resources are available in most areas and include:
   American Association for Retired Persons
   Association for Retarded Citizens
   Client's social network—friends, family, etc.
   Local job training and employment programs for homeless youths and adults
   Local youth and senior citizen programs
   Mental Health Association
   Private employment agencies
   State and local social service agencies
   Temporary employment agencies
   Urban League
   Veterans' employment and educational programs
   YMCA and YWCA
7. Develop a job search or vocational or educational plan including daily tasks.
8. Contact the local Department of Labor office and speak with a job counselor.
9. Bring your list of knowledge, skills, and abilities to a job counselor for review and discuss appropriate career paths or options.

Elaboration: Based on your identified knowledge, skills, and abilities, check job banks for any positions that may be suitable. Contact the companies identified and send a resume and cover letter.

10. Prepare a resume.

    Elaboration: Be specific about your abilities and skills. Consult a job counselor about a resume workshop.

11. Use other resources identified in task 6.

    Elaboration: Let friends, family members, and others in your social network know you are looking for a job and ask them for suggestions. Probably the majority of job hunters locate employment through their social networks (Burke 1998).

12. Prepare for job interview.

    Elaboration: Identify possible perceived weaknesses and develop ways of presenting them in the best light possible. These might include age, periods of unemployment, terminations, and disabilities (Burke 1998).

    Practitioner's Role: Use *role play* to help the client prepare for the interview.

13. Use the period of unemployment to consider new directions.

    Practitioner's Role: Some clients may experience long-term unemployment and severe financial and emotional stress. It is important to first help the client meet his or her perceived basic needs, but in addition, the client may benefit by reframing this period of unemployment as a time to consider learning a new and more marketable trade, changing career paths, or expanding his or her level of education.

Isabel Rose, Denise Jeremiah

Withdrawn Child

The withdrawn child's avoidance of peers and novel situations is more extreme than shyness. These behaviors result in distress for the child or others, and seem more pronounced when the child encounters the social and academic stress situation of school (Philadelphia Child Guidance Center 1994). The withdrawn child is reluctant to engage in peer-group activities, may have few friends, often appears to be daydreaming during school tasks, and may want to spend most of her or his time with parent(s) and siblings. Withdrawn children may be unhappy with their behavior because it isolates them from others.

According to Mokuau and Manos (1989), the withdrawn child has not received sufficient reinforcement for prosocial behaviors from significant others, especially parent(s). Withdrawn and aggressive behaviors are seen as predictable results of unsupportive or destructive early environments (Alpern & Lyons 1993; East 1991; Mills

& Allan 1992; Prino & Peyrot 1994). Children with low peer acceptance have been shown to be at risk for concurrent and later difficulties in terms of self-concept, social support, anxiety, depression, feelings of hostility, adolescent pregnancy, and behavioral problems (Koot & Verhulst 1992; Serbin et al. 1991; Vargo 1995).

Literature: In preschool classrooms, resilient peer treatment has been used effectively with withdrawn, maltreated children, as discussed in Fantuzzo et al. (1996). The Child Behavior Scale has been found useful for measuring aggressive, withdrawn, and prosocial behaviors in young children (Ladd & Profilet 1996, Mokuau & Manos 1989; Philadelphia Child Guidance Center 1994; Vargo 1995).

Task Menu Child

1. *Identify* people, situations, and events that seem to trigger discomfort.
   Elaboration: Learn to use *self-monitoring* practices to identify these items.
2. Learn *problem-solving* skills to decide what to do in social situations.
   Elaboration: For example, in brainstorming possible solutions to her problem of having too few friends, a shy girl seen at an elementary school came up with the idea of a "friends list." She would ask students she knew if they wanted their names on her list of friends. The two students she asked were quite willing to add their names. Indeed, another student whom she did not know also wanted her name included!
   Practitioner's Role: *Role play* with child effective strategies to use or ways to behave to encourage friendships and successful school and social interactions.
3. Use *applied relaxation* to reduce anxiety in social situations.
4. Use *self-verbalization* as needed to enhance your ability to interact with others.
   Elaboration: For example, say to yourself, "I will walk over to that person and say hello. Next, I will ask if they watched any good shows on TV last night. Then, after I listen to what they say, I will either say that I have seen that same show or, if not, I will say that I will have to watch it. Next, if our talk has gone well, I will ask them to play a game with me."
5. Learn to use verbal *self-reinforcement* for all successful interactions.
   Elaboration: For example, notice and say to yourself, "I asked Susan if she would have lunch with me and she did. I think I am doing well today."
6. To reward yourself for a good day, do something you particularly enjoy.
7. Learn *social skills.*
   Elaboration: Really listen to what others are saying. Notice how others react to you depending on what you are saying and doing. What seems to cause them to respond in a positive way?
   Practitioner's Role: *Role play* with child ways of interacting with peers that can lead to the development of social relationships.
8. Use *coping imagery* in situations that make you feel particularly uncomfortable.

Elaboration: When interacting with people you don't know well, you may wish to imagine that you are talking to someone you really like and feel comfortable with. When you are in a place where you feel uncomfortable, you may want to imagine a place where you always feel good.

9. Locate and participate in activities with peers (e.g., Scouts, local boys' or girls' clubs, etc.).

Practitioner's Role: Play *games* and do exercises with the child to encourage self-expression and age-appropriate *social skills* to use with peers. Such activities may include "Thinking, Feeling, Doing," sentence completion (e.g., "When I am by myself during recess, I think . . . ").

Task Menu Parents

1. Provide positive reinforcement of the child's prosocial activities and support for the child to express her or his feelings about engaging in such new behaviors.

2. Arrange for psychological or psychiatric consultation if the child evidences disturbance of clinical significance.

   Elaboration: Psychological testing may be needed to ascertain the exact nature of the child's problems and whether learning disabilities or emotional disorders exist.

3. Attend to physical characteristics that may prompt the child to use avoidance of social contact as a coping mechanism.

   Elaboration: Such characteristics may include hygiene, personal appearance, and speech impediments. If you cannot correct the characteristics, then you may be able to reassure the child. For example, one study (Sheerin, MacLeod, & Kusumakar 1996) suggests that there is no correlation between degree of disfigurement and level of psychosocial adjustment in cases of children with port-wine stains or prominent ears.

4. Discuss with school personnel (e.g., teacher, guidance counselor, or social worker) the child's functioning in specific situations.

   Elaboration: This may also open up the topic of the child's temperament and how the teacher could respond to it in the classroom (Bullock 1993).

5. Play and design regular activities that will reinforce prosocial behaviors.

   Practitioner's Role: Initially, monitor and guide such tasks. Discuss the family reaction to completing them and whether the tasks are successful in effecting behavioral change in the child.

6. Participate in *parent training* (Tanaka 1991).

   Elaboration: Most parents find that they gain additional ease in dealing with various child behaviors when they learn specific new skills, such as how to reward positive behavior or to notice the triggers that precede undesirable behavior.

Pamela Zettergren, Cynthia Morse

Common Procedures

Applied Relaxation   The technique of *progressive relaxation* is learned and then applied during periods of anxiety. Use of cues such as a self-instruction to relax can, with practice, be substituted for the actual tensing and relaxing of muscles. (For further discussion see Ost 1988 and Ost & Westling 1995).

Cognitive Restructuring   consists of the identification and change of dysfunctional cognitions or beliefs. Dysfunctional cognitions are those that contribute to a person's problems in one way or another. Many types of dysfunctional cognitions have been identified. Some of the more common are:

> **Automatic thoughts** Unarticulated, half-conscious beliefs that guide moment-to-moment behavior. They become dysfunctional if they cause unnecessary distress or interefere with task performance (Beck et al. 1979).
>
> **Faulty information processing** (Beck et al. 1979):
>> *Arbitrary inference* Drawing hasty conclusions from inadequate evidence
>> *Selective abstraction* Focusing too much on particular details
>> *Overgeneralization* Applying an idea to situations it does not fit
>> *Magnification and minimization* Blowing things out of proportion or downplaying them
>> *Personalization* Taking things personally
>> *Absolutist dichotomous thinking* Thinking in black-and-white terms
>
> **Erroneous beliefs about causation and responsibility** A common type is inappropriately blaming others. For example, Mrs. N reacts angrily toward her two-year-old because she feels he is deliberately trying to make her life miserable (Doherty 1981; Brehm & Smith 1986).
>
> **Problematic self-efficacy expectations** Ungrounded or untested beliefs about inability to carry out tasks, behaviors, etc. (Bandura 1986).
>
> **Dysfunctional assumptions** These may include core or underlying beliefs (schemata); for example, abandoned by his father as a child, Jerry assumes that close relationships are not to be trusted.

Once a possible dysfunctional cognition is identified, it is critically examined. The examination may take the form of a Socratic dialogue or "guided discovery" (Freeman et al. 1990) led by the practitioner. For example, the practitioner may ask the client to consider the evidence for or against the cognition, the quality of the evidence, or alternative ways of viewing the phenomena reflected by the cognition (Kuehlwein 1998). Distortions are brought to light and challenged. The purpose of the examination is to help the client develop cognitions that are better based in reality and more functional. A deeper level of cognitive restructuring consists of "schema-focused" treatment (Young, Beck, & Weinberger 1993), meant to elicit and alter dysfunctional assumptions.

Cognitive restructuring is usually seen as a collaborative process, with the client contributing actively. Once clients learn cognitive restructuring, they should be able to do it on their own.

Specific techniques that may be used include:

Developing counters or self-statements to offset or challenge dysfunctional cognitions (McMillan 1986). For example, counters may be statements disputing the cognition or suggesting alternatives to it.

Reattribution Developing more accurate and functional cognitions about cause and responsibility (Doherty 1981, Freeman et al. 1990)

Replacement imagery Developing more adaptive images of one's functioning in problem situations (Freeman et al. 1990) (see also *coping imagery*)

Seeing positives Focusing on positive aspects of adverse events or situations

Refocusing Focus on pleasant thoughts rather than dysfunctional cognitions (Freeman et al. 1990)

Thought stopping Use of *self-verbalization,* such as saying "stop!'" at the beginning of a train of dysfunctional or aversive thoughts

Role play The practitioner can express or argue for dysfunctional thoughts, and the client can respond critically.

Contingency Contracting   As applied to children and adolescents, contingency contracting involves developing an oral or written contract in which a parent or other caregiver agrees to provide a reward in the form of a privilege, tokens, etc., contingent upon the child or adolescent performing a given task or a particular kind of behavior. For example, if a child goes to bed quietly one night when asked to, he or she will be allowed to stay up a half hour longer the next night. To the extent possible, the child should be involved in developing the terms of the contract. Contingency contracting may be used as part of a *contingency management* system (see below).

Contingency Management   In a contingency management system (as applied to children and adolescents) the parent or caregiver rewards (reinforces) a child or adolescent for appropriate behavior, through praise, approval, extra privileges, tangibles, etc. Appropriate behavior should be rewarded with praise as soon as possible. Inappropriate behavior is ignored, if possible, or punished through such consequences as loss of privileges or *time out.* In implementing a contingency management system, the parent should have a clear idea of the target behaviors to be changed and the kinds of rewards and negative consequences to be given. Appropriate behavior should be rewarded with praise as soon as possible. The child or adolescent should be involved in the planning and implementation of the system to the extent possible, for example, in the selection of tangible rewards or punishments. Contingency management may also incorporate such behavioral control methods as *response cost, token economy,* and *contingency contracting.* (For additional techniques see *school problems: truancy,* task 6 and *parent training.* See also Briesmeister & Schaefer 1998.)

Coping Imagery   is a technique whereby the client, through repetition, alters negative images that induce anxiety or stress or creates positive images that are associated with a state of relaxation. Beck and Emery (1985) cite several coping imagery strategies, including substituting positive for negative imagery (for example, imagining a pleasant, peaceful event rather than one that provokes anxiety), exaggeration (carrying to an absurd conclusion a stress-inducing image), and goal *rehearsal* (imagining a new behavior that the client then rehearses with the practitioner and alone until it does not provoke anxiety).

Exposure   may be referred to as in vivo or real-life exposure or exposure therapy; clients experience distressful events or situations in order to learn to cope with them. Exposure is generally done in a graduated fashion, beginning with less aversive forms of the events or situations and slowly increasing the amount of exposure. For example, a person with anxiety about public speaking may begin graduated exposure by speaking informally to a small group of colleagues, or a school phobic child might start by spending a short time on the playground of the school. When the client experiences a beginning level of exposure without excessive difficulty, he or she progresses to a more stressful level. Exposure may be guided by a prearranged hierarchy of situations or events, ordered in terms of their degree of aversiveness; the client begins with the lowest on the hierarchy. Prior to exposure the client learns skills for coping with the events or situations; he or she develops these skills through progressively more difficult exposure experiences.

Exposure should be frequent, usually at least three times a week, and each exercise should last a substantial period of time (anywhere from thirty minutes to two hours). It is important that the anxiety engendered by the exposure subside before the exercise ends. The client may carry out exposure on his or her own or with a therapist or other helper in attendance. Intense exposure may be referred to as flooding. (For further discussion see Anthony, Craske, & Barlow 1995; Bouman & Emmelkamp 1996.)

Exposure is widely used in the treatment of anxiety disorders, for which its effectiveness has received considerable empirical support (DeRubeis & Crits-Christoph 1998; Reid 1997). Partners or family members can be involved in helping the client with exposure tasks. While such involvement may have beneficial consequences for the relationship, there is no convincing evidence that it increases the efficacy of exposure itself (Baucom et al. 1998).

Clients may also use imaginal exposure—imagining oneself coping with a feared object or re-creating anxiety associated with a traumatic event. The client can learn this kind of exposure method from the practitioner and then use it independently. For a related method, see *systematic desensitization.*

Uses of exposure for different types of problems are outlined below. Details and references may be found in the task planners related to the problems listed.

Uses of Exposure

Problem	How used
Agoraphobia	Increasing time spent in feared circumstances, e.g., in crowded places
Bulimia	Eating foods that produce anxiety but preventing purging; temptation exposure—exposing self to binge food but not eating it
Chronic grief	Experiencing stimuli associated with the deceased
Generalized anxiety disorder	Imagining the worst consequences of one's worries
Obsessive-compulsive disorder	Re-creating obsessive thoughts but preventing compulsive rituals
Post-traumatic stress disorder	Deliberate re-creation of and exposure to painful memories
School phobia	Gradually approaching school; increasing time in classroom
Social phobia	Increasing time spent in anxiety-producing social situations
Specific phobia	Gradually approaching the feared object, touching it, etc.

Games   Selected board and card games related to task planners in this volume are described below (prices may have changed since the data were obtained).

Names and numbers of suppliers: Childswork/Childsplay (1-800-962-1141); Creative Therapy Store (1-800-648-8857); Kidsrights (1-800-892-KIDS); Self Help for Kids (1-800-735-7323).

Controlling anger
Ready, Steady, Chill!: A Role-Playing Game for Teaching Anger Control Skills (for ages 7+); Childswork/Childsplay; $14.95

The Angry Monster Machine (board game for ages 5–10); Childswork/Childsplay; $49.00

The Anger Solution Game (board game for ages 7–12); Childswork/Childsplay; $49.00

The Self-Control Patrol Game (board game for ages 8–14); Childswork/Childsplay; $49.00

AD/HD
Stop, Relax and Think (board game); Childswork/Childsplay; $49.00
In Control: A Book of Games to Teach Children Self-Control Skills (board games for ages 7–12); Childswork/Childsplay; $36.95
AD/HD Self-Control Problem-Solving Cards (24 cards, manual); Childswork/Childsplay; $31.50
Look Before You Leap! (board game for ages 5–12); Childswork/Childsplay; $49.00

Resolving conflicts
The Conflict Resolution Game (board game for ages 6–12); Childswork/Childsplay; $49.00
A Case for Conflict Resolution (six games in one for ages 6–10); Childswork/Childsplay; $52.50

Family issues
My Two Homes (board game for ages 6–12); Childswork/Childsplay; $49.00
Talking, Trusting, Feeling (board game for children ages 6–12 from families torn by divorce or alcohol); Kidsrights; $39.95

Emotions and feelings
Face It! Card Deck (ten different feeling card games in one deck); Childswork/Childsplay; $25.00
The Talking, Feeling, and Doing Game (board game for ages 4–11); Childswork/Childsplay; only professionals with a master's degree in psychology or a related field may purchase this item; $49.00
The Talking, Feeling, and Doing Game (board game for ages 5–16); Creative Therapeutics; $35.00; Spanish Language Cards $10.00; only mental health professionals may purchase this item

Sexual abuse and sexual activity
Survivor's Journey (board game for ages 8 to adult); Kidsrights; $39.95

Identify   The client pins down factors bearing upon a problem. These might include possible causes, resources, consequences, and coping efforts. Such identifications are frequently the first steps in developing insights and solving problems. Often the practitioner initiates the identifying process in the session through exploration with the client or by giving examples. The practitioner may prompt the client or suggest additional possibilities, and may ask the client to continue the process at home by making a list and bringing it to the next session.

Identify Triggers   The process of identifying described above is focused on determining events that may precipitate problem behavior, such as aggressive outbursts, consumption of alcohol, etc. The client may begin the process of identifying triggers in the session and continue it at home. Once triggers are identified, tasks may be developed to avoid them or to cope with them when they occur.

Journal, Journaling   A journal is a record of personal experiences, thoughts, or feelings, in the form of a log, diary, unsent letter, essay, etc. *Journaling* allows clients to express themselves in a private manner, but also in a way that can be shared, at their discretion. It not only permits recording of actual experiences for later reflection or discussion but also enables exploration of thoughts and feelings and permits the development of new insights and problem-solving strategies.

Learn About   The client seeks information about a problem, condition, resources, or indeed anything that will facilitate task work and problem resolution. The learning may take a variety of forms: reading books or other materials suggested by the practitioner; asking questions of the practitioner, doctors, nurses, or other service professionals; or searching the Internet. The practitioner needs to consider with the client the possible values and risks of acquiring information. For example, for some clients learning about their illness furthers their ability to cope; for others it may simply produce anxiety. Practitioners can facilitate the learning process by helping clients acquire and understand source material, sharing their own expertise, and arranging for access to those who may have the necessary information.

Mutually Enjoyable Activity   Related clients, e.g., parent and child or marital partners, select an activity that each would find enjoyable. Such activities might include going out for dinner, attending a movie, playing a game together, or undertaking a home improvement project. The task may be used as a way of enabling conflicted participants to interact differently or to help rebuild an atrophied relationship. In setting up the task, the practitioner should ask clients to make suggestions about possible activities or to discuss possibilities with one another. The activity should be of interest to both (or all) clients. Some planning of the activity in the session is usually advisable—e.g., when it will take place and what it will consist of. If participants have a history of difficulty carrying out such plans, it may make sense to ask, "What could go wrong?" as a means of eliciting and dealing with potential obstacles.

Parent Training   is predicated on the notion that changing the behavior of the parent(s) leads to a change in the behavior of the child, and that behaviors can be learned and unlearned. The training is usually offered to parents of aggressive or noncompliant children (Magen & Rose 1994), but the basic skills are useful to every parent. Numerous techniques and training packages focus on altering parent behaviors; their common characteristics appear to be the following: 1) group training; 2) avoidance of aversive techniques (e.g., corporal punishment) because their success in altering behavior is time-limited and they must be intensified over time in order to achieve minimal results; 3) emphasis on reinforcement, or increasing the likelihood that a behavior will occur again in the future (Mokuau & Manos 1989); and 4) emphasis on discrimination, which channels the child's behavior in a particular way via commands or instructions (e.g., altering antecedent behavior) (Mokuau & Manos 1989). Parent-training programs for a range of specific problems, such as conduct disorder, school refusal behavior, AD/HD, and sibling conflict, may be found in Briesmeister & Schaefer (1998).

Although most parent training is offered in groups, the basic approach can be used in work with individual parents. The effectiveness of individualized parent training can often be enhanced by seeing parent(s) and child(ren) together. This affords the opportunity for the parent(s) to practice skills in the session under the guidance of the practitioner.

An illustration is the Parenting Skills Training program, which employs an ABC (antecedent, behavior, consequence) model of parent training that is useful to all caregivers. (For the most recent version of this program see Karant 1999). Training begins by helping parents identify a behavior that is seen or heard, not attributed (i.e., not based on what the parents feel or believe about the behavior). The practitioner explains that children use a particular behavior because it either helps them avoid something or helps them get something that they want. Therefore, parents practice identifying the trigger(s) (the events or conditions that occur beforehand) and the consequence(s) (the events or conditions that occur afterward) of a behavior. Parents also examine the consequence. Does it reinforce or punish the behavior?

Parents who have learned to track the ABCs of a child's undesirable behavior next learn to observe, count, and record its occurrences over a specific period of time (i.e., establish a baseline). This is useful in two respects. First, it may help to demonstrate to the parents that the undesirable behavior does not occur as frequently as they had thought. Second, it helps to set a realistic expectation of what initially will constitute positive change. That is, if a behavior occurs frequently (e.g., ten times a day, seven days a week), the parents may first work toward effecting a reduction in the unwanted behavior (e.g., five times a day, seven days a week).

The practitioner aids the parents in developing a "teaching goal" to extinguish the undesirable behavior. Rather than saying what should not be done (e.g., Jamel will not curse at his mother), the teaching goal states the positive, desired behavior, and is also incompatible with the unwanted behavior (e.g., Jamel will speak respectfully to his mother). Both reinforcers (social and nonsocial) and punishments should be identified before the teaching plan is presented to the child; reinforcers should be meaningful to him or her, otherwise the child will not work toward them. Also, parents should be prepared to identify reasonable punishments, to deliver them dispassionately, and to forget about the reason for the punishment after it has been given.

The plan to help a child extinguish an unwanted behavior should be explained to him or her in detail in a quiet setting. The parents identify the teaching goal; state when the plan will begin; identify the reinforcers and punishments, as well as the circumstances under which they will be delivered; and request that the child repeat the plan to ensure that he or she understands it. During implementation, the parents continue to document the target behavior and the delivery of the reinforcers and punishments.

Concomitant with the steps of teaching a goal to a child, the model incorporates "pure descriptive praise," "positive scan," and "uninterrupted listening" as parent skills to enhance the quality of the relationship between parents and child. Pure descriptive praise is unadulterated; there is no criticism at the end of the communication (e.g., "I liked that you set the table on time" versus "I liked that you set the table on time, but you forgot to pick up your toys again"). Also, behaviors are the focus (e.g., "You got up on time for the bus today" versus "You were a good boy today"), and the parents' comments are worthwhile to the child, providing positive attention and conveying warmth. Positive scan is parents' *planned*, overt recognition of the positive behaviors that the child uses daily (3:1 ratio of positive statements to negative observations every day). Finally, parents are encouraged to practice uninterrupted listening with the child at least ten minutes each day at a regular time. Parent training approaches for a variety of problems with children can be found in Briesmeister & Schaefer (1998).

Planned Activities Training (PAT)   is a form of parent training in which parents learn how to cope with a range of frequently occurring and often troublesome activities that they do with their children, such as shopping trips, meals, and bedtime routines. Parents learn to plan the activities in advance and to anticipate likely trouble spots; to instruct the child in the rules governing the activity; and to reward the child if the rules are followed. PAT can be used in place of or in combination with conventional parent training (see above). Studies have suggested that PAT can enhance the effectiveness of such training (Harrold et al. 1992).

Problem Solving   In developing problem-solving skills the individual learns to generate alternative solutions to a real-life problem situation and (ideally) to implement the alternative that has the best chance of solving the problem given his or her current resources and opportunities (D'Zurilla 1986; Goldfried & Goldfried 1980). The problem-solving process can be used in diverse settings, e.g., outpatient and inpatient clinical, educational, residential; for diverse problem situations, e.g., unipolar depression (Nezu, Nezu, & Perri 1990), caregiving (Toseland, Blanchard, & McCallion 1995), child behavioral disorders (Butterfield & Cobb 1994), family problems (Reid 1985, 1992); and in diverse formats, e.g., individual client and small group.

The problem-solving model has five components: 1) problem orientation; 2) problem definition and formulation; 3) generation of alternatives; 4) decision making; and 5) solution implementation and verification (D'Zurilla 1986; Nezu, Nezu, & Perri 1989, 1990). In problem-solving training, each of the five stages is presented sequentially over a period of time (Larson 1990). Problem orientation includes a determination of the client's general cognitive-affective-behavioral problem-solving style. Does the client recognize problem situations and their being a normal part of everyday life? Does the client believe that she or he can solve problems? Is the client's emotional response to problem situations mainly excitement and expectation of a new challenge, or fear of an insurmountable obstacle? Does the client engage in fight-or-flight behavior when confronted with problems? According to D'Zurilla (1986), the practitioner and client should understand the client's problem orientation at the outset because the cognitive, affective, and behavioral parameters influence problem formulations and solution implementation.

Problem definition and formulation involves organizing information about the problem situation so that it is concrete and yields an achievable problem-solving goal. Generation of alternatives, or brainstorming, includes identifying possible solutions or coping choices. Clients are encouraged to suspend their evaluation of the alternatives at this point, and instead to focus on maximizing their variety and number (D'Zurilla 1990).

Decision making is a two-part process. First, the client rejects alternatives that are clearly not viable solutions to the problem and then predicts the possible outcomes (positive and negative, short- and long-term consequences) for each of the remaining alternatives. Second, the client rates each alternative according to potential effectiveness. The "best" solution is the one that seems most likely to solve the problem and maximize benefits and minimize costs, or negative consequences. Solution implementation and verification entails acting on the solution and assessing its efficacy. D'Zurilla (1986) notes the importance of self-monitoring of implementation skills; self-evaluation, or evaluating the extent to which the outcome matches the prediction; and self-reinforcement, or acknowledging success if the problem has been solved.

Problem-solving assessment comprises ability and performance, knowledge about the steps of problem solving, and the ability to translate this knowledge into action (solving problems) (Nezu, Nezu, & Perri 1990). Ability-focused measures include the Problem-Solving Inventory (PSI; Heppner & Peterson 1982) and the Social Problem-Solving Inventory (SPSI; D'Zurilla & Nezu 1990). The Means-End Problem-Solving Procedure (MEPS; Platt & Spivak 1975) is a performance-focused measure. Supplemental measures include problem checklists (e.g., Personal Problems Checklist; Schinka 1984). A well-developed presentation of methods for helping individual clients learn problem-solving methods may be found in Hepworth, Rooney, & Larson (1997). This text also contains excellent overviews of other common procedures, including *cognitive restructuring, social skills training,* and *stress inoculation.*

Progressive Relaxation   is one means of achieving a state opposite to the physiological, cognitive, and emotional arousal concomitant with stress and anxiety. Progressive relaxation entails the methodical tensing and releasing of large and small facial and body muscles while lying down or sitting comfortably in a site free from distractions. The client tenses each muscle for about ten seconds and releases it for about twenty seconds, distinguishing the sensations of tenseness and relaxation. If an area is particularly tense, the cycle should be repeated two or three times. The overall sequence should be performed daily. According to Bourne (1995), this method is particularly useful for clients in whom stress leads to muscle tension. Additionally, Bourne (1995) notes that over time, the effects of progressive relaxation are generalized: i.e., the client experiences less stress throughout the day and in response to anxiety-provoking events. (See Bourne 1995 for further discussion.)

Steps in using *progressive relaxation* are:

1. Put yourself in a setting that is quiet and comfortable.
2. Take three deep abdominal breaths, exhaling slowly each time. As you exhale, imagine that tension throughout your body begins to flow away.
3. Clench your fists. Hold for seven to ten seconds and then release for fifteen to twenty seconds.
4. Tighten your biceps by drawing your forearms up toward your shoulders and "making a muscle" with both arms. Hold for several seconds and then relax.
5. Tighten your triceps by extending your arms out straight and locking your elbows. Hold for several seconds and then relax.
6. Tense the muscles in your forehead by raising your eyebrows as far as you can. Hold for several seconds and then relax. Imagine your forehead muscles becoming smooth and limp as they relax.
7. Tense the muscles around your eyes by clenching your eyelids tightly shut. Hold for several seconds and then relax. Imagine sensations of deep relaxation spreading all around the area of your eyes.
8. Tighten your jaw by opening your mouth so wide that you stretch the muscles around the hinges of your jaw. Hold for several seconds and then relax. Let your lips part and allow your jaw to hang loose.
9. Tighten the muscles in the back of your neck by pulling your head way back, as if you were going to touch it to your back. Focus only on tensing the muscles in your neck. Hold for several seconds and then relax. Repeat once.
10. Take a few deep breaths and tune in to the weight of your head sinking into whatever surface it is resting on.
11. Tighten your shoulders by raising them as if you were going to touch your ears. Hold for several seconds and then relax.
12. Tighten the muscles around your shoulder blades by pushing your shoulder blades back as if you were going to touch them together. Hold the tension for several seconds and then relax. Repeat once.
13. Tighten the muscles around your chest by taking in a deep breath. Hold for up to ten seconds and then release slowly. Imagine any excess tension in your chest flowing away with the exhalation.
14. Tighten your stomach muscles by sucking your stomach in. Hold for several seconds and then release. Imagine a wave of relaxation spreading through your abdomen.
15. Tighten your lower back by arching it. Hold for several seconds and then relax.

16. Tighten your buttocks by pulling them together. Hold for several seconds and then relax. Imagine the muscles in your hips going loose and limp.

17. Squeeze the muscles in your thighs all the way down to your knees. Hold for several seconds and then relax. Feel your thigh muscles smoothing out and relaxing completely.

18. Tighten your calf muscles by flexing your toes toward your head. Hold for several seconds and then relax.

19. Tighten your feet by curling your toes under. Hold for several seconds and then relax.

20. Mentally scan your body for any residual tension. If a particular area remains tense, repeat one or two tense-relax cycles for that muscle group.

21. Now imagine a wave of relaxation slowly spreading throughout your body, starting at your head and gradually penetrating every muscle group all the way down to your toes.

Reflect On   consists of thinking about an actual or possible course of action. In so doing clients may consider its actual or possible consequences, indicate how they think they would feel if they did or did not carry it out, or write out its pros and cons.

Rehearsal   is used within the session to enable the client to practice tasks to be carried out in real-life situations. The client may be asked to perform task behaviors, frequently through *role play* (see below).

Relaxation   See *applied relaxation* and *progressive relaxation.*

Response Cost System   According to Jones and Kazdin (1981), response cost involves the withdrawal of a reinforcer when an individual displays a specific undesirable behavior. The method is compatible with a token economy. Thus, a parent may contract with a child not only to award tokens for desirable behavior, but also to collect them for a behavior that is to be extinguished. For example, Mom might give Laurie ten chips, worth a trip to her favorite fast-food restaurant; five are worth staying up an extra half hour. Every time Laurie performs a desirable behavior, she is awarded a chip; every time she misbehaves, one chip is taken away. The target behaviors, value of tokens, rewards, and so on, should be discussed with the child before the response cost system is implemented.

Role Play   serves a variety of functions in task work. Practitioners may use role plays to help clients rehearse how they will cope with particular situations or learn and practice particular skills. The practitioner may first take the role of the client and model desired behavior. The client may then play him- or herself, while the practitioner takes the role of another—e.g., someone who may tempt or antagonize the client. The client can then practice the modeled behavior. In the role of other, the practitioner can present the client with a variety of challenges that may be gradually increased in difficulty. Role plays can also be used by couples or family members to re-create previous interactions, help one another rehearse responses to particular situations, or practice skills.

School-Home Notes   Teachers send parents a report card, brought home by the child, on a daily basis or so many times a week. The report card enables the teacher to rate the child on classroom behavior or academic performance. For children in kindergarten through second grade, teachers can use drawn happy faces, stars, or stickers. For older children, they may use points or a grading scale. Children can exchange positive ratings for extra privileges or money at home (Fowler 1993). The method is presented in detail in Kelley (1990).

Self-Monitoring   is the completion of a chart or diary that records the client's behavioral, cognitive, and emotional responses to people, situations, or events that induce stress or anxiety or result in problematic behavior (e.g., fighting in school). The technique is used to collect objective data necessary for the practitioner and the client to plan interventions and to indicate to the client that she or he can control responses to stimuli. Beck, Emory, & Greenberg (1985) note that monitoring may include the time of day when the response occurred as well as a rating of intensity (e.g., 0 to 100). A variation of self-monitoring includes recording the antecedent to the behavior, the behavior itself, and the consequence of the behavior.

Self-Reinforcement   requires that clients both evaluate their own behaviors (see *self-monitoring*) and reward themselves. A broad range of self-rewards includes positive self-statements (e.g., "I handled that difficult situation well") and tangible rewards (e.g., buying a new, coveted pair of sneakers after resisting a temptation to go out drinking with friends).

Self-Verbalization   consists of words and statements an individual utters to him- or herself as a means of enhancing ability to carry out tasks. It includes various forms of self-encouragement, self-praise, and self-instruction used by both children and adults. One format used to teach self-verbalization to a child involves the following steps: the practitioner or caregiver performs the task while talking aloud about the nature of the problem and the strategies to be used; the child observes. The child then performs the same task under the verbal direction of the caregiver. The child next performs the task while instructing himself aloud. The child performs the task again while whispering the instructions. The child performs the task once more while guiding his behavior with private speech (Johnson, Rasbury, & Siegel 1986).

Slow Diaphragmatic Breathing   As described by Anthony, Craske, & Barlow (1995), this procedure is used to allay anxiety in phobic or other fear-producing situations. It involves slow breathing (eight to twelve breaths per minute) from the abdomen. Clients are instructed to say "relax" after each inhalation.

Social Skills, Social Skills Training Social skills comprise appropriate and effective actions in social situations, e.g., being properly assertive, making conversation, following rules of social etiquette (Richey 1994). They also include verbal and non-verbal behavioral features (e.g., tone of voice, posture, speech content) that are recognized as socially acceptable in common interactions (Richey 1994). Social skills are more easily described than defined because they are culturally and situationally determined. Moreover, as Richey (1994) notes, social skills are usually employed to achieve a goal, e.g., increasing managerial effectiveness in the workplace or reducing aggressive or violent interpersonal behavior. Consequently, training focuses on the components of skills that are commensurate with the personal goals of the client. Most individuals are aware of the importance of their social skills and make efforts to improve them; social skills training can augment these efforts. Such training can be offered in individual or group formats. Whereas individual training affords the opportunity to refine the intervention to meet the unique needs of the client, the group format enables a greater amount of feedback and support from peers.

According to Sprafkin (1994), there are five components of social skills training: rationale, modeling, role play, feedback, and homework. The rationale includes a broad review of the skills to be learned and the reasons for learning them, if they are not already clear to the client. Modeling is teaching a new skill or strengthening an existing one. Modeling methods take into account whether the client lacks skills or does not apply them. In the former case, modeling is overt; i.e., the practitioner demonstrates the skill to be learned either personally or through the use of aids such as video- and audiotapes. In the latter case, the practitioner uses more abstract means (e.g., written case examples, vignettes) to show how and when the particular skill is used (Richey 1994). *Role play* allows the client to practice the skill, and the extent to which it is structured depends on the client's level of anxiety with the task. Thus, role play may be spontaneous with few cues or may include the use of scripts. Feedback is review, evaluation, and social reinforcement of the skill application. The practitioner offers specific suggestions on how to enhance use of the new skill and offers praise that underscores performance (e.g., "good eye contact" versus "good job"). Reinforcement may also be tangible (food, points) depending on the developmental level of the client (Cartledge & Milburn 1980). Richey (1994) and Sprafkin (1994) note the importance of self-evaluation and self-reinforcement. These not only help ensure that external feedback is not the sole stimulus for self-praise and skill use, but also cultivate generalization of the new skill. Homework extends skill performance beyond the training context and requires the client's agreement to apply the skill during a specific time and situation.

Although social skills training involves the acquisition of new behaviors, several writers (Richey 1994; Cartledge & Milburn 1980) point out that *cognitive restructuring* must be considered during each component of the training in order to enable the client to use the skill. Thus, for example, a shy child may know how to initiate a conversation with a new peer; however, her automatic thoughts about her inability to be interesting to another may prevent her from applying her skill.

Assessment of social skills may include written instruments (see Brady 1984; Richey 1994), self-reports, observation of the client, and analogue situations, e.g., *role plays* (Goldstein 1981). Additionally, there are numerous resources (*games,* kits, printed materials and books) available to help teach social skills (Cartledge & Milburn 1980). A model of social skills training that can be adapted for a range of populations may be found in *schizophrenia, chronic: social skills deficits.* See also L'Abate & Milan (1986) and Bellack et al. (1997).

Stress Inoculation   According to Meichenbaum and Fitzpatrick (1993:717), stress inoculation training (SIT) is based on the assumption "that bolstering an individual's repertoire for coping with milder stressors can reduce the likelihood of maladaptive coping responses to later exposure to more intense stressors." It has been used extensively to help clients cope with a variety of stressful events and experiences, such as anger- or anxiety-provoking situations, illnesses, unemployment, and stressful occupations. The three phases of the intervention are:

1. *Reconceptualization.* With the practitioner's help, the client reviews the stressful events or experiences and reframes his or her responses to them as constructive coping efforts. The client develops an explanation of the problem that fits with his or her cognitive, affective, physiological, and environmental characteristics and circumstances.
2. *Coping skills acquisition and rehearsal.* The client learns coping skills to deal with the stressful events or experiences. These might include imagery rehearsal, behavioral rehearsal, problem solving, and cognitive restructuring, as well as other skills found in the literatures on cognitive and behavioral therapies. Practitioner-client *role plays* may be used as a means of developing the skills.
3. *Application and follow through.* The client uses the coping skills, beginning—to the extent possible—with milder forms of the stressful events or situations. The principles of graded *exposure* may be used. Clients are encouraged to "take credit for the positive outcomes of their coping efforts" (719). Obstacles and setbacks are anticipated and ways of dealing with them are developed. (See also Meichenbaum 1985.)

Systematic Desensitization   entails gradually counterconditioning the client to experience relaxation in response to a stimulus that previously evoked stress and anxiety. The client is taught a deep relaxation technique (see *progressive relaxation*) and then requested to identify to the practitioner an anxiety hierarchy, i.e., aspects of a situation or event that evoke from minimal to the most extreme stress response. For example, a man who has a fear of learning to swim may state that walking around a pool is least threatening; he may most fear being in the deep end. An intermediate step might be immersion in the shallow end of a pool with a flotation device.

When the client is relaxed, the practitioner instructs her or him to envision the event that induces the least stress. This step—imagining the event and relaxing—is repeated until the image no longer evokes stress. The client and practitioner move up the anxiety hierarchy until the most stress-inducing image evokes not fear but relaxation. Once learned, the technique may be used by the client on his or her own.

Time Out   is a procedure used with toddlers and youth (i.e., ages three to eleven) to effect rapid change in a single disruptive behavior. The child is removed from people, objects, or situations that are positively reinforcing the problem behavior. Time out is time limited: a minute for each year of the child's age, and not exceeding fifteen minutes. According to Patterson (1976), the bathroom, cleared of toilet articles and of objects that might be damaged, is the best time out location in a household because it is familiar to the child. The effectiveness of time out depends, firstly, on its being used consistently and dispassionately by the parent or caregiver every time the child exhibits the disruptive behavior; and secondly, on the child's understanding the link between the disruptive behavior and the time out. Consequently, the parent or caregiver initiates the plan by identifying the target behavior to the child and rehearsing the procedure with him or her. Loss of privileges can be used as backup if the child refuses to go into time out or leaves time out prematurely. A discussion of time out methods may be found in Barkley (1997).

Token Economy   Point systems (token economies) may be used with older children or with less frequently occurring behavior. The child is given points (or tokens, e.g., plastic chips) contingent upon appropriate behavior, such as responding to the first parental request. Points/tokens can be accumulated and cashed in for rewards. In one variation (Barkley 1989), parents assign values of points or chips to each of the child's home responsibilities. The child is rewarded for carrying out these responsibilities. The child should have a say in the development of the point system and rewards (Barkley 1989; Reid 1992).

A token economy may be monitored with a behavior chart. In one variation, the desired behaviors for the day, including tasks that the child is likely to complete, are listed in chronological order. If the child cannot read, pictures can be used. The child is rewarded with special treats on a daily or weekly basis for the agreed-on level of completion. Targeted negative behaviors such as cursing, having a tantrum, or talking back can also be listed and their values subtracted from the child's scores. The parent can meet in the evening with the child to discuss the day's behavior and identify what the child needs to work on the next day (Fowler 1993).

Appendix

Task Schedule

Task Statement

_____

_____

(Begin statement with names of participants)

When developed? Session #_____ Date_____

1. Task selection_____

2. Establishing motivation_____

3. Task development and planning_____

4. Practice, rehearsal, problem solving, training_____

Client task behavior modeled/rehearsed through role play _____

  Couple or family members engaged in problem solving or skills training in face-to-face communication_____

5. Dealing with obstacles (to tasks already attempted)_____

6. Other activities

7. Task review

When task reviewed, sess. #) __ __ __ __ __ __ __ __ __ __ __ __ __ __ __
Progress rating (Use   __ __ __ __ __ __ __ __ __ __ __ __ __ __ __
additional lines if   __ __ __ __ __ __ __ __ __ __ __ __ __ __ __
different ratings for
different clients)

Scale for Task Evaluation

(No) no opportunity to carry out task
(1) minimally or not achieved
(2) partially achieved
(3) substantially achieved
(4) completely achieved

Details of implementation identified in review:
If rating of 1, include reasons for failure to do task.
If rating of 2, describe which aspects of the task were completed and which
    not.
If rating of 3 or 4, indicate how task was carried out.
Note instances of task substitution or reshaping.
Continue on reverse.

Task Schedule: Instructions

General

Use only one Task Schedule for each task. Check activities used. For each activity checked, indicate key interventions and client activities, preceded by session number. Continue on reverse if more space is needed. For tasks repeated over a number of sessions, describe the more important interventions or activities.

Task Statement

Tasks should be stated in single sentences with the subject the person doing the task. Verbs should indicate *actions* that the client or other task performer is to do. Avoid task statements that present simply goals, such as "J. will improve his ability to relate to women," without indicating steps to be taken.

Task selection

Indicate how task originated—e.g., was it suggested by client, practitioner, or task planner?

Establishing motivation

What was done to clarify or enhance client's motivation to undertake the task? For example, were concrete incentives used?

Task development and planning

Include in-session work on task not covered in other categories, such as identifying triggers or dysfunctional cognitions. What potential obstacles were considered to implementing the task between sessions?

Practice, rehearsal, problem solving, training

Include role plays and client-to-client communication. Task should be set out in Task Statement. For example, if task is "Initiate a conversation with peer," role play might be used to help client rehearse. Indicate if couple or family members (e.g., husband/wife, parent(s)/child) engage in face-to-face communication in the session to solve a problem, improve communication skills, etc. Task statement should describe activity—e.g., "Mary and Bob will try to resolve differences about their son's curfew."

Dealing with obstacles (to tasks already attempted)

What obstacles prevented a satisfactory level of task attainment and how were they dealt with? To what extent were they resolved?

Other activities

List other task-related activities not included in the above categories—e.g., client face-to-face activities expressing feelings or exchanging positives.

Task review

For repeated tasks in which there was considerable variation in client accomplishment from week to week, indicate key or representative aspects of client performance.

References

Abidin, R. R. 1983. *Parenting Stress Index.* Charlottesville, Va.: Pediatric Psychology Press.

Abikoff, H., R. Gittleman-Klein, and D. Klein. 1977. Validation of a classroom observation code for hyperactive children. *Journal of Consulting and Clinical Psychology* 45:772–783.

Abramovitz, M. 1984. Blaming women for unemployment: Refuting a myth. *Social Casework* 65:547–559.

Abrams, S. E. 1994. Response to "A theoretical model of independence for nursing home elders." *Scholarly Inquiry for Nursing Practice* 8(2): 225–228.

Abramson, J. 1990. Enhancing patient participation: clinical strategies in the discharge planning process. *Social Work in Health Care* 14(4): 53–71.

Abramson, J. S., J. Donnelly, M. A. King, and M. D. Mailick. 1993. Disagreements in discharge planning: a normative phenomenon. *Health and Social Work* 18(1): 57–64.

Achenbach, T. M. and C. Edelbrock. 1983. *Manual for the Child Behavior Checklist and Revised Behavior Profile.* Burlington: University of Vermont, Department of Psychiatry.

Adderholdt-Elliot, M. 1987. *Perfectionism.* Minneapolis: Free Spirit.

Adler, A. J. and C. Archambault. 1990. *Divorce Recovery: Healing the Hurt Through Self-Help and Professional Support.* Washington, D.C.: P.I.A. Press.

Adler, R., R. Nunn, E. Northam, V. Lebnan, and R. Ross. 1994. Secondary prevention of childhood firesetting. *Journal of American Child and Adolescent Psychiatry* 33(8): 1194–1202.

Agathon, M. 1994. Social anxiety: Occupational and life stressors. 2nd International Congress of Behavioral Medicine. *Homeostasis in Health and Disease* 35(1–2): 94–97.

Akiskal, H. S. and G. B. Cassano, eds. 1997. *Dysthymia and the Spectrum of Chronic Depressions.* New York: Guilford Press.

Al-Anon Family Group. 1978. *One Day at a Time in Al-Anon.* New York: Al-Anon Family Group Headquarters.

Albano, A. M., L. S. Knox, and D. H. Barlow. 1995. Obsessive–compulsive disorder. In A. R. Eisen, C. A. Kearney, and C. E. Shaefer, eds., *Clinical Handbook of Anxiety Disorder in Children.* Northvale, N.J.: Jason Aronson.

Albano, A. M., B. F. Chorpita, and D. H. Barlow. 1996. Childhood anxiety disorders. In E. J. Mash and R. A. Barkley, eds., *Child Psychopathology,* 196–241. New York: Guilford Press.

Alcoholics Anonymous. 1952. *Twelve Steps and Twelve Traditions.* New York: Alcoholics Anonymous World Services.

———. 1976. *Alcoholics Anonymous,* 3rd ed. New York: Alcoholics Anonymous World Services.

Alderman, L. 1997. Stand up for your rights on the job. *Money* 26(3): 130–134.

Allen-Meares, P. 1987. Depression in childhood and adolescence. *Social Work* 32(6): 512–516.

———. 1994. Social work services in schools: A national study of entry-level tasks. *Social Work* 39(5): 560–565.

Alpern, L. and K. Lyons-Ruth. 1993. Preschool children at social risk: Chronicity and timing of maternal depressive symptoms and child behavior problems at school and at home. *Developmental and Psychopathology* 5(3): 371–387.

Alyson, S., ed. 1991. *Young, Gay and Proud.* Boston: Alyson.

American Academy of Child and Adolescent Psychiatry. Problems with soiling and bowel control. http://www.psych.med.umich.edu:80/WEB/AACAP/FACTSFAM/bowel.htm (last updated 5/6/1996)

Amodeo, M. and L. K. Jones. 1997. Viewing alcohol and other drug use cross-culturally: A cultural framework for clinical practice. *Families in Society* 78(3): 240–254.

Anastopoulos, A. D. 1997. Attention deficit/hyperactivity disorder. In R. T. Michel, ed., *Handbook of Prevention and Treatment with Children and Adolescents,* 551–669. New York: Wiley.

———. 1998. A training program for parents of children with attention deficit/hyperactivity disorder. In J. M. Briesmeister and C. E. Schaefer, eds., *Handbook of Parent Training: Parents as Co-Therapists for Children's Behavior Problems,* 2nd ed., 27–60. New York: Wiley.

Anderson, C. M., D. J. Reiss, and G. E. Hogarty. 1986. *Schizophrenia and the Family.* New York: Guilford Press.

Anderson-Malico, R. 1994. Anger management using cognitive group therapy. *Perspectives in Psychiatric Care* 30(3): 17–20.

Andrews, D. A., I. Zinger, R. D. Hoge, J. Bonta, P. Gendreau, and F. T. Cullen. 1990. Does correctional treatment work? A clinically relevant and psychologically informed meta-analysis. *Criminology* 28(3): 369–386.

Anhalt, K., C. B. McNeil, and A. B. Bahl. 1998. The AD/HD Classroom Kit: A whole-classroom approach for managing disruptive behavior. *Psychology in the Schools* 35(1): 67–79.

Ansello, E. F. and N. N. Eustis. 1992. A common stake? Investigating the emerging "intersection" of aging and disabilities. In E. F. Ansello and N. N. Eustis, eds., *Aging and Disabilities: Seeking Common Ground,* 1–8. New York: Baywood.

Anshel, M. H. 1991. Cognitive-behavioral strategies for combating drug abuse in sport: Implications for coaches and sport psychology consultants. *Sport Psychologist* 5(2): 152–166.

Anthony, E. J. 1957. An experimental approach to the psychopathology of childhood encopresis. *British Journal of Medical Psychology* 30:146–175.

Antony, M., M. Craske, and D. Barlow. 1995. *Mastery of your specific phobia.* Albany, N.Y.: Graywind.

APA (American Psychiatric Association). 1994. *Diagnostic and Statistical Manual of Mental Disorders,* 4th ed. Washington, D.C.: American Psychiatric Association.

Apgar, K. and B. Nicholson Callahan. 1982. *Participant Workbook for Stress Management Training.* New York: Family Association of America.

Applied Medical Informatics, Inc. 1996. Encopresis. http://www.housecall.com/databases/ami/convert/001570.html

Arnold, S. J. 1997. *No More Bedwetting: How to Help Your Child Stay Dry.* New York: Wiley.

Artelt, T. A. and B. Thyer. 1998. Treating chronic grief. In B. A. Thyer and J. S. Wodarski, eds., *Handbook of Empirical Social Work Practice: Volume I: Mental Disorders,* 341–356. New York: Wiley.

Arthur, P. and R. Passini. 1993. *Wayfinding: People, Signs and Architecture.* New York: McGraw-Hill.

Atkinson, L., J. Quarrington, and J. Cyr. 1985. School refusal: The heterogeneity of a concept. *American Journal of Orthopsychiatry* 55(1): 83–101.

Auslander, G. 1988. Social networks and health status of the unemployed. *Health & Social Work* 13:191–200.

Azrin, N. F. et al. Job-finding Club: A group assisted program for obtaining employment. *Behavior Research and Therapy* 13(1): 17–27.

Bachman, R. and L. E. Saltzman. 1995. Violence against women: Estimates from the redesigned survey. Bureau of Justice Statistics press release. http://www.famvi.com.deptjust.htm

Badger, L. W. and E. H. Rand. 1998. Mood disorders. In J. B. W. Williams and K. Ell, eds., *Advances in Mental Health Research: Implications for Practice,* 49–117. Washington, D.C.: NASW Press.

Baer, L. and J. H. Greist. 1997. An interactive computer-administered self-assessment and self-help program for behavior therapy. *Journal of Clinical Psychiatry* 58(12): 23–28.

Baer, R. A. and M. T. Nietzel. 1991. Cognitive and behavioral treatment of impulsivity in children: A meta-analytic review of the outcome literature. *Journal of Clinical Child Psychology* 20(4): 400–412.

Bain, L. J. 1991. *A Parent's Guide to Attention Deficit Disorders.* New York: Dell.

Ballou, M. 1995. Assertiveness training. In M. Ballou, ed., *Psychological Interventions: A Guide to Strategies,* 125–135. Westport, Conn.: Praeger/Greenwood.

Bandura, A. 1982. Self-efficacy mechanism in human agency. *American Psychologist* 37:122–147.

———. 1989. *Social Foundations of Thought and Action: A Social Cognitive Theory.* Englewood Cliffs, N.J.: Prentice-Hall.

Barber, J. G. and R. Gilbertson. 1997. Unilateral interventions for women living with heavy drinkers. *Social Work* 42(1): 69–78.

Barker, P. J. 1993. *A Self-Help Guide to Managing Depression.* San Diego: Singular Publishing Group.

Barker, R. L. 1995. *Social Work Dictionary.* Washington, D.C.: National Association of Social Workers.

Barkley, R. A. 1989. Attention deficit/hyperactivity disorder. In E. Mash and R. T. Barkley, eds., *Treatment of Childhood Disorders,* 39–72. New York: Guilford Press.

———. 1995. *Taking Charge of AD/HD: The Complete, Authoritative Guide for Parents.* New York: Guilford Press.

———. 1996. Attention deficit/hyperactivity disorder. In E. J. Mash and R. A. Barkley, eds., *Child Psychopathology,* 63–112. New York: Guilford Press.

———. 1997. *Defiant Children: A Clinician's Manual for Assessment and Parent Training,* 2nd ed. New York: Guilford Press.

———. 1998. *Attention-Deficit Hyperactivity Disorder: A Handbook for Diagnosis and Treatment*, 2nd ed. New York: Guilford Press.

Barkley, R. A., G. H. Edwards, and A. L. Robin. 1999. *Defiant Teens: A Clinician's Manual for Assessment and Family Intervention.* New York: Guilford Press.

Barkley, R. A. and J. V. Murphy. 1991. Treating attention deficit/hyperactivity disorder: medication and behavior management training. *Pediatric Annals* 20:256–266.

Barlow, D. H. 1988. *Anxiety and Its Disorders.* New York: Guilford Press.

Barrett, P. M., M. R. Dadds, and R. M. Rapee. 1996. Family treatment of childhood anxiety: A controlled trial. *Journal of Consulting and Clinical Psychology* 64(2): 333–342.

Barrowclough, C. and N. Tarrier. 1998. Social functioning and family interventions. In K. T. Mueser and N. Tarrier, eds., *Handbook of Social Functioning in Schizophrenia.* Boston: Allyn and Bacon.

Barth, R. P. 1984. Reducing nonattendance in elementary schools. *Social Work in Education* 6(3): 151–166.

Barusch, A. S. 1991. *Elder Care: Family Training and Support.* Newbury Park, Calif.: Sage.

Basco, M. R., K. J. Prager, J. M. Pitra, L. M. Tamir, et al. 1992. Communication and intimacy in the marriages of depressed patients. *Journal of Family Psychology* 6(2): 184–194.

Bass, E. and L. Davis. 1988. *The Courage to Heal: A Guide for Women Survivors of Child Sexual Abuse.* New York: Harper and Row.

Bassuk, H. L. 1986. *The Mental Health Needs of Homeless Persons.* San Francisco: Jossey-Bass.

Baucom, D. H., N. Epstein, L. A. Rankin, and C. K. Burnett. 1996. Understanding and treating marital distress from a cognitive-behavioral orientation. In K. S. Dobson and K. D. Craig, eds., *Advances in Cognitive Behavioral Therapy,* 211–236. Thousand Oaks, Calif.: Sage.

Baucom, D. H., V. Shoham, K. T. Mueser, and A. D. Daiuto. 1998. Empirically supported couple and family interventions for marital distress and adult mental health problems. *Journal of Consulting and Clinical Psychology* 66(1): 53–88.

Beck, A. 1976. *Cognitive Therapy and the Emotional Disorders.* New York: New American Library.

Beck, A. T. and G. Emery. 1985. *Anxiety Disorders and Phobias: A Cognitive Perspective.* New York: Basic.

Beck, A. T., A. J. Rush, B. F. Shaw, and G. Emery. 1979. *Cognitive Therapy of Depression.* New York: Guilford Press.

Beck, A. T., C. H. Ward, M. Mendelsohn, J. Mock, and J. Ergaugh. 1961. An inventory for measuring depression. *Archives of General Psychiatry* 4:561–571.

Beck, R. and E. Fernandez. 1998. Cognitive-behavioral therapy in the treatment of anger: A meta-analysis. *Cognitive Therapy and Research* 22(1): 63–74.

Beckerman, A. 1994. Mothers in prison: Meeting the prerequisite conditions for permanency planning. *Social Work* 39:9–14.

Bednar, R. L. and S. R. Peterson. 1995. *Self-Esteem: Paradoxes and Innovations in Clinical Theory and Practice,* 2nd ed. Washington, D.C.: American Psychological Association.

Belcher, J. and P. Ephross. 1989. Toward an effective practice model for the homeless mentally ill. *Social Casework* 70:421–427.

Belfiore, P. J. and J. M. Hutchinson. 1998. Enhancing academic achievement through related routines: A functional approach. In W. T. Steuart and F. M. Gresham, eds., *Handbook of Child Behavior Therapy.* New York: Plenum Press.

Belgrave, L. L., M. M. Wykle, and J. M. Choi. 1993. Health, double jeopardy, and culture: the use of institutionalization by African-Americans. *The Gerontologist* 33(3): 379–385.

Bell, A. J., L. A. Rosen, and D. Dynlacht. 1994. Truancy intervention. *Journal of Research and Development in Education* 27(3): 203–211.

Bellack, A., K. Mueser, S. Gingerich, and J. Agresta. 1997. *Social Skills Training for Schizophrenia: A Step-by-Step Guide.* New York: Guilford Press.

Bellack, A. S., R. L. Morrison, and K. T. Mueser. 1992. Behavioral interventions in schizophrenia. In S. M. Turner, K. S. Calhoun, and H. E. Adams, eds., *Handbook of Clinical Behavior Therapy,* 2nd ed., 135–154. New York: Wiley.

Bell-Dolan, D. 1995. Separation anxiety disorder. In R. T. Ammerman and M. Hersen, eds., *Handbook of Child Behavior Therapy: In the Psychiatric Setting,* 217–238. New York: Wiley.

Ben, D. A. 1995. Family functioning and migration: considerations for practice. *Journal of Sociology and Social Welfare* 22(3): 121–137.

Benda, B. B. and P. Dattalo. 1990. Homeless women and men: Their problems and use of services. *Affilia* 5:50–82.

Benedict, H. 1994. *Recovery: How to Survive Sexual Assault for Women, Men, Teenagers and Their Families.* New York: Columbia University Press.

Benjamin, L. S. 1996. Introduction to the special section on structural analysis of social behavior. *Journal of Consulting and Clinical Psychology* 64(6): 1203–1212.

Bentley, K. J. 1998. Psychopharmacological treatment of schizophrenia: what social workers need to know. *Research on Social Work Practice* 8(2): 384–405.

Berg, I. K. and S. D. Miller. 1992. Working with Asian American clients: One person at a time. *Families in Society* 73:356–363.

Berg, I., A. Butler, J. Franklin, and H. Hayes. 1993. DSM-III-R disorders, social factors and management of school attendance problems in the normal population. *Journal of Child Psychology and Psychiatry and Allied Disciplines* 34(7): 1187–1203.

Berg, I. and J. Nursten. 1996. *Unwillingly to School,* 4th ed. London: Gaskell.

Berg-Cross, L. 1997. *Couples Therapy.* Thousand Oaks, Calif.: Sage.

Bergman, L. 1992. Dating violence among high school students. *Social Work* 37(1): 21–27.

Berlin, S. B., K. B. Mann, and S. F. Grossman. 1991. Task analysis of cognitive therapy for depression. *Social Work Research and Abstracts* 27:3–11.

Berliner, H. 1999. Clinical reference systems: Senior health advisor. http://www.patient education.com/level3/senorsa1.html

Berman, A. L. and D. A. Jobes. 1994. Treatment of the suicidal adolescent. Special issue: Suicide assessment and intervention. *Death Studies* 18(4): 375–389.

———. 1995. Suicide prevention in adolescents (age 12–18). Special issue: Suicide prevention: Toward the year 2000. *Suicide and Life Threatening Behavior* 25(1): 143–154.

Berman-Rossi, T. and M. B. Cohen. 1988. Group development and shared decision making: Working with homeless mentally ill women. *Social Work with Groups* 11(4): 63–78.

Bernheim, K. F. and A. F. Lehman. 1985. *Working with Families of the Mentally Ill.* New York: Norton.

Bernstein, G. A. and C. M. Borchardt. 1991. Anxiety disorders of childhood and adolescence: A critical review. *Journal of the American Academy of Child and Adolescent Psychiatry* 30(4): 519–532.

Berry, G. L. and A. Lizardi. 1985. The school phobic child and special services providers: Guidelines for early identification. *Special Services in the Schools* 2(1): 63–72.

Bersani, C. A., H. T. Chen, B. F. Pendleton, and R. Denton. Personality traits of convicted male batterers. *Journal of Family Violence* 7(2): 123–134.

Bertman, S. 1984. Helping children cope with death. In J. C. Hansen and T. T. Frantz, eds., *Death and Grief in the Family*, 48–60. Rockville, Md.: Aspen.

Berzon, B. 1992. *Positively Gay*, 2nd ed. Los Angeles: Mediamix Associates.

Biaggio, M. K. 1987. Clinical dimensions of anger management. *American Journal of Psychotherapy* 41(3): 417–427.

Biloon, S. and M. Quinn. 1996. Labor and management work together in Connecticut's vocational technical schools to create a safer school environment. *Public Personnel Management* 25(4): 439–451.

Birchler, G. R. 1986. Alleviating depression with "marital" intervention. Special issue: Depression in the family. *Journal of Psychotherapy and the Family* 2(3–4): 101–116.

Birchler, G. R. and S. H. Spinks. 1981. Behavioral systems for marital and family therapy: integration and clinical application. *The American Journal of Family Therapy* 8:6–28.

Birmaher, B., N. D. Ryan, D. E. Williamson, D. A. Brent, J. Kaufman, R. E. Dahl, J. Perel, and B. Nelson. 1996. Childhood and adolescent depression: A review of the past 10 years: Part I and Part II. *Journal of the American Academy of Child and Adolescent Psychiatry* 35 (11): 1427–1439; 35(12): 1575–1583.

Bisnaire, L. M., P. Firestone, and D. Rynard. 1990. Factors associated with academic achievement in children following parent separation. *American Journal of Orthopsychiatry* 60(1): 67–76.

Blagg, N. 1987. *School Phobia and Its Treatment*. New York: Croom Helm.

Blair, C. 1996. The Edinburgh Family Scale: A new measure of family functioning. *International Journal of Methods in Psychiatric Research* 6(1): 15–22.

Blankertz, L. E., R. A. Cnann, K. White, J. Fox, and D. Messinger. 1990. Outreach efforts with dually diagnosed homeless persons. *Families in Society* 71(7): 387–395.

Blasinsky, M. 1998. Family dynamics: influencing care of the older adult. *Activities: Adaptation and Aging* 22(4): 65–72.

Blatter, C. W. and J. J. Jacobsen. 1993. Older women coping with divorce: Peer support groups. Special issue: Faces of women and aging. *Women and Therapy* 14(1–2): 141–155.

Block, C. and R. Carter. 1998. White racial identity: theory, research, and implications for organizational contexts: Workplace diversity issues and perspectives. Washington, D.C.: NASW Press.

Bloom, J. 1990. *Help Me to Help My Child*. Boston: Little, Brown.

Bloomquist, M. L. 1996. *Skills Training for Youth with Behavior Disorders: A Parent and Therapist Guidebook*. New York: Guilford Press.

Bohlin, G. 1973. Interaction of arousal and habitation in the development of sleep during monotonous stimulation. *Biological Psychology* 1:99–114.

Boon, F. F. L. and N. N. Singh. 1991. A model for the treatment of encopresis. *Behavior Modification* 15(3): 355–371.

Bootzin, R. R. and M. A. Perlis. 1992. Nonpharmacological treatments of insomnia. *Journal of Clinical Psychology* 53(6): 37–41.

Borden, J. 1992. Behavioral treatment of simple phobia. In S. M. Turner, K. S. Calhoun, and H. E. Adams, eds., *Handbook of Clinical Behavior Therapy*, 2nd ed., 3–12. New York: Wiley.

Bornstein, M. H., ed. 1995. *Handbook of Parenting, Vol. 4: Applied and Practical Parenting*. Mahwah, N.J.: Lawrence Erlbaum Associates.

Borrero, M. 1980. Psychological and emotional impact of unemployment. *Journal of Sociology and Social Welfare* (7):916–934.

Bouman, T. K. and P. M. G. Emmelkamp. 1996. Panic disorder and agoraphobia. In V. B. Van Hasselt and M. Hersen, eds., *Sourcebook of Psychological Treatment Manuals for Adult Disorders*, 23–63. New York: Plenum Press.

Bourne, E. J. 1995. *The Anxiety and Phobia Workbook*, 2nd ed. Oakland: New Harbinger.

Boyd, G. M., J. Howard, and R. A. Zucker, eds. 1995. *Alcohol Problems Among Adolescents: Current Directions in Prevention Research*. Hillsdale, N.J.: Lawrence Erlbaum Associates.

Boyer, C. 1997. Sexually transmitted diseases. In J. Kagan and S. B. Gall, eds., *Gale Encyclopedia of Childhood and Adolescence*, 564–570). Detroit: Gale Research.

Brady, J. P. 1984. Social skills training for psychiatric patients I: Concepts, methods, and clinical results. *The American Journal of Psychiatry* 141(3): 333–340.

Branden, Nathaniel. 1994. *Six Pillars of Self-Esteem*. New York: Bantam.

Braswell, L. and M. Bloomquist. 1991. *Cognitive-Behavioral Therapy with AD/HD Children: Child, Family and School Interventions*. New York: Guilford Press.

Braun, D. L., S. R. Sunday, and K. A. Halmi. 1994. Psychiatric comorbidity in patients with eating disorders. *Psychological Medicine* 24(4): 859–867.

Braver S. L., B. S. Fogas, and S. A. Wolchik. 1992. Locus of control as a mediator of negative divorce-related events and adjustment problems in children. *American Journal of Orthopsychiatry* 62(4): 589–598.

Braver et al. 1991. Stability of quality of life events and psychological symptomatology in children of divorce. *American Journal of Community Psychology* 19(4): 501–521.

Brechling, B. G. and C. A. Schneider. 1993. Preserving autonomy in early state dementia. *Journal of Gerontological Social Work* 20:170–133.

Brehm, S. and T. Smith. 1986. Social psychological approaches to psychotherapy and behavior change. In S. L. Garfield and A. E. Bergin, eds., *Handbook of Psychotherapy and Behavior Change*. New York: Wiley.

Brendler, J., M. Silver, M. Haber, and J. Sargent. 1991. *Madness, Chaos, and Violence: Therapy with Families at the Brink*. New York: Basic.

Breton, M. 1988. The need for mutual aid groups in a drop-in for homeless women: The sistering case. *Social Work with Groups* 11(4): 47–61.

Breznitz, S. and L. Goldberger, eds. 1993. *Handbook of Stress: Theoretical and Clinical Aspects*, 2nd ed. New York: Free Press.

Briar, K. 1987. *Social Work and the Unemployed*. Silver Spring, Md.: National Association of Social Workers.

Brickman, P., V. Rabinowitz, J. Karuza, D. Coates, E. Cohn, and L. Kidder. 1982. Models of helping and coping. *American Psychologist* 37:368–384.

Briesmeister, J. M. and C. E. Schaefer, eds. 1998. *Handbook of Parent Training: Parents as Co-Therapists for Children's Behavior Problems*, 2nd ed. New York: Wiley.

Brigham, F. J., J. P. Bakken, T. E. Scruggs, and M. A. Mastropieri. 1992. Cooperative behavior management: Strategies for promoting a positive classroom environment. *Education and Training in Mental Retardation* 27(1): 3–12.

Bromley, D. B. 1990. *Behavioral Gerontology: Central Issues in the Psychology of Aging*. Chichester: Wiley.

Brouwers, M. 1990. Treatment of body image dissatisfaction among women with bulimia nervosa. *Journal of Counseling and Development* 69:144–147.

Brown, Anne. 1996. Mood disorders in children and adolescents. *NARSD Research Newsletter*. http://www.mhsource.com/advocacy/narsad/childmood.html

Brown, C. and G. J. Mazza. 1997. *Healing in Action: A Leadership Guide for Creating Diverse Communities*. Washington, D.C.: National Coalition Building Institute.

Brown, G. T. and K. Carmichael. 1992. Assertiveness training for clients with a psychiatric illness: A pilot study. *British Journal of Occupational Therapy* 55(4): 137–140.

Brown, J. G. 1991. *Central American Immigrants in New York: Settlement and Adjustment Issues*. Ph.D. diss., City University of New York.

Brown, K. S. and M. Ziefert. 1990. A feminist approach to working with homeless women. *Affilia* 5:6–20.

Brown, L. K. 1986. *Dinosaurs Divorce: A Guide for Changing Families*. Boston: Little, Brown.

Brown, P. A. and C. Dickey. 1992. Critical reflection in groups with abused women. *Affilia* 7:57–71.

Brown, S. A., M. G. Myers, and M. A. Mott. 1994. Correlates of success following treatment for adolescence substance abuse. *Applied and Preventive Psychology* 3(2): 61–73.

Brown, T. A., T. A. O'Leary, and D. H. Barlow. 1993. Generalized anxiety disorder. In D. H. Barlow, ed., *Clinical Handbook of Psychological Disorders: A Step-by Step Treatment Manual*, 2nd ed., 137–188. New York: Guilford Press.

Brownell, K. and C. Fairburn. 1995. *Eating Disorders and Obesity: A Comprehensive Handbook*. New York: Guilford Press.

Bryant, N. 1994. Domestic violence and group treatment for male batterers. Special issue: Men and groups. *Group* 18(4): 235–242.

Buchanan, C. M., E. E. Maccoby, and S. M. Dornbusch. 1996. *Adolescents After Divorce*. Cambridge: Harvard University Press.

Buglass, D. and J. W. McCulloch. 1970. Further suicidal behavior: The development and validation of predictive scales. *British Journal of Psychiatry* 116:483–491.

Bullock, J. R. 1993. Children's temperament: How can teachers and classrooms be more responsive? *Early Child Development and Care* 88:53–59.

Burke, A. C. 1998. Unemployment. In B. A. Thyer and J. S. Wodarski, eds., *Handbook of Empirical Social Work Practice* 2:199–223. New York: Wiley.

Burke, J. 1989. *Contemporary Approaches to Psychotherapy and Counseling: The Self-Regulation and Maturity Model*. Pacific Grove, Calif.: Brooks/Cole.

Burns, D. B. 1980. *The New Mood Therapy*. New York: The American Library.

Burns, D. D. and S. Nolen-Hoeksema. 1992. Therapeutic empathy and recovery from depression in cognitive-behavioral therapy: A structural equation model. *Journal of Consulting and Clinical Psychology* 60:441–449.

Burns, G. L., J. A. Walsh, and S. M. Owen. 1995. Twelve-month stability of disruptive classroom behavior as measured by the Sutter-Eyeberg Student Behavior Inventory. *Journal of Clinical Child Psychology* 24(4): 453–462.

Burroughs, M. S., W. W. Wagner, and J. T. Johnson. 1997. Treatment with children of divorce: A comparison of two types of therapy. *Journal of Divorce and Remarriage* 27 (3–4): 83–99.

Burt, M. R. and B. E. Cohen. 1988. *Feeding the Homeless: Does the Prepared Meals Provision Work?* Washington, D.C.: Urban Institute.

Bush, R. B. and J. Folger. 1994. *The Promise of Mediation: Responding to Conflict Through Empowerment and Recognition*. San Francisco: Jossey-Bass.

Bushy, A. 1994. When your client lives in a rural area: II. Rural professional practice—considerations for nurses providing mental health care. *Issues in Mental Health Nursing* 15(3): 267–276.

Butler, J. E. and R. I. Campise. 1998. Enurises and Encoprises. In B. A. Thyer and J. S. Wodarski, eds., *Handbook of Empirical Social Work Practice: Volume I: Mental Disorders,* 341–356. New York: Wiley.

Butterfield, W. H. and N. H. Cobb. 1994. Cognitive-behavioral treatment of children and adolescents. In D. K. Granvold, ed., *Cognitive and Behavioral Treatment: Methods and Applications,* 77–83. Pacific Grove, Calif.: Brooks/Cole.

Butterworth, J., J. Whitney-Thomas, and D. Shaw. 1997. The changing role of community-based instruction: Strategies for facilitating workplace supports. *Journal of Vocational Rehabilitation* 8:9–20.

Caldwell, K. 1995. Decreasing sensitivity to stressors: The lilac episode. *Journal of Family Psychotherapy* 6(2): 79–81.

Campbell, F. and D. C. Daley. 1993. *Coping with Dual Disorders: Addiction and Emotional or Psychiatric Illness.* Center City, Minn.: Hazeldon Educational Materials.

Campbell, F. and D. Lester. 1999. The impact of gambling opportunities on compulsive gambling. *Journal of Social Psychology* 139(1): 126–127.

Campbell, L. 1997. Child neglect and intensive family preservation practice. *Families in Society* 78(3): 280–290.

Cantos, A. L., L. T. Gries, and V. Slis. 1996. Behavioral correlates of parental visiting during family foster care. *Child Welfare* 76(2): 309–329.

Caplan, M., L. Bennetto, and R. P. Weissberg. 1991. The role of interpersonal context in the assessment of social problem-solving skills. *Journal of Applied Developmental Psychology* 12(1): 103–114.

Capps, L. and E. Ochs. 1995. *Constructing Panic.* London: Harvard University Press.

Carlson, B. E. 1996. Children of battered women: research, programs, and services. In A. R. Roberts, ed., *Helping Battered Women: New Perspectives and Remedies,* 172–187. New York: Oxford University Press.

———. 1997. A stress coping approach to intervention with abused women. *Family Relations* 46:1–8.

Carr, M. and C. Schellenback. 1993. Reflective monitoring in lonely adolescents. *Adolescence* 21(84): 737–747.

Carroll, K. M. 1997. Relapse prevention as a psychosocial treatment: A review of controlled clinical trials. In G. A. Marlatt and G. R VandenBos, eds., *Addictive Behaviors: Readings on Etiology, Prevention, and Treatment,* 697–717. Washington, D.C.: American Psychological Association.

Catalano, R. F., J. D. Hawkins, E. A. Wells, and J. L. Miller. 1991. Evaluation of the effectiveness of adolescent drug abuse treatment, assessment of risks for relapse, and promising approaches for relapse prevention. *International Journal of the Addictions* 25:1085–1140.

Carstensen, L. L., B. A. Edelstein, and L. Dornbrand. 1996. *The Practical Handbook of Clinical Gerontology.* Thousand Oaks, Calif.: Sage.

Cartledge, G. and J. F. Milburn, eds. 1980. *Teaching Social Skills to Children: Innovative Approaches.* New York: Pergamon Press.

Carton-LaNey, I. 1991. Some considerations of the rural elderly black's underuse of social services. *Journal of Gerontological Social Work* 16(1/2): 337–345.

Casper, E. S. and J. R. Regan. 1993. Reasons for admission among six profile subgroups of recidivists of inpatient services. *Canadian Journal of Psychiatry* 38(10): 657–661.

Cass, V. S. 1979. Homosexuality identity formation: A theoretical model. *Journal of Homosexuality* 4:219–235.

Catalano, R. F. et al. 1999. An experimental intervention with families of substance abusers: One-year follow-up of the focus on families project. *Addiction* 94(2): 241–254.

Cates, J. A. 1987. Adolescent sexuality: gay and lesbian issues. *Child Welfare* 66(4): 353–363.

Caton, C. 1984. *Management of Chronic Schizophrenia.* New York: Oxford University Press.

Caudill, M. A. 1995. *Managing Pain Before It Manages You.* New York: Guilford Press.

Centers for Disease Control and Prevention. 1998a. *HIV/AIDS Surveillance Report, U.S. and AIDS Cases Reported Through June 1998.* 10(1). Atlanta, Ga.: Centers for Disease Control and Prevention.

——. 1998b. *HIV Prevention Through Early Detection and Treatment of Other Sexually Transmitted Diseases, U.S. Recommendations of the Advisory Committee for HIV and STD Prevention.* MMWR 47(RR): 1–24. Atlanta, Ga.: Centers for Disease Control and Prevention.

Cervera, N. J. 1993. Serving pregnant and parenting teens. *Families-In-Society: The Journal of Contemporary Human Services* 74(6): 323.

Champlin, L. 1992. Inadequate analgesia: Patients endure pain, fear, addiction. *Geriatrics* 47(8): 71.

Charkin, W., V. Breitbart, and D. Elman. 1997. Integrating HIV, STD and family planning services, comment on Z. Stein. *American Journal of Public Health* 87:691–692.

Charney, L. 1993. Project achievement: A six-year study of a dropout prevention program in bilingual schools. *Social Work in Education* 15(2): 113–17.

Cheesbrough, M. and J. Hill. 1996. "Questions, questions, questions!" A comparison of therapist inferences and parental responses to systemic questions. *Journal of Family Therapy* 18(1): 79–97.

Cheung, M. 1989. Elderly Chinese living in the United States: Assimilation or adjustment? *Social Work* 34(5): 457–61.

Christiansen, L. and A. Poling. 1997. Using self-management procedures to improve the productivity of adults with developmental disabilities in a competitive employment setting. *Journal of Applied Behavior Analysis* 30:169–172.

Christopoulos, C., D. A. Cohn, D. S. Shaw, S. Joyce, J. Sullivan-Hanson, S. P. Kraft, and R. E. Emery. 1987. Children of abused women: I. Adjustment at time of shelter residence. *Journal of Marriage and the Family* 49(3): 611–619.

Chung, T. Y. and S. R. Asher. 1996. Children's goals and strategies in peer conflict situations. *Merrill Palmer Quarterly* 42(1): 125–147.

Cimmarusti, R. A., M. C. James, D. W. Simpson, and C. E. Wright. 1984. Treating the context of truancy. *Social Work in Education* 6(3): 201–211.

Clark, M. E. and J. P. Hornick. 1988. The child sexual abuse victim: Assessment and treatment issues and solutions. *Contemporary Family Therapy* 10(4): 235–242.

Clark, N. M. and W. Rakowski. 1983. Family caregivers of older adults: Improving helping skills. *The Gerontologist* 23:637–642.

Clark, W. G., and S. S. Travis. 1994. Early admissions to a state psychiatric hospital: Cohort characteristics, after-care needs, and discharge destinations. *Journal of Gerontological Social Work* 21(3–4): 101–115.

Clemens, E. L. 1995. Multiple perceptions of discharge planning in one urban hospital. *Health and Social Work* 20(4): 254–261.

Clements, M. L., A. D. Cordova, H. J. Markman, and J. P. Laurenceau. 1997. The erosion of marital satisfaction over time and how to prevent it. In R. J. Sternberg and M. Hojjat, eds., *Satisfaction in Close Relationships*, 335–355. New York: Guilford Press.

Cnaan, R. A. and V. C. Seltzer. 1989. Etiology of truancy. *Social Work in Education* 30:183–189.

Coburn, N., C. Martin, R. Thompson, and E. Nostrom. 1992. Guidelines for improvements to transit accessibility for persons with disabilities. Washington, D.C: Federal Transit Administration.

Coggan, C. and R. Norton. 1994. Reducing self-directed harm (suicide and attempted suicide) among young people: A public health approach? *Community Mental Health in New Zealand* 8(2): 26–31.

Cohen, B. E. and M. R. Burt. 1990. The homeless: Chemical dependency and mental health problems. *Social Work Research and Abstracts* 26:8–17.

Cohen, N., A. B. Gantt, and A. Sainz. 1997. Influences on fit between psychiatric patients' psychosocial needs and their hospital discharge plan. *Psychiatric Services* 48(4): 518–523.

Cohen, N. L. 1990. *Psychiatry Takes to the Streets.* New York: Guilford Press.

Cohen, M. B. 1988. Tenant organizing with the mentally ill homeless. *Catalyst* 4(22): 33–37.

———. 1989. Social work practice with homeless mentally ill people: Engaging the client. *Social Work* 54(6): 505–509.

Coke, M. M. and J. A. Twaite. 1995. *The Black Elderly: Satisfaction and Quality of Later Life.* New York: Haworth Press.

Coleman, J. C., ed. 1987. *Working with Troubled Adolescents: A Handbook.* Orlando, Fla.: Academic Press.

Collier, C. W. and G. A. Marlatt. 1995. Relapse prevention. In A. J. Goreczny, ed., *Handbook of Health and Rehabilitation Psychology,* 307–321. New York: Plenum Press.

Community of Mental Health Services. 1992. *Schizophrenia Information for Families.* Geneva: Division of Mental Health Services, World Health Organization.

Connell, C. M. and G. Gibson. 1997. Racial, ethnic, and cultural differences in dementia caregiving: Review and analysis. *Gerontologist* 37(3): 355–364.

Connelly, C. E. and J. D. Dilonardo. 1993. Self-care issues with chronically ill psychotic clients. *Perspectives in Psychiatric Care* 29(4): 31–35.

Conners, K. C. 1969. A teacher rating scale for use in drug studies with children. *American Journal of Psychiatry* 126(6): 884–888.

Contreras, R., S. S. Hendrick, and C. Hendrick. 1996. Perspectives on marital love and satisfaction in Mexican American and Anglo-American couples. *Journal of Counseling and Development* 74(4): 408–415.

Cook, A. C. and D. S. Dworkin. 1992. *Helping the Bereaved: Therapeutic Interventions for Children, Adolescents and Adults.* New York: Basic.

Corcoran, K. and Fischer, J. 1987. *Measures for Clinical Practice: A Source Book.* New York: Free Press.

Cotrell, V. 1996. Respite use by dementia caregivers: preferences and reasons for initial use. *Journal of Gerontological Social Work* 26(3–4): 35–55.

Cotterill, L., L. Hayes, M. Flynn, and P. Sloper. 1997 Reviewing respite services: some lessons from the literature. *Disability and Society* 12:775–788.

Courtois, C. 1989. *Healing the Incest Wound.* New York: Norton.

———. 1992. The memory retrieval process in incest survivor therapy. *Journal of Child Sexual Abuse* 1(1): 15–31.

Covey, S. 1989. *The Seven Habits of Highly Effective People: Powerful Lessons in Personal Change.* New York: Simon & Schuster.

Cox, C. 1997. Findings from a statewide program of respite care: A comparison of service users, stoppers and nonusers. *The Gerontologist* 37:511–517.

Craighead, W. E., D. D. Evans, and C. J. Robins. 1992. Behavioral interventions in schizophrenia. In S. M. Turner, K. S. Calhoun, and H. E. Adams, eds., *Handbook of Clinical Behavior Therapy,* 2nd ed., 99–116. New York: Wiley.

Craske, M. G., R. M. Rapee, and D. H. Barlow. 1992. Cognitive-behavioral treatment of panic disorder, agoraphobia, and generalized anxiety disorder. In S. M. Turner, K. S. Calhoun, and H. E. Adams, eds., *Handbook of Clinical Behavior Therapy,* 2nd ed., 39–68. New York: Wiley.

Crespi, T. D. and R. M. Sabatelli. 1993. Adolescent runaways and family strife: A conflict-induced differentiation framework. *Adolescence* 28(112): 867–878.

Crick, N. R. 1995. Relational aggression: The role of intent attributions, feelings of distress, and provocation type. *Development and Psychopathology* 7:313–322.

Crisafulli, A. 1999. *Managing Common Child and Adolescent Issues and Behavior Problems.* Albany, N.Y.: Schenectady Child Guidance Center.

Crockenberg, S. and A. Lourie. 1996. Parents' conflict strategies with children and children's conflict strategies with peers. *Merrill Palmer Quarterly* 42(4): 495–518.

Crose, R. 1990. Establishing and maintaining intimate relationships among nursing home residents. *Journal of Mental Health Counseling* 12(1): 102–106.

Cummings, S. M. and C. Cockerham. 1997. Ethical dilemmas in discharge planning for patients with Alzheimer's disease. *Health and Social Work* 22(2): 101–108.

Curtis, P. A. 1990. The consequences of acculturation to service delivery and research with Hispanic families. *Child and Adolescent Social Work Journal* 7:147–159.

Curtis, T. D. 1989. *Recovery Assistance Program: A Teacher's Guide to Drug and Alcohol Recovery Education.* Seattle: King County Division of Alcohol and Substance Abuse Services.

Cwik, M. S. 1996. The many effects of rape: The victim, her family, and suggestions for family therapy. *Family Therapy* 23(2) 96–116.

D'Zurilla, T. J. 1990. Problem-solving training for effective stress management and prevention. *Journal of Cognitive Psychotherapy: An International Quarterly* 4(4): 327–354.

D'Zurilla, T. J. and A. M. Nezu. 1990. Development and preliminary evaluation of the social problem-solving inventory. *Psychological Assessment: A Journal of Consulting and Clinical Psychology* 2:156–163.

D'Augelli, A. R. 1996. Lesbian, gay and bisexual development during adolescence and young adulthood. In R. P. Cabaj and T. S. Stein, eds., *Textbook of Homosexuality and Mental Health.* Washington, D.C.: American Psychiatric Press.

D'Zurilla, T. J. 1986. *Problem-Solving Therapy: A Social Competence Approach to Clinical Intervention.* New York: Springer.

Dadds, M. R. 1997. Conduct disorder. In R. T. Michel, ed., *Handbook of Prevention and Treatment with Children and Adolescents,* 521–550. New York: Wiley.

Dail, P. and R. Koshes. 1992. Treatment issues and treatment configurations for mentally ill homeless women. *Social Work in Health Care* 17:27–44.

Daley, C. 1993. *Preventing Relapse*. Center City, Minn.: Hazeldon Educational Materials.

Dalton, R., N. Haslett, and G. Daul. 1986. Alternative therapy with recalcitrant fire setters. *Journal of the American Academy of Child Psychiatry* 25(5): 713–717.

Dane, B. O. 1991. Death of a child. In A. Gitterman, ed., *Handbook of Social Work Practice with Vulnerable Populations*, 446–470. New York: Columbia University Press.

Danermark, B. and M. Ekstroem. 1990. Relocation and health effects on the elderly: a commented research review. *Journal of Sociology and Social Welfare* 17(1): 25–49.

Dangel, R. F. and R. A. Polster, eds. 1984. *Parent Training: Foundations of Research and Practice*. New York: Guilford Press.

Dare, C. and I. Eisler. 1997. Family therapy for anorexia nervosa. In D. M. Garner and P. E. Garfinkel, eds., *Handbook of Treatment for Eating Disorders*, 307–324. New York: Guilford Press.

Daro, D. 1988. *Confronting Child Abuse*. New York: Free Press.

Das, A. K. 1990. Counseling people with addictive behavior. *International Journal for the Advancement of Counseling* 13:169–177.

Dattilio, F. M. 1998. *Case Studies in Couple and Family Therapy: Systemic and Cognitive Perspectives*. New York: Guilford Press.

Dattilio, F. M., N. B. Epstein, and D. H. Baucom. 1998. An introduction to cognitive-behavioral therapy with couples and families. In F. M. Dattilio, ed., *Case Studies in Couple and Family Therapy: Systemic and Cognitive Perspectives*, 1–36. New York: Guilford Press.

Davenport, C., K. Browne, and R. Palmer. 1994. Opinions on the traumatizing effects of child sexual abuse: Evidence for consensus. *Child Abuse and Neglect* 18(9): 725–738.

Davis, L. V. and B. E. Carlson. 1987. Observation of spouse abuse: What happens to the children? *Journal of Interpersonal Violence* 2(3): 278–291.

Davis, L. V. and M. Strinivasan. 1995. Listening to the voices of battered women: What helps them escape. *Affilia* 10:49–69.

Davis, M., E. R. Eshelman, and M. McKay. 1995. *The Relaxation and Stress Reduction Workbook*. Oakland: New Harbinger.

Davison, T. 1997. *Life After Psychotherapy*. Northvale, N.J.: Jason Aronson.

Dawson, P. M., K. Griffith, and K. M. Boeke. 1990. Combined medical and psychological treatment of hospitalized children with encopresis. *Child Psychiatry and Human Development* 20(3): 181–190.

DeBellis, M. D. 1997. Post-traumatic stress disorder and acute stress disorder. In R. T. Michel, ed., *Handbook of Prevention and Treatment with Children and Adolescents*, 455–494. New York: Wiley.

Deblinger, E., S. U. McLeer, and D. Henry. 1990. Cognitive-behavioral treatment for sexually abused children suffering post-traumatic stress: Preliminary findings. *Journal of the American Academy of Child and Adolescent Psychiatry* 29(5): 747–752.

Deffenbacher, J. L. 1996. Cognitive-behavioral approaches to anger reduction. In K. S. Dobson and K. D. Craig, eds., *Advances in Cognitive-Behavioral Therapy*, 31–62. Thousand Oaks, Calif.: Sage.

Delmonte, M. M. 1995. The use of hypnotic regression with panic disorder: A case report. *The Australian Journal of Clinical Hypnotherapy and Hypnosis* 16(2): 69–73.

Dempsey, C. L. 1994. Health and social issues of gay, lesbian, and bisexual adolescents. *Families in Society* 75(3): 160–167.

DePanfilis, D. 1996. Social isolation of neglected families: A review of social support assessment and intervention models. *Child Maltreatment Journal* 1(1): 37.

Derogatis, L. 1986. *Manual for the Symptom Checklist-90, Revised* (SCL-90-R). Baltimore, Md.: Self-published.

DeRubeis, R. J. and P. Crits-Christoph. 1998. Empirically supported individual and group psychological treatments for adult mental disorders. *Journal of Consulting and Clinical Psychology* 66(1): 37–52.

DeSalvatore, G. and R. Hornstein. 1991. Juvenile fire setting: assessment and treatment in psychiatric hospitalization and residential placement. *Child and Youth Care Forum* 20(2): 103–115.

Deschner, J. P. 1984. *The Hitting Habit: Anger Control for Battering couples*. New York: Free Press.

Deschner, J. P., J. S. McNeil, and M. G. Moore. 1986. A treatment model for batterers. *Social Casework* 67(1): 55–60.

Dewhurst, A. M., R. J. Moore, and D. P. Alfano. 1992. Aggression against women by men: Sexual and spousal assault. Special issue: Sex offender treatment: Psychological and medical approaches. *Journal of Offender Rehabilitation* 18(3–4): 39–47.

deYoung, M. and B. A. Corbin. 1994. Helping early adolescents tell: A guided exercise for trauma-focused sexual abuse treatment groups. *Child Welfare* 73(2): 141–154.

Diamond, G. S. and H. A. Liddle. 1999. Transforming negative parent-adolescent interactions: From impasse to dialogue. *Family Process* 38(1): 5–26.

Diamond, R. J. 1983. Enhancing medication use in schizophrenic patients. *Journal of Clinical Psychiatry* 44(6) (sec. 2): 7–14.

Diekstra, R. F. 1992. The prevention of suicidal behavior: Evidence for the efficacy of clinical and community-based programs. *International Journal of Mental Health* 21(3): 69–87.

Dische, S., W. Yule, J. Corbett, and D. Hand. 1983. Childhood nocturnal enuresis: Factors associated with outcome of treatment with an enuresis alarm. *Developmental Medicine and Neurology* 25:67–80.

Dobson, K. S. 1989. A meta-analysis of the efficacy of cognitive therapy for depression. *Journal of Consulting and Clinical Psychology* 57:414–419.

Doherty, W. J. 1981. Cognitive processes in intimate conflict: I. Extending attribution theory. *American Journal of Family Therapy* 9:3–12.

Donahue, K. M. 1996. *Developing a Task-Centered Mediation Model*. Ph.D. diss., State University of New York at Albany.

Donavan, B. 1995. *Paraprofessional Home Visiting for High-Risk Adolescent Mothers: Effects on Social Support and Parenting*. Ph.D. diss., State University of New York at Albany.

Donnell, P. J. 1984. The abstinence violation effect and circumstances surrounding relapse as predictors of outcome status in male alcoholic patients. *Journal of Psychology* 117:257–262.

Donohue, B. C., V. B. Van Hasselt, and M. Hersen. 1994. Behavioral assessment and treatment of social phobia. *Behavior Modification* 18:262–288.

Donovan, D. and D. McIntyre. 1990. *Healing the Hurt Child: A Developmental-Contextual Approach*. New York: Norton.

Dowling, J. 1988. Counseling interventions with depressed children. *Elementary School Guidance and Counseling* 22(3): 231–239.

Drake, R. E., S. J. Bartels, G. B. Teague, D. L. Noordsy, and R. E. Clark. 1993. Treatment of substance abuse in severely mentally ill patients. *Journal of Nervous and Mental Disease* 181:606–611.

Drake, R. E., D. L. Noordsy, and T. Ackerson. 1995. Integrating mental health and substance abuse treatments for persons with chronic mental disorders: A model. In A. F. Lehman and L. D. Dixon, eds., *Double Jeopardy: Chronic Mental Illness and Substance Use Disorders,* 251–264. New York: Harwood.

Duggan-Ali, D. 1992. Social skills and assertiveness training integrated into high school sexuality education curriculum. In I. G. Fodor, ed., *Adolescent Assertiveness and Social Skills Training: A Clinical Handbook,* 219–233. New York: Springer.

Dumas, J. E. 1992. Conduct disorder. In S. M. Turner, K. S. Calhoun, and H. E. Adams, eds., *Handbook of Clinical Behavior Therapy,* 2nd ed., 285–316. New York: Wiley.

Dummit, E. S. et al. 1996. Fluoxetine treatment of children with selective mutism: An open trial. *Journal of the American Academy of Child and Adolescent Psychiatry* 35(5): 615–621.

DuPaul, G. J. and K. E. Hoff. 1998. Attention/concentration problems. In W. T. Steuart and F. M. Gresham, eds., *Handbook of Child Behavior Therapy.* New York: Plenum Press.

Durham, R. C. et al. 1999. One year follow-up of cognitive therapy, analytic psychotherapy and anxiety management training for generalized anxiety disorder: Symptom change, medication usage and attitudes to treatment. *Behavioural and Cognitive Psychotherapy* 27(1): 19–35.

Durrant, M. 1993. *Residential Treatment: A Cooperative Competency-Based Approach to Therapy and Program Design.* New York: Norton.

Dutton, M. A. 1992. *Empowering and Healing the Battered Woman: A Model for Assessment and Intervention.* New York: Springer.

Dziegielewski, S. F. 1998. Psychopharmacology and social work practice: Introduction. *Research on Social Work Practice* 8(4): 371–383.

East, E. 1992. Family as a resource: Maintaining chronically mentally ill members in the community. *Health and Social Work* 17(2): 93–97.

East, P. L. 1991. The parent-child relationships of withdrawn, aggressive, and sociable children: Child and parent perspectives. *Merrill Palmer Quarterly* 37(3): 425–443.

Eckman, T. A., R. P. Liberman, C. C. Phipps, and K. E. Blair. 1990. Teaching medication management skills to schizophrenic patients. *Journal of Clinical Psychopharmacology* 10(1): 33–38.

Edleson, J. L. 1992. *Intervention for Men Who Batter: An Ideological Approach.* Newbury Park, Calif.: Sage.

Edleson, J. L., Z. C. Eisikovits, E. Guttman, and M. Sela-Amit. 1991. Cognitive and interpersonal factors in woman abuse. *Journal of Family Violence* 6(2): 167–182.

Edelson, J. L. and R. J. Grusznski. 1988. Treating men who batter: Four years of outcome data from the domestic abuse project. *Journal of Social Service Research* 12(1–2): 3–22.

Edelson, J. L., D. M. Miller, G. W. Stone, and D. G. Chapman. 1985. Group treatment for men who batter. *Social Work Research and Abstracts* 21(3): 18–21.

Edelson, J. L. and M. Syers. 1990. Relative effectiveness of group treatments for men who batter. *Social Work Research and Abstracts* 26(2): 10–17.

———. 1991. The effects of group treatment for men who batter: An 18-month follow-up study. *Research on Social Work Practice* 1(3): 227–243.

EEOC Compliance Manual Bureau of National Affairs. Washington, D.C.: Government Printing Office.

Eerry, J. 1990. *Good Answers to Tough Questions About Divorce.* Sebastopol, Calif.: Living Skills Press.

Eisen, A. R., L. B. Engler, and B. Geyer. 1998. Parent training for separation anxiety disorder. In J. M. Briesmeister and C. E. Schaefer, eds., *Handbook of Parent Training: Parents as Co-Therapists for Children's Behavior Problems,* 2nd ed., 205–224. New York: Wiley.

Eisikovits, Z. C., E. Guttman, M. Sela-Amit, and J. L. Edleson. 1993. Woman battering in Israel: The relative contributions of interpersonal factors. *American Journal of Orthopsychiatry* 63(2): 313–317.

El Guebaly, N. and D. Hodgins. 1998. Substance-related cravings and relapses: Clinical implications. *Canadian Journal of Psychiatry* 43(1): 29–36.

Eldredge, K. L. and W. S. Agras. 1996. Weight and shape over concern and emotional eating in binge eating disorder. *International Journal of Eating Disorders* 19(1): 73–82.

Eldrid, J. 1993. The complementary roles of volunteers and professionals in suicide prevention. *Giornale Italiano di Suicidologia* 3(2): 107–109.

Ellis, A. 1963. *Reason and Emotion in Psychotherapy.* New York: Lyle Stuart.

——. 1977. *Anger: How to Live with and Without It.* New York: Citadel Press.

Emerson, S., L. Horne, and V. Vactor. 1991. Disturbed body image in patients with eating disorders. *Journal of American Psychiatry* 148:211–212.

Epstein, M. H. and D. Cullinan. 1986. Depression in children. *Journal of School Health* 56(1): 10–12.

Epstein, N. and S. E. Schlesinger. 1996. Treatment of family problems. In M. A. Reinecke and F. M. Dattilio, eds., *Cognitive Therapy with Children and Adolescents: A Casebook for Clinical Practice.* New York: Guilford Press.

Estes, L. Encopresis–soiling of the pants. Parenthood Web: http://www.parenthoodweb.com:80/askpros/laurie3.htm

Estes, N. J. and M. E. Heinemann. 1986. *Alcoholism: Development, Consequences, and Interventions.* St. Louis: C. V. Mosby.

Eth, S., and R. S. Pynoos. 1985. *Post-Traumatic Stress Disorder in Children.* Washington: American Psychiatric Press.

Evans, N. and H. Levine. 1990. Perspectives on sexual orientation. *New Directions for Student Services* 51:49–58.

Eyberg, S. M. and S. R. Boggs. 1998. Parent-child interaction therapy: A psychosocial intervention for the treatment of young conduct-disordered children. In J. M. Briesmeister and C. E. Schaefer, eds., *Handbook of Parent Training: Parents as Co-Therapists for Children's Behavior Problems,* 2nd ed., 61–97. New York: Wiley.

Fair Employment Practice: Cumulative Digest and Index: Cases from 1993–1989. 1989. Washington, D.C.: Bureau of National Affairs.

Fairburn, C. and G. Wilson. 1993. *Binge Eating: Nature, Assessment, and Treatment.* New York: Guilford Press.

Falicov, C. 1998. *Latino Families in Therapy: A Guide to Multicultural Practice.* New York: Guilford Press.

Fallon, J., L. Mark, and J. Olesen. 1993. *Groups: A Manual for Chemical Dependency and Psychiatric Treatment.* Santa Fe: CL Productions.

Fallon, P., M. Katzman, and S. Wooley. 1994. *Feminist Perspectives on Eating Disorders.* New York: Guilford Press.

Falloon, I. R. H., ed. 1988. *Handbook of Behavioral Family Therapy.* New York: Guilford Press.

Faludi, S. 1991. *Backlash.* New York: Doubleday.

Fanshel D., S. J. Finch, and J. F. Grundy. 1990. *Foster Children in a Life Course Perspective.* New York: Columbia University Press.

Fantuzzo, J., L. M. DePaola, L. Lambert, T. Martino, G. Anderson, and S. Sutton. 1991. Effects of interparental violence on the psychological adjustment and competencies of young children. *Journal of Consulting and Clinical Psychology* 59(2): 258–265.

Fantuzzo, J., B. Sutton-Smith, M. Atkins, and R. Meyers. 1996. Community-based resilient peer treatment of withdrawn maltreated preschool children. *Journal of Consulting and Clinical Psychology* 64(6): 1377–1386.

Fatout, M. F. 1993. Physically abused children: Activity as a therapeutic medium. *Social Work with Groups* 16(3): 83–96.

Fauber, R., R. Forehand, and A. M. Thomas. 1990. A mediational model of the impact of marital conflict on adolescent adjustment in intact and divorced families: The role of disrupted parenting. *Child Development* 61(4): 1112–1123.

Feather, J. 1993. Factors in perceived hospital discharge planning effectiveness. *Social Work In Health Care* 19(1): 1–14.

Feindler, E. 1991. Cognitive strategies in anger control intervention for children and adolescents. In P. C. Kendall, ed., *Child and Adolescent Therapy: Cognitive-Behavioral Procedures,* 67–97. New York: Guilford Press.

Feindler, E. and J. Guttman. 1994. Cognitive-behavioral anger control training. In C. W. LeCroy, ed., *Handbook of Child and Adolescent Treatment Manuals,* 170–199. New York: Lexington.

Feitel, B., N. Margetson, J. Chamas, and C. Lipman. 1992. Psychosocial background and behavioral and emotional disorders of homeless and runaway youth. *Hospital and Community Psychiatry* 43(2): 155–159.

Feldman, R. A., T. E. Caplinger, and J. S. Wodarski. 1983. *The St. Louis Conundrum: The Effective Treatment of Antisocial Youths.* Englewood Cliffs, N.J.: Prentice-Hall.

Felson, R. B. 1983. Aggression and violence between siblings. *Social Psychology Quarterly* 46: 271–285.

Felson, R. B. and N. Russo. 1988. Parental punishment and sibling aggression. *Social Psychology Quarterly* 5: 11–18.

Felthous, A. R. 1994. Preventing jailhouse suicides. *Bulletin of the American Academy of Psychiatry and the Law* 22(4): 477–488.

Ferreira de Mello, M. A. and W. C. Mann. 1995. The use of mobility devices by older individuals with developmental disabilities living in community residences. *Technology and Disability* 4: 275–285.

Filinson, R. and S. R. Ingman. 1989. *Elder Abuse—Practice and Policy.* New York: Human Sciences Press.

Finkelhor, D. 1986. *Child Sexual Abuse: New Theories and Research.* New York: Free Press.

Fiorentine, R. 1999. After drug treatment: Are 12-step programs effective in maintaining abstinence? *American Journal of Drug and Alcohol Abuse* 25(1): 93–116.

First, R. J., J. C. Rife, and B. G. Toomey. 1994. Homeless in rural areas: Causes, patterns, and trends. *Social Work* 39: 97–107.

Fischer, D. J., J. A. Himle, and B. A. Thyer. 1999. Separation anxiety disorder. In R. T. Ammerman and M. Hersen, eds., *Handbook of Prescriptive Treatments for Children and Adolescents,* 141–154. Boston: Allyn and Bacon.

Fischer, J. and K. Corcoran. 1994a. *Measures for Clinical Practice, 2nd ed. Vol. 1: Couples, Families, and Children.* New York: Free Press.

———. 1994b. *Measures for Clinical Practice, 2nd ed., Vol. 2: Adults.* New York: Free Press.

Fishman, H. C. 1988. *Treating Troubled Adolescents: A Family Therapy Approach.* New York: Basic.

Fleming, J. E. and D. R. Offord. 1993. *Childhood Depression.* Montreal: McGill-Queen's University Press.

Flener, B. S. 1993. The consultative-collaborative teacher for students with visual handicaps. *Review* 24(4): 173–182.

Fletcher, K. E. 1996. Childhood post-traumatic stress disorder. In E. J. Mash and R. A. Barkley, eds., *Child Psychopathology,* 242–276. New York: Guilford Press.

Flournoy, P. S. and G. L. Wilson. 1991. Assessment of MMPI profiles of male batterers. *Violence and Victims* 6(4): 309–320.

Foa, E. B., B. A. Rothbaum, and G. S. Steketee. 1993. Treatment of rape victims. *Journal of Interpersonal Violence* 8(2): 256–275.

Foder, I. G. 1992. *Adolescent Assertiveness and Social Skills Training: A Clinical Handbook.* New York: Springer.

Folberg, J. and A. Taylor. 1984. Family and divorce mediation. In *Mediation: A Comprehensive Guide to Resolving Conflicts Without Litigation,* 147–189. San Francisco: Jossey-Bass.

Force, R. and J. Sebree. 1985. The validation of outcome predictors used at the Saint Francis Boy's Homes. *Quality Review Bulletin* 1(9): 266–270.

Ford, C. V. 1996. *Lies! Lies! Lies! Lies!: The Psychology of Deceit.* Washington, D.C.: American Psychiatrist Press.

Ford, D. E. and D. B. Kamerow. 1989. Epidemiologic study of sleep disturbances and psychiatric disorders. *Journal of the American Medical Association* 262:1479–1484.

Forehand, R. and R. McMahon. 1981. *Helping the Noncompliant Child: A Clinician's Guide to Parent Training.* New York: Guilford Press.

Forehand, R., B. Neighbors, D. Devine, and L. Armisted. 1994. Inter-parental conflict and parental divorce: The individual, relative and interactive effects on adolescents across four years. *Family Relations* 43(4): 387–394.

Foreyt, J. P. and G. K. Goodrick. 1994. Attributes of successful approaches to weight loss and control. *Applied and Preventive Psychology* 3:209–215.

———. 1994. Impact of behavior therapy on weight loss. *American Journal of Health Promotion* 8(6): 466–468.

Forman, S. G. 1993. *Coping Skills Interventions for Children and Adolescents.* San Francisco: Jossey-Bass.

Fortune, A. 1985. *Task-Centered Practice with Families and Groups.* New York: Springer.

Foss, D. H. and O. D. Hadfield. 1993. A successful clinic for the reduction of mathematics anxiety among college students. *College Student Journal* 27(2): 157–165.

Foster, G. D. and P. C. Kendall. 1994. The realistic treatment of obesity: Changing the scales of success. *Clinical Psychology Review* 14(8): 701–736.

Fowler, M. 1991. *Attention Deficit Disorder.* National Information Center for Children and Youth Briefing Paper, September. Washington, D.C.: National Information Center for Children and Youth.

———. 1993. *Maybe You Know My Kid.* New York: Birch Lane Press.

Francis, A., J. P. Docherty, and D. A. Kahn. 1996. Treatment of schizophrenia. *Journal of Clinical Psychiatry* 57(Suppl 12 B): 5–58.

Francis, G. 1992. Behavioral treatment of childhood anxiety disorders. In S. M. Turner, K. S. Calhoun, and H. E. Adams, eds., *Handbook of Clinical Behavior Therapy*, 2nd ed., 227–243. New York: Wiley.

Francke, L. B. 1983. *Growing Up Divorced.* New York: Linden Press/Simon & Schuster.

Frank, J. R. 1990. High school dropouts: A new look at family variables. *Social Work in Education* 13(1): 34–47.

Fraser, M. W., K. E. Nelson, and J. C. Rivard. 1997. Effectiveness of family preservation services. *Social Work Research* 21:138–153.

Freedman, R. 1988. *Body Love: Learning to Like Our Looks and Ourselves.* New York: Harper and Row.

Freeman, E. M. 1984. Loss and grief in children: Implications for school social workers. *Social Work in Education* 6(4): 241–258.

———. 1984. Multiple losses in the elderly: An ecological approach. *Social Casework* 65(5): 287–296.

Freeman, K. A., C. D. Adams, and R. S. Drabman. 1998. Divorcing parents: Guidelines for promoting children's adjustment. *Child and Family Behavior Therapy* 20(3): 1–27.

Frey-Angel, J. 1989. Treating children of violent families: A sibling group approach. *Social Work with Groups* 12(1): 95–107.

Frick, A. 1983. *Reflections of a Rock Lobster: A Story About Growing Up Gay.* Boston: Alyson.

Friedman, H. S. 1998. *Encyclopedia of Mental Health,* vol. 3. San Diego: Academic Press.

Friedman, M. A. and K. D. Brownell. 1996. A comprehensive treatment manual for the management of obesity. In V. B. Van Hasselt and M. Hersen, eds., *Sourcebook of Psychological Treatment Manuals for Adult Disorders,* 375–422. New York: Plenum Press.

Friedrich, W. N., W. J. Luecke, R. L. Beilke, and V. Place. 1992. Psychotherapy outcome of sexually abused boys. *Journal of Interpersonal Violence* 7(3): 196–409.

Fuller, J. 1995. Getting in touch with your own heritage. In N. Vacce et al., eds., *Experiencing and Counseling Multicultural and Diverse Populations.* Bristol, Penn.: Accelerated Development.

Furnham, A. et al. 1996. Job search strategies, attitudes to school and attributions about unemployment. *Journal of Adolescence* 19(4): 355–369.

Gajria, M. and S. J. Salend. 1995. Homework practices of students with and without learning disabilities: A comparison. *Journal of Learning Disabilities* 28(5): 291–296.

Galan, F. J. 1985. Traditional values about family behavior: The case of the Chicano client. *Social Thought* 11:14–22.

Galloway, J. and S. M. Sheridan. 1994. Implementing scientific practices through case studies: Examples using home-school interventions and consultation. *Journal of School Psychology* 32(4): 385–413.

Galski, T., ed. 1987. *The Handbook of Pathological Gambling.* Springfield, Ill.: Charles C. Thomas.

Galvin, M. R. and S. Ferraro. 1991. *A Story for Children Who Soil.* Pasadena, Calif.: Magination Press.

Gambrill, E. 1995. Assertion training skills. In W. O'Donohue and L. Krasner, eds., *Handbook of Psychological Skills Training: Clinical Techniques and Applications,* 81–118. Boston: Allyn and Bacon.

Ganzarain, R. C. and B. J. Buchele. 1988. *Fugitives of Incest: A Perspective from Psychoanalysis and Groups.* Madison, Conn.: International Universities Press.

Garber, S., M. D. Garber, and R. F. Spizman. 1987. *Good Behavior.* New York: St. Martins Press.

Garff, J. T. and K. Storey. 1998. The use of self-management strategies for increasing the appropriate hygiene of persons with disabilities in supported employment settings. *Education and Training in Mental Retardation and Developmental Disabilities* 33:179–188.

Garland, A. F. and E. Zigler. 1993. Adolescent suicide prevention: Current research and social policy implications. Special issue: Adolescence. *American Psychologist* 48(2): 169–182.

Garner, D. 1991. *Eating Disorders Inventory 2.* Odessa, Fla.: Psychological Assessment Resources.

Garrett, J. et al. 1999. The "concerned other" call: Using family links and networks to overcome resistance to addiction treatment. *Substance Use and Misuse* 34(3): 363–382.

Gary, F., J. Moorhead, and J. Warren. 1996. Characteristics of troubled youths in a shelter. *Archives of Psychiatric Nursing* 10(1): 41–48.

Gatchel, R. J. and D. C. Turke, eds. 1996. *Psychological Approaches to Pain Management: A Practitioner's Handbook.* New York: Guilford Press.

Gaudin Jr., J. M., J. S. Wodarski, M. K. Arkinson, and L. S. Avery. 1990–1991. Remedying child neglect: Effectiveness of social network interventions. *The Journal of Applied Social Sciences* 15(1): 97–123.

Gavazzi, S. M. and D. G. Blumenkrantz. 1991. Teenage runaways: Treatment in the context of the family and beyond. *Journal of Family Psychotherapy* 2(2): 15–29.

GayellowPages: The National Edition. 1993. New York: Renaissance House.

Gelles, R. J. and M. A. Straus. 1988. *Intimate Violence.* New York: Simon & Schuster.

Gelso, C. J. and D. H. Johnson. 1983. *Explorations in Time-Limited Counseling and Psychotherapy.* New York: Teachers College Press.

Gendron, C., L. Poitras, D. P. Dastoor, and G. Perodeau. 1996. Cognitive-behavioral group intervention for spousal caregivers: findings and clinical considerations. *Clinical Gerontologist* 17(1): 3–19.

Gentry, C. E. and V. B. Eaddy. 1980. Treatment of children in spouse abusive families. *Victimology: An International Journal* 5(2–4): 240–250.

Giddan, J. J., G. J. Ross, L. L. Sechler, and B. R. Becker. 1996. Selective mutism in elementary school: multidisciplinary interventions. *Language, Speech, and Hearing Services in Schools* 28:102–112.

Gil, A. G., W. A. Vega, and J. M. Dimas. 1994. Acculturative stress and personal adjustment among Hispanic adolescent boys. *Journal of Community Psychology* 22(1): 43–54.

Gil, E. 1991. *The Healing Power of Play: Working with Abused Children.* New York: Guilford Press.

Gilligan, J. 1992. *Violence: Our Deadly Epidemic and Its Causes.* New York: Putnam.

Gillis, H. M. 1993. Individual and small-group psychotherapy for children involved in trauma and disaster. In C. F. Saylor, ed., *Children and Disasters,* 165–186. New York: Plenum Press.

Glass, S. P. and T. L. Wright. 1997. Reconstructing marriages after the trauma of infidelity. In W. K. Halford and H. J. Markman, eds., *Clinical Handbook of Marriage and Couple Interventions,* 471–507. Chichester, England: Wiley.

Glueckauf, R. L. and A. L. Quittner. 1992. Assertiveness training for disabled adults in wheelchairs: Self-report, role-play, and activity pattern outcomes. *Journal of Consulting and Clinical Psychology* 60(3): 419–425.

Golan, N. 1978. *Treatment in Crisis Situations.* New York: Free Press.

Gold, J. H. 1996. Intolerance of aloneness. *American Journal of Psychiatry* 153(6): 749–750.

Goldfried, M. R. and A. P. Goldfried. 1980. Cognitive change methods. In F. H. Kanfer and A. P. Goldstein, eds., *Helping People Change: A Textbook of Methods*, 2nd ed., 112–125. New York: Pergamon Press.

Gondolf, E. W. 1985. Fighting for control: A clinical assessment of men who batter. *Social Casework* 66(1): 48–54.

Gonsiorek, J. 1988. Mental health issues of gay and lesbian adolescents. *Journal of Adolescent Health Care* 9:114–122.

Gonzales, S., P. Steinglass, and D. Reiss. 1989. Putting the illness in its place: Discussion groups for families with chronic medical illnesses. *Family Process* 28:69–87.

Gonzalez, R. G. 1990. Examining the myth of Hispanic families' resistance to treatment: Using the school as a site for success. *Social Work in Education* 12:261–274.

Gordon, T. 1970. *P.E.T.: Parent Effectiveness Training.* New York: Van Rees Press.

———. 1976. *P.E.T. in Action: Inside P.E.T. Families: New Problems, Insights and Solutions in Parent Effectiveness Training.* New York: Wyden.

Gormally, J., S. Black, S. Daston, and D. Rardin. 1982. The assessment of binge eating severity among obese persons. *Addictive Behaviors* 7:47–55.

Gottman, J. 1993. The roles of conflict engagement, escalation, and avoidance in marital interaction: A longitudinal view of five types of couples. *Journal of Consulting and Clinical Psychology* 61(1): 6–15.

———. 1994. *Why Marriages Succeed or Fail.* New York: Simon & Schuster.

Graham, D. L. R. and E. I. Rawlings. 1991. Bonding with abusive dating partners: Dynamics of Stockholm Syndrome. In B. Levy, ed., *Dating Violence: Young Women in Danger*, 119–135. Seattle: Seal Press.

Gravitz, H. L. 1998. *Obsessive-Compulsive Disorder: New Help for the Family.* Santa Barbara: Healing Visions Press.

Green, R. J. and P. D. Werner. 1996. Intrusiveness and closeness-caregiving: Rethinking the concept of family enmeshment. *Family Process* 35(2): 115–136.

Greenberg, L. S. 1984. Task analysis: The general approach. In L. N. Rice and L. S. Greenberg, eds., *Patterns of Change: Intensive Analysis of Psychotherapy*, 124–148. New York: Guilford Press.

Greene, J. M. and C. Ringwalt. 1996. Youth and familial substance use's association with suicide attempts among runaway and homeless youth. *Substance Use and Misuse* 31(8): 1041–1058.

Greene, V. L. and D. J. Monahan. 1982. The impact of visitation on patient well-being in nursing homes. *The Gerontologist* 22:418–423.

Greenfield, W. L. 1984. Disruption and reintegration: Dealing with familial response to nursing home placement. *Journal of Gerontological Social Work* 8:15–21.

Greydanus, D. E. 1991. *American Academy of Pediatrics: Caring for Your Adolescent/Ages 12–21.* New York: Bantam.

Griffith, J. 1996. Relation of parental involvement, empowerment, and school traits to student academic performance. *Journal of Educational Research* 90(1): 33–41.

Grogan, G. 1991. Anger management: A perspective for occupational therapy: I. *Occupational Therapy in Mental Health* 11(2–3): 135–148.

Grossman, H. D. and A. Weiner. 1988. Quality of life: The institutional culture defined by administrative and resident values. *Journal of Applied Gerontology* 2(3): 389–405.

Gruszski, R. J., J. C. Brink, and J. L. Edelson. 1988. Support and education groups for children of battered women. *Child Welfare* 67(5): 431–444.

Grych, J. H. and F. D. Fincham. 1990. Marital conflict and the children's adjustment: A cognitive-contextual framework. *Psychological Bulletin* 108(2): 267–290.

Gunderson, J. G. 1996. Borderline patients' intolerance of aloneness: Insecure attachments and therapist availability. *American Journal of Psychiatry* 153(6): 752–758.

Haddock, C. K., W. R. Shadish, R. C. Klesges, and R. J. Stein. 1994. Meta-analysis: Treatments for childhood and adolescent obesity. *The Society of Behavioral Medicine* 16(3): 235–244.

Hagerty, B. M., R. A. Williams, J. C. Coyne, and M. R. Early. 1996. Sense of belonging and indicators of social and psychological functioning. *Archives of Psychiatric Nursing* 10(4): 235–244.

Hagopian, L. P. and K. J. Slifer. 1993. Treatment of separation anxiety disorder with graduated exposure and reinforcement targeting school attendance: A controlled case study. *Journal of Anxiety Disorders* 7(3): 271–280.

Haj-Yahia, M. M. 1994. Predicting the use of conflict resolution tactics among engaged Arab-Palestinian men in Israel. *Journal of Family Violence* 9(1): 47–62.

Hall, J. A. 1984. Empirically based treatment for parent-adolescent conflict. *Social Casework: The Journal of Contemporary Social Work* 65(8): 487–495.

———. 1987. Parent-adolescent conflict: An empirical review. *Adolescence* 22(88): 768–89.

Hall, J. A. and S. Rose. 1987. Evaluation of parent training in groups for parent-adolescent conflict. *Social Work Research and Abstracts* 23(2): 3–8.

Hallowell, E. 1995. *Psychotherapy of Adult Attention Deficit Disorder: A Comprehensive Guide to Attention Deficit Disorder in Adults.* New York: Brunner/Mazel.

Hallowell, E. and J. Ratey. 1994. *Driven to Distraction: Recognizing and Coping with Attention Deficit Disorder from Childhood Through Adulthood.* New York: Pantheon.

———. 1995. *Answers to Distraction.* New York: Pantheon.

Hamberger, L. and J. Hastings. 1991. Personality correlates of men who batter and nonviolent men: some continuities and discontinuities. *Journal of Family Violence* 6(2): 131–148.

Hamilton, B. 1994. A systematic approach to a family and school problem: A case study in separation anxiety disorder. *Family Therapy* 21(2): 149–152.

Hammen, C. and K. D. Rudolph. Childhood depression. In E. J. Mash and R. A. Barkley, eds., *Child Psychopathology,* 153–195. New York: Guilford Press.

Hammond, S. L. and B. L. Lambert. 1994. Communicating about medications: Directions for research. *Health Communication* 6(4): 247–251.

Hansen, D. J., D. B. Hecht, and K. T. Futa. 1998. Interpersonal family therapy for childhood depression. In G. R. Racusin, E. R. Carton, V. B. Van-Hasselt, and M. Hersen, eds., *Handbook of Psychological Treatment Protocols for Children and Adolescents.* Mahwah, N.J.: Lawrence Erlbaum Associates.

Hansen, S. S., M. A. Patterson, and R. W. Wilson. 1988. Family involvement on a dementia unit: The resident enrichment and activity program. *The Gerontologist* 28:508–510.

Hardy, F. C. and H. E. MacMahon. 1981. Adapting family therapy to the Hispanic family. *Social Casework* 62:138–148.

Hardy, K. and T. A. Laszloffy. 1995. Therapy with African Americans and the phenomenon of rage. *In-Session Psychotherapy in Practice* 1(4): 57–70.

Harris, H. 1996. Elective mutism: A tutorial. *Language, Speech, and Hearing Services in Schools* 27(1): 10–15.

Harris, P. B. 1997. A support group in a home for the elderly. In T. S. Kerson et al., eds., *Social Work in Health Care Settings: Practice in Context,* 2nd ed., 635–648. Binghamton, N.Y.: Haworth Press.

Harrold, M., J. R. Lutzker, R. V. Campbell, and P. E. Touchette. 1992. Improving parent-child interactions for families of children with developmental disabilities. *Behavior Therapy and Experimental Psychiatry* 23(2): 89–100.

Hartmann, A., T. Herzog, and A. Drinkmann. 1992. Psychotherapy of bulimia nervosa: What is effective? A meta-analysis. *Journal of Psychosomatic Research* 36(2): 159–167.

Hartmann, T. 1993. *Attention Deficit Disorder: A Different Perception.* Lancaster, Penn.: Underwood-Miller.

Hawkins, J. D. and R. F. Catalano, Jr. 1992. *Communities That Care: Action for Drug Abuse Prevention.* San Francisco: Jossey-Bass.

Hecker, L. L. and S. A. Deacon. 1998. *The Therapist's Notebook: Homework, Handouts, and Activities for Use in Psychotherapy.* Binghamton, N.Y.: Haworth Press.

Heggenhougen, H. K. 1997. *Reaching New Highs: Alternative Therapies for Drug Addicts.* Northvale, N.J.: Jason Aronson.

Heller, T. and A. Factor. 1988. Permanency planning among black and white family caregivers of older adults with mental retardation. *Mental Retardation* 26:203–208.

———. 1991. Permanency planning for adults with mental retardation living with family caregivers. *American Journal of Mental Retardation* 96:1630–1676.

Helphand, M. and C. M. Porter. 1981. Family group within the nursing home: Maintaining family ties of long-term care residents. *Journal of Gerontological Social Work* 4:51–62.

Henggeler, S. W. and C. M. Borduin. 1990. *Family Therapy and Beyond: A Multisystemic Approach to Treating the Behavior Problems of Children and Adolescents.* Pacific Grove, Calif.: Brooks/Cole.

Henriksson, M. M., H. M. Aro, M. J. Marttunen, M. E. Heikkinen, et al. 1993. Mental disorders and comorbidity in suicide. *American Journal of Psychiatry* 150(6): 935–940.

Heppner, P. P. and C. H. Peterson. 1982. The development and implications of a personal problem-solving inventory. *Journal of Counseling Psychology* 29:66–75.

Hepworth, D., R. Rooney, and J. Larson. 1997. *Direct Social Work Practice: Theory and Skills,* 5th ed. New York: Brooks/Cole.

Herdt, G. 1989. Gay and lesbian youth: Emergent identities and cultural scenes at home and abroad. *Journal of Homosexuality* 17:1–42.

Herdt, G., ed. 1989. *Gay and Lesbian Youth.* Binghamton, N.Y.: Harrington Park Press.

Herman, J. L. 1992. *Trauma and Recovery.* New York: Basic.

Heron, A., ed. 1983. *One Teenager in 10.* Boston: Alyson.

Hetrick, E. and A. Martin. 1987. Developmental issues and their resolution for gay and lesbian adolescents. *Journal of Homosexuality* 14:25–42.

Heward, W. L. and M. D. Orlansky. 1988. *Exceptional Children,* 3rd ed. Columbus, Ohio: Merrill.

Hewitt, S. K. 1994. Preverbal sexual abuse: What children report in later years. *Child Abuse and Neglect* 18(10): 821–826.

Hindman, J. 1985. *A Very Touching Book.* Durkee, Ore.: McClure-Hindman.

———. 1989. *Just Before Dawn.* Ontario, Ore.: AlexAndria.

———. 1991. *When Mourning Breaks.* Ontario, Ore.: AlexAndria.

Hines, P. M., N. Garcia-Preto, M. McGoldrick, and R. Almeida. 1992. Intergenerational relationships across cultures. *Families in Society* 73:323–338.

Hinshaw, S. P. and C. A. Anderson. 1996. Conduct and oppositional defiant disorders. In E. J. Mash and R. A. Barkley, eds., *Child Psychopathology,* 113–149. New York: Guilford Press.

Hinshaw, S. P. and D. Erhardt. 1991. Attention deficit/Hyperactivity disorder. In P. C. Kendall, ed., *Child and Adolescent Therapy: Cognitive-Behavioral Procedures,* 231–248. New York: Guilford Press.

Hirschmann, J. and C. Munter. 1995. *When Women Stop Hating Their Bodies.* New York: Ballantine.

Ho, D. K. 1990. An analysis of domestic violence in Asian American communities: A multicultural approach to counseling. In *Women and Therapy* 9(1–2): 129–150.

Hodges, W. F. 1986. *Interventions for Children of Divorce, Custody, Access, and Psychotherapy.* New York: Wiley.

Hoff, M. D., K. H. Briar, K. Knighton, and A. V. Ry. 1992. To survive and to thrive: Integrating services for the homeless mentally ill. *Journal of Sociology and Social Welfare* 19(4): 235–252.

Hogarty, G. E. 1993. Prevention of relapse in chronic schizophrenic patients. *Clinical Psychiatry* 54(3): 18–23.

Holliday, M. and R. Cronin. 1990. Families first: A significant step toward family preservation. *The Journal of Contemporary Human Services* 71(5): 303–306.

Hollin, C. R. and P. Trower, eds. 1986. *Handbook of Social Skills Training,* vol. 2. New York: Pergamon Press.

Holman, W. D. 1997. "Who would find you?" A question for working with suicidal children and adolescents. *Child and Adolescent Social Work Journal* 14(2): 129–137.

Hooker, K., D. J. Monahan, K. Shifren, and C. Hutchinson. 1992. Mental and physical health of spouse caregivers: The role of personality. *Psychology and Aging* 7:367–375.

Horne, A. M. and T. V. Sayger. 1990. *Treating Conduct and Oppositional Defiant Disorders in Children.* New York: Pergamon Press.

Horvath, A. T. 1998. *Sex, Drugs, Gambling, and Chocolate: A Workbook for Overcoming Addictions.* San Luis Obispo, Calif.: Impact.

Houtt, A. C., M. W. Mellon, and J. P. Whelan. 1988. Use of dietary fiber and stimulus control to treat retentive encopresis: A multiple baseline investigation. *Journal of Pediatric Psychology* 13:435–446.

Hovland, O. J. 1995. Self-defeating anxiety explored: The contribution of terror management theory and rational-emotive therapy. *Anxiety, Stress and Coping: An International Journal* 8(2): 161–182.

Howes, J. L. and C. A. Parrott. 1991. The application of cognitive therapy to post-traumatic stress disorder. In T. M. Vallis, J. L. Howes, and P. C. Miller, eds., *The Challenge of Cognitive Therapy: Applications to Nontraditional Populations,* 85–106. New York: Plenum Press.

Howing, P. T., J. S. Wodarski, J. M. Gaudin, Jr., and P. D. Kurtz. 1989. Effective interventions to ameliorate the incidence of child maltreatment: The empirical base. *Social Work* 34(4): 330–338.

Hoza, B., G. Vallano, and W. E. Pelham, Jr. 1995. Attention deficit/hyperactivity disorder. In R. T. Ammerman and M. Hersen, eds., *Handbook of Child Behavior Therapy: In the Psychiatric Setting,* 181–198. New York: Wiley.

Hudok, C. and B. Gallo. 1994. *Critical Care Nursing: A Holistic Approach.* Philadelphia: Lippincott.

Hughes, S. L. and R. A. Neimeyer. 1993. Cognitive predictors of suicide risk among hospitalized psychiatric patients: A prospective study. Special issue: Prevention and postvention of suicide. *Death Studies* 17(2): 103–124.

Hulewat, P. 1996. Resettlement: A cultural and psychological crisis. *Social Work* 41(2): 129–135.

Humphrey, L. L. 1982. Children's and parents' perspectives on children's self-control: The development of two rating scales. *Journal of Consulting and Clinical Psychology* 54: 61–72.

Hunt, F. M., C. R. Johnson, G. Owen, A. J. Ormerod, and R. L. Babbitt. 1990. Early intervention for severe behavior problems: the use of judgment-based assessment procedures. *Topics in Early Childhood Special Education* 10(3): 111–121.

Hunter, J. and D. Santos. 1990. The use of specialized cognitive-behavioral therapies in the treatment of adolescent sexual offenders. *International Journal of Offender Therapy and Comparative Criminology* 34(3): 239–247.

Husain, S. A. and J. H. Kashani. 1992. *Anxiety Disorders in Children and Adolescents.* Washington: American Psychiatric Press.

Hussey, L. C. 1991. Overcoming the clinical barriers of low literacy and medication noncompliance among the elderly. *Journal of Gerontological Nursing* 17(3): 27–29.

Hussian, R. A. and R. L. Davis. 1985. *Responsive Care: Behavioral Interventions with Elderly Persons.* Champaign, Ill.: Research Press.

Hutchinson, M. 1985. *Transforming Body Image.* Trumansburg, N.Y.: Crossing Press.

Ingersoll, B. D. and S. Goldstein. 1993. *Attention Deficit Disorder and Learning Disabilities.* New York: Doubleday.

Ingersoll-Dayton, B., R. Campbell, Y. Kurokawa, and M. Saito. 1996. Separateness and togetherness: Interdependence over the life course in Japanese and American marriages. *Journal of Social and Personal Relationships* 13(3): 385–398.

Interagency Council on the Homeless. 1992. *Outcasts on Main Street: Report of the Federal Task Force on Homelessness and Severe Mental Illness.* DHHS Publication No. ADM 92–1904. Washington, D.C.: U. S. Government Printing Office.

Irving, B. A. and M. Parker-Jenkins. 1995. Tackling truancy: An examination of persistent non-attendance amongst disaffected school pupils and positive support strategies. *Cambridge Journal of Education* 25(2): 225–235.

Isometsa, E. T., M. M. Henriksson, H. M. Aro, M. E. Heikkinen, et al. 1994. Suicide in major depression. *American Journal of Psychiatry* 151(4): 530–536.

Ivanoff, A. and M. Riedel. 1995. Suicide. In R. Edwards et al., eds., *Encyclopedia of Social Work,* 19th ed., 2358–2372. Washington, D.C.: NASW Press.

Ivanoff, A. and N. J. Smyth. 1992. Intervention with suicidal individuals. In K. Corcoran, ed., *Structuring Change: Effective Practice for Common Client Problems,* 111–137. Chicago: Lyceum.

Iverson, R. R. 1985. Winning against school phobia: team strategy. *School Social Work Journal* 10(1): 12–23.

Izzo, R. L. and R. R. Ross. 1990. Meta-analysis of rehabilitation programs for juvenile delinquents: A brief report. *Criminal Justice and Behavior* 17(1): 134–142.

Jackson, B. and D. Farrugia. 1997. Diagnosis and treatment of adults with attention deficit/hyperactivity disorder. *Journal of Counseling and Development* 75(4): 312–319.

Jackson, B. M. 1994. African-American women in the workplace: a personal perspective from African-American female EAPs. *Employee Assistance Quarterly* 9:11–19.

Jackson, D. and R. Sullivan. 1994. Developmental implications of homophobia for lesbian and gay adolescents: Issues in policy and practice. *Journal of Gay and Lesbian Social Services* 1(3–4): 93–109.

Jacob, R. G., K. D. O'Leary, and C. Rosenblad. 1978. Formal and informal classroom settings: Effects on hyperactivity. *Journal of Abnormal Psychology* 54: 47–59.

Jacobs, D. G., ed. 1999. *The Harvard Medical School Guide to Suicide Assessment and Intervention.* San Francisco: Jossey-Bass.

Jacobson, N. S. and A. Christensen. 1996. *Integrative Couple Therapy: Promoting Acceptance and Change.* New York: Norton.

Jacobson, N. S. and A. S. Gurman. 1995. *Clinical Handbook of Couple Therapy.* New York: Guilford Press.

Jacobsen, N. S. and G. Margolin. 1979. *Marital Therapy: Strategies Based on Social Learning and Behavior Exchange Principles.* New York: Brunner/Mazel.

Jaffe, P. G., M. Sudermann, D. Reitzel, and S. M. Killip. 1992. An evaluation of secondary school primary prevention program on violence in intimate relationships. *Violence and Victims* 7(2): 129–146.

Jaffe, P., D. Wolfe, S. K. Wilson, and L. Zak. 1985. Critical issues in the assessment of children's adjustment to witnessing family violence. *Canada's Mental Health* 33(4): 15–19.

Jaffe-Ruiz, M. 1984. A family systems look at the developmentally disabled. *Perspectives in Psychiatric Care* 22(2): 65–71.

Jahiel, R. I. 1992. *Homelessness: A Prevention-Oriented Approach.* Baltimore: Johns Hopkins University Press.

Janicki, M. P. and A. J. Dalton. 1999. *Dementia, aging, and intellectual disabilities: A handbook.* Philadelphia: Brunner/Mazel.

Janicki, M. et al. 1996. Help for caring for older people caring for adults with a developmental disability. Albany: New York State Developmental Disabilities Planning Council.

Jarry, J. 1998. The meaning of body image for women with eating disorders. *Canadian Journal of Psychiatry* 43(4): 367–374.

Jehu, D., C. Klassen, and M. Gazan. 1986. Cognitive restructuring of distorted beliefs associated with childhood sexual abuse. *Journal of Social Work and Human Sexuality* 4(1–2): 49–69.

Jencks, C. 1994. *The Homeless.* Cambridge: Harvard University Press.

Jennifer, A. J., N. J. Schwartz, and G. R Kaslow. 1998. Interpersonal family therapy for childhood depression. In G. R. Racusin, E. R. Carton, V. B. Van-Hasselt, and M. Hersen, eds., *Handbook of Psychological Treatment Protocols for Children and Adolescents.* Mahwah, N.J.: Lawrence Erlbaum Associates.

Jensen, C. 1994. Psychosocial treatment of depression in women: Nine single-subject evaluations. *Research on Social Work Practice* 4(3): 267–282.

Johnson, A. K. and R. A. Cnaan. 1995. Social work practice with homeless persons: State of the art. *Research on Social Work Practice* 5:340–382.

Johnson, D. W., R. Johnson, B. Dudley, and K. Acikgog. 1994. Effects of conflict resolution training on elementary school students. *Journal of Social Psychology* 134(6): 803–817.

Johnson, J. H., W. C. Rasbury, and L. J. Siegel. 1986. *Approaches to Child Treatment.* Elmsford, N.Y.: Pergamon Press.

Johnson, K. 1989. *Trauma in the Lives of Children: Crisis and Stress Management Techniques for Teachers, Counselors, and Student Service Professionals.* Claremont, Calif.: Hunter House.

Johnson, L. C. and C. L. Spinweber. 1983. Quality of sleep and performance in the Navy: A longitudinal study of good and poor sleepers. In C. Guilleminault and E. Lugaresi, eds., *Sleep/Wake Disorders: Natural History, Epidemiology, and Long-Term Evolution*, 13–28. New York: Raven Press.

Johnston, C. and W. Freeman. 1998. Parent training interventions for sibling conflict. In J. M. Briesmeister and C. E. Schaefer, eds., *Handbook of Parent Training: Parents as Co-Therapists for Children's Behavior Problems*, 2nd ed., 153–176. New York: Wiley.

Jongsma, A. E., Jr. and M. L. Peterson. 1995. *The Complete Psychotherapy Treatment Planner.* New York: Wiley.

Jongsma, A. E., Jr., M. L. Peterson, and W. P. McInnis. 1996. *The Child and Adolescent Psychotherapy Treatment Planner.* New York: Wiley.

Kadushin, G. and R. Kulys. 1994. Patient and family involvement in discharge planning. *Journal of Gerontological Social Work* 22(3–4): 171–199.

Kales, J. D., A. Kales, E. O. Bixler, C. R. Soldatos, R. J. Cadieux, G. J. Kashurbam, and A. Vela-Bueno. 1984. Biopsychobehavioral correlates of insomnia, V: Clinical characteristics and behavioral correlates. *American Journal of Psychiatry* 141:1371–1376.

Kalter, N. and S. Schreier. 1994. Developmental facilitation groups for children of divorce: The elementary school model. In C. W. LeCroy, ed., *Handbook of Child and Adolescent Treatment Manuals*, 307–342. New York: Lexington.

Kaminer, Y. 1994. Adolescent substance abuse. In M. Gallanter and H. D. Kleber, eds., *American Psychiatric Press Textbook of Substance Abuse Treatment.* Washington, D.C.: American Psychiatric Press.

Kane, J. and T. McGlashan. 1995. Treatment of schizophrenia. *Lancet* 346(8978): 820–828.

Kano, S. 1989. *Making Peace with Food: A Step-by-Step Guide to Freedom from Diet/Weight Conflict.* New York: Harper and Row.

Kanter, Joel. 1995. *Clinical Issues in Treating the Chronically Mentally Ill.* San Francisco: Jossey-Bass.

Kaplan, M. and G. Marks. 1990. Adverse effects of acculturation. *Social Science and Medicine* 31(12): 1313–1319.

Karant, R. 1999. *Home Base Program—Coordinated Children's Initiative.* Department of Health Promotion and Education, University of Utah. http://www.strengtheningfamilies.org/html/model_programs/mfp_pg27.html

Karls, J. M. and K. E. Wandrei, eds. 1994. *Person-in-Environment System*s. Washington, D.C.: NASW Press.

Kashani, J. H. and H. Orvaschel. 1988. Anxiety disorders in mid-adolescence: A community sample. *American Journal of Psychiatry* 145:960–964.

———. 1990. A community study of anxiety in children and adolescents. *American Journal of Psychiatry* 14:313–318.

Kasl, C. 1989. *Women, Sex, and Addiction.* New York: Harper and Row.

Katz, J. 1978. *White Awareness: Handbook for Anti-Racism Training.* Norman, Okla.: University of Oklahoma Press.

Katz, N. and J. Lawyer. 1993. *Conflict Resolution: Building Bridges.* The Practicing School Administrator's Leadership Series. Newbury Park, Calif.: Corwin Press/Sage.

Katzman, M., L. Weiss, and S. Wolchik. 1986. Speak don't eat! Teaching women to express their feelings. *Women and Therapy* 5(2–3): 143–157.

Katzman, R. 1987. Alzheimer's disease: Advances and opportunities. *American Geriatrics Society* 35:69–73.

Kauffer, S. 1996. *Resource Guide for Coming Out.* Washington, D.C.: Human Rights Campaign.

Kaufman, A. V., J. A. Adams, Jr., and V. A. Campbell. 1991. Permanency planning by older parents who care for adult children at home. *Mental Retardation* 29(5): 293–300.

Kayloe, J. C. 1993. Food addiction. Special issue: Psychotherapy for the addictions. *Psychotherapy* 30(2): 269–275.

Kazarian, S. S., S. B. McCabe, and L. W. Joseph. 1997. Assessment of service needs of adult psychiatric inpatients: A systematic approach. *Psychiatric Quarterly* 68(1): 5–23.

Kazdin, A. E. and J. R. Weisz. 1998. Identifying and developing empirically supported child and adolescent treatments. *Journal of Consulting and Clinical Psychology* 66(1): 19–36.

Kazdin, A. E., ed. 1995. *Conduct Disorders in Childhood and Adolescence,* 2nd ed. Thousand Oaks, Calif.: Sage.

Keane, T. M., R. J. Gerardi, S. J. Quinn, and B. T. Litz. 1992. Behavioral treatment of post-traumatic stress disorder. In S. M. Turner, K. S. Calhoun, and H. E. Adams, eds., *Handbook of Clinical Behavior Therapy,* 2nd ed., 87–97. New York: Wiley.

Kearney, C. A. and T. L. Roblek. 1998. Parent training in the treatment of school refusal behavior. In J. M. Briesmeister and C. E. Schaefer, eds., *Handbook of Parent Training: Parents as Co-Therapists for Children's Behavior Problems,* 2nd ed., 225–256. New York: Wiley.

Kearney, C. A. and W. K. Silverman. 1990. A preliminary analysis of a functional model of assessment and treatment for school refusal behavior. *Behavior Modification* 14:340–366.

Kearney, C. A. and D. Wadiak. 1999. Anxiety disorders. In S. D. Netherton and D. Holmes, eds., *Child and Adolescent Psychological Disorders: A Comprehensive Textbook,* 282–303. New York: Oxford University Press.

Keefe, T. 1984. Alienation and social work practice. *Social Casework* 65:145–153.

Kehoe, M. 1990. Loneliness and the aging homosexual: Is pet therapy an answer? *Journal of Homosexuality* 20(3–4): 137–142.

Keinz, L. A., C. S. Schwartz, B. M. Trench, and D. D. Houlihan. 1995. An assessment of membership benefits in the Al-Anon program. *Alcoholism Treatment Quarterly* 12(4): 31–38.

Kelley, M. L. 1990. *School-Home Notes: Promoting Children's Classroom Success.* New York: Guilford Press.

Kellner, M. H. and J. Tutin. 1995. A school-based anger management program for developmentally and emotionally disabled high school students. *Adolescence* 30(120): 813–825.

Kellogg, N. D. and T. J. Hoffman. 1997. Child sexual revictimization by multiple perpetrators. *Child Abuse and Neglect* 21(10): 953–964.

Kendall, P. C., ed. 1991. *Child and Adolescent Therapy: Cognizant Behavioral Procedures.* New York: Guilford Press.

Kendall, P. C. and L. Braswell. 1993. *Cognitive-Behavioral Therapy for Impulsive Children,* 2nd ed. New York: Guilford Press.

Kendall, P. C. and L. E. Wilcox. 1979. Self-control in children: Development of a rating scale. *Journal of Consulting and Clinical Psychology* 47: 61–71.

Kendall, P. C., A. Krain, and K. R. Treadwell. 1999. Generalized anxiety disorder. In R. T. Ammerman and M. Hersen, eds., *Handbook of Prescriptive Treatments for Children and Adolescents,* 155–171. Boston: Allyn and Bacon.

Kendall, P. C. et al. 1991. *Anxiety Disorders in Youth: Cognitive Behavioral Interventions.* New York: Pergamon Press.

Kennedy, M. R. 1991. Homeless and runaway youth mental health issues: No access to the system. Special issue: Homeless youth. *Journal of Adolescent Health* 12(7): 576–579.

Kennedy, S. H. and P. E. Garfinkel. 1992. Advances in diagnosis and treatment of anorexia nervosa and bulimia nervosa. *Canadian Journal of Psychiatry* 37:309–315.

Kennedy, W. A. 1995. Phobia. In R. T. Ammerman and M. Hersen, eds., *Handbook of Child Behavior Therapy: In the Psychiatric Setting,* 239–252. New York: Wiley.

Kerns, R. D. and M. C. Jacob. 1995. Toward an integrative diathesis-stress model of chronic pain. In A. J. Goreczny, ed., *Handbook of Health and Rehabilitation Psychology,* 325–340. New York: Plenum Press.

Kessler, R. C. and W. J. Mager. 1994. Childhood family violence and adult recurrent depression. *Journal of Health and Social Behavior* 35(1): 13–27.

Ketchel, J. A. 1986. Helping children cope with grief. *Daycare and Early Education* 14:24–27.

Killeen, M. 1990. The influence of stress and coping on family caregivers' perception of health. *International Journal of Aging and Human Development* 30:197–211.

Kim, Yoon-Ock. 1995. Cultural pluralism and Asian Americans: culturally sensitive social work practice. *International Social Work* 38:69–78.

Kinney, J. and G. Leaton. 1991. *Loosening the Grip: A Handbook of Alcohol Information.* St. Louis: Mosby Year Book.

Kinoshita, Y., K. Saito, and A. Matsunaga. 1993. Developmental changes in antecedents and outcomes of peer conflict among preschool children: A longitudinal study. *Japanese Psychological Research* 35(2): 57–69.

Kiselica, M. S., S. B. Baker, R. N. Thomas, and S. Reedy. 1994. Effects of stress inoculation training on anxiety, stress, and academic performance among adolescents. *Journal of Counseling Psychology* 41(3): 335–342.

Klingman, A. 1993. School-based intervention following a disaster. In C. F. Saylor, ed., *Children and Disasters,* 187–210.

Knell, S. M. 1995. *Cognitive-Behavioral Play Therapy.* Northvale, N.J.: Jason Aronson.

Knight, B. G., S. M. Lutzky, and U. F. Macofsky. 1993. A meta-analytic review of interventions for caregiver distress: Recommendations for future research. *The Gerontologist* 33(2): 240–48.

Knox, M. D. and C. H. Sparks. 1998. *HIV and Community Mental Healthcare.* Baltimore: Johns Hopkins University Press.

Koch, M. and S. Miller. 1987. Resolving student conflicts with student mediators. *Principal* (Middle School Notes) 6:59–62.

Koot, H. M. and F. C. Verhulst. 1992. Prediction of children's referral to mental health and special education services from earlier adjustment. *Journal of Child Psychology and Psychiatry and Allied Disciplines* 33(4): 717–729.

Kopelowicz, A., P. W. Corrigan, M. Schade, and R. P. Liberman. 1998. Social skills training. In K. T. Mueser and N. Tarrier, eds., *Handbook of Social Functioning in Schizophrenia.* Boston: Allyn and Bacon.

Kosberg, J. I. 1983. *Abuse and Maltreatment of the Elderly: Causes and Interventions.* Boston: John Wright PSG Inc.

Kostas, G. 1993. *The Balancing Act: Nutrition and Weight Guide.* Tennessee: Quebecor Printing Book Group.

Kournay, R. F. 1987. Suicide among homosexual adolescents. *Journal of Homosexuality* 13(4): 111–117.

Koverola, C. 1995. Post-traumatic stress disorder. In R. T. Ammerman and M. Hersen, eds., *Handbook of Child Behavior Therapy: In the Psychiatric Setting*, 389–408. New York: Wiley.

Kowitt, M. P., J. S. Sachs, M. G. Lowe, R. B. Schuller, M. Rubel, and D. M. Ellis. 1989. Predicting discharge and follow-up status of hospitalized adolescents. *Hospital and Community Psychiatry* 40(7): 724–731.

Kozak, M. J. and E. B. Foa. 1996. Obsessive-compulsive disorder. In V. B. Van Hasselt and M. Hersen, eds., *Sourcebook of Psychological Treatment Manuals for Adult Disorders*, 65–122. New York: Plenum Press.

Kozier, B., G. Erb, K. Blais, and J. Wilkinson. 1995. *Fundamentals of Nursing: Concepts, Process and Practice*. Redwood City, Calif.: Addison Wesley.

Kreitman, N. 1977. *Parasuicide*. London: Wiley.

Krementz, J. 1984. *How It Feels When Parents Divorce*. New York: Knopf.

Kris-Etherton, P. and D. Krummel. 1986. *Nutrition in Women's Health*. Gathersburg, Md.: Aspen.

Krown Buirsky, C. and P. Buirsky. The theurapeutic mobilization of mourning in a young child. *Bulletin of the Menninger Clinic* 58(3): 339–354.

Kruks, G. 1991. Gay and lesbian homeless/street youth: Special issues and concerns. *Journal of Adolescent Health* 12:515–518.

Krummel, S. 1996. Abuse of the elderly by adult children. In D. M. Busby, ed., *The Impact of Violence on the Family: Treatment Approaches for Therapists and Other Professionals*, 123–148. Boston: Allyn and Bacon.

Kubler-Ross, E. 1975. *Death: The Final Stage of Growth*. Upper Saddle River, N.J.: Prentice-Hall.

Kuehlwein, K. T. 1998. The cognitive therapy model. In R. A. Dorfman, ed., *Paradigms of Clinical Social Work* 2:125–148. Philadelphia: Brunner/Mazel.

Kufeldt, K. 1991. Social policy and runaways. Special issue: Homeless and runaway youth. *Journal of Health and Social Policy* 2(4): 37–49.

Kufeldt, K., M. Durieux, M. Nimmo, and M. McDonald. 1992. Providing shelter for street youth: Are we reaching those in need? VII International Congress on Child Abuse and Neglect (1988, Rio de Janeiro, Brazil). *Child Abuse and Neglect* 16(2): 187–199.

Kupych-Woloshyn, N., J. MacFarlane, and C. M. Shapiro. 1993. A group approach for the management of insomnia. *Journal of Psychosomatic Research* 37(Suppl. 1): 39–44.

Kurtz, P. D. and R. P. Barth. 1989. Parent involvement: Cornerstone of school social work practice. *Social Work* 33:407–413.

Kurtz, P. D., S. V. Jarvis, and G. L. Kurtz. 1991. Problems of homeless youths: Empirical findings and human services issues. *Social Work* 36(4): 309–314.

Kurtz, P. D., G. L. Kurtz, and S. V. Jarvis. 1991. Problems of maltreated runaway youth. *Adolescence* 26(103): 543–555.

Kyle, P. B. 1991. Developing cooperative interaction in schools for teachers and administrators. *Individual Psychology Journal of Adlerian Theory, Research and Practice* 47(2): 261–265.

L'Abate, L. and M. Milan. 1986. *Handbook of Social Skills Training and Research*. New York: Wiley.

L'Abate, L., J. E. Farrar, and D. A. Serritella, eds. 1991. *Handbook of Differential Treatments for Addictions*. Needham Heights, Mass.: Allyn and Bacon.

Lacks, P. and C. M. Morin. 1992. Recent advances in the assessment and treatment of insomnia. *Journal of Consulting and Clinical Psychology* 60(4): 586–594.

Ladame, F. 1992. Suicide prevention in adolescence: An overview of current trends. 5th Congress of the International Association for Adolescent Health (1991, Montreux, Switzerland). *Journal of Adolescent Health* 13(5): 406–408.

Ladd, G. W. and S. M. Profilet. 1996. The Child Behavior Scale: A teacher-report measure of young children's aggressive, withdrawn, and prosocial behaviors. *Developmental Psychology* 32(6): 1008–1024.

Lam, J. A. and R. Rosenheck. 1999. Social support and service use among homeless persons with serious mental illness. *International Journal of Social Psychiatry* 45(1): 13–28.

Lamb, H. R. 1984. *The Homeless Mentally Ill*. Washington, D.C.: American Psychiatric Association.

Lamb, M. E., K. J. Sternberg, and R. A. Thompson. 1997. The effects of divorce and custody arrangements on children's behavior, development, and adjustment. *Family and Conciliation Courts Review* 35(4): 393–404.

Lambert, M. J. and A. E. Bergin. 1994. The effectiveness of psychotherapy. In A. E. Bergin and S. L. Garfield, eds., *Handbook of Psychotherapy and Behavior Change*, 4th ed., 143–189. New York: Wiley.

Lamy, P. P. 1990. Adverse drug effects. *Clinical Pharmacology* 6(2): 293–307.

Landreth, G. L., L. E. Homeyer, G. Glover, and D. S. Sweeney. 1996. *Play Therapy Interventions with Children's Problems*. Northvale, N.J.: Jason Aronson.

Lane, P. 1995. *Conflict Resolution for Kids: A Group Facilitator's Guide. Accelerated Development*. Washington, D.C.: Taylor and Francis.

Larkin, K. T. and C. Zayfer. 1996. Anger management training with essential hypertensive patients. In V. B. Van Hasselt and M. Hersen, eds., *Sourcebook of Psychological Treatment Manuals for Adult Disorders*, 689–736. New York: Plenum Press.

Larson, L. M. 1990. A critique of problem-solving training: Where to from here? *Journal of Cognitive Psychotherapy: An International Quarterly* 4(3): 257–265.

Last, C. G., M. Hersen, A. E. Kazdin, R. Finkelstein, and C. C. Strauss. 1987. Comparison of DSM-III separation anxiety and overanxious disorders: Demographic characteristics and patterns of comorbidity. *Journal of American Academy of Child and Adolescent Psychiatry* 26:527–531.

Laursen, B., W. W. Hartup, and A. L. Koplas. 1996. Towards understanding peer conflict. *Merrill Palmer Quarterly* 42(1): 76–102.

Lavin, P. 1989. *Parenting the Overactive Child: Alternatives to Drug Therapy*. Lanhan, Md.: Madison.

Lawrie, M. 1998. Sibling conflict. Unpublished manuscript. Albany: The School of Social Welfare, the State University of New York.

Lawson, J. S. 1979. The Social Self-Esteem Inventory. *Educational and Psychological Measurement* 39:803–811.

Lawton, M. P. 1990. Residential environment and self-directedness among older people. *American Psychologist* 45(5): 638–640.

Leach, D. J. and R. Tan. 1996. The effects of sending positive and negative letters to parents on the classroom behavior of secondary school students. *Educational Psychology* 16(2): 141–154.

Lecompte, D. and I. Pelc. 1996. A cognitive-behavioral program to improve compliance with medication in patients with schizophrenia. *International Journal of Mental Health* 25(1): 51–56.

LeCroy, C. W. and C. C. Goodwin. 1988. New directions in teaching social work methods: A content analysis of course outlines. *Journal of Social Work Education* 24: 43–49.

Lee, M. I. and R. G. Miltenberger. 1996. School refusal behavior: Classification, assessment, and treatment issues. *Education and Treatment of Children* 19(4): 474–486.

Leff, J. 1989. Family factors in schizophrenia. *Psychiatric Annals* 19: 542–547.

Lehmann, P. and R. F. Dangel. 1998. Oppositional defiant disorder. In B. A. Thyer and J. S. Wodarski, eds., *Handbook of Empirical Social Work Practice: Volume I: Mental Disorders,* 91–116. New York: Wiley.

Lehrer, P. M. and R. L. Woolfolk. 1993. *Principles and Practices of Stress Management.* New York: Guilford Press.

Leitenberg, H., J. Rosen, S. Nudelman, and L. Vara. 1988. Exposure plus response-prevention treatment of bulimia nervosa. *Journal of Consulting and Clinical Psychology* 56: 97–105.

Leon, I. 1990. *When a Baby Dies.* New Haven: Yale University Press.

Lerner, H. 1985. *The Dance of Anger: A Woman's Guide to Changing the Patterns of Intimate Relationships.* New York: Harper and Row.

Leshner, A. I. 1992. *Outcasts on Main Street.* Washington, D.C.: Interagency Council on the Homeless.

Lester, D. 1994. Are there unique features of suicide in adults of different ages and developmental stages? *Omega Journal of Death and Dying* 29(4): 337–348.

———. 1995. Preventing suicide in women and men. *Crisis* 16(2): 79–84.

Leung, A., W. Robson, J. E. Fagan, and S. Lim. 1994. Attention deficit/Hyperactivity disorder. *Postgraduate Medicine* 95(2): 219–228.

Levine, I. S. and D. J. Rog. 1990. Mental health services for homeless mentally ill persons. *American Psychologist* 45(8): 963–968.

Levine, M. D. 1975. Children with encopresis. *Pediatrics* 56: 412–416.

Levine, R. S. 1984. An assessment tool for early intervention in cases of truancy. *Social Work in Education* 6(3): 133–150.

Levy, A. B., J. A. Aldaz, F. N. Watts, and K. Coyle. 1991. Case histories and shorter communications: Articulatory suppression and the treatment of insomnia. *Behavior Research and Therapy* 29(1): 85–89.

Levy, B. 1991. Support groups: Empowerment for young women in abused dating relationships. In B. Levy, ed., *Dating Violence: Young Women in Danger,* 232–239.

———. 1993. *In Love and in Danger: A Teen's Guide to Breaking Free of Abusive Relationships.* Seattle: Seal Press.

Levy, B., ed. 1991. *Dating Violence: Young Women in Danger.* Seattle: Seal Press.

Levy, B. and P. O. Giggans. 1995. *What Parents Need to Know About Dating Violence.* Seattle: Seal Press.

Lewinsohn, P., et al. 1991 *Adolescent Coping with Depression Course.* Eugene, Ore.: Castalia.

Lewis, M. 1993. The development of deception. In M. Lewis and C. Saarni, eds., *Lying and Deception in Everyday Life,* 90–105. New York: Guilford Press.

Libassi, M. F. 1995. The chronically mentally ill: A practice approach. In F. J. Turner et al., eds., *Differential Diagnosis and Treatment in Social Work,* 4th ed. New York: Free Press.

Liberman, R., W. DeRisi, and K. Mueser. 1989. *Social Skills Training for Psychiatric Patients.* New York: Pergamon Press.

Liebow, E. 1993. *Tell Them Who I Am: The Lives of Homeless Women.* New York: Penguin.

Lindemanscheli, B. 1993. *Employment and the Law,* 2nd ed. Washington, D.C.: American Bar Association: Labor and Employment Bureau of National Affairs.

Linehan, M. M. 1984. *Dialectical Behavior Therapy for Treatment of Parasuicidal Women: Treatment Manual.* Seattle: University of Washington Press.

———. 1987. Dialectical behavior therapy in groups: Treating borderline personality disorders and suicidal behavior. In C. M. Brody, ed., *Women's Therapy Groups: Paradigms of Feminist Treatment.* New York: Springer.

Lipovsky, J. A. 1991. Post-traumatic stress disorder in children. *Family and Community Mental Health* 14(3): 42–51.

Lipsey, L. W. 1992. Juvenile delinquency treatment: a meta-analytic inquiry into the variability of effects. In T. D. Cook et al., eds., *Meta-Analysis for Explanation: A Casebook,* 83–127. New York: Russell Sage Foundation.

Litman, R. E. 1995. Suicide prevention in a treatment setting. Special issue: Suicide prevention: Toward the year 2000. *Suicide and Life Threatening Behavior* 25(1): 134–142.

Locke, H. J. and K. M. Wallace. 1959. Short marital adjustment and prediction tests: Their reliability and validity. *Journal of Marriage and Family Living* 21: 251–255.

Loitz, P. A. and T. R. Kratochwill. 1995. Parent consultation: Evaluation of a self-help manual for children's homework problems. *School Psychology International* 16(4): 389–396.

Love, R. E. 1984. The Community Support Program: Strategy for reform? In J. A. Talbott, ed., *The Chronic Mental Patient: Five Years Later.* New York: Grune and Stratton.

Lum, D. 1996. *Social Work Practice with People of Color.* New York: Brooks/Cole.

Luster, T. and L. Okagaki. 1993. *Parenting: An Ecological Perspective.* Hillsdale, N.J.: Lawrence Erlbaum Associates.

Lutzker, J. R. 1998. *Handbook of Child Abuse Research and Treatment.* New York: Plenum Press.

Lutzker, J. R. and S. E. Steed. 1989. Parent training for families of children with developmental disabilities. In J. M. Briesmeister and C. E. Schaefer, eds., *Handbook of Parent Training: Parents as Co-Therapists for Children's Behavior Problems,* 2nd ed., 281–307. New York: Wiley.

Macarov, D. 1988. Reevaluation of unemployment. *Social Work* 3: 23–28.

Maccoby, E. E. 1996. Peer conflict and intrafamily conflict: Are there conceptual bridges? *Merrill Palmer Quarterly* 42(1): 165–176.

Mace, N. and P. Rabins. 1991. *The 36-Hour Day.* Baltimore: Johns Hopkins University Press.

Mack, A. 1989. *Dry All Night.* Boston: Little, Brown.

Magen, R. H. and S. D. Rose. 1994. Parents in groups: Problem solving versus behavioral skills training. *Research on Social Work Practice* 4(2): 172–191.

Maizels, M., D. Rosenbaum, and B. Keating. 1997. *Getting to Dry: How to Help Your Child Overcome Bedwetting.* Boston: Harvard Commons Press.

Mallon, G .P. 1994. Counseling strategies with gay and lesbian youth. *Journal of Gay and Lesbian Social Services* 1(3–4): 75–91.

Manaster, G. J. and R. J. Corsini. 1994. Individual psychology. In R. J. Corsini, ed., *Encyclopedia of Psychology,* 2nd ed., 3: 369–370. New York: Wiley.

Mann, J. A. 1994. Grief workshop intervention. *School Social Work Journal* 19: 24–33.

March, J. J., ed. 1995. *Anxiety Disorders in Children and Adolescents.* New York: Guilford Press.

Mares, M. L. and M. A. Fitzpatrick. 1995. The aging couple. In J. F. Nussbaum and J. Coupland, eds., *Handbook of Communication and Aging Research. LEA's Communication Series,* 185–205. Mahwah, N.J.: Lawrence Erlbaum Associates.

Maris, R. W. 1995. Suicide prevention in adults (age 30–65). Special issue: Suicide prevention: Toward the year 2000. *Suicide and Life Threatening Behavior* 25(1): 171–179.

Marlatt, G. A. 1996. Section I. theoretical perspectives on relapse: Taxonomy of high-risk situations for alcohol relapse: Evolution and development of a cognitive-behavioral model. *Addiction* 91(Suppl.): S37–S49.

Marlatt, G. A. and J. R. Gordon, eds. 1985. *Relapse Prevention: Maintenance Strategies in Addictive Behavior Change.* New York: Guilford Press.

Marlatt, G. A. and G. R. VandenBos, eds. 1997. *Addictive Behaviors: Readings on Etiology, Prevention, and Treatment.* Washington, D.C.: American Psychological Association.

Martin, A. and E. Hetrick. 1988. The stigmatization of the gay and lesbian adolescent. *Journal of Homosexuality* 15:163–182.

Martin, M. and C. Waltman-Greenwood, eds., 1995. *Solve Your Child's School-Related Problems.* New York: Harper Perennial.

Marvesti, J. 1989. Play therapy with sexually abused children. In S. A. Sgroi, ed., *Vulnerable Populations: Sexual Abuse Treatment for Children, Adult Survivors, Offenders, and Persons with Mental Retardation* 2:1–41. New York: Lexington.

Marzuk, P. M. 1994. Suicide and terminal illness. Special issue: Clinical and legal issues in suicide assessment. *Death Studies* 18(5): 497–512.

Mash, E. J. and R. A. Barkley. 1987. Assessment of family interaction with the response-class matrix. In R. Prinz, ed., *Advances in the Behavioral Assessment of Children and Families,* vol. 2. Greenwich, Conn.: JAI Press.

Mash, E. J., L. Terdal, and K. Anderson. 1973. The response class matrix: A procedure for recording parent-child interactions. *Journal of Consulting and Clinical Psychology* 40:163–164.

Massaro, J., B. Pepper, and H. Ryglewicz. 1994. Alcohol, street drugs and emotional problems. Center City, Minn.: Hazeldon Educational Materials.

Mattaini, M. A., B. G. McGowan, and G. Williams. 1996. Child maltreatment. In M. A. Mattaini and B. A. Thyer, eds., *Finding Solutions to Social Problems: Behavioral Strategies for Change.* Washington, D.C.: American Psychological Association.

Matthys, W. 1997. Residential behavior therapy for children with conduct disorder. *Behavior Modification* 21(4): 512–533.

McCallion, P., M. Janicki, and L. Grant-Griffin. 1996. Culture and acculturation: Exploring their impact on family caregiving for persons with developmental disabilities. Unpublished manuscript. Albany: School of Social Welfare, State University of New York.

McCallion, P. and S. S. Tobin. 1995. Social workers' perceptions of older parents caring at home for sons and daughters with developmental disabilities. *Mental Retardation* 33:153–162.

McCallion, P. and R. W. Toseland. 1995. Supportive group intervention with caregivers of frail older adults. *Social Work with Groups* 18(1): 11–25.

McColgan, E. B., R. L. Pugh, and D. D. Pruitt. 1985. Encopresis: a structural/strategic approach to family treatment. *The American Journal of Family Therapy* 13(3): 46–54.

McDaniel, S., J. Hepworth, and W. Doherty. 1993. A new prescription for family health care. *Networker* 17(1): 19–63.

McDermott, J. F. 1980. *Raising Cain (and Abel Too): The Parents' Book of Sibling Rivalry.* New York: Wyden.

McGoldrick, M. and B. Carter. 1988. Forming a remarried family. In M. McGoldrick and B. Carter, eds., *The Changing Family Life Cycle: A Framework for Family Therapy,* 2nd ed., 399–429. New York: Gardner Press.

McGoldrick, M., B. Carter, and M. Heiman. 1993. The changing family life cycle: A perspective on normalcy. In F. Walsh, ed., *Normal Family Processes,* 405–443. New York: Guilford Press.

McInerney, P., S. Stein, B. Barkow, and S. Wisernan. 1990. *Flight 201 Has Been Changed to Gate 102: Challenges Experienced by Travelers with Cognitive or Emotional Disabilities.* Ontario: Transport Canada.

McKay, M. and P. Fanning. 1987. *Self-Esteem.* New York: MJF.

McKay, S. et al. 1990. Unemployment: Some neglected dimensions in social work. *Journal of International and Comparative Social Welfare* 6(1–2): 16–37.

McLain, W. and F. Lewis. 1994. Anger management and assertiveness skills: An instructional package for persons with developmental disabilities. In M. J. Furlong and D. C. Smith, eds., *Anger, Hostility, and Aggression: Assessment, Prevention, and Intervention Strategies for Youth,* 473–507. Brandon, Vt.: Clinical Psychology Publishing.

McLellan, A. T., A. L. Alterman, D. S. Metzer, et al. 1997. Similarity of outcome predictors across opiate, cocaine, and alcohol treatments: Role of treatment services. In A. G. Marlatt and G. R. VandenBos, eds., *Addictive Behaviors: Readings on Etiology, Prevention, and Treatment,* 718–758. Washington, D.C.: American Psychological Association.

McLellarn, R. W. and J. Rosenzweig. 1998. Generalized anxiety disorder. In B. A. Thyer and J. S. Wodarski, eds., *Handbook of Empirical Social Work Practice: Volume I: Mental Disorders,* 385–397. New York: Wiley.

McNally, R. J. 1994. *Panic Disorder: A Critical Analysis.* New York: Guilford Press.

McShane, C. 1988. *Warning! Dating May Be Hazardous to Your Health!* Racine, Wisc.: Mother Courage Press.

McWhirter, B. T. and J. J. Horan. 1996. Construct validity of cognitive-behavioral treatments for intimate and social loneliness. *Current Psychology: Developmental, Learning, Personality, Social* 15(1): 42–52.

Medora, N. P. and J. C. Woodward. 1991. Factors associated with loneliness among alcoholics in rehabilitation centers. *Journal of Social Psychology* 131(6): 769–779.

Meeks, J. E. 1979. Fire setting. In J. D. Noshpitz, ed., *Basic Handbook of Child Psychiatry* 2:508–511. New York: Basic.

Meichenbaum, D. 1977. *Cognitive-Behavior Modification: An Integrative Approach.* New York: Plenum Press.

———. 1985. *Stress Inoculation Training.* New York: Pergamon Press.

———. 1994. *A Clinical Handbook/Practical Therapist Manual for Assessing and Treating Adults with Post-Traumatic Stress Disorder (PTSD).* Ontario: Institute Press.

Meichenbaum, D. and D. Fitzpatrick. 1993. A constructivist narrative perspective on stress and coping: Stress inoculation applications. In L. Goldberger and S. Breznitz, eds., *Handbook of Stress: Theoretical and Clinical Aspects,* 2nd ed., 706–723. New York: Free Press.

Meichenbaum, D. and D. C. Turk. 1987. *Facilitating Treatment Adherence: A Practitioner's Guidebook.* New York: Plenum Press.

Meiffren, M. 1993. The use of poetry and ritual with troubled adolescents. *Journal of Humanistic Psychology* 33(1): 24–44.

Mellinger, G. D., M. B. Balter, and E. H. Uhlenhuth. 1985. Insomnia and its treatment: Prevalence and correlates. *Archives of General Psychiatry* 42:225–232.

Mellins, C. A., M. J. Blum, S. L. Boyd-Davis, and M. Gatz. 1993. Family network perspectives on caregiving. *Generations* 17(1): 21–24.

Mellon, M. W. and A. C. Houtt. 1995. Elimination disorders. In R. T. Ammerman and M. Hersen, eds., *Handbook of Child Behavior Therapy: In the Psychiatric Setting,* 341–366. New York: Wiley.

Mellor, D. and S. Storer. 1995. Support groups for children in alternate care: A largely untapped therapeutic resource. *Child Welfare* 74(4): 905–918.

Mental Health Association in New York State. 1994. *Double Trouble in Recovery: How to Start a Double Trouble Recovery Group.* Prepared by Howard S. Vogel and Theresa M. Bonner. Albany: Mental Health Association.

Meyer, William. 1988. On the mishandling of anger in psychotherapy. *Clinical Social Work Journal* 16(4): 406–417.

MICA. 1989. *Problems and Solutions in Treating the Mentally Ill Chemically Addicted* (videotape). Burbank, Calif.: Avatar Productions.

Mikhail, M. L. 1992. Psychological responses to relocation to a nursing home. *Journal of Gerontological Nursing* 18(3): 35–39.

Miles, A. 1995. I want to see my son. *Associated Journal of Nursing* 5:58–59.

Milich, R. and J. Kramer. 1984. Reflections on impulsivity: An empirical investigating of impulsivity as a construct. In K. D. Gadow, ed., *Advances in Learning and Behavioral Disabilities* 3:57–94. Greenwich, Conn.: JAI Press.

Millan, F. and J. Chan. 1991. Group therapy with inner-city Hispanic acting-out adolescent males: Some theoretical observations. *Group* 15:109–115.

Miller, K. 1991. Body-image therapy. *Nursing Clinics of North America* 26(3): 727–736.

Miller, T. W. 1990. Effects of an intensive self-esteem building therapeutic model on adolescents in psychiatric treatment. *Child Psychiatry and Human Development* 21(2): 135–143.

Miller, T. W. and L. J. Veltkamp. 1998. *Clinical Handbook of Adult Exploitation and Abuse.* Madison, Conn.: International Universities Press.

Miller, W. R. and S. Rollnick. 1991. *Motivational Interviewing: Preparing People to Change.* New York: Guilford Press.

Mills, B. and J. Allan. 1992. Play therapy with the maltreated child: Impact upon aggressive and withdrawn patterns of interaction. *International Journal of Play Therapy* 1(1): 1–20.

Mintz, L. B. and N. E. Betz. 1988. *Journal of Counseling Psychology* 35(4): 463–471.

Minuchin, S. 1974. *Families and Family Therapy.* Cambridge: Harvard University Press.

Minuchin, S., B. L. Rosman, and L. Baker. 1978. *Psychosomatic Families: Anorexia Nervosa in Context.* Cambridge: Harvard University Press.

Minuchin, S., L. Baker, B. L. Rosman, R. Leibman, L. Melman, and T. C. Todd. 1975. A conceptual model of psychosomatic illness in children: Family organization and family therapy. *Archives of General Psychiatry* 32:1031–1043.

Mishne, J. 1992. The grieving child: Manifest and hidden losses in childhood and adolescence. *Child and Adolescent Social Work Journal* 9(6): 471–489.

Mitchell, J., H. F. Mathews, and L. W. Griffin. 1997. Health and community-based service use: Differences between elderly African Americans and whites. *Research on Aging* 19(2): 199–122.

Mokuau, N. and M. J. Manos. 1989. A behavioral model for training parents. *Social Casework: The Journal of Contemporary Social Work* 70(8): 479–87.

Monahan, D. J. and K. Hooker. 1995. Health of spouse caregivers of dementia patients: The role of personality and social support. *Social Work* 40(3): 305–314.

Monane, M. 1992. Insomnia in the elderly. *Journal of Clinical Psychology* 53(Suppl. 6): 23–28.

Moore, A. J., A. Eisenberg, and H. Eisenberg. 1992. *The Recovery Book*. New York: Workman.

Moore, E., R. Adams, J. Elsworth, and J. Lewis. 1997. An anger management group for people with a learning disability. *British Journal of Learning Disabilities* 25(2): 53–57.

Moore, L. A. and A. M. Waguespack. 1994. Mystery motivator: An effective and time efficient intervention. *School Psychology Review* 23(1): 106–118.

Moos, R. H., J. W. Finney, and R. C. Cronkite. 1990. *Alcoholism Treatment: Context, Process, and Outcome*. New York: Oxford University Press.

Morgan, R. 1987. *Nutrition Prescription: Strategies for Preventing and Treating 50 Common Diseases*. New York: Fawcett Crest.

Morgan, R. T. T. and G. C. Young. 1975. Parental attitudes and the conditioning treatment of childhood enuresis. *Behavior Research and Therapy* 13:197–199.

Morin, C. M. and S. E. Grambling. 1989. Sleep patterns and aging: Comparison of older adults with and without insomnia complaints. *Psychology and Aging* 4:290–294.

Morin, C. M., J. P. Culbert, and S. M. Schwartz. 1994. Nonpharmacological interventions for insomnia: A meta-analysis of treatment efficacy. *American Journal of Psychiatry* 151(8): 1172–1180.

Morin, C. M., R. A. Kowatch, T. Barry, and E. Walton. 1993. Cognitive-behavior therapy for late-life insomnia. *Journal of Consulting and Clinical Psychology* 61(1): 137–146.

Morris, R. J. and T. R. Kratochwill. 1983. Childhood fears and phobias. In R. J. Morris and T. R. Kratochwill, eds., *The Practice of Child Therapy*, 53–114. New York: Pergamon Press.

———. 1987. Dealing with fear and anxiety in the school setting: Behavioral approaches to treatment. *Special Services in the Schools* 3(3–4): 53–68.

Morrow, D. 1993. Social work with gay and lesbian adolescents. *Social Work* 38(6): 655–660.

Morse, G. A. 1992. Causes of homelessness. In J. Robertson and P. Ephross, eds., *Homelessness: A National Perspective*, 1–17. New York: Plenum Press.

Mostofsky, D. I. and J. Lomranz. 1997. *Handbook of Pain and Aging*. New York: Plenum Press.

Moyse-Steinburg, D. 1990. A model for adolescent pregnancy prevention through use of small groups. *Social Work with Groups* 2:57–68.

Mueller, C. W. 1993. Attention deficit/hyperactivity disorder and school social work practice. *Social Work in Education* 15(2): 104–112.

Mueller, C. W., R. Bidwell, S. Okamoto, and E. Mann. 1998. Preventing HIV disease in adolescents. In B. A. Thyer and J. S. Wodarski, eds., *Handbook of Empirical Social Work Practice* 2:105–121. New York: Wiley.

Murphy, B., H. Schofield, J. Nankervis, S. Bloch, H. Herrman, and B. Singh. 1997. Women with multiple roles: the emotional impact of caring for aging parents. *Aging and Society* 17(3): 277–291.

Nace, E. P. 1987. *The Treatment of Alcoholism*. New York: Brunner/Mazel.

Nathan, P. E. and A. H. Skinstad. 1987. Outcomes of treatment for alcohol problems: Current methods, problems and results. *Journal of Consulting and Clinical Psychology* 55:332–340.

National Alliance for Caregiving. 1997. *Family Caregiving in the U.S.: Findings from a National Survey*. Bethesda, Md.: National Alliance for Caregiving.

National Institute on Drug Abuse. 1994. *Clinical Report Series: Relapse Prevention*. Washington, D.C.: National Institute on Drug Abuse.

National Institutes of Health. 1985. Health implications of obesity. *Annals of Internal Medicine* 103:1073–1077.

National Society for the Prevention of Blindness. 1980. *Vision Problems in the U.S.* New York: National Society for the Prevention of Blindness.

Neidig, P. H., B. S. Collins, and D. H. Friedman. 1986. Attitudinal characteristics of males who have engaged in spouse abuse. *Journal of Family Violence* 1:223–233.

Neidig, P. H., D. H. Friedman, and B. S. Collins. 1985. Domestic conflict containment: A spouse abuse treatment program. *Social Casework* 66(4): 195–204.

Neilsen, J. M., R. K. Endo, and B. L. Ellington. 1992. Social isolation and wife abuse: A research report. In E. C. Viano, ed., *Intimate Violence: Interdisciplinary Perspectives*, 49–59. Washington, D.C.: Hemisphere.

Neimeyer, R. A. and G. Feixas. 1990. The role of homework and skill acquisition in the outcome of group cognitive therapy for depression. *Journal of Behavior Therapy* 21:281–292.

New York State Department of Labor. 1996. *Resume and Interview Preparation: Your Winning Edge*. Albany: New York State.

———. 1996. *The Job Seeker's Guide*. Albany: New York State.

New York State Department of Social Services. 1991. *HIV Infection and the Adolescent*. Albany: New York State Department of Social Services.

Nezu, A. M., C. M. Nezu, and M. G. Perri. 1990. Psychotherapy for adults within a problem-solving framework: Focus on depression. *Journal of Cognitive Psychotherapy: An International Quarterly* 4(3): 247–256.

———. 1989. *Problem-Solving Therapy for Depression Theory: Research and Clinical Guidelines*. New York: Wiley.

Nezu, C. M., A. M. Nezu, and P. Arean. 1991. Assertiveness and problem-solving training for mildly mentally retarded persons with dual diagnosis. *Research in Developmental Disabilities* 12(4): 371–386.

NiCarthy, G. 1991. Addictive love and abuse: A course for teenage women. In B. Levy, ed., *Dating Violence: Young Women in Danger*, 240–257. Seattle: Seal Press.

Nightingale, H. and P. Morrissette. 1993. Dating violence: attitudes, myths, and preventative programs. *Social Work in Education* 15(4): 225–232.

Nowinski, J. 1990. *Substance Abuse in Adolescents and Young Adults: A Guide to Treatment*. New York: Norton.

Nowinski, J. and S. Baker. 1992. *The Twelve-Step Facilitation Handbook*. New York: Lexington.

———. 1998. *The Twelve-Step Facilitation Handbook*. San Francisco: Jossey-Bass.

Nyberg, D. 1993. *The Varnished Truth: Truth-Telling and Deceiving in Ordinary Life*. Chicago: University of Chicago Press.

O'Brien, R. W., S. A. Smith, P. J. Bush, and E. Peleg. 1990. Obesity, self-esteem, and health locus of control in black youths during transition to adolescence. *American Journal of Health Promotion* 5(2): 133–139.

O'Connor, B. P., and R. J. Vallerand. 1994. Motivation, self-determination, and person-environment fit as predictors of psychological adjustment among nursing home residents. *Psychology and Aging* 9(2): 189–194.

Oest, L., A. Jerremalm, and J. Johansson. 1981. Individual response patterns and the effects of different behavioral methods in the treatment of social phobia. *Behavior Research and Therapy* 19(1): 1–16.

O'Gorman, G. 1993. Codependency explored: A social movement in search of a definition and treatment. *Psychiatric Quarterly* 64(2): 199–212.

O'Keefe, M. 1996. The differential effects of family violence on adolescent adjustment. *Child and Adolescent Social Work Journal* 13(1): 51–68.

O'Leary, K. D. 1984. *Mommy, I Can't Sit Still.* New Horizon Press.

Olfson, M. and J. Walkup. 1997. Discharge planning in psychiatric units of general hospitals. In D. Mechanic, ed., *Improving Inpatient Psychiatric Treatment in an Era of Managed Care,* 75–85. San Francisco: Jossey-Bass.

Olfson, M., S. Hansell, and C. A. Boyer. 1997. Medication noncompliance. In D. Mechanic, ed., *Improving Inpatient Psychiatric Treatment in an Era of Managed Care,* 39–49. San Francisco: Jossey-Bass.

Olney, M. F. and E. V. Kuper. 1998. The situation of women with developmental disabilities: Implications for practitioners in supported employment. *Journal of Applied Rehabilitation Counseling* 29:3–8.

Olympia, D. E., S. M. Sheridan, W. R. Jenson, and D. Andrews. 1994. Using student-managed interventions to increase homework completion and accuracy. Special section: Behavior analysis in school psychology. *Journal of Applied Behavior Analysis* 27(1): 85–99.

Orbach, S. 1978. *Fat Is a Feminist Issue.* New York: Berkley.

Ornduff, S. R., R. M. Kelsey, and K. D. O'Leary. 1995. What do we know about typologies of batterers? Comment on Gottman et al. *Journal of Family Psychology* 9(3): 249–252.

O'Rourke, K. 1990. Recapturing hope: Elementary school support groups for children of alcoholics. *Elementary School Guidance and Counseling* 25(2): 107–115.

Orr, V. L. and T. Guzie. 1995. Male batterers and psychological type. *Journal of Psychological Type* 34:3–7.

Osborn, A. F. 1963. *Applied Imagination.* New York: Scribners.

Osgood, N. J. 1991. Prevention of suicide in the elderly. *Journal of Geriatric Psychiatry* 24(2): 293–306.

Osher, F. C. and L. L. Kofoed. 1989. Treatment of patients with psychiatric and psychoactive substance abuse disorders. *Hospital and Community Psychiatry* 40:1025–1030.

Ost, L. G. 1988. Applied relaxation vs. progressive relaxation in the treatment of panic disorder. *Behavior Research and Therapy* 26(1): 13–22.

Ost, L. G. and B. E. Westling. 1995. Applied relaxation vs. cognitive behavior therapy in the treatment of panic disorder. *Behavior Research and Therapy* 33(2): 145–158.

Otto, M. W. and N. A. Reilly-Harrington. 1999. The impact of treatment on anxiety sensitivity. In S. Taylor, ed., *Anxiety Sensitivity: Theory, Research, and Treatment of the Fear of Anxiety. The LEA Series in Personality and Clinical Psychology,* 321–336. Mahwah, N.J.: Lawrence Erlbaum Associates.

Otto, M. W. Z., M. H. Pollack, G. S. Sachs, S. R. Reiter, S. Meltzer-Brody, and J. Rosenbaum. 1993. Discontinuation of benzodiazepine treatment: Efficacy of cognitive-behavioral therapy for patients with panic disorder. *American Journal of Psychiatry* 150(10): 1485–1490.

Overholser, J. C. 1995. Treatment of suicidal patients: A risk-benefit analysis. *Behavioral Sciences and the Law* 13(1): 81–92.

Paddison, P. L. 1993. *Treatment of Adult Survivors of Incest.* Washington, D.C.: American Psychiatric Press.

Page, R. M. 1991. Loneliness as a risk factor in adolescent hopelessness. *Journal of Research in Personality* 25(2): 189–195.

Page, R. M. and G. E. Cole. 1991. Loneliness and alcoholism risk in late adolescence: A comparative study of adults and adolescents. *Adolescence* 26(104): 925–930.

Palmer, D. S. 1991. Co-leading a family council in a long-term care facility. *Journal of Gerontological Social Work* 16:121–134.

Papadatou, D. and C. Papadatou. 1991. *Children and Death.* New York: Wiley.

Parks, A. L. and J. Fodor-Davis. 1997. Managing violent and disruptive students. In T. N. Fairchild et al., eds., *Crisis Intervention Strategies for School-Based Helpers,* 2nd ed., 245–277. Springfield, Ill.: Charles C. Thomas.

Parrot, A. 1996. Sexually assertive communication training. In T. L. Jackson, ed., *Acquaintance Rape: Assessment, Treatment, and Prevention,* 215–242. Sarasota, Fla.: Professional Resource Press/Professional Resource Exchange.

Passini, R., C. Rainville, N. Marchand, and Y. Joanette. 1998. Wayfinding and dementia: Some research findings and a new look at design. *Journal of Architectural and Planning Research* 15(2): 133–151.

Paulson, S. E. 1994. Relations of parenting style and parental involvement with ninth-grade students' achievement. Special issue: Middle grades schooling and early adolescent development: I. Early adolescents' psychological characteristics, relationships with others, and school performance. *Journal of Early Adolescence* 14(2): 250–267.

Penn, D. L. and K. T. Mueser. 1996. Research update on the psychosocial treatment of schizophrenia. *American Journal of Psychiatry* 153:607–617.

Perkinson, R. R. and A. E. Jongsma, Jr. 1998. *The Chemical Dependence Treatment Planner.* New York: Wiley.

Perlman, M. and H. S. Ross. 1997. The benefits of parent intervention in children's disputes: An examination of concurrent changes in children's fighting style. *Child Development* 68(4): 690–700.

Perozynski, L. and L. Kramer. 1999. Parental beliefs about managing sibling conflict. *Developmental Psychology* 35(2): 489–499.

Peterson, C. and H. Seligman. 1984. Causal explanations as a risk for depression: Theory and evidence. *Psychological Review* 91(3): 347–374.

Peterson, C. L., S. L. Patrick, and D. J. Rissmeyer. 1990. Social work's contribution to psychosocial rehabilitation. *Social Work* 35(5): 468–472.

Petretic-Jackson, P. and T. Jackson. 1996. Mental health interventions with battered women. In A. R. Roberts, ed., *Helping Battered Women: New Perspectives and Remedies,* 188–221. New York: Oxford University Press.

Peurifoy, R. 1992. *Anxiety Phobias and Panic.* Sacramento: Life Skills.

Pfeiffer, S. I. and S. C. Strzelecki. 1990. Inpatient psychiatric treatment of children and adolescents: A review of outcome studies. *Journal of the American Academy of Child and Adolescent Psychiatry* 29(6): 847–853.

Phelan, T. W. 1993. *All About Attention Deficit Disorder.* Glen Ellyn, Ill.: Child Management.

Philadelphia Child Guidance Center. 1994. *Your Child's Emotional Health: The Early Years.* New York: Macmillan.

Phillips-Hershey, E. and B. Kanagy. 1996. Teaching students to manage personal anger constructively. *Elementary School Guidance and Counseling* 30(3): 229–234.

Pikoff, H. B. 1996. *Treatment Effectiveness Handbook.* New York: Data for Decisions.

Pipher, M. 1994. *Reviving Ophelia.* New York: Ballantine.

Pirog-Good, M. A. and J. E. Stets, eds. 1989. *Violence in Dating Relationships: Emerging Social Issues.* New York: Praeger.

Platt, J. J. and G. Spiwack. 1975. Unidimensionality of the means-end problem-solving (MEPS) procedure. *Journal of Clinical Psychology* 31(1): 15–16.

Polich, J. M., D. Armor, and H. B. Braiker. 1981. *The Course of Alcoholism: Four Years After Treatment.* New York: Wiley.

Pomeroy, E. C., A. Rubin, and R. J. Walker. 1995. Effectiveness of a psychoeducational and task-centered group intervention for family members of people with AIDS. *Social Work Research* 19(3): 142–152.

Porter, E. J. and J. F. Clinton. 1992. Adjusting to the nursing home. *Western Journal of Nursing Research* 14(4): 464–481.

Post, P. and D. McCoard. 1994. Needs and self-concept of runaway adolescents. *School Counselor* 41(3): 212–219.

Postrado, L. and H. J. Nicholson. 1992. Effectiveness in delaying the initiation of sexual intercourse of girls aged 12–14: Two components of the Girls Incorporated Preventing Adolescent Pregnancy Program. *Youth and Society* 23:356–379.

Poulton, S. and J. Torrens. 1996. UHS care bulletin: Your child and encopresis. University Hospital School, University of Iowa. http://www.uiowa.edu/uhs/enco.html

Prino, C. T. and M. Peyrot. 1994. The effect of child physical abuse and neglect on aggressive, withdrawn, and prosocial behavior. *Child Abuse and Neglect* 18(10): 871–884.

Pristach, C. and C. Smith. 1990. Medication compliance and substance abuse among schizophrenia patients. *Hospital and Community Psychiatry* 41(12): 1345–1348.

Psychiatric Star Team on World Wide Web. 1996. The depressed child. American Academy of Child and Adolescent Psychiatry, http://www.psych.med.umich.edu

Purcell, D. W., A. S. DeGroff, and R. J. Wolitski. 1998. HIV prevention case management: Current practice and future direction. *Health and Social Work* 23:282–289.

Pyne, N., R. Morrison, and P. Ainsworth. 1985. A follow-up study of the first 70 admissions to a general purpose adolescent unit. *Journal of Adolescence* 8:333–345.

Qualls, S. H. 1995. Marital therapy with later life couples. *Journal of Geriatric Psychiatry* 28(2): 139–163.

Quay, H. 1986. *Psychopathological Disorders of Childhood.* New York: Wiley.

Ragg, M. 1991. Differential group programming for children exposed to spouse abuse. *Journal of Child and Youth Care* 5(1): 59–75.

Raines, J. C. and C. W. Foy. 1994. Extinguishing the fires within: Treating juvenile fire setters. *Families in Society* 75:595–606.

Rakos, R. F. 1991. *Assertive Behavior: Theory, Research, and Training.* London: Routledge.

Ralston, P. A. 1993. Health promotion and rural black elderly: A comprehensive review. *Journal of Gerontological Social Work* 20(1–2): 53–75.

Randall, E. J. 1994. *Using Guided Dialogue in the Treatment of Depression in Women.* Ph.D. diss., University of Georgia.

Randall, T. 1990. Domestic violence intervention calls for more than treating injuries. *Journal of The American Medical Association* 264:939–940.

Rando, T. A. 1993. *Treatment of Complicated Mourning*. Champaign, Ill.: Research Press.

Randolph, F. et al. 1997. Creating integrated service systems for homeless persons with mental illness: The ACCESS program. *Psychiatric Services* 48(3): 369–373.

Rehm, L. P. and P. Rokke. 1988. Self-management therapies. In K. S. Dobson et al., eds., *Handbook of Cognitive-Behavioral Therapies*, 136–166. New York: Guilford Press.

Reid, W. J. 1978. *The Task-Centered System*. New York: Columbia University Press.

———. 1985. *Family Problem Solving*. New York: Columbia University Press.

———. 1992. *Task Strategies: An Empirical Approach to Clinical Social Work*. New York: Columbia University Press.

———. 1994. Field testing and data gathering on innovative practice interventions in early development. In E. J. Thomas and J. Rothman, eds., *Integrative Perspective on Intervention Research*, 245–266. New York: Haworth Press.

———. 1997. Evaluating the dodo's verdict: Do all interventions have equivalent outcomes? *Social Work Research* 21:5–18.

Reid, W. J. and C. Bailey-Dempsey. 1995. The effects of monetary incentives on school performance. *Families in Society* 76:331–340.

Reid, W. J. and A. Crisafulli. 1990. Marital discord and child behavior problems: A meta-analysis. *Journal of Abnormal Child Psychology* 18:105–117.

Reid, W. J. and T. Donovan. 1990. Treating sibling violence. *Family Therapy* 71:49–59.

Reid, W. J. and L. Epstein, eds. 1977. *Task-Centered Practice*. New York: Columbia University Press.

Reif, S. F. 1993. *How to Reach and Teach ADD/AD/HD Children*. West Nyack, N.Y.: The Center for Applied Research in Education.

Reiff, D. and K. Reiff. 1992. *Eating Disorders: Nutrition in the Recovery Process*. Gathersburg, Md.: Aspen.

Remafedi, G. 1990. Fundamental issues in the care of homosexual youth. *Medical Clinics of North America* 74:1169–1179.

Reynolds, C. R. and T. B. Gutkin, eds. 1999. *The Handbook of School Psychology*, 3rd ed. New York: Wiley.

Reynolds, W. M. 1987. School-based intervention strategies for the treatment of depression in children and adolescents. *Special Services in the Schools* 3(3–4): 69–88.

Rhee, S. 1997. Domestic violence in the Korean immigrant family. *Journal of Sociology and Social Welfare* 24(1): 63–77.

Ricci, I. 1997. *Mom's House, Dad's House: A Complete Guide for Parents Who Are Separated, Divorced, or Remarried*. New York: Simon & Schuster.

Rice, L. N. and E. Saperia. 1984. Task analysis of the resolution of problematic reactions. In L. N. Rice and L. S. Greenberg, eds., *Patterns of Change: Intensive Analysis of Psychotherapy Process*, 3. New York: Guilford Press.

Richey, C. A. 1994. Social support skill training. In D. K. Granvold, ed., *Cognitive and Behavioral Treatment Methods and Applications*, 299–338. Pacific Grove, Calif.: Brooks-Cole.

Richlin, M. and J. G. Sholl. 1992. Physician anger. *Journal of Family Practice* 35(4): 382–384.

Richman, N. E. and R. L. Sokolove. 1992. The experience of aloneness, object representation, and evocative memory in borderline and neurotic patients. *Psychoanalytic Psychology* 9(1): 77–91.

Riddick, C. C., J. Cohen-Mansfield, E. Fleshner, and G. Kraft. 1992. Caregiver adaptations to having a relative with dementia admitted to a nursing home. *Journal of Gerontological Social Work* 19:51–76.

Ries, R. K. and T. Ellingson. 1990. A pilot assessment at one month of 17 dual diagnosis patients. *Hospital and Community Psychiatry* 41(11): 1230–1233.

Riggs, D. S. and E. B. Foa. 1993. Obsessive-compulsive disorder. In D. H. Barlow, ed., *Clinical Handbook of Psychological Disorders*. New York: Guilford Press.

Rihmer, Z. 1996. Strategies of suicide prevention: Focus on health care. *Journal of Affective Disorders* 39(2): 83–91.

Riskind, J. H. and M. A. Mercier. 1994. Phobias. In V. S. Ramachadran, ed., *Encyclopedia of Human Behavior* 3:489–497. New York: Academic Press.

Rite, J., R. First, R. Greenlee, L. Miller, and M. Feichter. 1991. Case management with homeless mentally ill people. *Health and Social Work* 16:58–67.

Robb, H. B. 1992. Why you don't have a "perfect right" to anything. *Journal of Rational-Emotive and Cognitive-Behavior Therapy* 10(4): 259–270.

Robert, A. H. 1990. Generic adaptations to blindness: an alternative method of rehabilitation. *Journal of Visual Impairment and Blindness* 84(4): 151–154.

Roberto, K. A., ed. 1993. *The Elderly Caregiver: Caring for Adults with Developmental Disabilities*. Thousand Oaks, Calif.: Sage.

Roberts, M. A. 1987. How is playroom behavior observation used in the diagnosis of attention deficit disorder? In J. Loney, ed., *The Young Hyperactive Child: Answers to Questions About Diagnosis, Prognosis, and Treatment*. New York: Haworth Press.

Robertson, J. and P. Ephross, eds. 1992. *Homelessness: A National Perspective*. New York: Plenum Press.

Robin, A. L. 1981. A controlled evaluation of problem-solving communication training with parent adolescent conflict. *Behavior Therapy* 12:593–609.

Robin, A. L., M. Bedway, and M. Gilroy. 1994. Problem-solving communication training. In C. W. LeCroy, ed., *Handbook of Child and Adolescent Treatment Manuals,* 92–125. New York: Lexington.

Robin, A. L., M. Gilroy, and A. B. Dennis. 1998. Treatment of eating disorders in children and adolescents. *Clinical Psychology Review* 18(4): 421–446.

Robins, A. L. 1981. A controlled evaluation of problem-solving communication training with parent-adolescent conflict. *Behavior Therapy* 12.

Robinson, L. A., J. S. Berman, and R. A. Neimeyer. 1990. Psychotherapy for the treatment of depression: A comprehensive review of controlled outcome research. *Psychological Bulletin* 100:30–49.

Rodriguez, C. and N. Moore. 1995. Perceptions of pregnant/parenting teens: reframing issues for an integrated approach to pregnancy problems. *Adolescence* 30(119): 685–706.

Roecker, C. E., E. F. Dubow, and D. Donaldson. 1996. Cross-situational patterns in children's coping with observed interpersonal conflict. *Journal of Clinical Child Psychology* 25(3): 288–299.

Rofes, E., ed. *The Kids' Book of Divorce, by, for and About Kids*. Lexington, Mass.: Lewis.

Rogers, A., J. C. Day, B. Williams, F. Randall, P. Wood, D. Healy, and R. P. Bentall. 1998. The meaning and management of neuroleptic medication: A study of patients with a diagnosis of schizophrenia. *Social Science and Medicine* 47(9): 1313–1323.

Rogers, B. 1994. Teaching positive behavior to behaviorly disordered students in primary school. *Support for Learning* 9(4): 166–170.

Rogers, K. T., E. A. Segal, and M. Graham. 1994. The relationship between academic factors and running away among adolescents. *Social Work in Education* 16(1): 46–54.

Rogers, R. L. and C. S. McMillin. 1991. *Relapse Traps.* New York: Bantam.

Rogler, L. 1991. Acculturation and mental health status. *American Psychologist* 46:331–349.

Rohr, M. E. and R. James. 1994. Runaways: Some suggestions for prevention, coordinating services, and expediting the reentry process. *School Counselor* 42(1): 40–47.

Rooney, R. H. 1981. A task-centered reunification model for foster care. In A. N. Malluccio and P. A. Sinanoglu, eds., *The Challenge of Partnership: Working with Parents of Children in Foster Care.* New York: Child Welfare League of America.

Rose, S. J. and W. Meezan. 1996. Variations in perceptions of child neglect. *Child Welfare* 75(2): 139.

Rosekind, M. R. 1992. The epidemiology and occurrence of insomnia. *Journal of Clinical Psychology* 53(6): 4–6.

Rosen, J. C., P. Orosan, and J. Reiter. 1995. Cognitive behavior therapy for negative body image in obese women. *Behavior Therapy* 26:25–42.

Rosen, J., E. Saltzberg, and D. Srebnik. 1989. Cognitive behavior therapy for negative body image. *Behavior Therapy* 20:393–404.

Rosen, K. H. and S. M. Stith. 1993. Intervention strategies for treating women in violent dating relationships. *Family Relations* 42(4): 427–433.

Rosenbaum, A. and K. D. O'Leary. 1981. Marital violence: characteristics of abusive couples. *Journal of Consulting and Clinical Psychology* 49:63–71.

———. 1981. Children, the unintended victims of marital violence. *American Journal of Orthopsychiatry* 51(4): 692–699.

Rosenstock, H. and K. R. Vincent. 1979. Parental involvement as a requisite for successful adolescent therapy. *Journal of Clinical Psychiatry* 40:132–134.

Rosenthal, C. and P. Dawson. 1992. Families and the institutionalized elderly. In G. M. Jones and B. M. Miesen, eds., *Caregiving in Dementia: Research and Applications.* London: Routledge.

Rosman, N. P. 1986. *Attention Deficit Disorder in Childhood: Diagnosis and Treatment: Feelings and Their Medical Significance.* Columbus, Ohio: Ross Laboratories.

Rossi, R. B. 1977. Helping a mute child. In W. J. Reid and L. Epstein, eds., *Task-Centered Practice,* 147–156. New York: Columbia University Press.

Rotheram-Borus, M. J., M. Gwadz, and I. M. Fernandez. 1998. Timing of HIV interventions on reductions in sexual risk among youth. *American Journal of Community Psychology* 26:73–96.

Rothstein, M. M. and P. J. Robinson. 1991. The therapeutic relationship and resistance to change in cognitive therapy. In T. M. Vallis, J. L. Howes, and P. C. Miller, eds., *The Challenge of Cognitive Therapy: Applications to Nontraditional Populations.* New York: Plenum Press.

Rouse, L. P. 1984. Models of self-esteem and locus of control as factors in spouse abuse. *Victimology: An International Journal* 9(1): 130–141.

Rowe, B. 1988. Practical treatment of adolescent sexual offenders. *Journal of Child Care* 3(6): 51–58.

Royce, R. A., A. Sena, W. Cates, Jr., and M. S. Cohen. 1997. Sexual transmission of HIV. *New England Journal of Medicine* 336:1072–1078.

Rubin, K. H. and R. S. Mills. 1990. Maternal beliefs about adoptive and maladaptive social behaviors in normal, aggressive, and withdrawn preschoolers. *Journal of Abnormal Child Psychology* 18(4): 419–435.

Rubin, K. H. and S. L. Stewart. 1996. Social withdrawal. In E. J. Mash and R. A. Barkley, eds., *Child Psychopathology,* 277–310. New York: Guilford Press.

Rue, N. N. 1989. *Coping with Dating Violence.* New York: Rosen Publishing Group.

Russell, D. E. H. 1986. *Healing the Incest Wound: Incest in the Lives of Girls and Women.* New York: Basic.

Rutherford, R. and C. Nelson. 1995. Management of aggressive and violent behavior in the schools. *Focus on Exceptional Children* 27:1–15.

Ryan, A. S. 1992. Social work with immigrants and refugees. *Journal of Multicultural Social Work* 2(1): 15–23.

Ryan, G. 1986. Juvenile sex offenders: Development and correction. *Child Abuse and Neglect* 11(3): 385–395.

Safford, F. 1980. A program for families of the mentally impaired elderly. *The Gerontologist* 20:656–660.

Sakheim, G. A., E. Osborn, and D. Abrams. 1991. Toward a clearer differentiation of high-risk from low-risk fire setters. *Child Welfare* 70(4): 489–503.

Saklofske, D. H. and M. Zeidner, eds. 1995. *International Handbook of Personality and Intelligence.* New York: Plenum Press.

Sales, E. 1995. Surviving unemployment: Economic resources and job loss duration in blue-collar households. *Social Work* 40:483–494.

Salter, A. C. 1988. *Treating Child Sex Offenders and Victims.* Thousand Oaks, Calif.: Sage.

Salzman, B. 1993. When you need to take psychiatric medications. In *The Handbook of Psychiatric Drugs* (1991; reprint, Center City, Minn.: Hazeldon).

Sanchez, Y. M. 1996. Distinguishing cultural expectations in assessment of financial exploitation. *Journal of Elder Abuse and Neglect* 8(2): 49–59.

Saposnek, D. 1983. *Mediating Child Custody Disputes.* San Francisco: Jossey-Bass.

Sappington, A. A. 1996. Relationships among prison adjustment, beliefs and cognitive coping style. *International Journal of Offender Therapy and Comparative Criminology* 40(1): 54–62.

Saunders, D. G. 1984. Helping husbands who batter. *Social Casework* 65(6): 347–353.

———. 1992. A typology of men who batter: Three types derived from cluster analysis. *American Journal of Orthopsychiatry* 62(2): 264–275.

Saunders, D. G. and D. Hanusa. 1986. Cognitive-behavioral treatment of men who batter: The short-term effects of group therapy. *Journal of Family Violence* 1(4): 357–372.

Saunders, R. 1985. Bulimia—an expanded definition. *Social Casework: Journal of Contemporary Social Work* 66(10): 603–615.

Saxena, V. 1992. Perceived maternal rejection as related to negative attention-seeking classroom behavior among primary school children. *Journal of Personality and Clinical Studies* 8(1–2): 129–135.

Saylor, C. F. 1993. *Children and Disasters.* New York: Plenum Press.

Scavo, R. 1989. Female adolescent sex offenders: A neglected treatment group. *Social Casework* 70(2): 114–117.

Schaefer, C. 1995. *Childhood Encopresis and Enuresis: Causes and Therapy.* Northvale, N.J.: Jason Aronson.

Schellenberg, T., R. L. Skok, and T. F. McLaughlin. 1991. The effects of contingent free time on homework completion in English with senior high school English students. *Child and Family Behavior Therapy* 13(3): 1–11.

Scheuer, M. L. and T. A. Pedley. 1990. The evaluation and treatment of seizures. *New England Journal of Medicine* 323(21): 1468–1474.

Schinka, J. A. 1984.*Personal Problems Checklist*. Odessa, Fla.: Psychological Assessment Resources.

Schinke, S. P., M. A. Forgey, and M. Orlandi. 1996. Teenage sexuality. In M. Mattaini and B. A. Thyer, eds., *Finding Solutions to Social Problems: Behavioral Strategies for Change*, 267–288. Washington, D.C.: American Psychological Association.

Schlundt, D. G. and W. G. Johnson. 1990. *Eating Disorders: Assessment and Treatment*. Boston: Allyn and Bacon.

Schmitt, B. D. 1984. Encopresis. *Primary Care* 11:497–511.

———. 1991. *Your Child's Health: The Parents' Guide to Symptoms, Emergencies, Common Illnesses, Behavior and School Problems*. New York: Bantam.

———. 1997. Bed-wetting (enuresis). Excerpted from *Your Child's Health*. Home Microsoft Essentials 97: http://family.starwave.com:80/experts/barton/ba05l496.html

Schneewind, E. H. 1990. The reaction of the family to the institutionalization of an elderly member: Factors influencing adjustment and suggestions for easing the transition to a new life phase. *Journal of Gerontological Social Work* 15:121–136.

Schneider, J. P. and R. Irons. 1997. Treatment of gambling, eating, and sex addictions. In N. S. Miller and M. S. Gold, eds., *Manual of Therapeutics for Addictions*, 225–245. New York: Wiley-Liss.

Schroeder, C. S. and B. N. Gordon. 1991. *Assessment and Treatment of Childhood Problems: A Clinician's Guide*. New York: Guilford Press.

Schubmehl, W. 1991. Davanloo's intensive short-term dynamic psychotherapy in the treatment of battered wife syndrome. *International Journal of Short-Term Psychotherapy* 6(2): 79–93.

Schutt, R. K. and G. R. Garrett. 1992. The homeless alcoholic, past and present. In M. J. Robertson et al., eds., *Homelessness: A National Perspective: Topics in Social Psychiatry*, 177–186. New York: Plenum Press.

Schutz, B. M. et al. 1989. *Solomon's Sword*. San Francisco: Jossey-Bass.

Schwartz, A. and R. M. Schwartz. 1993. *Depression Theories and Treatments*. New York: Columbia University Press.

Schwartz, J. M. 1997. *Brain Lock: Free Yourself from Obsessive-Compulsive Behavior: A Four-Step Self-Treatment Method to Change Your Brain Chemistry*. New York: HarperCollins.

Seaver, C. 1996. Muted lives: Older battered women. *Journal of Elder Abuse and Neglect* 8(2): 3–21.

Seifer, R., A. J. Sameroff, C. P. Baldwin, and A. Baldwin. 1992. Child and family factors that ameliorate risk between four and thirteen years of age. *Journal of the American Academy of Child and Adolescent Psychiatry* 31(5): 893–903.

Seligman, L. 1990. *Selecting Effective Treatments: A Comprehensive Systematic Guide to Treating Adult Mental Disorders*. San Francisco: Jossey-Bass.

Seltzer, M. M. 1992. Training families to be case managers for elders with developmental disabilities. *Generations* 16:65–70.

Serbin, L. A., P. L. Peters, V. J. McAffer, and A. E. Schwartzman. 1991. Childhood aggression and withdrawal as predictors of adolescent pregnancy, early parenthood, and environmental risk for the next generation. Special issue: Childhood disorders in the context of family. *Canadian Journal of Behavioral Science* 23(3): 318–331.

Sgroi, S., ed. 1989. *Handbook of Clinical Intervention in Child Sexual Abuse*. New York: Lexington.

———, ed. 1989. *Vulnerable Populations: Sexual Abuse Treatment for Children, Adult Survivors, Offenders, and Persons with Mental Retardation*. 2 vols. New York: Lexington.

Shankman, A. L. 1994. Can VT prevent suicide? *Journal of Optometric Vision Development* 25(3): 135–136.

Shapiro, E. S. and C. L. Cole. 1994. *Behavior Change in the Classroom: Self-Management Interventions.* New York: Guilford Press.

Sharlin, S. A. and M. Mor-Barak. 1992. Runaway girls in distress: Motivation, background, and personality. *Adolescence* 27(106): 387–405.

Sheafor, B. W., C. Horejsi, and G. Horejsi. 1997. *Techniques and Guidelines for Social Work Practice,* 4th ed. Boston: Allyn and Bacon.

Sheerin, D., M. MacLeod, and V. Kusumakar. 1996. Psychosocial adjustment in children with port-wine stains and prominent ears. *Annual Progress in Child Psychiatry and Child Development* 34(12): 342–366.

Shepard, M. F. 1992. Predicting batterer recidivism five years after community intervention. *Journal of Family Violence* 7(3): 167–178.

Sheras, P. L. and P. R. Koch-Sheras. 1998. New frontiers in treating couples. In L. Vande-Creek et al., eds., *Innovations in Clinical Practice: A Source Book,* 16 : 399–418. Sarasota, Fla.: Professional Resource Press/Professional Resource Exchange.

Sheridan, M. J., N. Gowen, and S. Halpin. 1993. Developing a practice model for the homeless mentally ill. *Families in Society* 74(7): 410–421.

Sherlock, J. and I. Gardner. 1993. Systemic family intervention. In A. Chapman and M. Marshall, eds., *Dementia: New Skills for Social Workers.* London: Jessica Kingsley.

Sherman, J. J. 1998. Effects of psychotherapeutic treatments for PTSD: A meta-analysis of controlled clinical trials. *Journal of Traumatic Stress* 11 : 413–435.

Shimizu, M., H. Takeuchi, T. Okumura, and T. Andoh. 1991. A nosological study of school refusal. *Japanese Journal of Child and Adolescent Psychiatry* 32(3): 37–44.

Shneidman, E. S. 1976. The components of suicide. *Psychiatric Annals* 6 : 51–66.

Showers, N., E. P. Simon, S. Blumenfield, and G. Holden. 1995. Predictors of patient and proxy satisfaction with discharge plans. *Social Work in Health Care* 22(1): 19–35.

Siegel, M., J. Brisman, and M. Weinshell. 1997. *Surviving an Eating Disorder: Strategies for Family and Friends.* New York: HarperCollins.

Silver, L. B. 1984. *The Misunderstood Child.* New York: McGraw-Hill.

———. 1993. *Dr. Larry Silver's Advice to Parents on Attention Deficit/Hyperactivity Disorder.* Washington, D.C.: American Psychiatric Press.

Silverman, M. M. and R. W. Maris. 1995. The prevention of suicidal behaviors: An overview. Special issue: Suicide prevention: Toward the year 2000. *Suicide and Life Threatening Behavior* 25(1): 10–21.

Silverman, W. H. 1990. Intervention strategies for the prevention of adolescent substance abuse. *Journal of Adolescent Chemical Dependency* 1(2): 25–34.

Silverstein, H. 1994. *Date Abuse.* Berkeley Heights, N.J.: Enslow Publishers.

Singer, M. and R. Needle. 1996. Preventing AIDS among drug users. *Journal of Drug Issues* 26(3): 521–523.

Sisson, R. W. and N. H. Agrin. 1986. Family member involvement to initiate and promote treatment of problem drinkers. *Journal of Behavior Therapy and Experimental Psychiatry* 17(1): 15–21.

Skinner, C. H. 1998. Preventing academic skills deficits. In W. T. Steuart and F. M. Gresham, eds., *Handbook of Child Behavior Therapy.* New York: Plenum Press.

Sloan, H. N. 1988. *The Good Kid Book: How to Solve the 16 Most Common Behavior Problems.* Champaign, Ill.: Research Press.

Smart, J. F. and D. W. Smart. 1995. Acculturative stress of Hispanics: Loss and challenge. *Journal of Counseling and Development* 73:390–396.

Smith, G. C., R. A. Majeski, and B. McClenny. 1996. Psycho-educational support groups for aging parents: development and preliminary outcomes. *Mental Retardation* 34(3): 172–181.

Smith, G. C. and S. S. Tobin. 1989. Permanency planning among older parents of adults with lifelong disabilities. *Journal of Gerontological Social Work* 14(3–4): 35–59.

———. 1993. Practice with older parents of developmentally disabled adults. *Clinical Gerontologist* 14(1): 59–77.

Smith, G. C., S. S. Tobin, and E. M. Fullmer. 1995. Assisting older families of adults with lifelong disabilities. In G. C. Smith et al., eds., *Strengthening Aging Families: Diversity in Practice,* 80–98. Thousand Oaks, Calif.: Sage.

Smith, J., I. O'Connor, and D. Berthelsen. 1996. The effects of witnessing domestic violence on young children's psycho-social adjustment. *Australian Social Work.* 49(4): 3–10.

Smith, L. L. and B. M. Beckner. 1993. An anger management workshop for inmates in a medium security facility. *Journal of Offender Rehabilitation* 19(3–4): 103–111.

Smith, L., J. Smith, and B. Beckner. 1994. An anger-management workshop for women inmates. *Families in Society* 75:172–175.

Smith, M. 1995. Mediation for children, youth, and families: A service continuum. Special issue: Victim and offender mediation: International perspectives on theory, research, and practice. *Mediation Quarterly* 12(3): 277–283.

Smyth, N. J. 1998. Alcohol abuse. In B. A. Thyer and J. S. Wodarski, eds., *Handbook of Empirical Social Work Practice: Volume I: Mental Disorders,* 181–204. New York: Wiley.

Soares, H. H. and M. Rose. 1994. Clinical aspects of case management with the elderly. *Journal of Gerontological Social Work* 22(3–4): 143–156.

Sommers-Flanagan, J. and R. Sommers-Flanagan. 1998. Assessment and diagnosis of conduct disorder. *Journal of Counseling and Development* 76(2): 189–198.

Sousa, C. 1991. The dating violence intervention project. In B. Levy, ed., *Dating Violence: Young Women in Danger,* 223–231. Seattle: Seal Press.

Spence, S. A. 1993. Rural elderly African-Americans and service delivery: A study of health and social service needs and service accessibility. *Journal of Gerontological Social Work* 20(3–4): 187–201.

Spencer, T., T. Wilens, and J. Biederman. 1995. Psychotropic medication for children and adolescents. *Pediatric Psychopharmacology* 4(1): 97–120.

Sperry, L. 1995. *Psychopharmacology and Psychotherapy: Strategies for Maximizing Treatment Outcomes.* New York: Brunner/Mazel.

Spirito, A. and J. C. Overholser. 1993. Primary and secondary prevention strategies for reducing suicide among youth. Special issue: Family treatment. *Child and Adolescent Mental Health Care* 3(3): 205–217.

Sprafkin, R. P. 1994. Social skills training. In R. Corsini, ed., *Encyclopedia of Psychology.* New York: Wiley.

Srebnik, D. S. and E. A. Saltzberg. 1994. Feminist cognitive-behavioral therapy for negative body image. *Women and Therapy* 15(2): 117–133.

Stanley, M. 1992. Obsessive-compulsive disorder. In S. M. Turner, K. S. Calhoun and H. E. Adams, eds., *Handbook of Clinical Behavior Therapy,* 2nd ed., 67–85. New York: Wiley.

Stanley, M. A. and P. M. Averill. 1998. Psychosocial treatments for obsessive-compulsive disorder: Clinical applications. In R. Swinson et al., eds., *Obsessive-Compulsive Disorder: Theory, Research, and Treatment,* 277–297. New York: Guilford Press.

Starck, P. L. 1992. Suffering in a nursing home: Losses of the human spirit. *International Forum for Logotherapy* 15(2): 76–79.

Stark, E., and A. Flitcraft. 1988. Violence among intimates: An epidemiological review. In V. B. Van Hasselt, R. L. Morrison, A. S. Bellack, and M. Hersen, eds., *Handbook of Family Violence*, 293–317. New York: Plenum Press.

Stark, L. J., J. Owens-Stively, A. Spirito, A. Lewis, and D. Guevremont. 1990. Group behavioral treatment of retentive encopresis. *Journal of Pediatric Psychology* 15(5): 659–671.

Stark, L. J., A. Spirito, A. V. Lewis, and K. J. Hart. 1990. Encopresis: Behavioral parameters associated with children who fail medical management. *Child Psychiatry and Human Development* 20(3): 169–179.

Stavans, I. 1995. *The Hispanic Condition.* New York: HarperCollins.

Stein, M. B., M. E. Tancer, C. S. Gelemter, B. J. Vittone, and T. W. Uhde. 1990. Major depression in patients with social phobia. *American Journal of Psychiatry* 147: 637–639.

Steinberg, L., S. D. Lamborn, S. M. Dornbusch, and N. Darling. 1992. Impact of parenting practices on adolescent achievement: Authoritative parenting, school involvement, and encouragement to succeed. *Child Development* 63(5): 1266–1281.

Steinhausen, H. C. and C. Juzi. 1996. Elective mutism: An analysis of 100 cases. *Journal of the American Academy of Child and Adolescent Psychiatry* 35(5): 606–614.

Steinmetz, S. K. 1978. The battered husband syndrome. *Victimology* 2(3 supp. 4): 499–509.

––, ed. 1993. *Random House Webster's Dictionary.* New York: Ballantine.

Steketee, G. 1987. Behavioral social work with obsessive-compulsive disorder. *Journal of Social Service Research* 10: 53–73.

Stevens, S. J. and A. L. Estrada. 1996. Reducing HIV risk behaviors: Perceptions of HIV risk stage of change. *Journal of Drug Issues* 26(3): 607–618.

Stewart, M. J. and R. E. Ray. 1984. Truants and the court: A diversionary program. *Social Work in Education* 10: 179–191.

Stewart, S. L. and K. H. Rubin. 1995. The social problem-solving skills of anxious-withdrawn children. *Development and Psychopathology* 7(2): 323–336.

Stillion, J. M. and E. E. McDowell. 1991. Examining suicide from a life span perspective. *Death Studies* 15(4): 327–354.

Straus, M. A. and R. J. Gelles. 1986. Societal change and change in family violence from 1975 to 1985 as revealed by two national surveys. *Journal of Marriage and the Family* 48: 465–479.

Straus, M. A., R. J. Gelles, and S. K. Steinmetz. 1980. *Behind Closed Doors: Violence in the American Family.* New York: Anchor.

Strauss, C. C. 1988. Behavioral assessment and treatment of overanxious disorder in children and adolescents. *Behavior Modification* 12(2): 234–251.

Stromgren, A. and P. H. Thomsen. 1990. Personality traits in young adults with a history of conditioning-treated childhood enuresis. *Acta Psychiatrica Scandinavica* 81: 538–541.

Stuart, R. B. 1980. *Helping Couples Change: A Social Learning Approach to Marital Therapy.* New York: Guilford Press.

Studer, J. 1996. Understanding and preventing aggressive responses in youth. *Elementary School Guidance and Counseling* 30(3): 194–203.

Subramanian, K. and S. Rose. 1988. Social work and the treatment of chronic pain. *Health and Social Work* 13: 49–60.

Sue, D. and D. W. Sue. 1991. Counseling strategies for Chinese Americans. In C. C. Lee and B. L. Richardson, eds., *Multicultural Issues in Counseling: New Approaches to Diversity*, 79–90. Alexandria, Va.: American Association for Counseling and Development.

Sugarman, D. B. and G. T. Hotaling. 1989. Dating violence: prevalence, context, and risk markers. In M. A. Pirog-Good and J. E. Stets, eds., *Violence in Dating Relationships: Emerging Social Issues,* 3–32. New York: Praeger.

Suinn, R. M. 1990. *Anxiety Management Training.* New York: Plenum Press.

Sullivan, T. and M. Schneider. 1987. Development and identity issues in adolescent homosexuality. *Children and Adolescent Social Work* 4(1): 13–24.

Susser, E., S. M. Goldfinger, and A. White. 1990. Some clinical approaches to the homeless mentally ill. *Community Mental Health* 26(5): 463–480.

Syrjala, K. L. and J. R. Abrams. 1996. Hypnosis and imagery in the treatment of pain. In R. J. Gatchel and D. C. Turke, eds., *Psychological Approaches to Pain Management: A Practitioner's Handbook,* 231–258. New York: Guilford Press.

Szabo, C. P. 1996. Selective mutism and social anxiety. *Journal of the American Academy of Child and Adolescent Psychiatry* 35(5): 555.

Taft, L. B. and M. F. Nehrke. 1990. Reminiscence, life review, and ego integrity in nursing home residents. *International Journal of Aging and Human Development* 10(3): 189–196.

Talbott, J. A., ed. 1976. *The Chronic Mental Patient: Five Years Later.* New York: Brunner/ Mazel.

Talbott, J. A., R. E. Hales, and S. C. Yudofsky, eds. 1988. *Textbook of Psychiatry.* Washington, D.C.: American Psychiatric Press.

Tanaka, S. 1991. Children's problem behaviors in the classroom from the standpoint of the structures of their norm-consciousness. *Japanese Journal of Criminal Psychology* 29(1): 1–17.

Taylor, B. and A. Taylor. 1993. Wayfinding in mental health: The transportation handicapped severely mentally ill. *Families in Society* 74:434–400.

———. 1996. Social work with transport disabled persons: A wayfinding perspective in health care. *Psychiatric Rehabilitation Journal* 20(2): 77–81.

Taylor, L. and H. S. Adelman. 1990. School avoidance behavior: Motivational bases and implications for intervention. *Child Psychiatry and Human Development* 20(4): 219–233.

Taylor, R. J. and L. M. Chatters. 1988. Correlates of education, income, and poverty among aged blacks. *The Gerontologist* 28(4): 435–441.

Taylor, S., ed. 1999. *Anxiety Sensitivity: Theory, Research, and Treatment of the Fear of Anxiety.* Mahwah, N.J.: Lawrence Erlbaum Associates.

Taylor, S. E. and L. G. Aspinwall. 1993. Coping with chronic illness. In L. Goldberger and S. Breznitz, eds., *Handbook of Stress: Theoretical and Clinical Aspects,* 2nd ed., 511–531. New York: Free Press.

Taylor-Brown, S. 1995. HIV/AIDS: Direct practice. In R. Edwards, ed., *Encyclopedia of Social Work,* 1291–1305. Washington, D.C.: NASW Press.

Taylor-Brown, S. and L. Wiener. 1993. Making videotapes of HIV-infected women for their children. *Families in Society* 74(8): 68–80.

Teare, J. F., K. Authier, and R. Peterson. 1994. Differential patterns of post-shelter placement as a function of problem type and severity. *Journal of Child and Family Studies* 3(1): 7–22.

Teare, J. F., D. W. Furst, R. W. Peterson, and K. Authier. 1992. Family reunification following shelter placement: Child, family, and program correlates. *American Journal of Orthopsychiatry* 62(1): 142–146.

Teare, J. F., R. W. Peterson, D. Furst, and K. Authier. 1994. Treatment implementation in a short-term emergency shelter program. *Child Welfare* 73(3): 271–281.

Teather, E. C. 1981. Social work with groups. *Practice-Digest* (entire issue) 4(1).

Terr, L. 1990. *Too Scared to Cry.* New York: Basic.

Tessler, R. C. and D. L. Dennis. 1989. *A Synthesis of NIMH-Funded Research Concerning Persons Who Are Homeless and Mentally Ill.* Rockville, Md.: National Institute of Mental Health.

Thase, M. E. 1996. Cognitive behavior therapy manual for treatment of depressed inpatients. In V. B. Van Hasselt and M. Hersen, eds., *Sourcebook of Psychological Treatment Manuals for Adult Disorders,* 201–231. New York: Plenum Press.

Thomas, E. J., K. B. Adams, M. R. Yoshioka, and R. D. Ager. 1990. Unilateral relationship enhancement in the treatment of spouses of uncooperative alcohol abusers. *The American Journal of Family Therapy* 18(4): 334–344.

Thomas, E. J., C. Santa, D. Bronson, and D. Oyserman. 1987. Unilateral family therapy with the spouses of alcoholics. *Journal of Social Service Research* 10:145–162.

Thompson, J. K., L. J. Heinberg, M. Altabe, and S. Tantleff-Dunn. 1999. *Exacting Beauty: Theory, Assessment, and Treatment of Body Image Disturbance.* Washington, D.C.: American Psychological Association.

Thyer, B. A. 1987. *Treating Anxiety Disorders.* Newbury Park, Calif.: Sage.

———. 1991. Diagnosis and treatment of child and adolescent anxiety disorders. *Behavior Modification* 15(3): 310–325.

Thyer, B. A. and K. M. Sowers-Hoag. 1986. The etiology of school phobia: A behavioral approach. *School Social Work Journal* 10(2): 86–98.

Tiedemann, G. L. and C. Johnston. 1992. Evaluation of a parent training program to promote sharing between young siblings. *Behavior Therapy* 23:299–318.

Timko, C. and R. H. Moos. 1989. Choice, control, and adaptation among elderly residents of sheltered care settings. *Journal of Applied Social Psychology* 12(8): 636–655.

Tipovsky, J. A. 1991. Post-traumatic stress disorder in children. *Family and Community Health* 14(3): 42–51.

Tobin, S. S. 1991. *Personhood in Advanced Old Age.* New York: Springer.

———. 1999. *Preservation of the Self When Very Old.* New York: Springer.

Tolson, E. R., W. J. Reid, and C. D. Garvin. 1994. *Generalist Practice: A Task-Centered Approach.* New York: Columbia University Press.

Tolson, E. R. (in press). The task-centered model. In P. Lehmann and N. Coady, eds., *Theoretical Perspectives in Direct Social Work Practice.* New York: Springer.

Toneatto, T. 1999. A metacognitive analysis of craving: Implications for treatment. *Journal of Clinical Psychology* 55(5): 527–537.

Toseland, R. W. and P. McCallion. 1998. *Maintaining Communication with Persons with Dementia.* New York: Springer.

Toseland, R. W. and G. Smith. 1991. Family caregivers of the frail elderly. In A. Gitterman, ed., *Handbook of Social Work Practice with Vulnerable Populations,* 549–583. New York: Columbia University Press.

Toseland, R. W., C. G. Blanchard, and P. McCallion. 1995. A problem solving intervention for caregivers of cancer patients. *Social Science and Medicine* 40(4): 517–528.

Trammel, D. L., P. J. Schloss, and S. Alper. 1994. Using self-recording, evaluation, and graphing to increase completion of homework assignments. *Journal of Learning Disabilities* 27(2): 75–81.

Tran, T. V. and R. Wright, Jr. 1986. Social support and subjective well-being among Vietnamese refugees. *Social Service Review* 60:449–459.

Trice, A. D. 1990. Adolescents' locus of control and compliance with contingency contracting and counseling interventions. *Psychological Reports* 67(1): 233–234.

Triolo, S. J. 1999. *Attention Deficit Hyperactivity Disorder in Adulthood: A Practitioner's Handbook.* Philadelphia: Brunner/Mazel.

Tucker, P. and A. Aron. 1993. Passionate love and marital satisfaction at key transition points in the family life cycle. *Journal of Social and Clinical Psychology* 12(2): 135–147.

Turk, D. C. 1996. Cognitive factors in chronic pain and disability. In K. S. Dobson and K. D. Craig, eds., *Advances in Cognitive-Behavioral Therapy,* 83–115. Thousand Oaks, Calif.: Sage.

————. 1996. Cognitive factors in chronic pain and disability. In K. S. Dobson and K. D. Craig, eds., *Advances in Cognitive-Behavioral Therapy,* 83–115. Thousand Oaks, Calif.: Sage.

Turk, D., D. Meichenbaum, and M. Genest. 1983. *Pain and Behavioral Medicine.* New York: Guilford Press.

Turner, S. 1995. Alcoholic women's self-esteem. *Alcoholism Treatment Quarterly* 12(4): 109–116.

Turner, J., R. Kessler, and J. House. 1991. Factors facilitating adjustment to unemployment: Implications for intervention. *American Journal of Community Psychology* 19:521–542.

Turner, S. M., K. S. Calhoun, and H. E. Adams, eds. 1992. *Handbook of Clinical Behavior Therapy,* 2nd ed. New York: Wiley.

U.S. Department of Agriculture. 1960. *The True Story of Smokey the Bear.* Washington, D.C.: Western.

U.S. Department of Health and Human Services. 1994. *Assessment and Treatment of Patient with Coexisting Mental Illness and Alcohol and Other Drug Abuse: Treatment Improvement Protocol Series #9.* Rockville, Md.: U.S. Department of Health and Human Services.

————. 1989. *The Homeless Mentally Ill: Service Needs of the Population.* Rockville, Md.: National Institute of Mental Health.

U.S. Department of Labor and Training Administration. 1994. *Employment and Training for America's Homeless: A Report on the Job Training for the Homeless Demonstration Program: A Report to Congress.* Washington, D.C.: U.S. Congress.

U.S. Federal Bureau of Investigation. 1992. *Crime in the United States, Annual.* Washington, D.C.: U.S. Federal Bureau of Investigation.

Ulene, A. 1995. *Take It Off! Keep It Off!* Berkeley: Ulysses Press.

Umoren, J. A. 1992. Maslow hierarchy of needs and OBRA 1987: Toward need satisfaction by nursing home residents. *Educational Gerontology* 18(6): 657–670.

Urbanska, W. 1991. Self-esteem: The hope of the future. *New Woman* 7:52–58.

Vaillant, G. E. 1966. A twelve-year follow-up of New York narcotic addicts: IV. Some characteristics and determinants of abstinence. *American Journal of Psychiatry* 123:573–584.

————. 1983. *The Natural History of Alcoholism.* Cambridge: Harvard University Press.

Van Brunt, D. L., B. W. Tiedel, and K. L. Lichstein. 1996. Insomnia. In V. B. Van Hasselt and M. Hersen, eds., *Sourcebook of Psychological Treatment Manuals for Adult Disorders,* 539–566. New York: Plenum Press.

Vandereycken, W. and R. Meermann. 1988. Chronic illness behavior and noncompliance with treatment: Pathways to an interactional approach. *Psychotherapy and Psychosomatics* 50(4): 182–191.

van der Kolk, B. A., A. C. McFarlane, and L. Weisaeth. 1996. *Traumatic Stress: The Effects of Overwhelming Experience on Mind, Body and Society.* New York: Guilford Press.

Van der Mey, B. J. 1988. The sexual victimization of male children: Review of previous research. *Child Abuse and Neglect* 12:61–71.

Vargo, B. 1995. Are withdrawn children at risk? *Canadian Journal of School Psychology* 11(2): 166–177.

Vaughn, C. and W. Long. 1999. Surrender to win: How adolescent drug and alcohol users change their lives. *Adolescence* 34(133): 9–24.

Vaux, A., J. Phillips, L. Holly, B. Thomson, D. William, and D. Steward. 1986. The Social Support Appraisals (SSA) Scale: Studies of reliability and validity. *American Journal of Community Psychology* 14:195–219.

Videka-Sherman, L. 1989. Therapeutic issues for physical and emotional child abuse and neglect: Implications for longitudinal research. Paper, Research Forum on Issues in the Longitudinal Study on Child Maltreatment. Toronto, Ontario, Canada, Oct. 15–18.

———. 1991. Child abuse and neglect. In A. Gitterman, ed., *Handbook of Social Work Practice with Vulnerable Populations,* 345–381. New York: Columbia University Press.

Viscott, D. 1976. *Anger, the Language of Feelings.* New York: Pocket.

Vonk, M. E. and B. L. Yegidis. 1998. Post-traumatic stress disorder. In B. A. Thyer and J. S. Wodarski, eds., *Handbook of Empirical Social Work Practice: Volume I: Mental Disorders,* 365–383. New York: Wiley.

Walker, L. 1978. Battered women and learned helplessness. *Victimology* 2 (3 supp. 4): 525–534.

———. 1979. *The Battered Woman.* New York: Harper and Row.

———. 1984. *The Battered Woman Syndrome.* New York: Springer.

———. 1994. *The Abused Woman: A Survivor Therapy Approach.* New York: Newbridge Communications.

———. 1995. Current perspectives on men who batter women—implications for intervention and treatment to stop violence against women: Comment on Gottman et al. *Journal of Family Psychology* 9(3): 264–271.

Walker, M. B. 1992. *The Psychology of Gambling.* Tarrytown, N.Y.: Pergamon Press.

Walkup, J. 1997. Family involvement in general hospital inpatient care. In D. Mechanic, ed., *Improving Inpatient Psychiatric Treatment in an Era of Managed Care,* 51–64. San Francisco: Jossey-Bass.

Wallace, B. and A. Nosko. 1993. Working with shame in the group treatment of male batterers. *International Journal of Group Psychotherapy* 43(1): 45–61.

Wallerstein, J. S. and S. Elakeslee. 1989. *Second Chances, Men, Women and Children: A Decade After Divorce.* New York: Ticknor and Fields.

Walsh, B. and P. Rosen. 1979. A network of services for severely disturbed adolescents. *Child Welfare* 58(2): 115–125.

Walters, J. and B. Neugeboren. 1995. Collaboration between mental health organizations and religious institutions. *Psychiatric Rehabilitation Journal* 19(2): 51–57.

Waltzer, F. 1984. Using a behavioral group approach with chronic truants. *Social Work in Education* 6(3): 193–200.

Wandrei, K. E. 1985. Identifying potential suicides among high-risk women. *Social Work* 30(6): 511–517.

Ward, M. A., P. H. Wender, and F. W. Reimherr. 1993. The Wender Utah rating scale: An aid in the retrospective diagnosis of childhood attention deficit/hyperactivity disorder. *American Journal of Psychiatry* 150: 885–890.

Wardle, J. 1995. The assessment of obesity: Theoretical background and practical advice. *Behavioral Research and Therapy* 33(1): 107–117.

Ware, C. 1982. *Sharing Parenthood After Divorce: An Enlightened Custody Guide for Mothers, Fathers, and Kids.* New York: Viking.

Warren, C. 1992. Perspectives on international sex practices and American family sex communication relevant to teenage sexual behavior in the United States. *Health Communication* 4(2): 121–136.

Warren, J. K., F. Gary, and J. Moorhead. 1994. Self-reported experiences of physical and sexual abuse among runaway youths. *Perspectives in Psychiatric Care* 30(1): 23–28.

Wasserman, D. 1993. Alcohol and suicidal behavior. *Nordic Journal of Psychiatry* 47(4): 265–271.

Webb, N. B. 1991. *Play Therapy with Children in Crisis: A Casebook for Practitioners.* New York: Guilford Press.

Webb, W. 1992. Treatment issues and cognitive behavior therapy techniques with battered women. *Journal of Family Violence* 7(3): 205–217.

Webster's New World College Dictionary. 1996. New York: Simon & Schuster.

Webster-Stratton, C. and L. Hancock. 1998. Training for parents of young children with conduct problems: Content, methods, and therapeutic processes. In J. M. Briesmeister and C. E. Schaefer, eds., *Handbook of Parent Training: Parents as Co-Therapists for Children's Behavior Problems,* 2nd ed., 98–152. New York: Wiley.

Webster-Stratton, C. and M. Herbert. 1993. *Troubled Families: Problem Children: Working with Parents: A Collaborative Process.* Chichester, England: Wiley.

Weeks, D. J. 1994. A review of loneliness concepts, with particular reference to old age. *International Journal of Geriatric Psychiatry* 9(5): 345–355.

Wehman, P. and W. Parent. 1996. Supported employment. In P. McLaughlin and P. Wehman, eds., *Mental Retardation and Developmental Disabilities,* 2nd ed., 317–338. Austin, Tex.: Pro-Ed.

Weidman, A. 1986. Family therapy with violent couples. *Social Casework* 67(4): 211–218.

Weishaar, M. E. and A. T. Beck. 1992. Hopelessness and suicide. *International Review of Psychiatry* 4(2): 177–184.

Weiss, L. and S. Wolchik. 1998. New Beginnings: An empirically-based intervention program for divorced mothers to help their children adjust to divorce. In J. M. Briesmeister and C. E. Schaefer, eds., *Handbook of Parent Training: Parents as Co-Therapists for Children's Behavior Problems,* 2nd ed., 445–478. New York: Wiley.

Weiss, R. L. and W. K. Halford. 1996. Managing marital therapy: Helping partners change. In V. B. Van Hasselt and M. Hersen, eds., *Sourcebook of Psychological Treatment Manuals for Adult Disorders,* 489–537. New York: Plenum Press.

Weiten, W. 1995. *Psychology: Themes and Variations.* Pacific Grove, Calif.: Brooks/Cole.

Wekerle, C. and D. A. Wolfe. 1996. Child maltreatment. In E. J. Mash and R. A. Barkley, eds., *Child Psychopathology,* 492–537. New York: Guilford Press.

Wells, A. 1998. Cognitive therapy of social phobia. In N. Tarrier and A. Wells, eds., *Treating Complex Cases: The Cognitive Behavioural Therapy Approach,* 1–26. Chichester, England: American Ethnological Press.

Wells, P. and B. Faragher. 1993. In-patient treatment of 165 adolescents with emotional and conduct disorders: A study of outcome. *British Journal of Psychiatry* 162:345–352.

Werry, J. S. and R. L. Sprague. 1970. Hyperactivity. In C. G. Costello, ed., *Symptoms of Psychopathology*. New York: Wiley.

Westen, D., M. J. Moses, K. R. Silk, N. E. Lohr, et al. 1992. Quality of depressive experience in borderline personality disorder and major depression: When depression is not just depression. *Journal of Personality Disorders* 6(4): 382–393.

Wheeler, J. R. and L. Berliner. 1988. Treating the effects of sexual abuse on children. In G. E. Wyatt and G. J. Powell, eds., *Lasting Effects of Child Sexual Abuse*, 227–247. Newbury Park, Calif.: Sage.

Whitbeck, L. B. and R. L. Simons. 1990. Life on the streets: The victimization of runaway and homeless adolescents. *Youth and Society* 22(1): 108–125.

Whitbread, J. and A. McGown. 1994. The treatment of bulimia nervosa: What is effective: A meta-analysis. *Indian Journal of Clinical Psychology* 21:32–44.

White, M. B. 1996. Don't just do something, stand there. *Journal of Family Psychotherapy* 7(4): 79–83.

Whiteman, M. D., D. Fanshel, and J. F. Grundy. 1987. Cognitive-behavioral interventions aimed at anger of parents at risk of child abuse. *Social Work* 32:469–474.

Wiederman, M. W. and E. R. Allgeier. 1996. Expectations and attributions regarding extramarital sex among young married individuals. *Journal of Psychology and Human Sexuality* 8(3): 21–35.

Wielkiewicz, R. M. 1995. Management of behavior excesses in the home. *Behavior Management in the Schools: Principles and Procedures,* 2nd ed., chapter 9. Boston: Allyn and Bacon.

Wierson, M., R. Forehand, and C. Frame. 1992. Epidemiology and treatment of mental health problems in juvenile delinquents. *Advanced Behavior Research Therapy* 14:93–120.

Wiesinger, H. 1985. *Dr. Weisinger's Anger Work-Out Book.* New York: Morrow.

Wilber, K. H. and S. L. Reynolds. 1996. Introducing a framework for defining financial abuse of the elderly. *Journal of Elder Abuse and Neglect* 8(2): 61–80.

Wilcox, D. and P. W. Dowrick. 1992. Anger management with adolescents. *Residential Treatment for Children and Youth* 9(3): 29–39.

Wilens, T., T. Spencer, and J. Giederman. 1995. *Pharmacotherapy of Adult Attention Deficit / Hyperactivity Disorder: A Comprehensive Guide to Attention Deficit Disorder in Adults.* New York: Brunner/Mazel.

Williamson, D. A., C. M. Champagne, L. P. Jackman, and P. J. Varnado. 1996. Lifestyle change: A program for long-term weight management. In V. B. Van Hasselt and M. Hersen, eds., *Sourcebook of Psychological Treatment Manuals for Adult Disorders,* 423–488. New York: Plenum Press.

Williamson, D. A., B. A. Cubic, and R. D. Fuller. 1992. Eating disorders. In S. M. Turner, K. S. Calhoun, and H. E. Adams, eds., *Handbook of Clinical Behavior Therapy,* 2nd ed., 355–371. New York: Wiley.

Wilson, G. T. 1994. Behavioral treatment of obesity: Thirty years and counting. *Advances in Behavior Research and Therapy* 16:31–75.

Wilson, G. T. and C. G. Fairburn. 1993. Cognitive treatments for eating disorders. *Journal of Consulting and Clinical Psychology* 61:261–269.

Wilson, K. 1997. *When Violence Begins at Home: A Comprehensive Guide to Understanding and Ending Domestic Abuse.* Alameda, Calif.: Hunter House.

Wilson, R. R. 1996. Imaginal desensitization and relaxation training. In C. Lindemann, ed., *Handbook of the Treatment of the Anxiety Disorders*, 263–290. Northvale, N.J.: Jason Aronson.

Wilson, S. K., S. Cameron, P. Jaffe, and D. Wolfe. 1989. Children exposed to wife abuse: An intervention model. *Social Casework* 70(3): 180–184.

Wodarski, J. S. 1987. An examination of spouse abuse: practice issues for the profession. *Clinical Social Work Journal* 15(2): 172–187.

Wolfe, D. A. 1993. Prevention of child neglect. *Criminal Justice and Behavior* 20(1): 90–96.

Wolfe, D. A. and C. Wekerle. 1993. Treatment strategies for child physical abuse and neglect: A critical progress report. *Clinical Psychology Review* 13: 473–500.

Wolfelt, A. D. 1996. *Healing the Bereaved Child: Grief Gardening, Growth Through Grief, and Other Touchstones for Caregivers*. Fort Collins, Col.: Companion Press.

Worden, J. W. 1991. *Grief Counseling and Grief Therapy: A Handbook for the Mental Health Practitioner*, 2nd ed. New York: Springer.

Wright, J. D. and E. Weber. 1987. Mental health. In *Homelessness and Health*. Washington, D.C.: McGraw-Hill.

Wyatt, G. E. and M. R. Mickey. 1988. The support by parents and others as it mediates the effects of child sexual abuse. In G. E. Wyatt and G. J. Powell, eds., *Lasting Effects of Child Sexual Abuse*, 211–226. Newbury Park, Calif.: Sage.

Yager, J. 1994. Psychosocial treatments for eating disorders. *Psychiatry* 57: 153–164.

Yank, G. R., K. J. Bentley, and D. S. Hargrove. 1993. The vulnerability-stress model of schizophrenia: Advances in psychosocial treatment. *American Journal of Orthopsychiatry* 63(1): 55–69.

Yoder, R. M., D. L. Nelson, and D. A. Smith. 1989. Added-purpose versus rote exercise in female nursing home residents. *American Journal of Occupational Therapy* 9: 581–586.

Young, J. E., A. T. Beck, and A. Weinberger. 1993. Depression. In D. H. Barlow, ed., *Clinical Handbook of Psychological Disorders: A Step-by-Step Treatment Manual*, 2nd ed., 240–277. New York: Guilford Press.

Zabrana, R. E. 1995. *Understanding Latino Families: Scholarship, Policy, and Practice*. Thousand Oaks, Calif.: Sage.

Zarit, S. H. and A. B. Edwards. 1996. Family caregiving: Research and clinical intervention. In R. T. Woods, ed., *Handbook of the Clinical Psychology of Aging*, 333–368. New York: Wiley.

Zarit, S. H. and C. J. Whitlach. 1992. Institutional placement: Phases of the transition. *The Gerontologist* 32: 665–672.

Zeidner, M. and D. Saklofske. 1995. Adaptive and maladaptive coping. In M. Zeidner and N. Endler, eds., *Handbook of Coping: Theory, Research and Applications*, 506–527. New York: Wiley.

Zerbe, K. J. 1992. Eating disorders in the 1990s: Clinical challenges and treatment implications. *Bulletin of The Menninger Clinic* 56: 167–187.

Zide, M. R. and A. L. Cherry. 1992. A typology of runaway youths: An empirically based definition. *Child and Adolescent Social Work Journal* 9(2): 155–168.

Ziesmer, C. 1984. Student and staff perceptions of truancy and court referrals. *Social Work in Education* 6: 167–178.

Zimbardo, P. 1977. *Shyness*. New York: Addison-Wesley.

Zimberg, S., J. Wallace, and S. B. Blume. 1982. *Practical Approaches to Alcoholism Psychotherapy*. New York: Plenum Press.

Zimmerman, R. B. 1988. Childhood depression: New theoretical formulations and implications for foster care services. *Child Welfare* 67(1): 37–46.

Zlotnick, C., A. L. Zakriski, M. T. Shea, and E. Costello. 1996. The long-term sequelae of sexual abuse: Support for a complex post-traumatic stress disorder. *Journal of Traumatic Stress* 9(2): 195–205.

Zuger, A. 1998. The other drug problem: Forgetting to take them. *New York Times,* September 10.

Index